D0810168

Twilight
of
Liberty

William A. Donohue

Twilight of Liberty

The Legacy of the ACLU

Transaction Publishers
New Brunswick (U.S.A.) and London (U.K.)

Library of Congress Catalog Number: 93:16796
ISBN: 1-56000-049-X
Printed in the United States of America

Library of Congress Cataloging-in-Publication Data
Donohue, William A., 1947-
   Twilight of liberty : the legacy of the ACLU / William A. Donohue
      p. cm.
   Includes bibliographical references (p.   ) and index.
   ISBN 1-56000-049-X
   1. American Civil Liberties Union.   I. Title.
JC599.U5D663   1993
323'.06'073—dc20
                                                93-16796
                                                CIP

This book is dedicated to my daughters, Caryn and Caitlin

Contents

Preface

Over the years, I have had basically two central criticisms of the American Civil Liberties Union: (a) it is not the nonpartisan organization it pretends to be and (b) it hurts the cause of liberty by taking an extremist interpretation of individual rights. Having dealt with the first issue in *The Politics of the American Civil Liberties Union*, it made sense to do a sequel, one that would address the second issue.

This book is different from my first book on the ACLU in several ways. The first book sought to debunk the idea that the ACLU is above politics; this book tries to show how the ACLU undermines the process of liberty. The first book was both thematic and historical, covering the years 1920 to 1984; this book is a contemporary analysis of the ACLU, focusing on events of the last ten years. Those who have read the first book will find that almost all the work in this book is new. Unavoidably, there are some events that must be restated; otherwise, the reader is left without a sense of how events have unfolded. But because this book is fundamentally different from my previous effort, it does not presuppose that the reader has already read *The Politics of the American Civil Liberties Union*.

The purpose of this preface is to discuss some important material that does not directly relate to the thesis of this book; the introductory section that follows will do that.

Since my first book on the ACLU was published, I have met many former ACLU members, most of whom joined in the 1940s, 1950s, or early 1960s. Virtually without exception, the reason they left was the increasing politicization of the Union. As my previous book showed, the years these members joined were the most balanced in the ACLU's history. But beginning in the late 1960s, the ACLU steered left, leaving behind those civil libertarians who joined for principled reasons.

Perhaps the most famous person who parted ways with the ACLU was Dick Thornburgh, former board member in Pittsburgh, governor of Pennsylvania, and former attorney general of the United States. Other former officials, like Eugene Feldman of Pennsylvania, have gone public with their denunciations of the Union, holding that the ACLU's new agenda is "politics, foreign policy and sociology."[1] To Alan Dershowitz, a former board member of the Union, the problem is that "the ACLU and many of its local affiliates have increasingly become captives of feminists and leftists in recent years."[2] Some of those leftists, like William Kunstler, raise disturbing questions about how seriously the ACLU takes its own constitution.

Kunstler is a long-time member of the National Advisory Council, and according to the ACLU's constitution, that means that he must be "unequivocally committed" to civil liberties.[3] But as Kunstler has admitted, he only takes those cases "whose goals I share."[4] Here is a man who boasts "I don't think America is a democracy" and maintains that "the Constitution is now a myth." He believes that "the government is totally bankrupt, morally," and that the way to change things is through violence: "Violence is natural. I think the threat of violence has to be there" [if the system is to change].[5] Kunstler's contribution to the destruction of the system comes by way of his acting as "a double agent." To be exact, he describes himself as "a double agent" who wants to "bring down the system through the system."[6] The ACLU, obviously, provides Kunstler with just the sort of legitimate outpost he wants.

Over the past several years, I have mentioned to several ACLU officials the incongruity of allowing partisans like Kunstler to serve on one of the Union's governing boards. The usual reply is that (a) the National Advisory Board is not one of the governing boards, or (b) Kunstler has little influence, or (c) it doesn't matter a whole lot. Those who give the first reply are unaware that the ACLU's constitution lists the National Advisory Board as one of its governing bodies.[7] As to the second reply, the point is not whether Kunstler has much influence; rather, it is whether he ascribes to the principles of the organization. And to say that it doesn't matter is unconvincing. It is doubtful that the ACLU would accept an extreme right-winger as a member of one of it's governing boards (with good reason). So why permit extreme leftists?

Part of the problem is that the ACLU's interpretation of ideological extremism is narrowly drawn. To be specific, the Union sees extremism as emanating from just one direction: the right. That is why it continues to have a policy on "The Ultra-Right" but none on "The Ultra-Left." For example, its policy on "The Ultra-Right" speaks about "the problem of extremist organizations" without ever acknowledging that organizations on the left might also fit the mold.[8]

Perhaps a better index of the ACLU's politics can be gleaned from the scorecard that it tallies on the voting record of congressmen and senators. Each year the ACLU presents a list of what it determines to be the key civil liberties issues as voted on by Congress. It scores each representative and senator as either agreeing or disagreeing with its position. Data from 1983 to 1990 reveal the following scores: Senator Edward Kennedy of Massachusetts and Congressman Don Edwards of California agreed with the ACLU's position 93 and 99 percent of the time, respectively. But Senator Alfonse D'Amato of New York and Congressman Henry Hyde of Illinois garnered a rating of only 16 and 12 percent, respectively.[9] To those who claim the ACLU is nonpartisan, these results must be seen as an anomaly; to those who know better, the results are as unremarkable as they are predictable.

The standard ACLU response to charges of partisanship is a citation of its defenses of Nazis, Klansmen, and conservatives like Lt. Col. Oliver North. Now the record will show that there are both principled and politically expedient reasons why the ACLU has made these exceptions. Though they are in a minority, there are still some officials who are principled civil libertarians; hence, their willingness to defend people independent of political bent. The reader should know that although I admire the consistency of this position, I personally think it important to distinguish between Nazis and non-Nazis on the right. In the concluding section, a full explanation of this position is offered. In any event, there is nothing noble about the way some others in the ACLU view the issue.

To most ACLU activists, the occasional defense of a Nazi or Klansman costs little. After all, these extremists are hardly in a position to win. Furthermore, it is good for public relations to appear nonpartisan, especially when the case in point is sure to garner high visibility. Consider, too, what the ACLU founder Roger Baldwin had to say about this matter in 1934: "If I aid the reactionaries to get free speech now and then, if I go outside the class struggle to fight against censorship, it is only because those liberties help to create a more hospitable atmosphere for working class liberties."[10] In other words, the occasional defense of right-wing extremists opens up the courts, thereby making it easier for the ACLU to defend its ideological kinfolk on the left. [The ACLU opposed the Wagner Act, so it cannot seriously be maintained that by "working class liberties" Baldwin was implying elementary rights for workers.]

The case of Oliver North is more complicated. There is no dispute as to what the ACLU did, only as to why it did it. In 1988, the ACLU filed an amicus brief urging dismissal of the criminal charges against Oliver North for his role in the Iran-Contra affair. The Union's stated reason was that North's testimony, which had been compelled by congressional investigators, was being used against him by Judge Gerhard Gesell. The ACLU argued that the Fifth Amendment means that no one can be forced to testify before Congress and then be criminally prosecuted on the basis of such testimony. This is an admirable position to take, and it would be unfair to say that there were none in the ACLU who weren't prepared to defend North on principle alone. But there is reason to believe that the ACLU may have decided to come to the defense of North for reasons extrinsic to its stated purpose.

On July 7, 1987, North began six days of testimony before the Congressional committees investigating the Iran-Contra affair. He did so under a grant of limited immunity. On March 16, 1988, North was indicted on charges of conspiring to defraud the government by illegally providing the *contras* (the anti-Sandinista rebels) with funds from the sale of American weapons to Iran; the trial did not begin until January 31, 1989. In the end, on September 16, 1991, criminal charges against North were dropped after prosecutors decided it would be too hard to prove that testimony used to convict North was not tainted by his testimony before Congress.

When did the ACLU enter the picture? It filed its amicus brief on July 20, 1988. But to put the issue in context, we need to know what transpired between the day North was indicted and the day the ACLU filed its amicus brief, namely the period between March 16 and July 20, 1988. Before doing so, mention must first be made of an event that preceded the North indictment by several months.

In May 1987 in Los Angeles, and again in August 1987 in Spencer, Iowa, Governor Michael Dukakis of Massachusetts mentioned his membership in the ACLU while campaigning for the Democratic nomination for president. In both instances Dukakis boasted, "I'm a card-carrying member of the American Civil Liberties Union."[11] As the presidential campaign took form the following spring, these words would come back to haunt Dukakis and ultimately play a role in his defeat to George Bush.

As the spring of 1988 wore on, it was becoming increasingly clear that Michael Dukakis was going to be the choice of the Democratic party for president. The Bush campaign, therefore, began concentrating its attacks on Dukakis, offering the view that the Governor was a radical liberal, not in step with mainstream American values. Dukakis, on the other hand, fought back, saying that he was a competent manager of public policy, not an ideologue as charged. To make its case stick, the Bush campaign began to cite Dukakis's membership in the ACLU, repeatedly citing his boastful remark about being a card-carrying member of the organization. Focus groups organized by the Bush campaign showed quite convincingly that the ACLU was a "hot-button" issue, one that benefited Bush at the expense of Dukakis. It didn't take long before the radio talk shows, journalists, and news reporters began calling me for interviews and information on the ACLU. The Bush campaign wasted no time either.

On May 17, 1988, two months after North was indicted and two months before the ACLU filed its amicus brief, I supplied the Bush campaign headquarters with information on the ACLU that showed just how extremist the organization was on many important policy issues. That began my contact with the Bush campaign, an odyssey that lasted right up to election day. During the spring, summer, and fall of 1988, I supplied the Bush headquarters with virtually all the information on the ACLU that it used during the campaign. I also appeared on dozens of television and radio shows explaining various ACLU policies. The July 16 cover article I wrote for *Human Events*, which listed some of the most incredible policies of the ACLU, found its way into the hands of journalists and talk show hosts around the country, becoming the basis of criticism during the campaign; it was also entered into the *Congressional Record*.

The Politics of the American Civil Liberties Union also became a hot item during the campaign as it was the only critical book ever to be published on the Union. The thesis of the book—that the ACLU was not nonpartisan—was widely repeated during the campaign. Stung by this criticism, the Union began fighting back, maintaining that its past willingness to defend Nazis and Klansmen demonstrated its nonpartisanship. But there was no current case of any significance that the Union could cite that showed its nonpartisan approach to civil liberties, not, at least, until it decided to enter an amicus on July 20 in Ollie North's behalf.

Once the ACLU filed its amicus, it never missed an opportunity to cite its defense of North as proof of its nonpartisanship. There is little doubt that the decision to defend North paid dividends in public relations: many in the media repeated the Union's action as evidence of the ACLU's neutrality. How much this weighed on the ACLU's decision to enter the case in the first place is not certain. But before deciding, the reader should be apprised of two related matters.

If it were fidelity to principle alone that motivated the ACLU, and especially its fidelity to the Fifth Amendment right against self-incrimination, then how does one explain the Union's earlier reaction to Richard Nixon's Fifth Amendment right? In the spring of 1974, when it appeared for a while that there might be a Senate trial of President Nixon, the ACLU board of directors met to decide what its reaction to the trial should be if it were to take place. On June 12, 1974, a *majority* of board members voted that Nixon should not be given the right to claim the Fifth Amendment privilege against self-incrimination.[12] Given this, are we now to believe that the ACLU's decision to defend North's Fifth Amendment right, coming as it did in the midst of the most heated criticism ever directed at the organization, was without any political motive whatsoever?

It is also interesting to note that after the ACLU decided to defend North, it presented itself to the media as *the* defender of North. Its role, however, was that of a friend of the court. This is not an insignificant role, but it is not the same as playing the lead role, either. This point takes on special relevance in light of the Union's tendency to elevate the role of amicus when it is convenient to do so (as in the North case) and then de-emphasize this role when it is useful to distance itself from unpopular cases.

For example, when the ACLU affiliate in New Jersey entered an amicus on behalf of Richard Kreimer, a homeless man who was living in the Morristown, New Jersey, library in the 1990s (see chapter six for more details), it was roundly criticized for its insensitivity to the library's patrons and for making a mockery of the law. In reply to a *Wall Street Journal* editorial denouncing the Union's action, Lisa Glick Zucker, staff attorney for the ACLU, wrote that the editorial "incorrectly states that the ACLU assisted Mr. Kreimer in the suit." The ACLU attorney then said the charge was "incorrect," contending that the Union was merely "participating as amicus curiae" in the lawsuit.[13] If she is right, then the ACLU never assisted Ollie North.

How much of the ACLU's willingness "to defend" North was motivated by principle, and how much was motivated by politics, may not be known, but there is no doubt that it was Dukakis, not Bush, who first cited the ACLU in the 1988 presidential campaign. But this would never be known by reading some accounts of the campaign. For example, in August 1988, left-wing writer and ACLU "medal winner"[14] I.F. Stone wrote that it was improper for Bush to say before the Republican platform committee that Michael Dukakis was "a card-carrying member of the American Civil Liberties Union." By making this statement, Stone charged, Bush had "injected into the campaign a pale whiff of the witch-hunting McCarthyite 50's."[15] One month later, the editors of the *New York Times* agreed, charging that Bush was guilty of a McCarthyite "smear" by mentioning Dukakis's "card-carrying" membership in the ACLU.[16] And ACLU official and chronicler Samuel Walker later wrote that it was Bush who "introduced the ACLU into the 1988 presidential campaign."[17]

But as I have already pointed out, it was Dukakis, not Bush, who first made an issue of the ACLU. The question needs to be asked: If it was legitimate for Dukakis to score points by choosing to characterize himself as a "card-carrying member of the American Civil Liberties Union," why was it illegitimate—indeed McCarthyite—for Dukakis's critics to score points by repeating Dukakis's own description of himself?

"It sometimes seems as though the election is more about the ACLU than anything else." This is the way Tom Brokaw of NBC News characterized the ACLU's role in the fall of 1988,[18] and judging from the way the ACLU was reacting, it was on the defensive. The Union took out full-page ads in the *New York Times* and the *Los Angeles Times* defending its positions and secured the services of ACLU member Burt Lancaster to make several television appeals.[19] The shots that Bush and others were taking at the ACLU were beginning to hurt, as witnessed by Michael Dukakis's strategy of distancing himself from ACLU policies. As the campaign developed, Dukakis found it necessary to openly disagree with the ACLU on several issues, including the Union's defense of child pornography and its opposition to metal detectors in the airports, sobriety road checks, the tax-exempt status of churches, and the inscription "In God We Trust" on coins.[20]

Though it was Dukakis's membership in the ACLU that provoked the greatest controversy, the fact that his campaign manager, Susan Estrich, was also an ACLU member gave additional clout to Dukakis's critics. Estrich, in fact, had been elected to serve on the ACLU's board of directors in 1984.[21] I had the opportunity to disclose some of her more extreme positions on *Crossfire* in August 1988. Estrich had earlier co-authored a piece with Virginia Kerr entitled "Sexual Justice," wherein she made the case for lesbian motherhood.[22] Like others in the ACLU, she had no problem defending her ideas before other Union members or before her colleagues at Harvard Law School (she has since left), but when the public spotlight was put on her politics, she, like Dukakis, began to back off.

It was not only Dukakis and Estrich that felt under the gun; the ACLU itself began to pull back, refusing to verify Dukakis's status as a member and refusing—at least initially—to distribute its policy guide to the public. Its refusal to verify Dukakis's status (it was never really in doubt) was made on the grounds of privacy rights.[23] Ironically, the ACLU was already on record criticizing a law that made it illegal to disclose the names of active covert intelligence agents, even though the disclosure of some names by Philip Agee had already resulted in the death of an innocent agent.[24] But now it was saying that "we do not make our lists available to partisan political groups, or to groups whose programs are incompatible with ACLU policies."[25] What was most curious, however, was the Union's refusal to disclose its own policies.

Throughout the campaign, when reporters would call me for verification of an ACLU policy, I would make a copy of the requested documents and send it to them. Some wanted to access the files I had, and while I never denied anyone to personally see them, the extent of my files is simply too voluminous to send to anyone. When reporters would query the ACLU about seeing a copy of the policy guide, it said it would make them available in its offices to anyone who wanted to see them. But when reporters tried to access them, they were refused.[26] So, too, were many others. As a result, Allan Ryskind of *Human Events* began to encourage readers to call the ACLU demanding copies of its policies.[27] The flood of calls proved to be too much, and late in the campaign, with only a few weeks remaining, the ACLU reversed its position and provided copies of its policy guide on request (for a modest fee).

If there was one episode in the campaign that really brought the ACLU into focus, it was what happened during the first presidential debate. To this day, many in the media and in academe continue to say that Bush misrepresented the ACLU's positions during the debate. Before dealing squarely with this issue, it would be helpful to know exactly what Bush said about the ACLU.

During the first debate, Peter Jennings of ABC News asked candidate George Bush why he continued to make an issue out of Michael Dukakis's membership in the ACLU. Bush replied that he didn't like most of the ACLU's positions and offered four of them. "I simply don't want to see the ratings on movies—I don't want my ten-year-old grandchild to go into an X-rated movie. I like those ratings systems. I don't think they're right to try to take the tax exemption away from the Catholic Church. I don't want to see the kiddie pornographic laws repealed. I don't want to see under God come out from our currency. Now, these are all positions of the A.C.L.U., and I don't agree with them."[28]

Norman Dorsen accused Bush of distorting the ACLU's policies. With regard to whether children should be admitted to X-rated movies, Dorsen said, "We believe that's a decision that should be made by each family." He added that the ACLU opposes tax exemption for all churches, not just the Catholic Church. As for child pornography, Dorsen said, "Our view is that the government can prosecute the makers of pornography [for] the improper use of children for this purpose." He then added, "We don't feel that the material itself can be censored." The inscription "In God We Trust," Dorsen contended, had never been the object of an ACLU lawsuit, though he admitted that it ran afoul of the organization's principles.[29]

Ira Glasser was more caustic. He said Bush mentioned four ACLU positions and "managed to get three wrong." Glasser had this to say regarding the issue of the Catholic Church's tax-exempt status: "There is a case trying to do that, but it happens not to be an ACLU case. The ACLU had not taken a position on the merits of that case." The Union's child pornography policy, Glasser said, was also misrepresented. "The ACLU supports making it a crime to exploit children that way. What we have opposed are laws which also have the effect of interfering with the rights of reputable publishers to publish sex education books, for example; and that is not fanciful." As for the admission of children to X-rated movies, Glasser complained, "As if somehow the ACLU was really anxious to have his [Bush's] 10-year-old granddaughter go to X-rated movies all she could." He never addressed the Union's opposition to "In God We Trust" on the coins.[30]

After the election was over, David Margolick of the *New York Times*, in his "At the Bar" column, cited Bush's comments on the ACLU during the first debate. He then wrote, "None of these represented group's [sic] position," and he said that Norman Dorsen and Ira Glasser "sought to set the record straight."[31] Then in 1990, a college textbook published by Harper and Row and entitled *American Democracy: Institutions, Politics and Policies* listed Bush's remarks and concluded that "(The ACLU subsequently pointed out that Bush was wrong in attributing to it all but the last of these four positions.)" The book then proceeded to give a highly favorable account of the ACLU's history. For the record, the editor of the volume is Lauren Silverman, and the authors are William J. Keefe, William H. Flanigan, Morris S. Ogul, Henry J. Abraham, Charles O. Jones, and John W. Spanier.[32]

Only the account offered by Dorsen even comes close to being accurate; the others are simply wrong. I know because I was the one who suggested these very policies to the Bush operatives who briefed the candidate before the first debate, and I made sure to double-check my sources. I have the proof, taken from ACLU documents, that verifies that Bush was right.

Here's where I got the material. In Policy #18, "Rating Systems Sponsored by the Communications Industries," the ACLU lists its objections to the movie rating system. Though the Motion Picture Association of America (MPAA) is a purely voluntary nongovernmental body—with no censorial powers whatsoever—the Union holds that the effect of the MPAA "is to restrict the marketplace of ideas." The policy further states that "some subsidiary markets for films (hotels, airlines, pay television) frequently refuse to accept X-rated films."[33] So when Bush said that he liked the ratings system, he was calling attention to the ACLU's opposition to it.

Bush's mention of his granddaughter was truly gratuitous, the kind of remark designed to score political points. But his statement that he didn't want his ten-year-old granddaughter going to see X-rated movies did not imply that the ACLU was anxious to have her see such movies (as Glasser said); it only suggested that if the ACLU had things its way, there would be no way to bar minors from legitimately seeing these movies.

Policy #4, "Censorship of Obscenity, Pornography and Indecency," lists the ACLU's qualified objections to the use of children in sexually explicit movies. But it also says that "the First Amendment protects the dissemination of all forms of communication," meaning that the sale and distribution of kiddie porn should be legal.[34] Indeed, in 1982, in *New York v. Ferber*, the ACLU was on the losing side of a unanimous decision that held that the First Amendment did not protect the production, sale, and distribution of child pornography.[35] As was true then, the issue is not whether pictures of naked children can be shown in medical textbooks; rather it is whether pictures of children performing various sex acts with adults and animals should be legal. Glasser's attempt to conflate these matters is done to obfuscate the issue and make Bush appear to be distorting ACLU policy.

Glasser says that although there is a case trying to challenge the right of the Catholic Church to a tax-exempt status, "it happens not to be an ACLU case." He adds that the ACLU "has not taken a position on the merits of that case." Technically this is true, but again Glasser is less than forthcoming. The fact is that at that time the ACLU Foundation and the New York Civil Liberties Union had filed an amicus in support of the Abortion Rights Mobilization to secure standing in its lawsuit directed at the tax-exempt status of the Catholic Church.[36] Glasser never mentioned this before his audience at the National Press Club.

So here again we have the ACLU downplaying its role as an amicus. In addition, we have the ACLU pretending that it hasn't really ruled on the merits of the case; we are to believe that it is just supporting the right of the respondent to secure standing. If it is wrong to deduce the ACLU's position on the merits of a case by citing its willingness to support standing for the respondent, could we then expect that the ACLU might agree to file an amicus in support of a respondent seeking standing in a case that challenged the legality of, say, gay bathhouses? Of course not. Dorsen, to his credit, didn't try to pretend what the ACLU's real position was. As he said, the ACLU opposes the tax-exempt status of all churches; it is one of its official policies.[37]

ACLU opposition to "In God We Trust" on coins is long-standing: Union founder Roger Baldwin mentioned it to me in the 1970s as one of the most foolish statements ever made by the ACLU.[38] Just because the ACLU hasn't litigated a case over it doesn't mean that the organization isn't opposed to it, and that is why Bush was entirely correct to mention the Union's position.

The same day that David Margolick's piece appeared in the *New York Times*, I called to ask him where he had gotten his information that Bush was wrong and the ACLU was right about the four policies in question. He didn't return my phone call so I wrote a letter explaining that I was the source of Bush's comments. More than that, I sent a copy of all the relevant documents that sustained my case.[39] He never answered my letter and never printed a retraction of his error.

I had the same experience with the editor and authors of the textbook on American government. I wrote to all seven of them and provided each with a copy of the policies in question.[40] None of them responded.

The inaccuracies mentioned must be weighed alongside the favorable media treatment the ACLU received during the campaign. In addition to Anthony Lewis and Tom Wicker of the *New York Times*, William Raspberry and Richard Cohen of the *Washington Post* also defended the ACLU from its critics. And as Colleen O'Connor of the ACLU admitted, "*Time* and *Newsweek* carried favorable profiles of the group, as did most major newspapers and the four national television networks."[41]

As a result of the coverage it received, the ACLU registered an impressive gain in membership. But the overall effect of its exposure during the presidential campaign was mixed. O'Connor mentions that 50,000 people joined the ACLU for the first time during this period.[42] Other estimates, like those offered by Jeffrey T. Leeds, put the figure at exactly half that amount.[43] What may prove to be more important in the end, however, is how many prospective office seekers will want to identify themselves with the ACLU. It is not likely to be seen as an asset.

Was the public image of the ACLU enhanced as a result of the Union's visibility during the campaign? At the time of the election, some surveys showed that somewhere between 56 and 83 percent of the public held an unfavorable view of the ACLU.[44] But the ACLU would have us believe that following the campaign, "a public opinion survey showed 72 percent of Americans voicing opinions about the ACLU generally had a favorable impression of the organization."[45] The figure, however, is spurious.

Consider the poll that was conducted by Peter D. Hart Research Associates in February 1989; the ACLU commissioned the survey itself. The results showed that 47 percent of Americans had a favorable view of the Union and 18 percent had an unfavorable view.[46] There is reason to believe that even the figure of 47 percent is inflated. For example, the Hart survey never asked the respondents whether they first had enough knowledge about the ACLU to make an informed judgment. Pollsters have often found the public reacts favorably to any organization that has words like "American" or "Freedom" in its name. Indeed, Joseph Napolitan, the political consultant who wrote the questions for the survey, admitted that the respondents were reacting as much to the words "American Civil Liberties Union" as to what the organization actually did.[47]

More important is the results of a *New York Times*/CBS poll taken in October of 1988. In this poll, the public was first asked whether they had sufficient knowledge to comment on the ACLU. Of those who did, 11 percent had a favorable view and 19 percent had an unfavorable view.[48] With good reason, the ACLU never cites this survey, even though it offers a more informed view of the Union's reputation.

There is no question that the ACLU is far more protective of its image today than it was before the election of 1988. When Mark S. Campisano was doing research for an article in the *New Republic* on the ACLU during the fall campaign, he was refused access to past annual reports when he visited ACLU headquarters in New York.[49] In 1990 Charles Oliver of *Reason* magazine tried for three months to interview Ira Glasser but was never given the opportunity to do so.[50] When Jon Carroll of the *San Francisco Chronicle* asked Ira Glasser in 1990 if he could sit in on one of the Union's board meetings, he was denied.[51] My treatment accords with the experiences of these men. While writing my first book on the ACLU, I was allowed to see the entire transcript of the minutes of the board of directors, but after the book appeared, all that would be made available were summaries of the meetings.

The fact that the ACLU does not take criticism well, even when it comes from friendly sources, was learned by the late CBS newsman Eric Sevareid. In October 1987, Sevareid told me what had happened when he had spoken at a recent ACLU dinner. After speaking kindly about the ACLU, he began to take issue with the Union for adopting some of its extremist policies and for neglecting a proper balance between rights and responsibilities. The reaction stunned him. ACLU activists began to mutter, in unison and ever so loudly, "fascist, fascist, fascist."

It is not expected, therefore, that there will be many in the ACLU who will take well to the criticisms contained in this book. Nonetheless, there are some civil libertarians who will respond constructively, either by directly confronting my arguments or by seeking some needed reforms. It is they, along with the reading public, that I seek to persuade.

Notes

All references to the *New York Times* and *Wall Street Journal* are to the national editions of the newspapers.

1. Letter to the editor, *New York Times*, October 18, 1988, p. 26.
2. Alan Dershowitz, "ACLU Takes a Wrong Turn," in Alan Dershowitz, *Taking Liberties* (Chicago: Contemporary Books, 1988), 140–41.
3. See ACLU Constitution, Policy #501, sections 2 and 7 (E).
4. Quoted by Sam Howe Verhovek, "At 69, Kunstler Is Still Moved by Fervor," *New York Times*, July 28, 1988, p. B1.
5. Ron Chepesiuk's interview with Kunstler appeared in *Gallery*, December 1987, pp. 27–30, 118.
6. Quoted by Robert Reinhold, "Radical Lawyers Adopt New Life-Style," *New York Times*, August 2, 1971, p. 13.
7. Policy #501, "Constitution." See section 7.
8. Policy #46, "The Ultra-Right."
9. For the data, see the following editions of *Civil Liberties Alert*: January 1984; November 1984; January/February 1986; January 1987; November 1988; December 1989; November/December 1990.
10. Roger Baldwin, "Freedom in the U.S.A. and the U.S.S.R.," *Soviet Russia Today*, September 1934, p. 11.
11. The first journalist to take note of Dukakis's boast was Joe Klein. See his piece "Ready for the Duke?" *New York*, August 17, 1987, p. 30. Mention of Dukakis's Los Angeles statement is recorded by Jeffrey T. Leeds, "Impeccable Judgments or Tainted Policies?" *New York Times Magazine*, September 10, 1989, p. 72.
12. Minutes of the Board of Directors, June 12, 1974, pp. 10–13.
13. Lisa Glick Zucker, letter to the editor, *Wall Street Journal*, December 2, 1991, p. A13.
14. I.F. Stone received the ACLU's Medal of Liberty at the 1987 Biennial Conference. Mention of this can be found in Stone's piece, "We Can Claim to be the Real Americans. We Can Wave the Flag," *Civil Liberties*, Fall 1987, p. 10.
15. I.F. Stone, "Bush vs. A.C.L.U.," *New York Times*, August 16, 1988, p. A27.
16. "Card-Carrying Smears," *New York Times*, September 18, 1988, section E, p. 22.
17. Samuel Walker, *In Defense of American Liberties: A History of the ACLU* (New York: Oxford University Press, 1990), 368.
18. Brokaw made his comment on the NBC nightly news broadcast of September 27, 1988.
19. Ruth Marcus, "ACLU Unexpectedly Finds Itself in Cross Fire of '88 Campaign," *Washington Post*, October 3, 1988, p. A8.
20. These were the five most often cited departures from ACLU policy as stated by Dukakis. He made his comments at various stops along the way. I made a note of them as they occurred.
21. "10 Elected to ACLU Board of Directors," *Civil Liberties*, Fall 1984, p. 2.
22. Susan Estrich and Virginia Kerr, "Sexual Justice," in Norman Dorsen, ed., *Our Endangered Rights: The ACLU Report on Civil Liberties Today* (New York: Pantheon Books, 1984), 98–133.
23. "GOP Pounds ACLU Despite Its Causes For Right As Well As Left," *Pittsburgh Press*, September 4, 1988, p. B12.
24. William A. Donohue, *The Politics of the American Civil Liberties Union* (New Brunswick, New Jersey: Transaction Press, 1985), 206.

25. See "Membership Lists," *Civil Liberties*, Fall 1990, p. 7. See also Policy 518a, "Outside Requests for Distribution of Material to Board and Affiliates," and Policy #519, "Political Non-Partisanship."

26. Gordon Crovitz of the *Wall Street Journal* supplied me with this information.

27. See "Media Covering Up ACLU's Extremist Agenda," *Human Events*, September 10, 1988, pp. 1, 17.

28. This is taken from the transcript of the first debate as reported in the *New York Times*, September 26, 1988, p. 11.

29. "ACLU Says Bush Distorts Views," *Newsday*, September 27, 1988, pp. 5, 35.

30. Glasser made his remarks before the National Press Club on October 6, 1988.

31. David Margolick, "At the Bar," *New York Times*, January 27, 1989, p. 21.

32. The cited academics are the authors of *American Democracy: Institutions, Politics, and Policies* (3rd edition) (New York: Harper and Row, 1990). The reference to the ACLU is on pp. 132-33.

33. Policy #18, "Rating Systems Sponsored by the Communications Industries."

34. Policy #4, "Censorship of Obscenity, Pornography and Indecency."

35. *New York v. Ferber*, 458 U.S. 747 (1982).

36. *United States Catholic Conference and National Conference of Catholic Bishops v. Abortion Rights Mobilization*, No. 87-416.

37. Policy #92, "Religious Bodies' Tax Exemption."

38. Donohue, *The Politics of the American Civil Liberties Union*, 309.

39. The letter was dated January 27, 1989, the same day that Margolick's article appeared.

40. The letters were sent February 1, 1990.

41. Colleen O'Connor, "State of Siege," *Civil Liberties*, Winter 1989, p. 6.

42. Ibid.

43. Jeffrey T. Leeds, "Impeccable Judgments or Tainted Policies?" p. 78.

44. George Grant, *Trial and Error: The American Civil Liberties Union and Its Impact on Your Family* (Brentwood, Tennessee: Wolgemuth and Hyatt, Inc., 1989), 19.

45. ACLU Annual Report for 1988, p. 2.

46. E.J. Dionne Jr., "A.C.L.U. Studies Its Image and Finds It Intact," *New York Times*, May 14, 1989, p. 23.

47. Ibid.

48. See E.J. Dionne Jr. "Latest Poll Finds Dukakis Is Closing The Gap With Bush," *New York Times*, October 5, 1988, p. A1, A14. Dionne later reported the unfavorable rating at 17 percent (see previous citation) and not 19 percent, so it is not clear which figure is right, though it hardly matters substantively to the point being made.

49. Mark S. Campisano, "Card Games," *New Republic*, October 31, 1988, p. 12.

50. Charles Oliver, "The First Shall Be Last?" *Reason*, October 1990, p. 25.

51. Jon Carroll, "Doing Something To Offend Me," *San Francisco Chronicle*, February 2, 1990.

Acknowledgments

This book would not have been written without the prodding and support of Irving Louis Horowitz, founder and editor-in-chief of Transaction Publishers and Hannah Arendt Distinguished Professor of Sociology and Political Science at Rutgers University. It was his idea to write an update to *The Politics of the American Civil Liberties Union*, and it was his willingness to accept my desire to write this book on the ACLU instead. From what I know of other authors, the relationship they have with their publishers is remote and impersonal. That has not been my experience with Irving Horowitz: I count him as one of my best friends. More than that, he has had a profound influence on my life. For that I am eternally grateful.

I would like to thank Lawrence Cranberg, who, next to Irv Horowitz, has done more than anyone to urge me to continue my study of the ACLU. Larry is a dear friend and an endless source of wisdom and inspiration.

Many thanks, too, to my wife Valerie. She is always in my corner, ready to support my many endeavors, and willing to listen to my latest ideas, worthy or not. Thanks must also be given to my children, Caryn and Caitlin, to my mother and sister, Anna and Tara, and to my in-laws, Althea and Bob Fowlie. As always, I am grateful for the support that I have received from my best friends, Mans and Duff, as well as from their wives, Maggie and Nancy.

Parts of chapters 4 and 6 were previously published in "The New Agenda of the ACLU," *Society*, January/February 1991. Parts of chapter 6 also appeared in an article co-written with James Taranto, "The Assault on Public Order: How the Civil Liberties Union Goes Astray," *City Journal*, Winter 1992.

Introduction

Perspectives on Liberty

The prevailing view among students of freedom holds that nothing is more important to the cause of liberty than individual rights. This book hopes to challenge that assumption. It is not that the rights of the individual do not matter; it is just that, standing alone, they do not make for a free society. Indeed, it is quite possible to have a social order wherein each individual possesses unheralded rights, and still have a society that lacks freedom. It seems plain that if social institutions lose their autonomy, and if libertinism reigns in the culture, all the rights in the world cannot stave off the onslaught of liberticide. Unfortunately, there are signs in the United States that we have come dangerously close to realizing this condition, so much so that we may have entered the twilight of our liberty.

The reasons for this predicament are multiple, but none is more evident than in our contemporary approach to the subject of freedom. To be specific, our singular fixation on civil liberties has blunted our vision, allowing for the neglect of many other constitutive elements of freedom. In this regard, the positions of the American Civil Liberties Union best express our failed perspective on freedom. The ACLU not only defines the mindset of civil liberties, it more generally defines the way important sectors of American society have come to think about the meaning of freedom. That is why it will command the attention of this book. But it cannot be said too forcefully that the ACLU is only the most conspicuous outpost of our current malaise. It is one thing to assert that the ACLU is emblematic of our inability to think of freedom in terms other than individual rights, quite another to maintain that it is the *only* reason why the state has triumphed and deracinated individuals abound. It is the former position, not the latter, that is being made here.[1]

The current wisdom on liberty begins and ends with a discussion of the rights of the individual. It assumes that civil liberties are exhaustive of freedom and that the conceptual framework of freedom need not be placed within a social context. This view, which will be labeled the atomistic conception of liberty, sees individual rights as existing within

1

a social, and therefore, moral, vacuum. Asocial in its orientation, the atomistic school of thought is highly legalistic: state anointed rights, crafted either by executive agencies, the legislature, or the judiciary—it matters little what the source is—are all that seem to matter.

An alternative perspective, what can be called the social conception of liberty (it is the one favored here),[2] posits that any discussion of freedom must start with society, not the individual. Of utmost importance is the kind of social order that is best suited to the establishment of liberty; this entails an examination of the desired relationship between the state and society. Equally critical to this conception of liberty are the type of characterological outcomes that are most desirable in the citizenry and how they might best be fulfilled. Once this framework has been established, the subject can then turn to rights.

Individual rights may be the cornerstone of liberal democracy, but the proper exercise of rights is limited by the parameters of society. Moreover, society is not a mere aggregation of individuals; rather it is a constellation of groups and communities, all of which are defined by moral boundaries. And whatever moral boundaries there are require steady enforcement, the kind of quality insurance traditionally provided by the mediating institutions of family, school, church, and voluntary associations.[3] It is in these structures that social authority rests.

There is another kind of authority available in society, namely the authority of the state. The centralization of authority, in the hands of government, can be total, or it can coexist with social authority; it is also possible to have nothing but total social authority. But there are no other choices (having no authority of any kind abets anarchy, which soon turns to despotism). Authority, being necessary to the minimal operations of society, must be lodged somewhere. If it is lodged totally—either with the state or with the social—there is no hope for liberty. Therefore, the coexistence of authority between the state and the social is the only avenue that yields realistic prospects for liberty.

The present danger is that, in the name of individual rights, we are moving toward the eclipse of social authority by the authority of the state. Quite frequently these days, when individuals win rights, they win them against authority, resting either in the state or in the social order. Problems emerge when the final outcome means that the state continuously and relentlessly sustains individual rights at the expense of social authority. When that occurs, there is nothing left to ward off encroachments of the state on the individual. "If the rights of such groups as family, community, and province are invaded by the central state," writes sociologist Robert Nisbet, "and almost predictably in the name of individuals assertedly robbed of their natural rights—the true walls of individual freedom will in time crumble."[4]

If the atomistic conception of liberty were to go unchallenged, the social authority that is lodged within mediating institutions would be decimated. All that would be left in society is the individual and the state. There is a name for that kind of outcome, and it is called totalitarianism. If every injustice spawned by mediating institutions against the individual is seen as cause for governmental redress, the end result of such a fractious exercise is statism, pure and simple. It is nothing if not post-Orwellian to think that a society dedicated to individual rights might conclude in despotism. But it is a thought worth thinking about, especially considering the extent to which we continue to conceive of liberty in purely individualistic terms.

The social order that is best suited to the establishment of liberty is one that strikes a balance between the social authority of mediating institutions and the rights of the individual. This means, first and foremost, that students of freedom need to give as much recognition to the vital role of mediating institutions as they presently give to civil liberties. And this, quite naturally, calls for a more informed sociological insight into the crafting of constitutional law.

To discourse on what rights individuals should have without first asking what characterological attributes they should possess is a major mistake, and it is one we continue to make. To be exact, only morally responsible individuals are capable of exercising their rights in a way that liberates. Morally irresponsible individuals do not use rights, they abuse them. And because their abuse occurs in society, it unavoidably means that others lose their rights in the process. It therefore makes no sense to claim that rights liberate: they do so only for those who are morally responsible in the first place.

What character traits are desirable in a free society? Many, but none more than the capacity for self-restraint. Without self-restraint, or a sense of self-discipline, all the other desirable virtues that come to mind will matter little in the end. The reason for the primacy of self-restraint has to do with the societal need for social control. And what that means is this: either people police themselves or the police will do the job for them.

The only alternative is anarchy, which is no alternative in a society that seeks to be free. That explains why self-restraint commands our attention: without it, self-policing is impossible, thus beckoning the hand of the state.

In addition to self-restraint, there is a host of other characterological attributes that are desirable in a free society. Responsibility, duty, obligation, commitment—anything that turns the eyes of the individual away from himself—should be given high priority. A society that fails to nourish a strong sense of responsibility in its citizens is one that is ill-prepared to distribute rights to individuals. For once the traditional link between rights and responsibilities has been severed, there is little that can be done to ensure that the exercise of rights will be done in a matter that liberates. And if duty, obligation, and commitment to others isn't properly socialized, it is not likely that people will learn to give as much as they take, making tenuous the condition of freedom for all.

How, then, should we proceed? What is the most efficacious method for achieving these desirable characterological attributes? And what means is the most felicitous to the prospect of liberty? The values of self-restraint, responsibility, duty, obligation, and commitment—what might be called core moral values—are best transmitted through the mediating institutions of family, school, and church; to a lesser extent, neighborhood voluntary associations can play this role as well. If, for whatever reason, parents, teachers, and clergy fail in this endeavor, the mission of liberty is undermined. No compensation can be found in the distribution of a new round of rights, for only morally responsible individuals can be expected to add to the fund of liberty.

One of the most effective and pernicious ways to undermine the social authority of mediating institutions is to inflate the powers of the state. If this happens, not only do the individual and the state reign supreme, so too does libertinism. For once the mediating institutions atrophy, there is no source left to instill core moral values. Hence, self-restraint fails to develop and the exercise of liberty turns to license. This condition, the natural progeny of an atomistic conception of liberty, is one in which everyone loses.

Once the social and moral requisites of freedom have been established, at least to a modest degree, discussion can turn to civil liberties. The rights of the individual, as embodied in the Bill of Rights, are exactly the kind of rights that are necessary for liberty to take hold. Those rights are rights against government, insurances that allow the individual to cordon off a circle of autonomy that even the state cannot trespass. But since the exercise of those rights can only take place in a moral community, bound by a normative order, it makes little sense to treat them as absolutes. Liberty depends as much on the proper exercise of rights as it does their sheer presence in society.

The ACLU: Past and Present

More than any single source, the American Civil Liberties Union exemplifies the atomistic conception of liberty. It interprets freedom exclusively in terms of rights and sees the concerns of peace, order, security, justice, and social solidarity as being the responsibility of other segments of society. The ACLU's focus on rights has much to do with its political interest in fostering a radical egalitarianism: the pursuit of individual rights is a useful means to effect equal outcomes. Indeed, it is the ACLU's animus against hierarchy, or, more exactly, the hierarchy associated with traditional liberal values, that drives the organization. The Union is committed to leveling—advancing political, economic, social, and cultural equality—all in the name of civil liberties. It is the redistribution of power, not the cause of freedom, that is at the heart of the ACLU's mission.

For example, when it comes to socio-economic issues, the ACLU seizes on statist prescriptions to further its agenda, warmly embracing the centralization of authority that marks left politics. In doing so, the ACLU openly departs from its alleged commitment to individual rights but makes good on its real goal of radical egalitarianism. On moral issues, the ACLU also seeks equality, preferring to use individual rights to promote a doctrine of moral neutrality against the conventional moral hierarchy associated with the Judeo-Christian ethos.

The final outcome of this war on hierarchy is not liberty but a statist society wherein libertinism thrives. If it is true that this condition is not an accurate description of contemporary American society, it is because resistance to this effort is commonplace. But that is where the assault on a moral nucleus inexorably leads—to statism and libertinism.

The statism and libertinism that the ACLU currently promotes is in keeping with the affectations of its founder, Roger Baldwin, who was both a socialist and a nudist. Baldwin was executive director from 1920, when the Union was founded, until 1950, and he remained active in the

Union until his death in 1981. He was succeeded by Patrick Murphy Malin, John dePemberton, Jr., Aryeh Neier, and Ira Glasser. None but dePemberton was a lawyer, a characteristic that has become a signature of ACLU officials in general. As captured by Jeffrey T. Leeds, "most board members [of the current ACLU directorship] are neither lawyers, scholars, academics nor historians."[5]

The unbounded affection that the founding members of the ACLU showed for Leninism and Stalinism is further proof that the Union was never serious about curbing the powers of the state. But one would never know this by reading books on the ACLU written by ACLU activists. For instance, in Samuel Walker's recent history of the ACLU (he serves on the board of directors of the Union), there is hardly any indication that the founding members of the Union were statists of the worst kind: they defended Soviet repression and explained away its ugly record of human rights abuses.

Walker would have us believe that the founder of the ACLU, Roger Baldwin, made only two short statements in his lifetime that showed support for the communist "experiment" in the Soviet Union.[6] But that is flatly wrong. Indeed, Baldwin wrote two books defending Soviet terror and was a self-described "fellow traveler" of the Communists. Baldwin's *Letters from Russian Prisons* records his sentiment that the Russian Revolution "was the greatest and most daring experiment yet undertaken to recreate society in terms of human values," adding that Russia was "a great laboratory of social experimentation of incalculable value to the development of the world."[7]

Baldwin went beyond fawning when he wrote *Liberty Under the Soviets*: "Repressions in Western democracies are violations of professed constitutional liberties, and I condemn them as such. Repressions in Soviet Russia are weapons of struggle in a transition period to socialism."[8] Interestingly, Walker's only comment on this work was that it was "an informative book."[9] That it was, but for reasons Walker chose not to discuss.

It will not do to say that Baldwin had no knowledge of the terror that was sweeping the Soviet Union at the time. He was informed by his friend Emma Goldman and by his tour guide in the U.S.S.R.[10] But, like many intellectuals at that time, Baldwin was so profoundly disillusioned with his own country, and with the West in general, that the most horrible conditions in the Soviet Union could be justified as a temporary aberration on the road to Utopia. Baldwin's belief in the communist cause was so strong that even when many others on the left began to have second thoughts, he kept the faith. Here again, Walker gives the wrong impression. Walker says that by 1937 Baldwin cut his ties with Popular Front groups. But, as the ACLU founder admitted to his biographer, Peggy Lamson, he was active in United Front groups as late as the 1940s.[11]

Even before the ACLU was formally founded, Baldwin was scheming to shroud his real objectives in patriotic dress. Three years before the ACLU was launched, Baldwin, in his role as director of the National Civil Liberties Bureau (a unit of the American Union Against Militarism), wrote to Louis Lochner explaining his strategy: "Do steer away from making it look like a Socialist enterprise. Too many people have gotten the idea that it is nine-tenths a Socialist movement." And it was important to look like patriots: "We want also to look like patriots in everything we do. We want to get a good lot of flags, talk a good deal about the Constitution and what our forefathers wanted to make of this country, and to show that we are really the folks that really stand for the spirit of our institutions."[12] By wrapping themselves in the flag, then, civil libertarians could pursue their political objectives while feigning loyalty to the nation.

Was the ACLU a Communist organization in the 1920s and 1930s? No, but it certainly did not lack for Communists in its leadership. Harry F. Ward, Louis Budenz, Elizabeth Gurley Flynn, William Z. Foster, Robert W. Dunn, Anna Rochester, A.J. Isserman, and Mary Van Kleeck were all members of the Communist party. If one includes the number of fellow travelers (the multi millionaire Corliss Lamont comes quickly to mind), it is no exaggeration to say that the most active members of the ACLU, in its formative years, were partisans of communism. In fact, the ACLU loaned money and provided bail for many Communist party members and Front organizations.[13] Was the ACLU a communist front? Yes, according to Earl Browder, general secretary of the Communist party, the ACLU functioned as a "transmission belt" for the Communist party.[14]

It needs to be asked, how was it that an organization founded on the alleged purpose of promoting liberty could have in its leadership so many persons who were committed to communism? One would think that an organization that made civil liberties its raison d'etre would have nothing but principled students of liberty in its senior positions. How could it be that so many were in fact associated with a political doctrine that was responsible for the wholesale annihilation of human rights, and that, after being apprised of the carnage that their doctrine yielded, they remained recalcitrant? The answer is that the leadership of the ACLU was driven by an insatiable appetite for power, not liberty: the Bill of Rights was a useful instrument to effect the redistribution of power.

From 1940 to the late 1960s, the ACLU moved to the center and practiced a principled commitment to civil liberties. Ironically, the Union's carefully balanced posture during those years is now looked upon with contempt by contemporary ACLU activists. Walker, for instance, regards Norman Thomas—probably the most sensible, committed, and principled civil libertarian official the ACLU ever had—as a "pathetic figure," one who was "obsessed" with his Communist rivals.[15] Similarly, Walker accuses Baldwin's successor, Patrick Murphy Malin, as indulging in "the ritualistic denunciations of the Communist menace."[16] This is in keeping with Walker's preference for dubbing the anti-Communists within the ACLU as "the devious ones."[17] And as to be expected, Walker blames the United States for the Cold War.[18]

Beginning in the late 1960s, the ACLU became repoliticized, embracing every statist prescription that advanced equal outcomes. But unlike that of founding period, the ACLU of this period began promoting moral equality as well. The establishment of this new domain can be traced to two forces: (a) the cultural winds of moral neutrality that began in the late 1960s hit the ACLU with a fury and (b) growing resources made it possible for the Union to expand its reach and add moral equality to its list of egalitarian objectives.

Today the ACLU has 300,000 members and has affiliates in all fifty states and the District of Columbia; there are over 400 chapters nationwide. In one sense, there are actually two ACLUs: the lobbying wing and the nonlobbying wing, represented respectively by the ACLU and ACLU Foundation. The ACLU is a not-for-profit corporation that is sustained by dues and contributions from its members; it lobbies in Washington on issues ranging from national security to Supreme Court appointees. On the other hand, the ACLU Foundation is a tax-deductible entity, supported mostly by large grants from the Rockefeller, Ford, Carnegie, John D. and Catharine T. MacArthur Foundations, the tobacco industry as well as smaller grants from the likes of the Playboy Foundation; it handles litigation and public education. Indeed, according to Marvin Olasky, the

ACLU is one of the biggest recipients of left-wing philanthrophy in the nation.[19]

The national staff has approximately 300 salaried members, including about 70 staff attorneys, and depends on 5000 volunteer lawyers to handle much of the litigation. Involved in about 6,000 cases annually, the ACLU also receives free litigation assistance from its law school affiliates, including places like Harvard, the University of California-Davis, Indiana University, and the University of Colorado.[20] In addition, the ACLU benefits when law students are given lucrative fellowships, paid mostly with federal dollars, to do research at the ACLU on issues like gay rights.[21] It is for reasons like these that the ACLU can manage to do so much on a budget of approximately $30 million (this figure includes revenues from the ACLU Foundation).

Another source of Union revenue comes from being compensated for its services through the allotment of contingency fees. Indeed, the ACLU is officially on record supporting "statutes and other laws which adequately provide for attorneys' fees for successful plaintiffs in civil rights and civil liberties litigation."[22] The Union's idea of what constitutes adequate compensation is a matter of some dispute: in 1990, Richard Emery filed a claim against the City of New York amounting to $1,004,559. Emery, who worked on the case that ultimately abolished the New York City Board of Estimate, said most of the award he was seeking would go to the New York Civil Liberties Union, the place where he worked for most of the eight-year life of the suit. Not surprisingly, the attorneys for the City thought the amount excessive.[23]

Policy is set quarterly by the 83 members of the board of directors; 51 of the seats are held by the heads of the affiliates, with one each going to the national treasurer and the chair of the national advisory council, the rest going to at-large members. Despite the fact that the ACLU has quite stringent and exact policies regarding minority representation on its governing staffs,[24] few minorities play an active role in the organization. The ACLU gets around its own internal affirmative action policy by periodically granting itself a waiver[25] or by simply ignoring its policy altogether, a practice that has led some minority members to quit in disgust.[26]

The ACLU has put an increasing amount of money into its office of public education and into its many "projects." The public education department, headed by Colleen O'Connor, was essentially a one-person office until the late 1980s. Then, given the heavy attack that the Union labored under during the 1988 presidential campaign, the staff quickly ballooned to 12.

The "projects" represent a brand of special interest groupings within the ACLU. They exist independent of the basic work of the organization and concentrate on a variety of issues.

There is an AIDS Project, a Capital Punishment Project, a Children's Rights Project, an Immigrant's Rights Project, a Lesbian and Gay Project, a National Security Project, a National Prison Project, a Reproductive Freedom Project, a Women's Rights Project, a Civil Liberties in the Workplace Project, a Privacy and Technology Project, and an Arts Censorship Project. What with all the special interest groupings, former board member Alan Dershowitz has let, "Perhaps the Civil Liberties Union needs a civil liberties project."[27]

The ACLU's Methodology: Working the Courts

In order to accomplish its objective of reordering society, the ACLU has focused primarily on the courts. The Union understands that its goal of political, economic, social, and cultural equality is most likely to be realized by circumventing the will of the people, and that is why it is wary of taking its case to the executive and legislative branches of government. Similarly, the ACLU's preference for judicial activism is born of a desire to escape the considered judgments of others and rewrite law according to right results. So by taking its case to the most un-democratic branch of government, and by ignoring the intent of the Framers, the ACLU is in a position to superimpose its vision of liberty on society, despite the lack of public support for many of its efforts.

The ACLU's excessive reliance on a judicially active court explains why it greets Supreme Court nominees with the utmost seriousness. Indeed, nothing galvanizes the energies of ACLU officials more than the appointment of a justice to the high court. It is a matter of some saliency that until the nomination of Robert Bork to the Supreme Court, the ACLU had had a policy of not opposing any candidate for elected or appointed office. Bork officially changed all that, though he was not the first prospective justice the ACLU sought to discredit. In fact, the Union's disdain for judicial restraint antedates Bork by decades.

Even before the ACLU officially changed its policy regarding its refusal to take a stand on any candidate for elected or appointed office, it violated its own policy on nonpartisanship. For example, in 1971, the Union sent letters to each member of the Senate Judiciary Committee publicly attacking the nomination of William Rehnquist to the Supreme Court.[28] And in a different manner, Ira Glasser berated President Reagan in 1985 for considering the promotion of William Bradford Reynolds within the Justice Department.[29] The ACLU's "Stop Meese" campaign, a fundraiser that was waged with characteristic hyperbole against Attorney General Edwin Meese,[30] and its practice of issuing bumper stickers proclaiming "LONG LIVE JUSTICE(S) BLACKMUN, BRENNAN, MARSHALL,"[31] are other examples of ACLU departures from its policy of nonpartisanship.

It was the prospect of having Robert Bork on the Supreme Court, however, that caused the ACLU to make a formal change in policy. It was known for years that Bork was on the short list of virtually every Republican candidate for president, so when President Reagan nominated him, it took no time at all for his critics to rally. What made Bork such a threat was more than his erudition—it was his detailed and principled objection to judicial activism that made him persona non grata among the liberal-left elite; he was the antithesis of everything the ACLU represented.

On August 31, 1991, Norman Dorsen, president of the ACLU, announced that the board of directors of the Union had decided to drop its 51-year policy against involvement in Supreme Court confirmation battles. As previously discussed, the ACLU had already broken its policy on several occasions, though this was the first admission that it was going to officially oppose a nominee for elected or appointed office. From now on, the Union would oppose any Supreme Court nominee "whose record demonstrates a judicial philosophy that would fundamentally jeopardize the Supreme Court's critical and unique role in protecting civil liberties in the United States." Once the new policy was approved, the board voted 61 to 3 to oppose Bork's nomination. Interestingly, only a minority on the board were lawyers, and none was a judge.[32]

To get some idea of what a threat Bork was to the ACLU agenda, it is worth recalling what the ACLU used to say about taking a partisan stand on Supreme Court nominations. Just two years before the ACLU reversed its official policy of nonpartisanship, Ira Glasser stated that "if we get involved in partisan politics to the extent of supporting or opposing a particular candidate or nominee, then everything we say later about what that person does becomes suspect."[33] Evidently, the defeat of Bork was worth the risk.

On the same day that the ACLU announced its opposition to Bork, Glasser sent a letter, via Western Union, to the Union membership. It included such lines as: "DETAILED RESEARCH REVEALS BORK FAR MORE DANGEROUS THAN PREVIOUSLY BELIEVED . . . WE RISK NOTHING SHORT OF WRECKING THE ENTIRE BILL OF RIGHTS . . . HIS CONFIRMATION WOULD THREATEN OUR SYSTEM OF GOVERNMENT . . . TIME IS SHORT." And in closing there was the predictable "URGE YOU TO RUSH EMERGENCY CONTRIBUTION AT ONCE."[34]

The tactic that the ACLU used to discredit Bork was to paint him as a "radical," someone who was "well outside the mainstream of conservative judicial philosophy." According to the Union, Judge Bork posed "an extraordinary threat to individual liberty and to the Court's special role in protecting minority rights against the will and whim of the majority." Dorsen warned that "if Robert Bork's views were to prevail, the most critical function of the Supreme Court—the protection of individual rights—would atrophy, and the system of checks and balances that protects such rights would be upset." Glasser, tapping into the charge of "majoritarianism," contended that Bork "believes the highest right in society is for the majority to impose its moral views on the minority." Then Glasser really unloaded: "Had he [Bork] been around in the 18th century, he would have been against adding the Bill of Rights to the Constitution."[35]

Throughout the Bork proceedings, the ACLU deliberately chose not to oppose Bork on the basis of his adherence to the doctrine of original intent, though everyone knew that that was why his critics were so exercised about him. Ironically, the few times the ACLU did mention original intent, it chided Bork for *not* adhering to the philosophy of original understanding. Colleen O'Connor explains that the Union opposed Bork because he "did not reflect the true intent of the founders in drafting the Bill of Rights,"[36] suggesting not only that the ACLU has a better understanding of what the Framers wanted but that the Union has an interest in following it. Even its most ardent supporters must find this posturing amusing, for in reality the ACLU has never taken original intent jurisprudence seriously.

The Bork debacle left its scars on all the participants, leaving the ACLU and others wary for another fight over a Supreme Court nominee.

That is why in the nominations that followed, the ACLU took a low profile, though it would be incorrect to suggest that it remained totally on the sidelines. Indeed, in the wake of Bork's defeat, even before Douglas Ginsburg was nominated, Morton Halperin of the ACLU sent a "Dear Joe" letter to Senator Joseph Biden, chairman of the Senate Judiciary Committee, urging a delay in the process; the ACLU wanted more time to chart the prospective nominees.[37] Glasser publicly asked for a stay of two months, mentioning the need for research and the preparation of reports.[38] But all this was mooted when Ginsburg was forced to withdraw upon revelations of his former drug use.

Neither Anthony Kennedy nor David Souter ran into trouble with the ACLU. But Clarence Thomas almost did. On August 17, 1991, the board of directors of the ACLU voted 36 to 25 to oppose the nomination of Thomas, one vote short of the 60 percent needed (as determined by ACLU policy) to formally oppose a Supreme Court nominee. ACLU policy states that nominees should be rejected only when there is a finding of "a grave and imminent threat" to civil liberties.[39] Not to be misunderstood, Colleen O'Connor was quick to add that the vote, which followed four hours of debate, was not "in any way an endorsement." And Glasser made it clear that "if this were a vote on Thomas alone, it would have probably been 61 to nothing."[40] There is little doubt that Thomas would not have survived the vote had it been taken after Anita Hill made her allegations of sexual misconduct against him.

There are other ways the ACLU can accomplish its goals without reliance on like-minded federal judges: the use of state constitutions and international human rights laws. Ever since Presidents Reagan and Bush succeeded in staffing the majority of seats on the federal bench, the ACLU has looked for new venues to practice its convictions. The use of state constitutions to secure an expansion of civil liberties, long urged by former Supreme Court Justice William Brennan, has been utilized by the ACLU in recent years to effect, among other things, changes in the school systems of Alabama and Connecticut, changes in the handling of rights of mental patients in Montana, and changes in police behavior in New Jersey.

The ACLU not only sees in state constitutions a great opportunity to go beyond the liberties prescribed in the U.S. Constitution, it sees state courts as a new venue to apply international human rights laws. And no one has been more outspoken in her advocacy of this approach than the

ACLU's new president, Nadine Strossen. Strossen, who succeeded Norman Dorsen on February 1, 1991, has fingered gay rights and capital punishment as issues she would like to bring before state courts, applying international human rights laws.[41]

The ACLU's determination to use state constitutions and international human rights laws to advance its cause is in keeping with the charge being made here: the ACLU does not believe in limited government, and that is why it continually searches for new ways for the judiciary to expand the reach of the state. A commitment to the principle of separation of powers and respect for the rights of the people to determine their own public policies would not allow for the application of expanded state powers through international human rights laws. The very fact that it is willing to impose on the American people laws not crafted by its own legislators and judges—and only vaguely found in state constitutions—is testimony to just how far removed the ACLU is from the republican notion of representative government.

The Road to Liberticide

Over the past few decades, the ACLU has exhibited a strong strand of both collectivism and libertarianism. Indeed, this strange admixture, the result of which is statism and libertinism, is what defines civil libertarianism today. At bottom, what links the ACLU's espousal of collectivism and libertarianism is an unabiding hostility to the constitutive properties of the social order.

All societies are hierarchical in nature. The social institutions that shape our lives—and the traditions, customs, and social conventions that we share—are as natural as they are inevitable. But from the atomistic perspective of the ACLU, these are just the properties that stand in the way of full-blown individual liberation. That is why it prefers the authority of the state to the authority of mediating institutions, and that is why it finds objectionable traditional norms and values.

The fundamental problem with the atomistic conception of liberty is that it interprets freedom exclusively through the prism of rights. By neglecting the social context of freedom, the ACLU pursues a reckless liberty. The caretakers of moral responsibility are the mediating institutions, and that is why it is critical that social authority not be undermined by the courts in the pursuit of individual rights.

The chapters that follow attempt to demonstrate how a flawed idea of liberty works against the very goal its proponents seek to advance. Not included here are many of the mundane matters that the ACLU attends to. The focus is on those issues that define the organization's *Weltanschauung*, or world view. To be sure, there are many outstanding contributions that the ACLU has made to the cause of liberty. When it comes to defending serious violations of individual rights, the ACLU has an honorable record. Where the record is tainted, however, is in the Union's extremist interpretation of what constitutes individual rights. By making a fetish of individual rights, the ACLU corrupts the social foundation that freedom depends upon, thereby sadly contributing more to liberticide to liberty.

Notes

1. The ACLU is not solely responsible for promoting an impoverished conception of liberty. The problem is largely cultural in nature and is discussed more thoroughly in my book, *The New Freedom: Individualism and Collectivism in the Social Lives of Americans* (New Brunswick, New Jersey: Transaction Press, 1990).
2. I intentionally reject the term "communitarian" even though I share many of the positions that communitarians hold. The problem I have with "The Responsive Communitarian Platform," as sponsored by Amitai Etzioni, editor of *The Responsive Community*, is its queasiness regarding religion: it totally ignores the role religion plays in the formation of a truly communitarian society.
3. The term "mediating structures" was popularized by Peter Berger and Richard John Neuhaus to describe a concept that was first broached by Edmund Burke and Alexis de Tocqueville and given fresh insight by Robert Nisbet.
4. Robert Nisbet, *Conservatism: Dream and Reality* (Minneapolis: University of Minnesota Press, 1986), 49.
5. Jeffrey T. Leeds, "The ACLU: Impeccable Judgments or Tainted Policies," *New York Times Magazine*, September 10, 1989, p. 78.
6. Samuel Walker, *In Defense of American Liberties: A History of the ACLU* (New York: Oxford University Press, 1990), 119.
7. See chapter three of my book, *The Politics of the American Civil Liberties Union* (New Brunswick, New Jersey: Transaction Press, 1985).
8. Ibid.
9. Walker, *In Defense of American Liberties*, 63.
10. Donohue, *The Politics of the American Civil Liberties Union*, 134.
11. Peggy Lamson, *Roger Baldwin: Founder of the American Civil Liberties Union* (Boston: Houghton Mifflin, 1976), 204.
12. Quoted by William H. McIlhany II, *The ACLU on Trial* (New Rochelle, New York: Arlington House, 1976), 194.
13. Donohue, *The Politics of the American Civil Liberties Union*, chapters two and three.
14. Frederick R. Barkley, "Calls New Deal Communist 'Front," *New York Times*, September 7, 1939, p. 26.

15. Walker, *In Defense of American Liberties*, 130.
16. Ibid., 206.
17. Ibid., 128.
18. Ibid., 120.
19. Marvin Olasky, "Philanthrophic Correctness," *Heterodoxy*, October 1992, p. 13.
20. For more information on the role that the law schools play in assisting the ACLU and other left activist organizations, see the Washington Legal Foundation report entitled, *In Whose Interest? Public Interest Law Activism in the Law Schools*, 1990.
21. See Salma Abdelnour, "Programs for Community Service by College Students Get U.S. Aid," *Chronicle of Higher Education*, September 16, 1992, p. A28.
22. Policy #220a, passed April 15-16, 1988.
23. See George James, "Lawyer Asks $1 Million Fee For Ending Estimate Board," *New York Times*, September 13, 1990, p. B10.
24. Policy #526, passed October 14-15, 1989. There were other internal affirmative action policies before this one, though none that were as strict.
25. See Board Minutes for June 12-13, 1982, p. 3.
26. In 1985, Roger Wilkins quit as chairman of the search committee for the post of Washington director when Ira Glasser appointed Morton Halperin as the acting director. Wilkins, as well as board member and minority activist Michael Meyers, were convinced that Glasser did not want an honest search for qualified minority candidates. Glasser denied the charges, but Halperin eventually got the job. See David Burnham, "Civil Liberties Group Embroiled in Hiring Dispute," *New York Times*, January 24, 1985, p. A19.
27. Quoted by Leeds, "The ACLU: Impeccable Judgments or Tainted Policies," p. 76.
28. Dan Popeo, *Not OUR America . . . The ACLU Exposed* (Washington, D.C.: Washington Legal Foundation, 1989), 21-25. Ira Glasser tried to deny that the ACLU ever took a position for or against a candidate for elected or appointed office but then had to admit error when Paul Kamenar of the Washington Legal Foundation presented him with evidence regarding ACLU opposition to Rehnquist.
29. See Glasser's letter of June 19 1985, to the *New York Times*, written in his official capacity as executive director of the ACLU.
30. See ACLU fund-raising letter of December 1986. Walker admits that the Executive Committee hastily met to consider whether the "Stop Meese" campaign violated its policy on nonpartisanship. It concluded that it didn't. See Walker, *In Defense of American Liberties*, 364.
31. I have photocopies of the bumper stickers in my possession. They were given to me by former ACLU activist Lawrence Cranberg.
32. Linda Greenhouse, "A.C.L.U., Reversing Policy, Joins the Opposition to Bork," *New York Times*, September 1, 1987, p. A10.
33. Glasser's remarks were made in an interview that was published in the Winter 1985 edition of *Civil Liberties*, p. 3.
34. Quoted in Robert Bork, *The Tempting of America* (New York: Free Press, 1990), 287-88.
35. All quotes are from "ACLU Opposes Bork," *Civil Liberties*, Summer 1987, p. 1.
36. Quoted by Jeffrey Leeds, "The ACLU: Impeccable Judgments or Tainted Policies?" p. 78.
37. See the *Wall Street Journal* editorial "Do They Dare Again?" of November 2, 1987, p. 28.
38. Ira Glasser, "Stop This Headlong Rush To Judgment on Ginsburg," *New York Times*, November 4, 1987, p. A31.

39. Policy #519 "Political Non-Partisanship."

40. Quoted by Karen De Witt, "A.C.L.U. to Remain Neutral on Nomination of Thomas," *New York Times*, August 19, 1991, p. A7.

41. Phil Gutis, "ACLU Elects First Woman President in 71-Year History," *Civil Liberties*, Winter 1990–91, p. 3. See also Nadine Strossen, "The President's Word," *Civil Liberties*, Summer–Fall 1992, p. 11.

PART I

Mediating Structures and Liberty

1

The Family

Surrogate Motherhood

Those who hold to an atomistic conception of liberty tend to understate the role that mediating structures play in the production of a free society. For them, freedom is understood in terms of the distribution of rights, meaning that the more, the better. This describes the ACLU's vision of liberty and accounts for its reticence regarding the family's contribution to freedom. When Harvard law professor Mary Ann Glendon complains that nothing has negatively impacted on marriage and the family more than radical individualism, she might well have been thinking about the ACLU's approach to the subject.[1]

The Book of Genesis records that Ishmael was begot by Abraham and his maid Hagar, who acted as a surrogate for Abraham's barren wife, Sarah. Today, a new form of adultery is practiced, known as rent-a-womb. The business, though not flourishing, is growing, with the result that it is standard practice to pay a woman well in excess of $10,000, plus expenses, just for the rent of her womb (payments of over $100,000 are no longer unusual). The lucrative nature of the business, however, has set off a storm of controversy, resulting in legal problems both at home and abroad.[2]

Ethicists have raised serious questions regarding surrogate motherhood, contending that it promotes dehumanization by effectively criminalizing any bonding that may take place between the surrogate (who is in fact the mother) and her child. Serious questions remain, as well, over whether single people, including homosexuals and lesbians, should have the right to "contract out" for such services. And what should be done if the surrogate wants to keep the baby? What happens if the adoptive parents change their mind, or divorce, or die, during gestation? This is fertile ground for lawyers, if for no one else.

The ACLU's policy on surrogate parenting is indicative of its atomistic vision regarding family issues: nowhere in the Union's lengthy policy is there any mention of the term "family." What we get instead is a policy that discusses the rights of the "gestational mother," the "genetic father," and the "genetic mother," as well as such civil libertarian ideas as "right to privacy and bodily integrity" and "associational rights." Even the Fourteenth Amendment is given a chilly cast, as when the Union proclaims that "equal protection principles dictate that an egg donor mother who, like the sperm donor father, participates in a surrogacy arrangement, contributing genetic material for the purpose of becoming a parent, be like the father, a parent to the resulting child."[3]

In 1988, the ACLU challenged a Michigan law outlawing surrogate mother contracts for payment. Though Judge John H. Gillis Jr. of Wayne County Circuit Court ruled that the law was constitutional, the state's attorney general agreed to an interpretation of the law that closely resembled the ACLU's position. Surrogacy, it was decided, could be permitted, providing the gestational mother did not give up her rights to be a parent until after the child was born.[4] Official ACLU policy holds that "a surrogacy agreement that conditions payments to the gestational mother on her termination of parental rights is void." However, the Union does not oppose "agreements to compensate the mother for providing gestational services."[5] In other words, baby selling is taboo with the ACLU, but not wombs-for-rent.

As far as the ACLU is concerned, a child born of a surrogate agreement where there is a genetic mother who is not also the gestational mother, has three parents, all of whom have equal rights. If, upon birth, the surrogate mother yields her parental rights, she may do so, but she may not do so in advance. The Union reasons that "an agreement to waive a fundamental right in the future . . . is inappropriate until a person is in a position to know the meaning, importance, or value of a particular right."[6]

The same logic regarding the waiver of parental rights for the surrogate holds true for abortion: the ACLU wants to deny women who agree to be surrogate mothers the right to waive their right to an abortion. It is a matter of same salience that, though the ACLU says that there is no legitimate societal reason for state legislation in the area of "reproductive choice," it adamantly contends that "free choice" should not apply to a woman who chooses to waive her right to an abortion in surrogate agreements. In a policy that can only be labeled innovative, the civil libertarians justify their reasoning by stating that "allowing a woman to waive her right to an abortion would violate her constitutional privacy rights, along with the Thirteenth Amendment's prohibition against involuntary servitude." And so what rights should the prospective adoptive parents have against a woman who chooses to abort the baby? None, according to the ACLU.[7]

Adding more controversy to its position, the ACLU defends the right of the surrogate mother to change her mind and opt to keep the baby after he or she is born. What about her previous decision to relinquish her rights at birth? The ACLU dubs it "irrelevant," maintaining that "holding her to that previous intention chills the exercise of her right to reproductive choice (the entry into a surrogacy arrangement) and penalizes the exercise of her relational right (her decision not to relinquish the child)." What about the father's rights? The Union argues that the father's entrance into the surrogate agreement "should not give him an equitable right to custody arising from his thwarted expectation that the mother would relinquish her parental rights." So while the ACLU holds that the father is one of the parents and believes that both "women and men have the right to reproductive choice," it is entirely legitimate to trump his parental rights and award custody to the reneging surrogate mother.[8]

Questions regarding parental suitability, as determined by custom, are not considered germane to the ACLU. It does not matter to the ACLU that a couple entering a surrogate agreement may not be married. Nor does it matter that single persons may want to acquire a child through this procedure. Homosexuals and lesbians are also entitled to participate in a surrogacy agreement, as well as the mentally retarded. What is at work here is a highly atomistic conception of liberty, one that places exclusive value on the exercise of individual rights, independent of social context or cultural prerogatives.

Abortion

The ACLU's policy on surrogate motherhood is the logical derivative of the Union's position on abortion. For the ACLU of the 1990s, abortion-on-demand is an unqualified right, deserving of no restrictions of any kind and entitled to full Medicaid coverage. As will become evident, this issue has done more to galvanize the ACLU than any other. "The deliberate killing of a human being has no place in a society that calls itself civilized and humane." Though that is an official position of the ACLU's, it expresses the Union's sentiments toward capital punishment,[9] not abortion. When asked to explain why the ACLU's logic on capital punishment does not extend to abortion, official statements stress that the abortion issue involves "disagreement between basically religious beliefs" without also mentioning disputes among biologists and physicians.[10] The central question in the whole debate—when life begins—is not only not addressed, the Union acts as if there were no legitimate grounds for a debate: the only party that it recognizes is the woman (the fetus as potential life is not even acknowledged).

Glasser has said that the ACLU's position on abortion "*preceded* the women's rights movement by many years."[11] Not so. The ACLU did not adopt a "pro-choice" position until 1967, a year after the founding of the National Organization for Women (NOW). Aryeh Neier, Glasser's predecessor, was more candid about the Union's politics when he stated that the ACLU was "the legal branch of the women's movement."[12] Former ACLU board member Alan Dershowitz has even accused the Union of harboring "a preference for abortion."[13]

Abortion is no ordinary issue for the ACLU—it is the organization's top priority. It is almost impossible to find a fund-raising letter written by Glasser in the last decade and a half that hasn't mentioned abortion. Moreover, when attorney Jeffrey T. Leeds was working on a piece on the ACLU for the *New York Times Magazine*, he was struck by the extent to which Union leaders boasted that the ACLU handles 80 percent of the abortion rights litigation cases nationwide.[14] Similarly, *Reason* writer Charles Oliver was taken aback when he learned from John Powell, the Union's national legal director, that he considered abortion to be the ACLU's number one priority; the defense of the First Amendment, the alleged heart and soul of the ACLU's mission, was listed third, after civil rights. Oliver's conclusion cuts to the question why:

> Abortion may indeed be a civil liberties issue, but it seems strange to make it the ACLU's top priority. After all, Planned Parenthood, NOW, and the National Abortion Rights Action League ably fight for abortion rights. Only the ACLU speaks for the First Amendment. But defending abortion rights may seem like a much more lucrative venture than defending the speech rights of Nazis. Or of anti-abortion protesters.[15]

The charge that Oliver makes is not without foundation. One of the reasons why the ACLU is so fiercely committed to abortion rights is greed: nothing works to garner more dollars than an "EMERGENCY MEMO" citing some alleged restriction on abortion rights. If it were principle that fired the ACLU, then surely it would not sacrifice the First Amendment rights of antiabortion activists for the sake of financial gain. But as Alan Dershowitz sees it, that's exactly what the ACLU does: "You can make more money supporting reproductive rights than you can supporting civil liberties. It's as simple as that."[16] Dershowitz believes that the very existence of a Reproductive Freedom Project within the ACLU creates an inherent conflict of interest.

Janet Benshoof commanded the ACLU's Reproductive Freedom Project from 1977 to 1993 and has had much to do with why the ACLU has been so reluctant to defend the rights of antiabortion protesters. Armed with a budget of approximately $2 million and a staff of 17 employees, Benshoof was the Union's most devoted activist in behalf of abortion rights, willing to pull out all the stops at any given moment. Frequently, her style became demagogic, as when she blamed opponents of abortion not only of having "engineered" the conservative majority on the Supreme Court but of conspiring to police the bedrooms of Americans as well: "They want to get into your bedroom and tell you exactly what you can do there."[17] Benshoof became so overextended in her approach that she was not above recommending disrespect for the process of law, as, for example, in her advocacy of applying mob pressure on the judiciary; she pushed for "pro-choice" activists to march on courtrooms where abortion cases were being heard.[18]

Benshoof's extremism is tolerated by her superiors because the question of abortion is not a difficult one for the ACLU: it's a matter of a woman's right to choose, not a conflict between her right to abort and the right of someone else to live. Antiabortion protesters, therefore, are not seen as analogous to civil rights demonstrators in the 1960s but as lunatic fascists out to destroy freedom. Hence, the reluctance of the ACLU to defend principle, that is, the exercise of First Amendment rights by antiabortion activists. Ironically, real fascists—like American Nazis and Klansmen—have had their rights protected more often and with greater vigor by the ACLU than antiabortion demonstrators.

To be sure, there are bona fide crazies in the antiabortion movement, and many of them have engaged in acts of violence and sheer thuggery, a far cry from the civil disobedience practices of Martin Luther King. But that was true of the civil rights movement, and the anti-war crusade of the 1960s, as well: every dissident outfit has its fringe element. Yet the ACLU never flinched from defending the most egregious violations of law in any of these movements. But when it comes to the opponents of abortion having their First Amendment rights violated by the authorities, the most noticeable thing about the ACLU is its absence from the fray. Not even having the Racketeer Influenced and Corrupt Organizations Act (RICO) thrown at antiabortion protesters has moved the ACLU to action.

The reason why RICO was originally passed in 1970 was to root out the Mafia from legitimate business. Unfortunately, the wording of the statute was so vague that it soon came to be used for purposes having nothing to do with weakening organized crime; for example, couples undergoing a divorce have sued each other as racketeers, and a speeding California motorist has sued the city of Huntington Beach as a criminal enterprise for awarding him three tickets. Bad as these abuses are, they at least don't gut the heart out of the First Amendment, as has happened to those who protest abortion.

The ACLU is nominally opposed to the RICO statute, and there are some senior members, like Washington official Antonio Califa, who are truly opposed to the invocation of RICO against any protesters, including opponents of abortion.[19] However, due largely to the influence of Benshoof, the ACLU's record is grievously stained in this area. It was her Reproductive Freedom Project that in 1986 issued an infamous booklet entitled "Preserving the Right to Choose: How to Cope with Violence and Disruption at Abortion Clinics." In it was the suggestion that abortion clinics might want to use RICO against antiabortion protesters; it was further stated that abortion clinics might want to hire off-duty police officers as security guards. If this were a radical feminist group making the suggestions, it would be understandable, if still questionable. But this was the nation's number one civil liberties organization at work. The booklet was eventually pulled and has since been understood as "something that slipped through" out of "zeal."[20]

The ACLU would not tolerate the use of RICO against nuclear weapons dissidents, but in the case of antiabortion protesters the matter is different. In fact, the ACLU has actually used RICO against abortion demonstrators. When antiabortion protesters were sued under RICO in

Philadelphia, the local chapter of the ACLU filed an amicus brief on behalf of the plaintiffs, the Northeast Women's Center. By chance, another ACLU attorney, Christine Smith Torre, was retained to represent the protesters in appealing the case to the U.S. Supreme Court. Smith Torre wrote to Glasser in New York outlining the dangers of having the ACLU use RICO to squash First Amendment rights and asked him to enlist the national office on her side. But the national office refused to get involved.[21] Barry Steinhardt, then executive director of the state affiliate, justified using RICO against the abortion foes by arguing that the dissidents were "interfering with the constitutional rights of others." Pittsburgh ACLU attorney and Duquesne University law professor Bruce Ledewitz saw it differently: "The ACLU is so obsessed with the right to abortion that they don't recognize the implications of these suits."[22]

The ACLU missed another opportunity to defend civil liberties in 1989 in West Hartford, Connecticut. It was on June 17 that 261 persons were arrested, and then physically abused by the police, for staging a sit-in at the Summit Women's Clinic. Though the events of that day were largely overlooked by the press, John Leo of *U.S. News and World Report* gave it the attention it deserved.[23]

The police used so-called "come-a-long" holds, or "pain compliance holds," with the result that many of the protesters claimed permanent nerve damage. Some were denied medical care, while others were held incommunicado for two days and arraigned in a court closed to the public. One woman had to have surgery after police damaged her uterus, and others were kept for days without making a phone call. The ACLU, which on other occasions has sued municipalities for failing to adequately discipline and train its police force,[24] did nothing.

When John Spear, the publisher of a small upstate New York community newspaper, wrote an editorial against the police brutality, he too was slapped with a RICO suit. He was charged with extortion, that is, attempting to extort from the police better protection! Another person named in the suit was a woman whose only crime was opening her home to the relatives and friends of those arrested. The Connecticut affiliate of the ACLU knew all this (a letter was even sent regarding the arrest of Spear) but chose to do nothing.

"Why do they still call it a civil-liberties union?" commented ACLU member and nemesis Nat Hentoff. When pressed about cases like the West Hartford one, the ACLU typically responds that it can't get involved with the defense of antiabortion protesters because it is already committed to the side of the abortion clinics. When John Leo asked Alan Dershowitz, "Can it be that affiliates sometimes deliberately involve themselves early on one side so they will have an excuse not to help victims on the other?" the Harvard Law professor replied, "Absolutely. They go to the pro-choice people and say, 'Get us in right away,'" thereby giving them the excuse of conflict of interest in the event they are contacted by the antiabortion side. And what does the ACLU say when asked specifically about its duplicity regarding RICO? Lynn Paltrow, who works for Benshoof, explained the Union's attitude: "It's ACLU policy to oppose application of RICO, but there are those on staff who feel that as long as RICO exists, this kind of behavior (Operation Rescue tactics) does fit." "In other words," as John Leo put it, "RICO is totally bad, but sort of useful."[25]

When 25,000 antiabortion protesters showed up in Wichita, Kansas, in the summer of 1991 with the express purpose of shutting down the city's three abortion clinics, little did they know that Judge Patrick Kelly would make a federal case out it. Judge Kelly drew on a little-used 1871 law, originally intended to halt the terrorism of the Ku Klux Klan, to ban the demonstrators. Not only did the ACLU not come to their defense, it filed an amicus brief in support of the blocked clinics. However, in 1993 the Supreme Court ruled that the Reconstruction-era law did not give federal judges jurisdiction to bar antiabortion protesters from blockading abortion clinics.[26]

It is not just antiabortion protesters who have felt the sting of the ACLU's pro-abortion zealotry. Congressman Henry Hyde was followed into a Catholic church in the 1970s and subjected to ACLU surveillance, all because the Union wanted to demonstrate that it was his religious beliefs that undergirded his antiabortion position; a judge threw the suit out, finding no breach of church-state lines.[27] But no one knows the ACLU's reaction to those who take an antiabortion position better than Nat Hentoff.

Hentoff, an avid writer on everything from jazz to civil liberties, has become somewhat persona non grata within the ranks of the ACLU for his antiabortion views. A pure libertarian and civil rights activist if there ever was one, Hentoff sees a direct line between support for disenfranchised blacks in the 1960s and support for disenfranchised unborn children today. But his rallying for the rights of the underdog has come up short with his colleagues in the ACLU when the subject turns to the unborn. It is no secret that Hentoff's failure to win reelection to the board of the New York Civil Liberties Union in the late 1970s was due to his emerging antiabortion position.

Hentoff has also been criticized for his defense of the rights of handicapped children. Though the ACLU has no official policy on the right of handicapped children to live, its inaction in cases where such children have been denied medical treatment has been reported by Hentoff and others.[28] And the fact that it provided the attorney, William Colby, to the family of Nancy Cruzan (she was comatose and her parents wanted doctors to "let her die") is only one example of the ACLU's new position endorsing euthanasia, as well.[29] In cases where the person is not competent, the ACLU accepts "advance directives" *and* "proxy decisions"; the latter includes members of the immediate family or life partner, providing that "there is a consensus among health care providers, family members, and other relevant parties that the person is in a persistent vegetative state."[30]

Notwithstanding the protests of Hentoff, there is not a single ancillary issue regarding abortion rights that the ACLU hasn't tackled. True to its atomistic conception of liberty, the ACLU sees abortion as purely a matter of individual choice, requiring no concurrence from the father or, in the case of minors, from parents. The ACLU has fought waiting periods in several states and has opposed requirements that doctors perform certain tests on women seeking abortion if the doctor believes the woman to be at least 20 weeks pregnant. Requirements that all abortions be performed in hospitals have also been resisted by the ACLU, as have restrictions on fetal-tissue transplants.

The Union has also sought to declare unconstitutional a New York prenatal funding law, a statute aimed at reducing infant mortality among indigent women. Why? Because the law doesn't provide monies for abortion (this is the Union's way of using an existing program to create a "right to abortion" under the state constitution). The ACLU has even sued over an Illinois birth questionnaire: according to the ACLU, new mothers in maternity wards should not be required to disclose the number of their previous live births, miscarriages, and abortions, nor should they have to answer questions about alcohol and tobacco.

ACLU litigation in abortion cases has been extensive. Two days after George Bush became president, the ACLU found reason to sound the alarms. The reason? Attorney General Dick Thornburgh asked the Supreme Court to hear *Webster v. Reproductive Health Services*, a Missouri case aimed at making abortion more difficult to obtain. The possibility that *Roe v. Wade* might be overturned was real, so the ACLU wasted no time in launching an all-out effort aimed at overturning the Missouri law. The ACLU's Reproductive Freedom Project, led by Janet Benshoof, teamed up with Faye Wattleton of Planned Parenthood to begin a massive nationwide "pro-choice" campaign. With pro bono assistance from New York advertising executives, the ACLU placed full-page ads in the *New York Times, Washington Post* weekly, *New Republic*, and *USA Today*; college campuses were also hit with poster-size copies of the ad. It was a success: the campaign quickly netted 100,000 letters, followed by another 100,000 letters in the four-month period after the ads were run.[31]

But in the end, the ads didn't matter: ACLU attorney Kathryn Kolbert lost in her amicus bid to overturn the Missouri law. On July 3, 1989, the U.S. Supreme Court upheld three key provisions of the Missouri statute and, though it didn't overturn *Roe*, set back the "pro-choice" movement more than any decision in the post-*Roe* period. Specifically, the Court upheld the declaration that life begins from the moment of conception; the prohibition that barred the use of public buildings for performing abortions, even if the abortions were themselves paid for privately; and the provisions regarding viability testing.[32] The ACLU claimed that the decision to uphold the Missouri declaration that life begins at conception "may harm women's freedom and both maternal and fetal health in a variety of ways." The ACLU, which up until this point never had anything to say regarding the state's interest in fetal health, did not say how the health of the fetus would be harmed by recognizing that life begins at conception.[33]

In the two years following the *Webster* decision, state legislatures across the country considered some 600 bills restricting abortion. It was in the U.S. territory of Guam, and in Utah, that the ACLU pressed its case. On March 8, 1990, the Guam legislature unanimously passed a law (21-0) that allowed for abortions only in the rare cases where "there is a substantial risk that the continuance of the pregnancy would endanger the life of the mother or would gravely impair [her] health." Eight days later, Janet Benshoof flew to Guam to assist Guamanian lawyer Anita Arriola in her effort to convince Guam Governor Joseph Ada to veto the bill. Benshoof's trip ended in failure; she also had criminal charges filed against her for "solicitation" of abortion.[34] But in 1992, a federal court of appeals ruled that *Roe v. Wade* was still binding and that the Guam law was in conflict with it; the Supreme Court let the decision stand.

In Utah, a bill was passed in the spring of 1991 that effectively banned abortion-on-demand, allowing for abortion in only narrow circumstances. The ACLU was energized, charging in a full-page ad in the *New York Times*, "IN UTAH, THEY KNOW HOW TO PUNISH A WOMAN WHO HAS AN ABORTION. SHOOT HER."[35] The law, however, said nothing of the kind.[36] In fact, women were clearly exempt from any penalties. Commenting on the law, Utah Governor Norman H. Bangerter said, "The ACLU's recent allegation, made in a fundraising ad, that this law subjects women who have abortions to murder charges is simply false. The law is quite specific that *no* woman is to be punished in any manner for obtaining an abortion; the only penalty is for physicians." Just to be certain that no one misinterpreted the law to penalize women, the Utah legislature clarified the law during a special session of the legislature.[37] Perhaps this explains why the ACLU eventually lost in its effort to overturn the law.

The rancor caused by the Guam and Utah cases was nothing compared to the outburst that followed the 1991 Supreme Court decision in *Rust v. Sullivan*. In *Rust*, the Court held that 1988 federal regulations that ensured that Title X funds be used solely to assist women in pre-pregnancy family planning, and not to subsidize abortion counseling or prenatal care, were in keeping with the intent of Congress when it enacted the 1970 Title X program. The ACLU maintained that the federal regulations imposed a sort of "gag rule," prohibiting physicians from partaking in abortion referrals.

The 1970 law had two goals: delivery of contraceptive services to indigent families, and contraceptive research. The law explicitly said that "none of the funds . . . shall be used in programs where abortion is a method of family planning." It was later determined, however, that Title X providers were promoting and performing abortions. The 1988 regulations, issued by the Department of Health and Human Services, prohibited abortion counseling and referral in Title X programs but did not stop Title X grantees from counseling, referring, or performing abortions; if they chose to do so, it had to be in settings that were "physically and financially separate" from their Title X-funded program.

As for the alleged "gag rule" part of the regulations, the Court said that the regulations do not suppress speech but merely reflect the limits of a program created and paid for by the federal government.[38] Ira Glasser disagreed, arguing that the decision in *Rust* was "an especially cruel waiver of rights" for poor women.[39]

Rust was effectively gutted in 1992, however, when a federal appeals court invalidated the Bush administration's modifications of the ban on abortion counseling. The modifications, made in the spring of 1991, were held by the panel of judges to substantially amend and even repudiate part of the original regulation. And if there were any doubt about the legality of abortion counseling at federally funded clinics, it was removed altogether when President Bill Clinton, in one of his first acts as president, revoked the regulations in question.

Perhaps the most controversial abortion case since *Roe* was the 1992 decision affecting Pennsylvania law. In October 1991, a federal appeals court upheld several provisions of a strict antiabortion law passed by the Pennsylvania legislature in 1989. The provisions that were upheld included the requirement that women under 18 years of age had to have parental consent before obtaining an abortion and the stipulation that a 24-hour waiting period must evolve so that women have a chance to consider information on the risks of and alternatives to abortion. The ACLU, along with Planned Parenthood, appealed the case to the U.S. Supreme Court.

On June 29, 1992, the Supreme Court upheld both the parental consent provision of the Pennsylvania law and the waiting period provision (as well as two other sections of the law), but it reaffirmed what it called the "essence" of the constitutional right to abortion. Offering a new analysis, the court specifically said that no law would be considered constitutional if it placed an "undue burden" on women seeking an abortion.[40] Though the decision left *Roe* fully intact, Ira Glasser immediately hit members with another "EMERGENCY LEGAL BULLETIN," this time warning of impending dangers and the need for more money.[41]

Perhaps the most dramatic aspect of the *Casey* decision was the language that the court used in rendering its decision. By declaring marriage to be only an "association" of individuals, the high court embraced an atomistic vision of liberty. As the editors of *First Things* said, "The notion of the unburdened, unencumbered, autonomous self drives the entirety of the Court's opinion."[42] Now the fundamental problem with this atomistic perspective is its asocial character: it reduces a social institution, complete with primary group relationships and moral strictures, to nothing more than an "association" of independent and disconnected individuals. Marriage, then, is given the same social and moral standing as any dyadic relationship.

The ACLU wasn't satisfied with *Casey* because it didn't proclaim an absolute right to abortion in every state of the union. But the ACLU's absolutist approach to abortion rights is not shared by most Americans. In those surveys that get beyond "yes or no" answers, and allow respondents to express their mixed feelings about the subject (they are the only meaningful polls), it is evident that a clear consensus has emerged on this difficult moral issue. It is this: Most Americans do not want a return to the days of a near-absolute ban on abortions, but fully eight in ten oppose abortion-on-demand. If a woman's health is endangered by a pregnancy, or if there is a strong chance of a defect in the baby, most Americans favor abortion. But only a minority favor abortion when (a) the family has a very low income and cannot afford a baby, (b) the woman is unwed and does not want to marry the man, and (c) the pregnancy interferes with the woman's work or education. In short, the public seems to be saying that abortion should be legal only for reasons of health, not for reasons of convenience. Not surprisingly, single men, who no doubt see abortion rights as a way to escape the consequences of their own irresponsibilities, are the nation's biggest supporters of a woman's right to choose.[43]

If there is ambivalence about abortion, it is because most Americans do not view the subject through the kind of atomistic lens that the ACLU favors. Not only do most people see abortion as a conflict of rights, a majority believe that pregnant women have responsibilities to the unborn child. The ACLU fully rejects both positions, casting all fetal protection laws as oppressive and illegal. The courts, as well as the court of public opinion, hold that it is one thing to exclude pregnant women from jobs thought to be harmful to the health of the unborn, quite another to exculpate pregnant women from engaging in drug abuse. In 1991, a unanimous Supreme Court agreed with the ACLU by striking down a 1982 policy of Johnson Controls that excluded "all women except those whose inability to bear children is medically documented" from working in high lead-exposure positions; the company said it had a "moral obligation" to protect unborn children from dangerous elements, but the high court saw the policy as amounting to "overt discrimination against women."[44]

Fetal protection laws that seek to protect unborn children from substance-abusing mothers are another matter altogether. In these cases, the ACLU has proved to be far less successful, as serious questions have been raised over the mounting number of infants born with AIDS and addicted to crack. But to the ACLU, it does not matter what substance, or how much of it, is introduced into the blood supply of an innocent unborn child. As Kary L. Moss of the ACLU's Women's Rights Project sees it, requiring a pregnant woman to abstain from substance abuse is analogous to requiring a woman to risk her life by rushing to save the life of a child in a burning building.[45] It could be pointed out, of course, that when a woman gets pregnant, she reasonably assumes responsibilities toward her unborn child that no stranger incurs when children are at risk in a burning building.

"It is dangerous and counterproductive," says the ACLU, "to treat women and the fetuses within them as independent beings with opposed and competing interests."[46] This is an interesting position to take, but it is a rather strange one for the ACLU to be voicing. Is the Union maintaining that the unborn are dependent on their mothers, possessing similar interests, such as health? If so, then how can the ACLU logically argue that "women who are drinking excessively, abusing drugs, smoking, or eating inadequately are first and foremost hurting themselves," without ever mentioning the harm done to the children that the women are carrying?[47] It is because the ACLU is bent on seeing substance-abusing pregnant women as victims that it dismisses their culpability in harming their unborn children.

In what way are pregnant drug abusers victims? Why don't they just stop taking drugs? To this the ACLU replies that ending an addiction "without help is virtually impossible"; it cites the opinion of one nurse to substantiate this remarkable claim.[48] The Union contends that drug users are drawn to their habit by forces outside their control, emphasizing such things as "genetic predispositions and environmental factors outside the addicts' control." It follows, then, that "to treat pregnant addicts as indifferent and deliberate wrongdoers is to misunderstand addiction."[49] Moreover, the Union says that "80 to 90 percent of female drug addicts and alcoholics have been victims of rape and incest"[50] and that "women of color, poor women and battered women are primarily the victims of these prosecutions."[51] Not only has the ACLU succeeded in transposing the victimizer for the victim, it maintains that laws aimed at "fetal abusers" could be used against "women who fly to Europe and clean their cat's litter box."[52]

A social conception of freedom closely ties rights to responsibilities and holds wrongdoers accountable for their actions. But the ACLU rejects such a position, even in extreme cases. When Jennifer Clarise Johnson, a 25-year-old woman, gave birth to her third drug-inflicted baby, she was sentenced to 14 years' probation and participation in a drug treatment program, over the objections of the ACLU. The Union argued in 1991 that the cocaine-using recidivist should not be held accountable for the damage done to her child and protested vehemently when a judge ordered Ms. Johnson to use Norplant, a long-term birth control implant.[53] A year later, a state appeals court ruled that the order was moot because Ms. Johnson had already been sent to prison for using cocaine during her probation period. Her alleged right to bodily integrity, then, was never fully tested in court.[54]

If there is one aspect of the abortion issue where there is a clear consensus, it is the matter of a minor obtaining parental consent before obtaining an abortion. Fully 76 percent of the public supports parental consent laws (the figure jumps to 83 percent when only one parent's approval is required), while only 21 percent oppose such a requirement.[55] The ACLU sides with the 21 percent. But do such laws work? The results from Minnesota indicate that they do. In the five years (1975–1980) prior to Minnesota's 1981 parental consent law, pregnancies for 10 to 17 year olds had increased by 22 percent, with abortions up 71 percent. In the five years after the law was passed, there was a 20.5 percent drop in pregnancy rates, and a 27.4 percent decrease in the abortion rate, for the same age group.[56]

The ACLU knows that the Minnesota law has been a success in reducing the number of pregnancies and abortions among teenagers, but instead of crediting the law, it incredibly blames it for "preventing many minors from exercising their constitutional right to avoid teen motherhood through abortion."[57] Commenting on the effect of parental consent laws, the Union states that "there are no benefits which can be balanced against the traumatic impact of these laws on minors."[58] This could only be true, of course, if we assume an absolutist position and maintain that the unborn pose no competing right to the mother; that the unborn child might be traumatized by the injection of a saline solution never seems to enter the thinking of the ACLU.

One of the ACLU's prime objections to parental consent laws is that they "significantly increase health risks to minors . . . by impairing the ability of health providers to give quality care."[59] But health issues have never stood in the way of the ACLU's support for abortion, even when it is clear that the woman incurs certain risks. For example, in Illinois in the 1980s the state sought to bring abortion clinics into line with the standards set for other outpatient surgical facilities. It sought regulations for building heating, ventilating, air conditioning, hot water, and plumbing systems, as well as insulation for fire safety purposes; such regulations already governed such surgical procedures as plastic surgery, hernia repairs, and the removal of cysts and tumors.

But the ACLU objected nonetheless and sued the state, claiming that the law "discriminates" against abortion facilities and inhibits a woman from obtaining an abortion. It noted that the estimated increase in cost for an abortion in one of the approved facilities was in the neighborhood of $25 to $40, a price deemed too high by the ACLU. Ironically, the net result of the ACLU's position is to further jeopardize the health and safety of women undergoing abortion, thereby contributing to an already serious problem.[60]

For the ACLU, "a decision not to reveal the fact of the pregnancy or abortion is often best for many reasons including . . . preventing a breakdown in the family relationship."[61] Exactly what the quality of the family relationship is likely to be when parents are kept ignorant of their daughters' health is not addressed by the ACLU. But no matter, the ACLU objects that parental consent laws are designed "to protect minors, foster family structure and protect parental rights." In its atomistic vision, the ACLU dismisses such functions as "paternalistic,"[62] without explaining why that should be sufficient grounds for objection. Are we not discussing minors, after all? And are not all laws designed to protect minors inherently "paternalistic" (the Consumer Product Safety Commission recalls over 200 items a year because they are deemed dangerous to children)?

The Union says it is "false and misleading" to claim that minors often lack the maturity necessary to make an informed judgment on a subject like abortion.[63] Drawing on the highly contentious work of psychologist Lawrence Kohlberg, known mostly for his "value-free" approach to moral issues, the ACLU asserts that "by age 14, adolescents have developed their own sense of conscience and morality"[64] and are thus in a position to make a decision regarding abortion. But if adolescents have a full-blown morality by age 14, why does the ACLU maintain that they must be shielded from habit-wearing nuns in a public school classroom?[65] In any event, to say that "it is incongruous to allow minors to make independent health care decisions in some areas while requiring parental involvement for abortion,"[66] begs the question: Why, if the ACLU were to have its way, does it make sense for a minor to have parental consent to get her ears pierced but not to have an abortion? Adolescents have died from abortions, in hospitals, though none have died from having their ears pierced.[67]

It hardly needs mentioning that the ACLU thinks parental consent laws discriminate against women. But in the end, it is nature—not the law— that really disturbs the Union. Speaking of women's position in general, Isabelle Katz Pinzler, director of the ACLU's Women's Rights Project, contends that no amount of rights can ever stop women from being "vulnerable to attack simply because it is the women of the species who bear children."[68] As for parental consent laws, specifically, the Union says that the effect of these laws "is to single out unmarried minor women whose sexual activity results in a pregnancy and subject them to burdensome and often traumatic requirements."[69] Of course, the law singles out women precisely because it is they, not men, who get pregnant. If this is unfair, the ACLU will need to appeal its case to a higher source than the Supreme Court.

So what does the ACLU say we should do about unwanted pregnancies? Spend more money on social programs. Besides repealing parental consent laws, we should provide more money for the following programs: health care, education, services, and counseling for minors; sex education; sex education and counseling for parents; day care; food supplement programs; family therapy services; battering and alcoholism programs; literacy programs; bilingual education; student school grants; work/study and loan programs; and job training. Without offering any evidence that such programs have worked in the past, or are likely to do so in the future, the ACLU sublimely concludes that they "may reduce pregnancy rates."[70]

Family Integrity

Family integrity is not a civil liberties issue, but there are civil libertarian decisions that have a direct impact on it. How people deal with family integrity depends partly on the conception of liberty that they hold. From the perspective of a social conception of liberty, parental prerogative is seen as a virtue, to be interfered with only in those instances when the minor's welfare might otherwise be jeopardized. An atomistic perspective places a premium on servicing the rights of the individual and is generally unsupportive of parental authority. The ACLU, though clearly of the atomistic school, occasionally departs from its preferred position, but for reasons that are at least questionable.

To those who favor a social conception of liberty, even the cause of family integrity cannot justify the involuntary placement of a child in the hands of despots. But in the case of Walter Polovchak, the ACLU sought to do just that. In 1982, when Walter was just 12 years old, his Ukranian parents decided to leave the United States and return to the Soviet Union, after spending just two years in Illinois. Walter resisted and obtained legal counsel, though not from the ACLU; in fact, the Union sided with Walter's parents, citing its allegiance to family integrity. In the end, the case became moot when Walter turned 18 and legally made the decision to stay in the United States.

Why would the ACLU want to send Walter back to the U.S.S.R. against his will? To Alan Dershowitz, it reflects the ACLU's "unwillingness to criticize communism."[71] The evidence supports Dershowitz's charge: at the same time that the ACLU was seeking to export Walter Polovchak to the U.S.S.R., it was seeking to prevent the parents of another minor from taking their unwilling child back to Chile. According to the ACLU, Chile was a dictatorship; it did not opine what it thought the Soviet Union was under Brezhnev. Henry Mark Holzer, Walter's attorney, saw another anomaly: the same ACLU that opposes parental notification laws for minors considering an abortion (on the grounds that minors are competent), held in this instance that young Walter was too immature to decide whether he wanted to return to the U.S.S.R. Holzer saw it this way: "The ACLU likes abortion, and it likes the Soviet Union."[72]

The issue of parental rights versus children's rights also surfaces in debates over what movies are appropriate for youngsters to watch. Now it is hardly controversial to say that most parents want to know whether a particular movie is appropriate for their children, and that is why they like to consult the movie rating system before making a decision. But the ACLU sees a problem in this. Why? In its own novel way, the ACLU opposes the Motion Picture Association of America (MPAA) because it does not allow parents to decide if their underage children should be allowed to see a pornographic film.

To be explicit, the Union says that "the MPAA rating system, through its X and R ratings, interferes with the autonomy of the family. These ratings deprive parents of the right to determine what films their children may see. Such restrictions on parents' freedom to raise their children as they see fit are particularly offensive."[73] That most parents would find it far more difficult to raise their children without the guidance of the movie rating system is not addressed by the ACLU. Similarly, the ACLU does not explain why an organization committed to limitations on the power of the federal government ought to be concerned about the business of a private, voluntary organization, which is precisely what the MPAA is.

The ACLU opposes curfew laws and laws that ban minors from driving late at night for the same reason it opposes the movie rating system: they deprive parents of making choices for their children. The Union is unimpressed with detailed stories of violence in crime-ridden neighborhoods, maintaining that curfew laws are "unjustifiable government intrusions on the rights of children and young people and on parental rights to control and direct the movements of their children."[74] Now it would be one thing if the ACLU were simply objecting to the unfair enforcement of curfew ordinances. But its opposition is total. It is not without cause that many inner-city black parents wonder just whose side the ACLU really is on when it attempts to thwart community sentiment by opposing curfew restrictions in high-crime areas. This was exactly the reaction many blacks in Atlanta had when the ACLU stood firm against curfew laws after scores of black children were found missing or dead in the early 1980s.[75]

There is much more to family integrity than parental prerogative: solidarity among family members, and the status of the nuclear family vis-a-vis its alternatives, tells us a great deal about the value that a modern society places on the integrity of the family. Since the late 1960s, there have been many disturbing signs that the American family has fallen on hard times, what with record levels of divorce, illegitimacy, and single parenthood, to say nothing about the record number of persons who have either suffered or died as a result of sexually transmitted diseases. While it is still true that most children live with two parents, the likelihood that youngsters will live some part of their childhood in a one-parent family has grown dramatically. And though most mothers either are not in the labor force or are working part-time, the number of children who return home from school to an empty house has definitely increased. The nuclear family, though far from dying (as some pundits would have us believe), has certainly seen better days.[76]

Due to the large number of women working outside the home, employers have come under considerable governmental pressure to provide maternity leave or, more inclusively, family leave. Even though leave policies are not usually thought of as a civil liberties concern, and should therefore be of little interest to the ACLU, the Union has not been able to resist lobbying and litigating over the issue; any problem bearing on a woman's freedom from traditional domestic work is seen as a civil liberties matter by the ACLU, regardless of the wording of the Bill of Rights.

Support for parental leave may come from either the atomistic or social schools of thought, albeit for entirely different reasons. Those of the social school who are pro-parental leave may argue that it is in the best interests of society that a mother and child have a chance to bond before the mother returns to the work force; the emphasis would clearly be on the interests of society's new entrant, namely the child. The atomistic approach to liberty would stress the liberating effect parental leave would have on the temporarily disabled female employee. This last position represents the thinking of the ACLU.

Nowhere in the ACLU's policy governing parental leave does it address the social interests that are at stake when a child is born. Indeed, in true atomistic form, its policy speaks exclusively to the interests of women employees. In fact, the Union's ruling on this subject appears not in a policy on parental leave (which might address real family concerns) but in a policy called "Employment and Education"; the matter of parental leave is seen strictly from the perspective of civil liberties in the workplace and not from the vantage of mother-child bonding. Its policy also makes understandable its opposition to maternity leave.

Why would the ACLU, the much vaunted defender of women's rights and a proponent of family leave, sue the state of California for passing legislation that allowed employed women up to four months leave for the purpose of childbirth? Because the law was gender-specific. Here's what happened: In the mid-1980s, the ACLU teamed up with the National Organization for Women to defeat the California law on the grounds that all laws designed to benefit women, no matter how well-intentioned or effective, must be resisted for fear that gender-specific legislation might be passed stripping women of certain rights. The position taken by the ACLU and NOW was not universally endorsed by feminists, never mind most women: Betty Friedan, the intellectual godmother of the feminist movement, and the organization 9 to 5 (the national association of working women) supported the law. The Chamber of Commerce sided with the ACLU and NOW, making a strictly business-oriented decision in opposing the law.

That men really are different from women is such a pedestrian observation that it hardly merits comment. But to the ACLU, such differences should never be acknowledged in law: "The fact that only women become pregnant has been used historically to prove that men and women are not really similarly situated, and thus cannot be treated equally under the law."[77] But is not the situation of pregnant women inherently dissimilar from that of the men who impregnated them? The ACLU does not want to distinguish between the unequal condition of pregnancy and unfair treatment of women under the law. Equality and equity, it needs to be restated, refer to sameness and fairness, hardly identical values. Friedan understands all of these differences and at the time of the battle over maternity leave let go a salvo at the Union's stance. She lambasted the ACLU's idea of gender equality, stating that "the time has come to acknowledge that women are different from men, and that there has to be a concept of equality that takes into account that women are the ones who have the babies."[78]

It is consistent with ACLU thinking on this subject that when it comes to child care, the emphasis is not on the alleged benefits that the child might accrue from a leave policy. No, the entire issue is seen exclusively in terms of a battle of the sexes. Official ACLU policy frames the issue in a similar way, centering its concerns on advancing opportunities for women in the workplace; it even calls for government-funded day care centers for working mothers, removing any doubt as to who the real beneficiary of this policy is supposed to be and why it is advocated in the first place.[79]

It is striking—though entirely predictable from an atomistic perspective—that ACLU policy on family issues is mostly silent on the needs of children. Ironically, the one area where the ACLU is expressive of the interests of children concerns the subject of prisoners' rights. A strong proponent of prisoners' rights, the Union favors so-called "family unity demonstration projects," or what are known as community placement and family visitation centers, sites where incarcerated mothers can have steady access to their children. In making its case for legislation in this area, the ACLU uncharacteristically makes a psychological brief in behalf of mother-child bonding. It begins by saying that though male and female prisoners would be eligible to participate in this program, the Union recognizes that "a majority of prisoners with primary caretaker responsibility for their children are women," and therefore it is they who are the targeted group.

It is refreshing, even at the risk of being inconsistent, to hear the ACLU speak of the "irreparable harm" that befalls "a child's psychological and intellectual development" when separated from his mother. If bonding is not fulfilled, the ACLU says that juvenile delinquency and a lack of security and trust are likely to develop later in life. It quite correctly notes that "parent-child bonding is especially crucial during the first few years of an [sic] child's life" and that "normal child development depends upon the formation of an attachment bond through continuous care by a single caretaker."[80] Unfortunately, the Union doesn't let this social conception of liberty permeate its thinking on all family matters; it surfaces only when the rights of female prisoners are concerned, suggesting that it is expediency, not principle, that is at work.

The ACLU's amicus brief was of little help in the end: in 1987, the Supreme Court, by a vote of 6-3, upheld the California law granting pregnant women preferential treatment. Eleanor Smeal, president of NOW, welcomed the high court decision as "a clear win" for women[81] even though NOW filed suit to overturn the law; to its credit, the ACLU did not feign joy in defeat.

A truly social conception of liberty sees the family as a friend of liberty, the bedrock of moral responsibility, without which license reigns and freedom is negated. But to those who prefer an atomistic interpretation, the family is seen at best as unrelated to the cause of freedom, at worst as an impediment to liberty itself. The latter approach is dismissive of the family because its vision of liberty centers exclusively on the rights of the individual, having little if anything to say about the role of the family in a liberal democracy.

The social perspective not only values the family, it especially values that family form that is best suited to the needs of a modern democratic society. The empirical evidence suggests that the nuclear family, above all alternative family types, is not only best suited to the demands of a developed market economy, it is best equipped to deal with the psychological and social needs of children, as well. Children raised in one-parent families, for instance, are disproportionately represented among the ranks of the poor, school dropouts, juvenile delinquents, criminals, drug users, the academically impaired, unwed mothers and fathers, the accident prone, and so forth.[82] Almost all of the homeless population is composed of single persons or mothers with children, as opposed to intact families.[83] And the institution of cohabitation has a track record of breakup that far exceeds the rate among married couples, both in the United States and abroad.[84] None of the other "alternatives" to the nuclear family compares favorably as well, on virtually any index.

It is not just that the life chances of youngsters are less when they are reared in settings other than the nuclear family; it is the risks to the social order, and to the process of liberty, that matter as well. Social control is a requirement in any social order, and it is best achieved when individuals are socialized to control themselves, lest the police do the job for them. This is particularly true in a free society, where the fear of beckoning the hand of the state is a major concern. That is why mediating institutions are so important, for it is within the confines of institutions like the family that the individual is most likely to learn social control and a measure of individual liberty. If these attributes go unlearned, then liberty falters and social disorder prevails. The family, then, is inextricably bound to the makings of a free society, and no model of the family is better prepared for the demands of freedom than the nuclear family.[85]

The ACLU's atomistic outlook means that it does not take a holistic approach to family issues. Put differently, the ACLU is neglectful of family interests not because it is anti-family but because it does not see the family as a social unit; it sees the family as a small aggregate of individuals, each with competing claims. This vision of social life illustrates why the Union fails to give primacy to the nuclear family over any of its competitors and explains why it thinks prostitution should be legalized, including street solicitation.[86]

The laws against prostitution serve the social interest in maintaining stable marriages and families. But to the ACLU, such laws represent undue interference with the consensual rights of adults. It is because the Union collapses the social interest in family solidarity to matters of individual choice that it cannot appreciate the logic of anti-prostitution statutes. This accounts for the fact that it once filed a lawsuit against a Nevada house of prostitution for refusing to service a black customer.[87] To the ACLU, discrimination is wrong and not to be tolerated. But prostitution is nobody's business but that of the parties to the exchange.

The ACLU not only objects to laws that proscribe adultery (it's a privacy right),[88] cohabitation, and gay and lesbian marriages, it has recently sought to legalize polygamy as well; those who disagree with the Union's thinking are regarded as atavistic.[89] Some of the affiliates are even more "progressive" than the national office: the New Jersey affiliate has advanced a definition of the family that is so broad that it includes households of recovering alcoholics and drug addicts, much to the dismay of the residents of Cherry Hill.[90]

From 1946, when the ACLU filed an amicus brief in *Musser et al. vs. State of Utah*, to 1991, the Union's official policy on polygamy stated that "a line must be drawn between expression of belief and the actual practice of an act which has been proscribed by the community through its legislative representatives (the test of a 'clear and present danger')."[91] Official policy now holds that laws that prohibit plural marriages "violate constitutional protections of freedom of expression and association, freedom of religion, and privacy for personal relationships among consenting adults."[92] Thus, the Union now sees plural marriages as constituting nothing more than individual decisions with individual effects, thus reversing its longstanding belief that a community's interest in maintaining monogamous relationships may legitimately override individual preferences for polygamy.

Michele Parish-Pixler, executive director of the Utah affiliate, cogently sums up the ACLU's new attitude: "I can't see that there's any rational justification for prohibiting it [polygamy]. As long as it is between consenting adults, it ought to be permitted."[93] From the days of Jean-Jacques Rousseau, it has been a source of chagrin among rationalists that all societies embody such patently "irrational" features as custom, tradition, and social convention. And now the ACLU has added monogamy to the list. From the vantage of Parish-Pixler, the only thing that matters is that consenting adults be satisfied, thus relegating the social interest in marriage and child-rearing to the dustbin of history.

Constitutional law experts Bruce Fein and William Bradford Reynolds have caught the import of the ACLU's new policy on polygamy. They maintain that when the ACLU declares that "the State has no business enforcing the moral judgments of the majority of its citizens on the minority unless the actions of the minority have some deleterious effect on society," the Union really means that laws against polygamy are unconstitutional unless "the degradation [of women] causes some impact on society." According to Fein and Reynolds, the broad sweep of the ACLU's new stance on polygamy is tactical: "Its real game is to secure . . . a veritable constitutional juggernaut that can topple a host of laws on the books in numerous states—for instance, prohibitions on homosexual sodomy, obscenity, indecency, and use of marijuana or similar drugs." Even laws against peonage and prostitution, they maintain, would not survive such a broad constitutional principle.[94]

Gay Rights

To put it in a slightly different way, once the ACLU took the plunge and immersed itself in gay rights, there was no holding back on other forms of consensual sexual expression: everything had to be sanctioned. The agenda of gay activists is broad, and it is one the ACLU has wholeheartedly endorsed. All across the country, gays have campaigned for antidiscrimination laws, recognition in law of gay and lesbian marriages, parental and adoptive rights, "domestic partnership laws," the legalization of sodomy, and the like.

With support from Planned Parenthood, the Sex Education and Information Council of the United States, the National Organization for Women, and the ACLU, leaders in the gay and lesbian communities have worked the courts and state legislatures to achieve their goals, having done poorly in local referenda. And in every year since 1975, legislation has been introduced in Congress that would add sexual orientation to the Civil Rights Act of 1964,[95] meaning that not only would gays and lesbians be entitled to federal protection from discrimination, they might also qualify for affirmative action, the way women and minorities presently do—this despite the plain wording of the Act against preferential treatment.

It was in 1975 that the ACLU came out four-square in favor of gay rights. Prior to that time, the Union voiced several misgivings about homosexuality, including fears that minors might be subjected to "adult corruption." Indeed, in the Union's first policy on homosexuality, passed in 1957, it openly said that the issue was beyond its province. The board of directors said that it was not the business of the ACLU "to evaluate the social validity of laws aimed at the suppression or elimination of homosexuals." Referring to gays as a "deviant group," the ACLU said that it was entirely proper to consider homosexuality as a security risk in sensitive positions. But beginning in the 1960s, the Union's reservations about homosexuality declined in almost exact proportion to the assertiveness of gay rights in the homosexual community.[96]

Although midway through the 1970s the ACLU was on record as a pro-gay rights organization, in 1977 Matt Coles of the San Francisco affiliate was still trying to convince the national office of the need for gay rights legislation. The Union, Coles said, was skeptical, wanting to know what constitutional principle would be vindicated by such legislation. Coles pressed for more representation of gays and lesbians on the Union's affiliate boards and on the board of the national organization; in 1989, the same demands were restated, complete with the suggestion that ACLU officials attend Gay Rodeos so as to recruit new members.[97]

If it is true that gay activists have not been completely satisfied with the ACLU's dedication to their cause, it is nonetheless true that the Union is among the most pro-gay rights organizations in the country. Alan Dershowitz has even gone so far as to charge the ACLU with making "an alliance with lesbianism,"[98] so blatant is the Union's habit of almost always siding with the demands of gay and lesbian activists. The ACLU's "alliance with lesbianism" is a tribute to the extent that gay activists have penetrated the Union's positions of influence. Duncan Donovan of the Southern California affiliate, for instance, succeeded in the 1980s in establishing the first gay chapter within an affiliate in the nation. Other ACLU officials, like Tom Stoddard (previously of the New York CLU), have left the Union to become more active in the gay rights movement; Stoddard is now executive director of the Lambda Legal Defense and Education Fund.

ACLU gay activists have also succeeded in fostering change outside the ranks of the Union. In Florida, gay militants from the ACLU were maneuvered to chair the American Bar Association's Committee on Rights of Gay People, eventually leading to an ABA endorsement of gay rights.[99] In Atlanta, when adult bookstores were being closed down after hundreds of homosexuals were arrested for engaging in indecent behavior, the local ACLU affiliate began a dialogue with the police chief, the result of which was that Union activists wound up staffing an Advisory Task Force Committee to the Police.[100] And as important as any measure, the Lesbian Rights Project has compiled a list of expert medical witnesses—psychiatrists who can be relied upon to offer ACLU-correct testimony.[101] The Union, it should be pointed out, elects to see homosexuality as an orientation and not as a preference,[102] though some ACLU gay and lesbian activists still insist that their sexual identity is chosen.[103]

The ACLU has worked to combat discrimination in employment, and to change immigration laws and military policies that exclude gays, but most of its efforts have concentrated on the more controversial issues of gay and lesbian rights as "guardians," "parents," and "spouses." In short, should gays and lesbians be given the same rights as heterosexuals in marital and familial affairs? Though the public has clearly not endorsed such legislation, the ACLU has, and it is actively seeking to change the status quo.

What accounts for the ACLU's wide disagreement with most Americans on this subject is its atomistic vision of liberty: it simply does not regard the nuclear family as having any special role to play in society. When civil libertarians hear the word "family," what they picture is a constellation of people who live together. They do not see father, mother, and children, or even mothers with their children. From this perspective, it makes no sense to prize the solidarity of a social unit, nor does it make any sense to be respectful of social convention or the mores of the people. What counts are the rights of the individual. To be more honest about it, what counts is the right of dissenting individuals to neutralize the expressed will of the public on matters of marriage and the family.

Given the ACLU's orientation on the subject, it was only logical that the Union would file suit against Big Brothers for excluding homosexuals. One of the central goals of Big Brothers is to provide young boys with what it regards as suitable role models, that is, men who sponsor traditional values and lifestyles. Homosexuals, the organization reasons, do not fit that description and are thus not welcome. But according to Paul Hoffman, legal director of the Southern California affiliate that filed suit against Big Brothers, it does not matter what the mission of Big Brothers is—homosexuals should not be excluded.

While Hoffman finds it ludicrous that gays "would destroy an organization that let them in," others, like journalist William Raspberry, have been quick to reply that "they could very well destroy an organization like Big Brothers." Raspberry notes that between 1982 and 1987, five Los Angeles area Big Brothers were convicted of sex offenses involving boys they were assigned to, making it implausible to maintain that Big Brothers doesn't have a vested interest in excluding gays. Though Raspberry finds "gay bashing" offensive and would oppose the arbitrary discrimination against homosexuals in employment and housing, he would "draw the line at accepting gay couples as foster or adoptive parents and in positions in which the function of role model is primary."[104]

Raspberry's reservations are not shared by the ACLU. It has successfully challenged laws, like the one in Florida, that barred gays from adopting children; New Hampshire is the only state left that prohibits homosexuals from adopting children. In 1992, the ACLU was successful in persuading a surrogate court judge in New York to approve the adoption of a 6-year-old boy by the lesbian partner of the child's natural mother; the child was conceived by artificial insemination.[105] Some of these cases get quite intricate, even for the ACLU. For example, in June 1980 a child was born to a Nancy S., after her lover, Michele G., had secured a sperm donor for "their" child; Michele G. took part in the artificial insemination and was officially listed on the child's birth certificate under "father." Five years and a second child later, the women split up, with both seeking parental rights.

The lawyer for the "mother," Nancy S., was a long-time member of the ACLU. Attorney Carol Amyx argued that her client had the right to raise her child as she saw fit. But to her dismay, the ACLU not only saw things differently, it filed a brief on behalf of the "father," Michele G., contending that the constitutional rights to privacy and freedom of association permit lesbians to form families and enjoy all the traditional protections afforded heterosexual parents.

Amyx was perplexed by the ACLU's action but shouldn't have been. After all, the organization that she belonged to was only practicing what it preached. For Amyx to hold that "these children were produced by Nancy, and Michele is not the legal or biological anything to them"[106] may be true, but it is not the kind of position that is very convincing to an organization that rejects social conceptions of liberty. The ACLU scoffs at arguments like Amyx's for the same reason that it challenges state laws that inquire into the nature of the sexual orientation of day care applicants: it isn't relevant from the atomistic perspective on liberty.[107] Many of these issues are subsidiary, of course, to the question of gay marriages, a matter of utmost importance to the ACLU.

In June 1986, the Lesbian and Gay Rights Project was created under the direction of Nan Hunter. Four months later, the ACLU became the first mainstream organization in the United States calling for the legalization of gay marriages.[108] Claiming that gay and lesbian marriages were not only desirable but "imperative," the Union sought a complete panoply of rights: foster parenthood, employee fringe benefits, insurance benefits, income tax benefits, visitation rights, and survivorship and other economic benefits that normally accompany the hospitalization of one's spouse.[109] In July 1989, the Union got much of what it wanted when New York's highest court, the court of appeals, held that a gay couple that had lived together for a decade could be considered a family under New York City's rent-controlled regulations.

Writing for the majority, Judge Vito J. Titone, opined that protection against eviction "should not rest on fictitious legal distinctions or genetic history, but instead should find its foundation in the reality of family life." So what constitutes a "family"? Such factors as "exclusivity and longevity" of a relationship, the "level of emotional and financial commitment," how a couple conducts their "everyday lives," and the "reliance placed upon one another for daily family services."

Anticipating his critics, Judge Titone added that the enumerated factors should not be the only issues considered. "It is the totality of the relationship as evidenced by the dedication, caring and self-sacrifice of the parties which should, in the final analysis, control," he wrote. Just how those affective qualities were to be measured, he did not say, but one thing was certain: traditional concepts of the family were fully overthrown. William B. Rubenstein, the ACLU staff lawyer who argued the case, rightly concluded that the decision "marks the most important single step forward in American law toward legal recognition of lesbian and gay relationships."[110] "Domestic partnership" laws have since sprung up around the nation, mostly in college towns and cities with large gay communities.

AIDS

It is ironic to note that at about the same time that AIDS was first detected—in the early 1980s—the ACLU began pressing for the reform of sodomy laws throughout the country. Indeed, the predecessor to the Lesbian and Gay Rights Project was the Ad Hoc Task Force to Challenge Sodomy Laws, a clear indication of the Union's priorities. The ACLU knew, obviously, that anal sexual intercourse was one of the major ways in which AIDS was transmitted, but that had little effect on changing its course of action. It suffered a defeat, however, when in 1986 the Supreme Court, in *Bowers v. Hardwick*, refused to grant sodomy constitutional protection. The Union then switched strategies by trying to amend various state constitutions' to include a general right to privacy, a tactic most legislators have thus far been reluctant to sanction.

It is because AIDS is a behavior-specific disease that it makes little sense to approach the subject without understanding how and why the disease surfaced in the first place. The ACLU, however, as with virtually every other pro-homosexual organization nationwide, prefers not to engage in robust freedom of speech on this issue. The feeling seems to be that whatever the cause, we must deal seriously with present conditions. But there are some voices in the gay community, like Marshall Kirk and Hunter Madsen,[111] who are trying to end the reticence over gay lifestyles and thus bring out into the open some of the notorious practices that have contributed to the transmission of AIDS.

Kirk and Madsen list ten "misbehaviors" that gays either are known to exhibit or are idealized by gay leaders for doing. The personality traits and practices they describe can generously be labeled disoriented, including as they do vivid illustrations of a population literally obsessed with its own sexuality. Add to this the tenuousness of most gay relationships (almost all gays cheat on their mates), and the picture that emerges is that of a population saddled with severe problems. At base, Kirk and Madsen attribute most gay problems to a rejection of morality, a condition they say is widespread in the homosexual population. It is not without cause that Kirk and Madsen (who are themselves gay) label the gay lifestyle as "the pits."[112]

Why do many gays reject morality? Because "amorality is damned convenient. And the moral enemy of that convenience is the value judgment." The logical consequence of this perception, Kirk and Madsen rightly point out, is that "anything goes," leading ineluctably to a host of physical and emotional problems.[113] Regrettably, the willingness to shun all morality has even led some gays to sanction the North American Man-Boy Love Association, an organization dedicated to the goal of securing young boys for adult sexual purposes.[114]

According to Kirk and Madsen, the most common effects of the gay rejection of morality are narcissism and self-indulgent and self-destructive behavioral patterns. Pathologically self-absorbed, many gays find it almost impossible to form lasting relationships, finding it more attractive to ventilate their sexual drives among a number of partners. The idea that self-restraint equals self-hatred is also prevalent, leading inevitably to "drugs and kinky sex." The typical pattern, Kirk and Madsen stress, is for young gays to experiment with cuddling and mutual masturbation and then progress to multiple partners and new sexual acts. Having become bored with this, they now turn to raunch and aggression, meaning coprophilia and "mere wallowing in filth," as well as a resort to "whips, executioner's masks, and fist-fucking." This is what it takes to "stay excited," they add.[115]

Given this brief insight into the lifestyle that many gays have adopted, it is disconcerting not to hear the ACLU comment on the reasons why homosexuals account for the lion's share of AIDS victims. It talks endlessly about the root causes of crime and other social pathologies but is noticeably silent on the social atmospherics that give rise to AIDS transmission. Worse still is the ACLU's cover-up of the seamy side of the gay lifestyle. To argue in court, as the ACLU has, that gay bars are "social meetinghouses that provide gays and lesbians the opportunity to engage in a form of expressive conduct that is protected by the First Amendment"[116] is to pretend innocence. Kirk and Madsen are more honest: "The gay bar is the arena of sexual competition, and it brings out all that is most loathsome in human nature. Here, stripped of the facade of wit and cheer, gays stand nakedly revealed as single-minded, selfish sexual predators . . . and enact vignettes of contempt and cruelty that make the Comte de Sade look like a Red Cross nurse."[117]

As astonishing as it is sad, the ACLU,[118] the editors of the *New York Times*,[119] and the leadership in the gay community all begged and pleaded to keep the bathhouses open, after it had been well established that such places were, in the words of gay journalist Randy Shilts, "biological cesspools for infection." As Shilts notes, "Common sense dictated that bathhouses be closed down," but, alas, that was the very ingredient lacking on this subject.[120] Kirk and Madsen recall that the bathhouses were shut down "not as they should—voluntarily, as soon as it became evident to a reasonable person that what they were selling was death, and in abundance—but under legal duress, kicking and screaming in protest, and spewing out a sewer system of cheap rationales for their continued operation."[121]

In 1986, the ACLU issued its first policy on AIDS. It listed AIDS as a threat to public health and one that had "serious implications for civil liberties such as control over one's body, freedom of association and the right to privacy of one's medical records." The board of directors went on record opposing breaches of confidentiality, mandatory testing, compulsory contact tracing of HIV infected partners, and a quarantine. In January 1987, it added that "the right to individual privacy which extends to the sexual acts of consenting adults prohibits government regulation including criminalization of sexual activity and restrictions on nonpublic places where sex takes place, although it does not necessarily bar civil remedies in tort." A few months later, it added its opposition to compulsory testing, segregation, and treatment of prison inmates with the AIDS virus. In 1988, the Union endorsed the distribution of sterile hypodermic needles to drug addicts.[122]

In gaining protection for AIDS carriers, the ACLU has been successful in persuading the Supreme Court that communicable diseases such as tuberculosis and AIDS are handicaps subject to federal antidiscrimination statutes.[123] Nan Hunter, the director of the AIDS and Civil Liberties Project, has since sought to expand coverage of the federal Rehabilitation Act of 1973, as amended ("section 504"), by trying to convince the Congress to bring the private sector under the Act's coverage.[124] The ACLU's commendable interest in protecting AIDS victims from unwarranted discrimination is, however, not matched by a similar interest in protecting the public from unwarranted risks. Its opposition to contact tracing is a case in point.

In 1988, after a Kansas man tested positive for AIDS, his doctors decided to inform his divorced wife of his test results. The man secured an ACLU attorney, and a judge complied with the Union's request: a permanent injunction was granted barring the doctors from informing the man's former wife of the test results. William Rubenstein of the ACLU expressed content with the knowledge that the woman's health provider had also done an HIV test on her, after her husband had tested positive, and found that she had not been exposed. The fact that the woman had expressed an interest in reconciliation amounted to nothing, so adamant was the ACLU's position on the issue.[125] No one in the ACLU has been more explicit on this subject than Janlori Goldman, director of the Privacy and Technology Project: "The benefits of confidentiality outweigh the possibility that somebody may be injured."[126] Or die.

"Interests of privacy and self-expression may be involved in any individual's choice of activities or possessions, but these interests are attenuated where the activity, or the object sought to be possessed, is inherently dangerous to others." This is official ACLU policy, but it is not a commentary on lethal sexual practices, it is the Union's policy on gun control.[127] It would be totally out of character for the ACLU to speak this way about anal sexual intercourse, though of course it might make a great deal of sense, given what we know about the transmission of AIDS. No, when it comes to the subject of sexual behavior, the ACLU, true to its atomistic roots, thinks only in terms of rights. And the right it most trumpets on this issue is the right to privacy.

Lawyer Charles Rembar and journalist Nat Hentoff have impeccably good civil libertarian credentials. But when it comes to the ACLU's dogmatic position on AIDS, they break company, asserting that the Union has lost the true meaning of liberty. Rembar chastises the ACLU for becoming a "backward-looking organization, trapped in vested doctrine." Taking the same position that most Americans take, Rembar argues that it is good to identify and report those who carry the AIDS virus; it is just as good to allow for contact tracing. Privacy rights, he holds, should not prevail in light of what we know about AIDS.

Offering a social vision of liberty, Rembar charges that the only persons who might disagree with this are those "so infatuated with personal rights as to ignore the sorest community needs." He then takes the ACLU to task: "The A.C.L.U., rather than receding from a cherished doctrine, would allow a number of people—perhaps a very large number—to die this horrid death. The organization apparently believes in a divine right of privacy, which reigns supreme above reason and common decency."[128] Hentoff, too, is critical, charging that the ACLU "is becoming an icon to itself," forgetting that privacy rights are not the whole of civil liberties. A strict civil libertarian, Hentoff nonetheless questions the wisdom of opposing contact tracing.[129]

It is not just in recent times that the ACLU has ruled on issues that intersect sexuality and public health. In 1945, the Union opposed laws requiring prostitutes to submit to examinations and vaccinations, citing an allegiance to what it called "medical liberty."[130] Today it has gone further than ever before in promoting "medical liberty." For example, in 1988 the ACLU sued in Maryland because court officers donned gloves before handling a murder suspect with AIDS (this was allegedly prejudicial to the jury)[131]; it has sued dentists in Philadelphia for refusing to treat HIV-infected persons[132]; it has protested amendments to federal law that would allow employers to transfer an employee with a communicable disease out of food handling positions[133]; it has registered complaints against government policies that exclude HIV-infected persons from entering the United States as travelers or visitors[134]; and it has protested state legislation requiring arrested prostitutes to be tested for AIDS.[135]

Should doctors who test positive for AIDS be forbidden to practice? A majority of Americans say yes. And by a margin of 63 to 28 percent, the public favors barring surgeons who test positive for AIDS.[136] The ACLU not only does not agree, it has defended doctors who have been proscribed from practicing, arguing that it is a violation of the Rehabilitation Act to do so.[137] To the ACLU, it does not matter even when invasive procedures are involved: those who test positive for the HIV virus should be allowed to conduct surgery. When the Senate voted 81-8 to impose a fine of $10,000 and a prison term of 10 years on such persons, the ACLU protested, claiming that "the net effect of this proposal would condemn those convicted to die in jail."[138] It did not allude to what might happen to the patients of these surgeons, if they were permitted to practice.

If a woman is raped, should the suspected rapist be tested for AIDS? If he tests positive, should the woman be informed of the results? Should it be a crime if someone with AIDS intentionally tries to transmit the disease to an innocent, unsuspecting person? On all three questions, the ACLU answers a resounding "no." Aside from gay organizations, it would be difficult to find many other organizations that would be prepared to sacrifice the lives of innocent persons on the mantle of privacy rights. But to the ACLU, to run a test on a suspected rapist is simply "an unnecessary and unwarranted infringement of rights."[139] And in Pennsylvania, the Union has gone to court to protest the release of the results of an HIV test performed on a rape suspect. To ACLU staff attorney Scott Burris, the confidentiality rights of the accused outweigh the rights of rape victims.[140]

In a 1989 radio debate I had with ACLU official Gara LaMarche, I asked him why the ACLU was officially on record as opposing state laws that criminalize the intentional transmission of AIDS to innocent, unsuspecting persons.[141] All LaMarche could offer was that "homosexuals have rights." To which I replied, the issue is murder, not the rights of homosexuals. When I asked LaMarche whether it should be illegal for someone to intentionally pour a toxic substance into the water supply of a city, he languidly conceded that it should be. My follow-up was to ask him to explain the moral difference between that and someone who intentionally transmitted the AIDS virus to an innocent, unsuspecting person. And again, all he could do was say that "homosexuals have rights."[142]

LaMarche's response is as good an example as any of how the ACLU arrives at its atomistic conclusions on liberty. It is hardly surprising, then, to read of the ACLU coming to the defense of a prison inmate who intentionally bit a guard, and did so with the belief that he could transmit his AIDS virus in that manner.[143] Nor is it surprising to read that the ACLU's National Prison Project regards the fear of AIDS transmission in the prisons as a "phantom" and a "phobia."[144] In none of these instances has the ACLU shown the slightest interest in the consequences of its position for the rights of innocent persons, so thoroughly wed is it to the gay rights agenda.

So what does the ACLU recommend we do about the spread of AIDS? More research and education are needed.[145] More research may lead to a cure, but in the meantime the prospects for relying on education are not encouraging. And by education, the ACLU means having the government publish information that gives a positive spin to homosexuality,[146] as well as information on how AIDS is transmitted. Unfortunately, the data give little credence to the ACLU's position: it was the most well-educated segment of the gay population that wound up with AIDS, as they proved to be more reckless in their behavior than poorly educated gays.[147] Even more discouraging is the fact that among young gays, there has been a striking return to the high-risk behavioral patterns that resulted in AIDS in the first place.[148]

If the family has a special role to play in the establishment of a free society, it cannot be learned by examining ACLU policies on this issue. The rights of the individual often conflict with social interests, and this is particularly true when civil liberties clash with the need for a stable family structure. Think of it this way: If an organization dedicated to strong families were to be dismissive of all competing rights that individual family members might have, we would probably brand it as too one-sided, even unfair. The same can be said of organizations dedicated to civil liberties that treat family matters as though they were of slight significance. The end result is neither strong families nor, tragically, a freer society.

Notes

1. Mary Ann Glendon, *The Transformation of Family Law, State Law, and Family in the United States and Western Europe* (Chicago: University of Chicago Press, 1989).
2. George J. Annas, "Making Babies without Sex: The Law and the Profits," *American Journal of Public Health* (December 1984): 1415–17.
3. Policy #262a, "Surrogate Parenting."
4. See John Holusha, "Judge Upholds Ban on Surrogate Birth Contracts," *New York Times*, Septmeber 20, 1988, p. A15.
5. Policy #262a, "Surrogate Parenting."
6. Ibid.
7. Ibid.
8. Ibid.
9. See ACLU Briefing Paper on "Crime and Civil Liberties," Number 2. It is not dated but was issued in the late 1980s.
10. See the official response to an inquiry over this issue in *Civil Liberties*, Winter 1986, p. 2.
11. See Mary Meehan's interview with Glasser in "Ira Glasser: ACLU's Main Man," *National Catholic Register*, June 19, 1988, p. 8.
12. Quoted by J. Anthony Lukas, "The A.C.L.U. Against Itself," *New York Times Magazine*, July 9, 1978, p. 26.
13. Alan Dershowitz, "ACLU Takes a Wrong Turn," in Alan Dershowitz, *Taking Liberties* (Chicago: Contemporary Books, 1988), 141.
14. Leeds told me about the ACLU's boasting while he was preparing his article, "The A.C.L.U.: Impeccable Judgments or Tainted Policies?" *New York Times Magazine*, September 10, 1989, p. 72.
15. Charles Oliver, "The First Shall Be Last?" *Reason*, October 1990, p. 25.

16. Quoted by John Leo, "One Watchdog Missing in Action," *U.S. News and World Report*, November 5, 1990, p. 23.
17. See the letter sent by Benshoof accompanying a March 1990 membership drive, p. 3.
18. She made this remark during the "Life and Choice After Roe v. Wade" segment of the PBS special "That Delicate Balance II: Our Bill of Rights," Fred and Ruth Friendly, executive producers. This segment first aired on WNET/New York, February 4, 1992.
19. See the September 27, 1990, letter sent by Halperin and Califa to a select group of congressmen protesting the use of RICO against antiabortion activists and others. They called for a reform of RICO. Califa has been one of the most consistent critics of RICO in the ACLU.
20. See the interview between Mary Meehan and Ira Glasser in *National Catholic Register*, June 19, 1988, p. 8.
21. Smith-Torre's comments appeared in a letter to the editor, *Insight*, January 22, 1990, p. 7.
22. The comments by Steinhardt and Ledewitz appear in "Protesters Fear More Racketeering Lawsuits," *Pittsburgh Press*, May 7, 1989, p. B5.
23. John Leo, "One Watchdog Missing in Action," p. 23.
24. One of the most recent examples occurred in Philadelphia. In 1991, the ACLU sued the City of Philadelphia for not adequately disciplining and training its police force after ACT-UP members were roughed up at a demonstration. See "City Pays Up to ACT-UP," *Civil Liberties Record* (of Pennsylvania), Spring 1992, p. 3. As a result, the city awarded $75,000 to the injured parties.
25. John Leo, "One Watchdog Missing in Action," p. 23.
26. *Bray v. Alexandria Women's Health Clinic, et al.*, 113 S.Ct. 753 (1993).
27. See my book, *The Politics of the American Civil Liberties Union* (New Brunswick, New Jersey: Transaction Press), 102-103.
28. See the interview with Hentoff, *National Catholic Register*, July 15, 1984, p. 1. See also Richard Vigilante and Susan Vigilante, "Taking Liberties: The ACLU Strays from Its Mission," *Policy Review*, Fall 1984, pp. 32-33.
29. Nat Hentoff, "Two Cheers for the ACLU," *Washington Post*, March 3, 1990, p. A25.
30. Policy #271a, "The Right To Have Medical Treatment Withheld or Withdrawn."
31. Lisa Beattie, "Letters, He Got Letters," *Civil Liberties*, Spring 1989, p. 5.
32. *Webster v. Reproductive Health Service*, 492 U.S. 490 (1989).
33. See "Summary of *Webster v. Reproductive Health Services*," a document prepared by the ACLU's Reproductive Freedom Project, 1989, pp. 8-9.
34. Lisa Beattie, "Guam Government Strikes Blow Against Choice," *Civil Liberties*, Summer 1990, pp. 1, 5.
35. *New York Times*, March 24, 1991, section E, p. 18.
36. The law said that women would not face criminal penalities for having an abortion, but the ACLU dismissed this altogether and maintained that since the abortion statute was tied to the state's homicide law (which allows for capital punishment in cases of murder), it could be inferred that women who obtained an abortion would be shot.
37. The Governor's response is contained in correspondence to Anna M. Donohue (and in my possession); it is dated April 25, 1991.
38. *Rust v. Sullivan*, 111 U.S. S.Ct. 1759 (1991).
39. Ira Glasser, *Visions of Liberty* (New York: Arcade Publishing, 1991), 268.
40. *Planned Parenthood v. Casey*, 112 S.Ct. 2791 (1992).

41. The bulletin was dated June 30, 1992, and was sent to all ACLU members.
42. "Abortion and a Nation at War," *First Things*, October 1992, p. 9.
43. One of the most comprehensive surveys on this subject was a Gallup study, "Abortion and Moral Beliefs Survey," May 1990. See also the New York Times/CBS survey, "Poll on Abortion Finds Nation Is Sharply Divided," *New York Times*, April 26, 1989, p. A1.
44. *Automobile Workers v. Johnson Controls*, 111 S.Ct. 1196 (1991).
45. Moss's statement was entered into testimony by Wendy Chavkin, MD, MPH, in her presentation before the House Select Committee on Children, Youth, and Families, April 27, 1989.
46. See ACLU Memo from the Washington Office to Interested Persons on "Possible Amendment on Drug Bill to Subject Women Substance Abusers to Criminal Sanctions for Giving Birth to Impaired Infants," October 3, 1989. p. 1.
47. Testimony of Lynn M. Paltrow, Kary Moss, and Judy Crockett of the ACLU on The President's National Drug Abuse Strategy Before The Subcommittee on Health and the Environment of the United States House of Representatives Committee on Energy and Commerce, April 30, 1990, p. 28.
48. Ibid., p. 6.
49. Ibid., p. 9.
50. Ibid., p. 29.
51. Ibid., p. 3.
52. Ibid., p. 18. The ACLU quotes a doctor as saying that he would not recommend pregnant women to fly to Europe because of the danger of radiation from the sun and stars.
53. "Affiliate Notes," *Civil Liberties*, Spring 1990, p. 14.
54. See Don Feder, "ACLU Gives Civil Liberties a Bad Name," *Heritage Features Syndicate*, June 13, 1988. See also Charlotte Allen, "Norplant—Birth Control or Coercion?" *Wall Street Journal*, September 13, 1991, p. A14. For a story on how the order was declared moot, see "No Precedent Is Seen in Birth-Control Order," *New York Times*, April 15, 1992, p. A16.
55. See the New York Times/CBS poll, reported in "Abortion Ruling to Lead to Hearings," *New York Times*, June 27, 1990, p. A9. See also the NBC News/ Wall Street Journal poll of July 1990, as reported in "Abortion, Inc.," *New Dimensions*, Septmeber/October 1991, p. 19.
56. See James L. Rogers, et al., "Impact of the Minnesota Parental Notification Law on Abortion and Birth," *American Journal of Public Health*, March 1991, pp. 294–98. See also "Restoring Parental Rights," *AUL Insights*, November 1990. The newsletter is a publication of Americans United for Life.
57. The pamphlet, *Parental Notice Laws: Their Catastrophic Impact on Teenagers' Right to Abortion*, was prepared by Janet Benshoof, et al., of the Reproductive Freedom Project of the ACLU. It was published in 1986, and the citation for the noted remark is on p. 7.
58. Ibid., p. 1.
59. Ibid.
60. For a good discussion of the effects of abortion on women see the work of Paige Comstock Cunningham and Clarke D. Forsythe, "Is Abortion the 'First Right' for Women?: Some Consequences of Legal Abortion," in J. Douglas Butler and David F. Walbert, eds., *Abortion, Medicine, and the Law*, 4th ed. (New York: Facts on File, 1992).
61. *Parental Notice Laws*, p. 8.

62. Ibid., p. 3.
63. Ibid., p. 3.
64. Ibid., p. 5.
65. Donohue, *The Politics of the American Civil Liberties Union*, pp. 304–305.
66. *Parental Notice Laws*, p. 5.
67. For a tragic case that was well documented, see the case of 13-year-old Dawn Ravenell, a black girl who died after having an abortion in New York's Eastern Women's Center. Her mother, who had no previous knowledge that her daughter was even pregnant, was contacted by the hospital for one reason: to pick up the body. See "Parental Lament," *First Things*, February 1992, p. 66–67.
68. Isabelle Katz Pinzler, "Liberty, Equality and Maternity," *Civil Liberties*, Fall/Winter 1989, p. 1.
69. *Parental Notice Laws*, p. 10.
70. Ibid., p. 20.
71. Dershowitz, "ACLU Takes a Wrong Turn," 141.
72. Quoted by Charles Oliver in "The First Shall Be Last?" p. 21.
73. Policy #17, "Film Classification."
74. Policy #206, "Curfew Ordinances."
75. William A. Donohue, *The Politics of the American Civil Liberties Union*, 264.
76. It has often been said that only about 27 percent of American households live today in the nuclear family. This is usually broached as a way of convincing the reader that we need to be more accepting of alternative lifestyles. But even in the so-called heyday of the family—the 1950s—only 33 percent of all households were constituted by the nuclear family. These low figures are derived by falsely comparing nuclear families to all households, instead of to other families with children, and therefore include millions of newlyweds and empty-nesters. This is the kind of intellectual dishonesty that is all too common in family studies these days.
77. Policy #315, "Employment and Education."
78. Quoted by Tamar Lewin, "Pregnancy-Leave Suits Has Divided Feminists," *New York Times*, June 28, 1986, p. 52.
79. Policy #315, "Employment and Education."
80. See Memo to Interested Persons, sent by the ACLU Washington Office, ACLU National Prison Project, ACLU Capital Area, ACLU Southern California, and other organizations, on the subject of "Family Unity Demonstration Projects for Children and Their Incarcerated Parents," July 26, 1990.
81. Smeal is quoted by Stuart Taylor, Jr., "Job Rights Backed in Pregnancy Case," *New York Times*, January 14, 1987, p. B10.
82. See my book, *The New Freedom: Individualism and Collectivism in the Social Lives of Americans* (New Brunswick, New Jersey: Transaction Press, 1990), ch. 11. See also the work of psychologist Urie Bronfenbrenner, "What Do Families Do?" *Family Affairs*, Winter/Spring 1991, p. 1. The publication is published by the Institute for American Values. And especially good is the piece by Barbara Dafoe Whitehead, "Dan Quayle Was Right," *Atlantic Monthly*, April 1993, pp. 47–50.
83. Bryce Christensen, "On the Streets: Homeless in America," *Family in America*, June 1990. See also Dan McMurry, "The Myth of the Homeless Family," *Chronicles*, October 1990, pp. 52–54.
84. Bryce Christensen, "No Promises: Cohabitation in America," *Family in America*, December 1989
85. For an excellent account of the relationship between the nuclear family and the makings of a free society, see Brigitte Berger and Peter Berger, *The War Over the*

Family: Capturing the Middle Ground (Garden City, New York: Anchor Press, Doubleday, 1984).

86. Policy #211, "Prostitution."
87. Ed Rowe, *The ACLU and America's Freedoms* (Wheaton, Illinois: Church League of America, 1984), p. 43.
88. See Alan Dershowitz, "The Adultery Cops Are Watching," in Alan Dershowitz, *Contrary to Popular Opinion* (New York: Pharos Books, 1992), 72–74. The Wisconsin affiliate argued in 1990 that the adultery laws invaded the privacy rights of individuals.
89. Ira Glasser, though speaking for himself, accurately conveys ACLU policy on this matter. See his *Visions of Liberty*, 257–58.
90. "Affiliate Notes," *Civil Liberties*, Fall 1990, p. 10.
91. Policy #91, "Marriage."
92. Ibid. This policy, passed April 6–7, 1991, is a revision of its 1978 policy.
93. Quoted in "ACLU Wants to Legalize Polygamy," *Christians and Society TODAY*, June 1990, p. 4.
94. Bruce Fein and William Bradford Reynolds, "Polygamy Stand Exposes ACLU's Agenda," *Legal Times*, Week of May 22, 1989, p. 22.
95. "Lesbian and Gay Civil Rights Bill Introduced in Both Houses," *Civil Liberties Alert*, December 1991, p. 6.
96. See the discussion of ACLU policy on homosexuality in my book, *The Politics of the American Civil Liberties Union*, 281–85.
97. See the tape of the ACLU's 1989 Biennial Conference on "Rights of Gays and Lesbians."
98. Alan Dershowitz, "ACLU Takes a Wrong Turn," 141.
99. See the tape on "Rights of Gays and Lesbians" of the 1989 Biennial Conference of the ACLU.
100. Ibid.
101. 1985 Biennial Conference tape #7 on "Gay Rights."
102. Policy #264, "Sexual Orientation."
103. 1985 Biennial Conference tape #7 on "Gay Rights."
104. William Raspberry, "A Special Case of Discrimination," *Washington Post*, October 14, 1987, p. A19.
105. Ronald Sullivan, "Judge Says Lesbian Can Adopt Companion's Child," *New York Times*, January 31, 1992, p. A16.
106. David Margolick, "Lesbian Child-Custody Cases Test Frontiers of Family Law," *New York Times*, July 4, 1990, pp. 1, 10.
107. 1985 Biennial Conference tape #7 on "Gay Rights."
108. "Lesbian and Gay Rights Project Focuses on AIDS Discrimination," *Civil Liberties*, Fall 1987, p. 5.
109. Policy #264, "Homosexuality."
110. Philip Gutis, "Court Widens Family Definition to Gay Couples Living Together," *New York Times*, July 7, 1989, p. 1.
111. Marshall Kirk and Hunter Madsen, *After the Ball: How America Will Conquer Its Fear and Hatred of Gays in the '90s* (New York: Doubleday, 1989).
112. Ibid., p. 276.
113. Ibid., p. 292.
114. Ibid., p. 306.
115. Ibid., pp. 297–305.
116. Phil Gutis, "Ohio CLU Creates Gay Rights Office," *Civil Liberties*, Fall 1990, p. 6.

117. Kirk and Madsen, *After the Ball*, p. 313.
118. 1985 Biennial Conference tape #7 pm "Gay Rights."
119. *New York Times* editorial, "Morality, AIDS and the Bathhouses," October 19, 1985, p. 26.
120. Randy Shilts, *And the Band Played On* (New York: St. Martin's Press, 1987), 154, 306.
121. Kirk and Madsen, *After the Ball*, pp. 301-302.
122. Policy #268, "Communicable Diseases and AIDS."
123. Annual Report of the ACLU, 1986-87, p. 28.
124. See the testimony of Nan Hunter before The United States Commission on Civil Rights, an ACLU document of the Washington Office, May 17, 1988, pp. 16-18.
125. Dennis Hevesi, "Kansas Judge Bars Doctors' Release of Positive Test for AIDS Virus," *New York Times*, October 19, 1988, p. A16.
126. Quoted by Lindsey Gruson, "Privacy of AIDS Patients: Fear Infringes on Sanctity," *New York Times*, July 30, 1987, p. D20.
127. Policy #47, "Gun Control."
128. Charles Rembar, "The A.C.L.U.'s Myopic Stand on AIDS," *New York Times*, May 15, 1987, p. A31. In a move that was as unusual as it was revealing, the *New York Times* ran an Op-Ed page response to Rembar's piece by Ira Glasser, just eight days later. The normal response to an Op-Ed article is a letter to the editor, not an Op-Ed opportunity at rebuttal. See Glasser's article (which doesn't mention Rembar by name but is clearly directed at him), "Where the A.C.L.U. Stands on AIDS," *New York Times*, May 23, 1987, p. 27.
129. Nat Hentoff, "Two Cheers for the ACLU," *Washington Post*, March 3, 1990, p. A25.
130. Samuel Walker, *In Defense of American Liberties* (New York: Oxford University Press, 1990), 309.
131. "AIDS Hysteria and Due Process," *Free State Liberties*, a publication of the Maryland CLU, Summer 1988, p. 4.
132. "ACLU Hits Dentists' Discrimination," *Civil Liberties Record*, a publication of the Pennsylvania CLU, Fall 1990, p. 2.
133. "Civil Rights," *Civil Liberties Alert*, legislative newsletter of the ACLU/Washington Office, November/December 1990, p. 14.
134. See the Washington office "Consensus Proposal for Amending INS Procedures for the Inspection of Aliens Suspected of Being HIV Infected," sent to Commissioner Gene McNary, January 24, 1990, p. 8.
135. "Prostitution-related AIDS tests under fire," *Pittsburgh Press*, March 22, 1992, p. A9.
136. "Doctors and AIDS," *Newsweek*, July 1, 1991, p. 54.
137. "Affiliate Notes," *Civil Liberties*, Summer 1989, p. 10.
138. "Public's Fear at AIDS Provokes Draconian Measures in Senate," *Civil Liberties Alert*, July/August 1991, p. 10.
139. "President's AIDS Commission Repudiates Reagan's AIDS Policy," *Civil Liberties*, Spring/Summer 1988, p. 5.
140. "AIDS," *Civil Liberties Record* of Pennsylvania, Winter 1990, p. 4.
141. The ACLU opposed this idea when the President's AIDS Commission made it in June 1988. See "President's AIDS Commission Repudiates Reagan's AIDS Policy," *Civil Liberties*, Spring/Summer 1988, p. 5.
142. The radio debate took place in New York on The Barry Farber Show, WMCA, August 8, 1989.

143. Joseph F. Sullivan, "AIDS-Infected Prisoner Receives 25 Years for Biting a Jail Guard," *New York Times*, May 19, 1990, p. 25.
144. See the pamphlet, "AIDS & Prisons: The Facts for Inmates and Officers," 1988, a publication of the National Prison Project, p. 2.
145. "AIDS and Civil Liberties," *ACLU Briefing Paper*, issued by the national office.
146. The ACLU objected to an amendment by Senator Jesse Helms (it carried in the Senate) that barred funding for AIDS information that was seen as promoting or encouraging homosexuality. See "ACLU Condemns Anti-Gay AIDS Vote," *ACLU News*, a release from the Washington Office, October 14, 1987.
147. Randy Shilts, *And the Band Played On*, pp. 414–15, 481, 492.
148. "Relapses into Risky Sex Found in AIDS Studies," *Society*, September/October 1990, p. 3.

2

The Schools

Moral Education

The cultivation of citizenship is central to liberty, a necessary antecedent to the formal structures of democracy. Institutional mechanisms providing for a balance of power can be written into law, but civic virtue and a sense of duty require constant nourishment and reinforcement. In this respect, the role of mediating institutions is critical; they are a natural locus for the transmission of values. While there is no substitute for the family, the schools are a prime agent of socialization, one that in the past, at least, could be relied upon to transmit a value-centered education. But for some time now, the schools have opted for "value-free" education and have thus relinquished their traditional role as transmitter of the nation's culture.

In addition to jettisoning a commitment to value-centered education, the schools have also deserted a commitment to accountability. Misconduct is commonplace in the schools, and not just in the inner cities. There are many reasons for this problem, and among them is the failure of administrators and teachers to hold students accountable for their behavior. What makes this cycle of despair so complete is the elevation of students' rights over students' responsibilities, leaving dropouts, as well as graduates, with a depraved sense of liberty. At the heart of both of these developments is the perception of freedom as a cache of individual rights, an arsenal to be drawn upon at will.

A social vision of liberty would never countenance a curriculum that did not first and foremost stress the inculcation of a value-centered education. From this perspective, if the schools turned out students who were at once academically literate but morally illiterate, it would surely be labeled as a failed effort. Indeed such students would be seen as a threat to liberty, as persons who would use their knowledge in a way that worked against the public weal. But, alas, there is every indication that this is not the dilemma we face: the evidence suggests that the schools are producing students who are not only morally illiterate, they are underprepared academically as well, leaving us with the worst of all possible worlds.

Though clear to the ancients, the relationship between moral education and academic achievement is today either rejected or taken very lightly. For the past few decades, most schools have come to think of moral education as a matter outside their purview. But at the same time, ironically, the schools are spending many more resources—in time and money—on trying to cope with the social consequences of a society increasingly bereft of a moral nucleus. Thus the explosion of courses dealing with drugs and sex, and the endless workshops for administrators and teachers on how to deal with issues of chemical dependency, violence, unwed motherhood, herpes, and AIDS.

It hardly needs to be said that the real reason why the schools are in such disarray is not the ACLU. However, it would be equally wrong to suggest that the Union's role has been trivial, especially given its activism in behalf of students' rights; its rejection of a value-centered education has also had an impact. At issue is the ACLU's willingness to use the authority of the state, via the courts, to check the social authority of school administrators.

Because the public schools are an entity of the state, it might be objected that the schools qualify as a mediating institution, thus blunting charges that the ACLU could in any way be responsible for elevating state power over the social power of the schools. But as legal scholar Bruce C. Hafen has argued, there are several reasons why the public schools can properly be regarded as mediating institutions.

Hafen notes that "the traditional commitment of the schools to teach children such fundamental civic and moral virtues as integrity, coopera- tion, self-reliance, and responsibility remains central to the task of public education," thus fulfilling a "core mediating role of value transmission." He also emphasizes the "custodial and child-nurturing functions" that the schools play. Perhaps most important, "schools can be understood to be mediating institutions because, despite their battered present state, they function as 'little republics'—tiny communities of learning in which all the participants have the interactive opportunity . . . of developing those 'habits of the heart' without which there is no larger community."[1]

If the public schools can rightly be seen as a mediating institution, it can also be said that the ACLU is wary of the authority they possess, or seek to exercise. More than anything else, it is the ACLU's atomistic conception of liberty that best explains its position toward the social authority that is lodged within the schools. In particular, the Union has focused on challenging the wisdom of moral education and the supremacy of school administrators.

In its own characteristic way, the ACLU sees the process of learning as being independent of a value-centered education and looks upon the rights of students as being nearly absolute. The Union does not see itself as a barrier to quality education, only as a force for individual rights. What the determinants of education are, or what makes for a milieu that is conducive to learning, is seen by the ACLU as being irrelevant to its mission. But to many school superintendents, principals, teachers, and school board members, it is just this kind of myopia that has allowed the ACLU to thwart *their* mission, which is the education of students.

If freedom depends upon citizenship, and if citizenship requires the successful inculcation of core moral values, then it is only logical that we look to the schools to play a central role in the establishment of liberty. But to the mind of the civil libertarian, such a position is, at best, tangential to the meaning of freedom. ACLU officials are not opposed to good citizenship, they simply do not see it as one of their areas of concern. It is this tendency to separate the cause of liberty from the cause of citizenship that marks the atomistic approach to liberty, something a social perspective would find unintelligible. The ACLU, however, fixes its eyes exclusively on individual rights and is deterred from its atomistic vision only when the competing issue of group equality emerges.

It would be one thing if the ACLU's unwillingness to support moral education in the schools simply left it removed from the issue altogether. But that is not the case. The Union has been very much involved in this matter, filing suit, lobbying school officials, and unleashing the resources of its public education office. From its vantage point, the ACLU thinks that the importation of values, or more accurately, traditional values, is a threat to constitutional rights and to the meaning of liberty itself. It casts attempts at moral education as anathema to the spirit, if not the letter, of the establishment clause of the First Amendment.

New York Governor Mario Cuomo, the National Education Association, and People for the American Way are the kinds of people and organizations that are generally in sympathy with the ACLU's positions on a variety of issues; all are emblematic of liberalism. But quite unlike the ACLU, they have sounded the alarm over the dearth of values being taught in the schools. They are troubled, as are most Americans, over the mounting psychological and social pathologies that so many young people experience. That is why at the beginning of the 1986 school year, Governor Cuomo announced that he was prepared to propose a value-centered curriculum for New York's public schools, one that advanced values such as "love thy neighbor" and respect for the law. Predictably, the New York Civil Liberties Union expressed its "nervousness" over the idea, citing church-state concerns.[2] Just two years later, Colleen O'Connor expressed the ACLU's reservations about character education by saying that the Union felt that "values education is sometimes a ruse for teaching religious values."[3]

Sex Education

Throughout the country, the ACLU has fought any school program designed to promote abstinence as the best and only way to check the problems associated with drugs and sex. As Ira Glasser once put it, "Abstinence makes as little sense in the drug context as it does in the fight against AIDS."[4] Given this cast of mind, it makes sense for the ACLU to oppose laws that require written parental consent before instruction in sex education can commence; its insistence that referral to abortion clinics be incorporated in the curriculum is also understandable. No wonder, then, that some affiliates even blame the nation's high rate of teenage pregnancy on programs that teach that the only appropriate method of birth control for teenagers is abstinence.[5] ACLU officials are aware, naturally, that sex education programs that emphasize contraceptives and abortion are the rule and curricula that stress abstinence are the exception, but that has not been enough to dissuade them from their view.

In 1992, in New York City, the local affiliate of the ACLU labeled as censorship a vote taken by the Board of Education ordering that all AIDS education in the public schools stress abstinence. Norm Siegel of the New York CLU announced that a suit would be filed to overturn the new rules. Siegel said that the NYCLU would argue that the rules violated the teachers' freedom of expression in the classroom and attempted to impose "an orthodoxy of values" on students.[6]

Siegel's own idea as to what constitutes "an orthodoxy of values" is itself anything but orthodox. The NYCLU did not object to the multicultural curriculum that says that first graders should be taught "to be aware of various family structures, including gay or lesbian parents" and "to acknowledge the positive aspects of each type of household." (Books such as *Daddy's Roommate* and *Heather Has Two Mommies*, two of the most popular pro-gay books for children, were adopted by the Board of Education.) Indeed, the NYCLU actually said that when some school districts protested the inclusion of this material in their curriculum they were guilty of censorship.[7] It seems plain, then, that it is not the imposition of "an orthodoxy of values" that angers the NYCLU, rather it is the transmittance of traditional values that it regards as objectionable.

The 1990 confrontation between the school system of Chesapeake, Virginia, and the ACLU is another good illustration of how this issue transpires around the country. Alarmed by increasing rates of unwanted teenage pregnancies and the failure of a "value-free" sex education program, school authorities adopted a brochure for ninth graders that called virginity a gift from God and premarital sex a sin. Despite the fact that this alternative viewpoint was not presented as the school system's position, and despite the inclusion of the conventional referencing of contraceptives and abortion in other parts of the sex education curriculum, the local ACLU affiliate vowed to file suit. In the words of Stephen B. Pershing, legal director of the Virginia CLU, the school superintendent and administration "ought to start squirming immediately because our suggestion that they might face legal action is not a threat. It's a promise."[8] Had the school administrators decided to distribute condoms to the youngsters, as they have in New York City, it's a safe bet that the state affiliate would have risen to their defense.

One person who knows firsthand the ACLU's reaction to abstinence-based sex education programs is Jo Ann Gasper. In the 1980s, Gasper worked in the Reagan administration, first in the Department of Health and Human Services and then in the Department of Education. It was at that time that she became aware of a newly established sex education program in Pennsylvania. The program taught that abstinence was *not* beneficial to a person's health, strength, wisdom, or character and instructed students that "you deserve love and sexual pleasure—and you can get exactly what you want"; the context of marriage was never mentioned.[9] It was encounters with material like this that led Gasper to do something about the status of sex education. Upon leaving government, she founded a program called Teen Choice—one that stressed abstinence—in Falls Church, Virginia. Like most sex education programs, Teen Choice received some federal funding. It wasn't long before Gasper heard from the ACLU.

The Union was disturbed to learn that one of Teen Choice's pamphlets advised students to "pray together and invite God on every date." There was also the matter of books that asked pregnant teenagers to consider whether it was "God's will" that they give their child up for adoption. These instances were among only a few isolated references to religion in the program, but that was sufficient to provoke a reaction from the ACLU. According to Gasper, "The ACLU maintains that because we're encouraging kids to abstain from sex outside marriage that we're promoting religiosity, and that's crazy. We are teaching good health."[10] The ACLU saw it differently, stating that Teen Choice was objectionable because it received some federal money from the so-called teen chastity program created by the Adolescent Family Life Act (AFLA); from the beginning, the AFLA has been a source of contention with the ACLU.

The AFLA was introduced as legislation by former Senator Jeremiah Denton in 1981 as an alternative method to the Planned Parenthood policy of providing teenagers with counseling on contraceptives and abortion. In the eyes of some, what made the AFLA controversial was the fact that it was designed to allow religious organizations the right to receive federal funds for the promotion of self-discipline as a form of birth control for teenagers. Notwithstanding the record- level statistics on teenage pregnancies and the obvious need to try a new approach, the ACLU, along with the American Jewish Congress and three Methodist ministers, went to court to stop Catholic participation in this government effort at curbing illegitimacy.

Central to the legislation was the belief that "prevention of adolescent sexual activity and adolescent pregnancy depends upon developing strong family values and close family ties."[11] That is why the AFLA sought to promote sexual restraint among teenagers in the context of parental involvement in sex education. Other aspects of the program included pregnancy testing and maternity counseling, adoption counseling and referral services, prenatal and postnatal care, nutrition information, referral for screening and treatment of venereal disease, referral to appropriate pediatric care, and mental health services. The target population, as the act stipulated, was the poor. It sought to offer low-income individuals the same kinds of services that the affluent already have.

Given the magnitude of the problem, it seemed reasonable that the government try multiple remedies. Over $150 million is spent each year on the Title X (the Public Health Service Act) contraception program, with more than a quarter of the funding going to Planned Parenthood. But the Title V funds do not compose the majority of governmental funding for Planned Parenthood, which also manages to receive funding under Title V (the Maternal and Child Health program of the Social Security Act), Title XIX (Medicaid), and Title XX (the Social Services program under the Social Security Act). The monies appropriated for the AFLA never totaled more than $14 million a year, with the bulk of it going to state and local health agencies, private hospitals, community health associations, privately operated health care centers, and community and charitable organizations. But because some of the grantees were organizations with institutional ties to religious denominations, the ACLU objected.

The ACLU had made up its mind: the AFLA amounted to nothing more than an attempt to offer a privileged position to the Catholic Church. To the ACLU, the legislation discriminated in favor of Catholicism because, by granting money only to programs that didn't promote abortion, it excluded religions that favor abortion. However, the AFLA was not a religious program; it was a program for abstinence. Abstinence was presumably not a Catholic prerogative; Jews, Hindus, and others have been known to be in favor of abstinence and even to abstain. Further, while it is true that the Catholic Church, as well as the AFLA, opposes abortion, it does not follow that the legislation was "Catholic" in nature. The Catholic Church also accepts elementary algebra; schools that teach algebra are not, on that account, proselytizing in the classroom. The point is that sexual restraint and rejection of abortion are not exclusively Catholic beliefs. But none of this mattered to the ACLU, which filed suit challenging the constitutionality of the AFLA.

In the spring of 1987, Washington, D.C., judge Charles Richey sustained the ACLU's complaints that the AFLA amounted to a federal subsidy for religious indoctrination. This was the first time in the nation's history that any court invalidated an act of Congress as an impermissible establishment of religion. However, on June 29, 1988, the Supreme Court ruled 5-4 that the AFLA was, with qualification, constitutional. What the court decided was that religious affiliation is constitutional but the injection of religious content or indoctrination into the federal program was not.[12] The case was sent back to the district court to determine whether individual AFLA grantees met these requirements. Since that time, the ACLU has registered its objections to further fact-finding, asking that the entire program be found unconstitutional in practice.

The ACLU's challenge to the AFLA highlights the organization's attitude toward sex education programs and the legal approach it prefers to take. Following a highly atomistic conception of liberty, the ACLU shows little appreciation for school curricula that emphasize self-control, as opposed to self-liberation. By opposing any connection between public monies and religious institutions, even in instances where there is clearly no religious indoctrination taking place, the Union seeks to limit the range of public policy options that are available in dealing with serious social problems. Its attempt to thwart a fairly innocuous sex education program in California is a case in point.

In 1988, Marjorie C. Swartz and Francisco Lobaco of the California Legislative Office of the ACLU wrote a letter to the members of the Assembly Education Committee in the State Capitol of Sacramento, expressing their dismay at a recently proposed bill (SB 2394) concerning sex education in the public schools. "It is our position," they said, "that teaching that monogamous, heterosexual intercourse within marriage is a traditional American value is an unconstitutional establishment of a religious doctrine in public schools. There are various religions which hold contrary beliefs with respect to marriage and monogamy. We believe that SB 2394 violates the First Amendment."[13] The prime reason why the ACLU reacted this way had nothing to do with the Constitution: it was due to the Union's professed belief that the bill stigmatized children born out of wedlock. But in order to gain a constitutional handle on the issue, it resorted to its familiar church-state objection.

Former ACLU board member Nat Hentoff said that the letter was representative of the Union's "bizarre notion of the separation of church and state," adding that the ACLU could use some "remedial education" in this area. Hentoff wondered why anyone would question whether monogamous heterosexual intercourse was a traditional American value.

"It's not?" he asked. "And is it not possible for atheists to believe in—and practice—this old-time value?"[14]

Hentoff's charges incensed Colleen O'Connor of the New York office, who replied that the Union was not objecting to the teaching of monogamous heterosexual intercourse as a traditional American value but only to "a highly prescriptive bill . . . designed to prevent teachers from discussing other kinds of families—single-parent families, gay relationships, families in which children are born out of wedlock . . . ."[15] However, in the original letter sent to the Education Committee, these concerns were not noted. And O'Connor still did not explain how gay relationships could in any way be defended as a traditional American value.

In a debate with Dennis Prager, the author of the quarterly journal *Ultimate Issues*, Ira Glasser commented that he personally rebuked the California office for the "outrageous letter" it sent to members of the Assembly Education Committee and had it withdrawn.[16] But apparently Glasser's "rebuke" mattered little in the end.

The letter was written May 26, 1988, and by the end of the year it was still being defended by the California affiliate, though with the new qualifications offered by O'Connor. On December 20, 1988, in a reply to a *New York Post* editorial of December 7 that was critical of the ACLU's letter, Ramona Ripston, executive director of the Southern California CLU, and Dorothy Ehrlich, executive director of the Northern California CLU, explained their position. "The language of that letter (but not the position)," they said, "was repudiated by both national and state ACLU officials and we have clarified our positions for state legislators." What they meant by this was that although the wording of the letter "contains an unfortunate characterization of the ACLU evaluation of a then-pending sex-education bill," it is nonetheless accurate to say that the Union opposes any teaching that says that monogamous heterosexual marriages are the only acceptable lifestyles.[17]

The ACLU's position—that so-called alternative lifestyles could in any way be labeled an acceptable model or a traditional American value—shows how thoroughly imbued it is with the atomistic approach to liberty. To civil libertarians, the institution of marriage is itself simply an alternative lifestyle, it being an alternative to homosexual liaisons, heterosexual cohabitation, and out-of-wedlock teenage relationships. But the reason why the institution of monogamous heterosexual marriage has always been prized, and these other variants have been seen as either dysfunctional or deviant, is precisely that a more social conception of liberty has been in force, valuing the traditional model of marriage as being the most appropriate institution in society for the rearing of children. The ACLU's rejection of this verity tells much about its thinking.

A more complete rendering of the ACLU's position on sex education was its reaction to the abstinence-based program known as Project Respect. The Union not only expressed its outrage over the program, it engaged in an unprecedented book banning effort, seeking to prevent inclusion of the program in the state curriculum in Wisconsin.

In 1985, Kathleen Sullivan founded Project Respect, an abstinence-based sex education program headquartered in Golf, Illinois. The book that is used in the program is called *Sex Respect*, written by educator Colleen Kelly Mast, and was developed subsequent to a grant issued by the Office of Adolescent Pregnancy Programs, Department of Health and Human Services. The purpose of the program is to present abstinence as a positive and rewarding alternative to premarital sex. Lesson plans include segments on the need to differentiate between sexual freedom and sexual impulsiveness; recognition of the various influences on sexual decision making; identification of emotional, psychological, and physical consequences of teenage sexual activity; discussion of dating guidelines—with an emphasis on how to say NO; and exploration of the responsibilities of parenthood.

Does *Sex Respect* work? The facts are incontrovertible. Among the 3,500 students in Midwestern schools that adopted the curriculum in the period 1985–1990, there was a dramatic decline not only in attitudes regarding sexual experimentation but in teenage pregnancies as well. A pronounced attitudinal change was evident in all 26 schools in the federal pilot study as well as in 46 schools funded by the state of Illinois, covering 9,500 students. Among participating female students, only 5 percent had become pregnant one to two years afterward, as compared to 9 percent of girls who had not participated. For males, only 4 percent of the boys had caused a pregnancy after one year of completing the course, compared to 7 percent of the boys who were in the control group and did not take part in the program. By contrast, the Planned Parenthood sex education programs have typically resulted in increased teenage pregnancies.[18]

So what irked the ACLU? In 1991 the Union filed suit on behalf of two Wisconsin parents following the adoption of *Sex Respect* in the public schools of East Troy, claiming that the book violated state laws prohibiting discriminatory stereotyping in curricular materials and should therefore be removed from the classrooms. According to the ACLU, "Bias and stereotyping pervade *Sex Respect*: the curriculum portrays all boys as sexual aggressors, and all girls as virginity protectors; the curriculum states that males 'aggressively seek sexual release with whatever person they can persuade or force to accommodate them,' and 'use love to get sex.'"[19] But what the fictional psychologist in the book actually says is, "Boys tend to use love to get sex. Girls tend to use sex to get love."[20] It is fair to say that this is not the kind of characterization that most people outside the ranks of the ACLU would find remarkable, much less meriting a lawsuit.

The ACLU's reading of *Sex Respect* leads it to believe that the book is guilty of presenting girls "as incapable of sexual fantasy, and motivated solely by needs for 'warmth, closeness, and security.'" The Union is perhaps most adamant in its conviction that "the two-parent heterosexual couple" should not be presented as "the sole model of a healthy, 'real' family." It also finds objectionable the portrayal of AIDS "as the sexually transmitted disease most common among homosexuals, and as nature's way of making 'some kind of statement on sexual behavior,'" without explaining the grounds upon which it finds these statements to be incorrect. And, of course, the Union finds that *Sex Respect* "promotes one religious perspective regarding the 'spiritual dimension' of sexuality," not saying what religious perspective might regard abstinence as an objectionable teaching construct.[21]

Even if one were to agree with the substance of the ACLU's complaints, it is not at all clear why an organization supposedly dedicated to free speech would want to be associated with efforts at book banning. To put it bluntly, having the courts police school textbooks is something the ACLU accuses fascists of doing. Moreover, it is revealing that the same ACLU that has long defended the most obscene public expressions as a First Amendment right—and to be paid for at public expense (for example, through the National Endowment of the Arts)—cannot bring itself to accept the teaching of traditional moral values in the schools. It is not for nothing that *Newsweek* calls into question the ACLU's commitment to its own much-vaunted principle of "defending the thought it hates": "Is the ACLU following that admonition, or looking for an excuse to excise the thought it hates?"[22]

Students' Rights

For those who share the atomistic perspective on liberty, the subject of responsibility rarely merits more than cursory attention, the focus being on individual rights. The subject of students' rights is no exception, as a reading of ACLU policies and actions in this area testifies. It was in New York City, in the late 1960s, that the ACLU first targeted the schools as an "enclave" to be penetrated. According to Samuel Walker, it was Ira Glasser, following the dictates of Executive Director Aryeh Neier, who actively pushed the Union's new strategy: "Identify a problem and frame it in civil liberties terms."[23] In Neier's view, then, there was hardly a social problem that the ACLU wouldn't have at least something to say about and, presumably, litigate about as well.

One of the first people to experience the ACLU's newfound interest in students' rights was Howard L. Hurwitz. Beginning in the 1960s, the New York affiliate of the ACLU worked for about a decade to oust Hurwitz as principal of Long Island City High School. Hurwitz, known back then as "the strongest principal in the city," took a hard line against student misbehavior and won the overwhelming respect and support of students and parents alike; this was nowhere more true than among minority students and parents. But to the officers at the NYCLU, Hurwitz was seen as a threat to the civil liberties of miscreant students.

Hurwitz, who spent half a century in the public school system of New York (1938–88), incurred the wrath of the ACLU for doing exactly what most of the residents of Long Island City praised him for doing: refusing to tolerate the relatively small band of unruly students who made it nearly impossible for serious learning to take place. The ACLU's preoccupation with the alleged rights of offending students set off a storm of controversy, engendering the criticism not only of teachers, parents, and students, but of the New York Council of Supervisors and Administrators as well. This august group censured the NYCLU "for its continuing efforts to disrupt discipline in the schools and to undermine the exercise of reasonable authority of principals and teachers."[24]

Hurwitz sees the situation the same way, charging that the NYCLU "has done much to harass school principals by assuring retention in schools of disruptive students."[25] By continuing to bring suit over the slightest matters, the ACLU, according to Hurwitz, "has had a chilling effect on the freedom of principals to act in a principled way."[26] This might indeed be the worst consequence of ACLU challenges to the legitimate authority of school officials. Once the fear of an ACLU lawsuit sets in, decisions that ought to be made are frequently shelved in favor of a more expedient approach. While it is difficult to measure just how prevalent and serious this matter is, it would be dishonest to say that it isn't an issue most principals haven't thought much about during the course of their tenure.

"Simple civility so essential to fostering a climate of learning," argues Hurwitz, has been "destroyed on an altar of civil liberties designed by American Civil Liberties Union zealots."[27] This may sound harsh, but there is cause for concern, if not alarm, at many ACLU policies on this subject. What angers Hurwitz are things like the NYCLU's "Student Rights Handbook for New York City." In it, students learn much about their rights, real and contrived, and little about their responsibilities. For example, prior to recent court decisions strengthening administrative authority, the NYCLU advised students that "the use of the word fuck could not be prohibited in a high school newspaper since it also appeared in magazines and books in the school library."[28] Just as notorious was the situation in Boston's public schools, where in the 1980s students were given a twenty-five-page pamphlet on their rights called "The Book." Culled from such sources as the ACLU, the pamphlet contained eleven lines of type on students' responsibilities.

In fairness to the ACLU, it would be wrong to suggest that the Union has not done some good work in protecting students' rights from serious and blatant abuses of powers. Where there are clear violations of elementary students' rights, a civil liberties organization ought to get involved. But too often that is not the issue. The issue is whether the educational process can continue to stand the kind of micromanagement the ACLU wants to foster. Quite simply, the atomistic approach favored by the ACLU is attentive neither to questions of student responsibilities nor to issues bearing on the requisites of a successful learning environment.

It was the New York CLU's Student Rights Project that laid the groundwork for the national organization's handbook on *The Rights of Students*.[29] In it, students learn that school officials have no authority in addressing their off-campus behavior. The Union disagrees, for example, with the decision of a federal court in Texas that schools have a right to expel a student for the remainder of the school year for "using, selling, or possessing a dangerous drug." To the ACLU, this represents "unnecessary extension of the responsibility of school officials for off-school activities."[30]

In another instance, the Union cites a New Hampshire case that ruled on the matter of suspending a student for drunkenness at school. The court took note of strained family relations at home, holding that it was "fundamentally unfair to keep a student out of school indefinitely because of difficulties between the student and her parents, unless those difficulties manifest themselves in a real threat to school discipline." The ACLU's read on this case concludes that "the school had no business interfering with a student's problems at home, although it did have the right to punish a student for misconduct in school that might be the result of those problems."[31] But school officials never tried to interfere with the student's problems at home; they confined themselves, quite properly, to the student's misbehavior in school. The latitudinal rendering of the court's decision offered by the ACLU is informative of its expansive notion of students' rights.

Here's another example of what the ACLU says is a student's right: it's okay to skip study hall during a free period and head off to the local amusement park, providing no one says this is forbidden. In fact, the ACLU instructs that "it would be illegal" to punish the student "without prior warning."[32] Given this cast of mind, it was only logical that the Union would protest a faculty decision, made in a rural Colorado school, requiring that students maintain a little "daylight" between them, this in response to increasing amounts of kissing and necking in the halls.[33] It is instances like these that sustain the charge being made here: too often, ACLU decisions are made in a social vacuum, independent of real-life contexts.

Students' rights is but a part of a much wider phenomenon, namely the subject of children's rights. Throughout the ages, most students of liberty have drawn clear distinctions between the rights of adults and the rights of children. Because of their dependent state, and owing to their lack of emotional and intellectual maturity, children have not been seen as the equal of adults in terms either of rights or responsibilities. For example, John Stuart Mill explicitly excluded children from his principle of liberty, and Jefferson also took note of children's limitations. But in the contemporary period, a radical children's rights movement has emerged, one that regards the traditional wisdom on this subject as antiquated and obsolete. The ACLU, needless to say, has signed on to this movement.

In times past, children were informed of their responsibilities, almost never about their rights. Today, the exact opposite has occurred. Beginning with the rights revolution of the 1960s, educators and social scientists pushed for a radical reinterpretation of the status of children in society. Educator John Holt and psychologist Richard Farson, for example, promoted the idea that children should be given the same rights as adults (but not responsibilities) in virtually every aspect of society. Voting, working, owning property, traveling, driving, taking drugs, sex— there is nothing these children's rights advocates wouldn't sanction as appropriate for children.[34] Though these ideas have not come into practice, the logic of granting children more rights has gained in the culture and in some institutional settings as well.

The goal is nothing less than a radical redistribution of power, using rights as the fulcrum. Having defined children as "the most oppressed of all minorities,"[35] children's rights advocates seek to equalize the rights of children and thereby undercut the legitimate authority of parents. Unfortunately, this extremely atomistic approach to liberty provides for an environment that few child psychologists would be prepared to defend as beneficial to children's needs. It is bonding, not autonomy, that children seek, the deprivation of which is associated with a host of pathological conditions. Only a very lawyerly view of the world could conclude otherwise.

The ACLU's role in the children's rights movement has centered mostly on the question of students' rights. The Union has been particularly active in matters of freedom of expression, participating either directly or as an amicus in virtually every significant Supreme Court case. It was in the 1969 case *Tinker v. Des Moines Independent Community School District* that the Supreme Court first gave the ACLU what it wanted: the establishment of a First Amendment right for students to express themselves in school. The high court ruled that students had a right to express their politics in school by wearing black armbands to protest American involvement in the war in Vietnam. It was this affirmation of "symbolic speech" on the part of students that led Justice Hugo Black, an "absolutist" on free speech, to dissent, maintaining that issues of discipline and educational quality were sufficient to override any alleged First Amendment right of the students.[36]

Almost twenty years later, in 1986, the Supreme Court delivered a ruling in *Bethel School District No. 403 v. Fraser* that considerably narrowed *Tinker*. Students, the court said, could be disciplined for "vulgar and offensive" language. In 1983, Matthew Fraser, a high school senior, was suspended after using indecent language in a speech before an assembly of students. The ACLU defended Fraser's vulgarities, citing First Amendment protections, but the Supreme Court ruled otherwise, claiming that school authorities were within their rights in ordering the suspension. The difference between *Tinker* and *Fraser* was this: the former was a matter of the students' political discourse, and one that did not unduly effect the educational process, whereas the latter was a matter of vulgar speech made at an officially sponsored school event. Though the ACLU did not see the difference, seven of the nine justices did.

The *Fraser* decision meant that the Supreme Court was willing to broaden its horizons regarding the proper regulation of student expression. It would look heretofore to the inculcation of "the habits and manners of civility as values . . . conducive to happiness and . . . indispensable to the practice of self-government" as the basis of its determinations. In doing so, it took a position on the First Amendment that evinced a truly social conception of liberty, one that was inclusive of the goals of the public school system.[37]

Tinker was further limited in the *Kuhlmeier* case. This suit involved the right of students to print in the school newspaper material the principal deemed inappropriate. The court held, 5–3, that school officials have the right to censor school newspapers, plays, and other "school-sponsored expressive activities." The decision, made in 1988, concluded that there was no First Amendment violation. Writing for the majority, Justice Byron White contended that a school need not tolerate student speech inconsistent with its "basic educational mission," even though "the government could not censor similar speech outside the school." White reaffirmed the principle of *Tinker* that students do not "shed their constitutional rights to freedom of expression at the schoolhouse gate," but he went on to say that there is a difference between a student's own speech and that which occurs in the school curriculum; the latter might seem "to bear the imprimatur of the school."[38]

The ACLU quickly branded *Kuhlmeier* as "undoubtedly the worst civil liberties decision" rendered in the first half of the 1987–88 term of the Supreme Court. In a demonstration of just how far out of touch the ACLU is with public sentiment on this matter, it stated that "it is possible that public outcry produced by this decision will encourage local school boards to adopt policies that guarantee the First Amendment rights of students."[39] It is safe to say that the only sustained outcry has come from the ACLU, the public being overwhelmingly on the side of increased control by school authorities.

After the *Fraser* decision, but before *Kuhlmeier*, the ACLU instructed students that if they wanted to use language that school officials might object to, it might be helpful "to point out that many books and articles in the school library contain the same words to which the principal is objecting in school literature." Even after *Kuhlmeier*, the Union found little reason to pare back its advice, this time advising student editors to show that potentially controversial subjects are already available "in places such as school library books, local newspapers, rap groups, counseling programs," and the like.[40] The unmistakable message is that students should not give up on their right to engage in highly offensive speech. This is the kind of civics lesson that is taught throughout the ACLU's handbook on *The Rights of Students*.

The ACLU's idea of free speech rights for students has also led it to resist the imposition of a dress code in the schools. For instance, there is not a T-shirt so vile and obscene that the Union wouldn't defend as fit to wear to school. Here are a few examples. When in 1988 students at a Rockville, Maryland, high school were barred from wearing T-shirts with the inscription "Big Pecker," the ACLU threatened a lawsuit.[41] In 1990, the Union protested when an East Islip Long Island student was forbidden to wear a T-shirt inscribed with the legend "Adolf Hitler European Tour 1939–1945."[42] And in 1992, the Virginia affiliate of the ACLU filed a federal lawsuit on behalf of a student who was suspended for wearing a T-shirt saying "Drugs Suck."[43] In each case, the ACLU saw no competing interest to the students' alleged First Amendment right.

The ACLU's defense of vulgar T-shirts in the classroom is at one with its thinking on dress codes in general. Ira Glasser, for instance, speaks derisively of the days when dress codes were enforced with regularity in the public schools. He attributes to the advocates of a dress code the belief that "the structure of public education would crumble if a boy were allowed another quarter-inch of hair or a girl permitted to wear pants."[44] Of course, no one has seriously said that "the structure of public education would crumble" if students' appearance or dress were unconventional. What many have said is that proper decorum bears some relationship to academic success, and to the extent that dress and appearance codes help facilitate that process, they play a role in meeting educational objectives. In other words, if a tone of seriousness is desirable in the classroom, then the way students present themselves must matter.

What does the ACLU advise principals, teachers, and students to do when a student wears a vulgar T-shirt to school? "If you don't like the message on a T-shirt," says Alan Schlosser, a staff lawyer with the San Francisco CLU, "you should turn your head or talk to someone about it rather than speculate that there may be some problem."[45] Now the ACLU would never counsel someone who was offended by the placement of a crèche on public property to simply "turn his head." On the contrary, the Union would sue in his behalf. But now offended educators and students are told that the only proper remedy for combating the public display of obscenities is to cease in their speculation that there is a problem.

ACLU resistance to dress codes has especially impacted on the educational achievement of minority students. In one black neighborhood after another, parents and school boards have demanded dress and appearance codes in the schools, only to face challenges by the local affiliate of the ACLU. At issue is whether students can be expected to learn when daily violence erupts over the wearing of flashy jewelry and coveted shoes and clothes. Most parents and educators think not. The ACLU does not necessarily disagree, it simply says that such concerns should in no way trump the right of students to express themselves.

Violence in the schools occurs for many reasons, and when school officials attempt to deal with such problems they typically find themselves dealing with the ACLU as well. There is much to deal with, as the scope and level of school violence has reached unprecedented proportions. The experience of Glen Kirkland offers ample testimony to the ways things have changed.

Kirkland graduated in the 1980s from Thomas Jefferson High School in Brooklyn and a decade later was a city police officer assigned to his alma mater. When he was at Jefferson, Kirkland says, the guys used to "duke it out." But now the guys say, "'Hey, you stole my girlfriend, boom!' Then his friends say, 'Hey, you shot my friend, boom!' Pretty soon it's boom, boom, boom!" It is for reasons like this that guns have become the leading cause of death among older teenage boys. Even more disturbing is the fact that one in twenty students comes to class armed; some are now toting .357 magnums, 9-mm semiautomatics, and Uzi assault rifles. While the problem is nationwide, it is the inner cities that have been most plagued with the problem of school violence. An estimated 43 percent of inner-city children age 7 to 19 have witnessed a homicide.[46]

School officials, often in response to intense community pressure, have tried a number of preventive measures aimed at stopping violence before it occurs. In New York City, the Joint Commission on Integrity in the Public Schools, a government commission aimed at restoring the public's confidence in the schools, decided in 1989 that it was time to do an investigation to determine the extent of violence, drugs, and guns in the schools. Five undercover officers spent seven months in the nine schools ranked highest in violent incidents by the Board of Education and the United Federation of Teachers. No one complained but the ACLU. Norman Siegel, head of the New York affiliate, wrote a letter to Schools Chancellor Joseph A. Fernandez and Police Commissioner Lee P. Brown, protesting that such investigations "manifest a gross insensitivity and serious disregard for fundamental constitutional values respecting privacy, fairness and intellectual freedom within the school community."[47]

Just about every action taken to combat school crime—metal detectors, locker searches, bans on beepers and gold jewelry—has been rebuffed by the ACLU. The Union has gone into federal district court in Michigan to defend the right of a high school student to carry a beeper and has threatened lawsuits in Chicago and elsewhere. Now it is well known that beepers are often used by drug pushers to contact drug dealers on school property, and that is why Philadelphia's school board banned students from carrying beepers in 1988; exceptions were made for health or family reasons. Though most educators support beeper laws, the ACLU fears that kids might be detained for reasons that are illegal. But the Philadelphia experience shows that legitimate needs can be accommodated without prohibiting beeper laws altogether.[48]

The ACLU, which thinks metal detectors should be banned from the airports,[49] thinks they should be banned from the schools as well. As Norm Siegel sees it, metal detectors in the schools "violate constitutional rights,"[50] and no amount of innocent human life that is saved is worth the minimal loss of privacy incurred by walking through one of the devices. The same logic is used to oppose locker searches. Official ACLU policy demands that a search warrant be obtained before school authorities can search a student's locker, save for exigent or emergency conditions.[51] Worse still, the Union cannot bring itself to advise students not to traffic in guns and drugs. No, the best it can offer is "never to carry on you or keep in school anything that you wouldn't want the police or school officials to know about for any reason." And to top it off, it adds, "Never consent to any search. Say in a loud, clear voice, so that witnesses can hear, that you do not consent."[52]

"What is an appropriate balance between the need to keep drugs and weapons out of schools and your *right* to privacy?" To this eminently reasonable question, posed by the ACLU, come answers that unfortunately show little interest in finding a balance. The Union's handbook on *The Rights of Students* is replete with castigation of preventive measures used by school authorities. What is striking is that the ACLU argues against most security tactics because they make education "difficult if not impossible" to achieve.[53] It does not say, or even imply, that it is criminal behavior that makes education "difficult if not impossible to achieve." But that is what happens when an atomistic approach to liberty is followed: individual rights, shorn of any other concern, are all that matters. Tragically, it does not matter that by following the ACLU's prescriptions on individual rights, most students experience less liberty, not more.

The ACLU is not only opposed to most of the favored measures that would curtail crime in the schools, it opposes most disciplinary actions as well. It is against corporal punishment and, more important, it disapproves of expulsion as a disciplinary option. The ACLU opposes expulsion because it "might have a lifetime effect, depriving a student of a chance to go to college or to obtain many kinds of jobs."[54] The ACLU is correct. But it is also correct to say that chronically misbehaving students might deprive other students of learning and thus inhibit their chances of going to college, the effect of which is a lifetime penalty. That the ACLU chose not to make a statement in behalf of the innocent students who are prohibited from learning gives us some idea of its priorities. Even more regrettable is the advice the ACLU gives to students on how to beat the system. "If you disrupt a class and school officials try to expel you," the handbook opines, "you might bring witnesses to testify at your hearing that other students received only short suspensions for such misconduct."[55]

The human cost of the ACLU's atomistic idea of freedom is perhaps nowhere more well known than in Detroit. In late 1984, the Detroit school board authorized a policy of surprise "sweeps," a program that allowed school security personnel and Detroit police to be posted at school entrances with hand-held and walk-through metal detectors. The reason for this drastic action was the drastic rise in school violence. During the 1983–84 school year, 325 weapons were seized inside the city's schools. The next year the number of weapons seized jumped to 456; the cache included 155 handguns, 222 knives, eight sawed-off shotguns, one hand grenade, and a host of wrenches, ice picks, razors, and brass knuckles. Almost everyone was relieved that the surprise "sweeps" had been authorized. Everyone but the ACLU.

The 1985–86 school year began with the ACLU in court challenging the constitutionality of the surprise "sweeps." Because the searches were not based on probable cause, the Union said, the Fourth Amendment protection against unreasonable searches and seizures had been violated. Due to a legal technicality, the federal district court averted a direct ruling on the ACLU's challenge, but it nonetheless agreed to put a temporary halt on the "sweeps." Judge Avern Cohn lectured school authorities for their methods, the police presence, and the surprise nature of the searches; the metal detectors, however, could stay. The school board reconsidered its actions and drafted a new set of guidelines.

The new guidelines authorized searches only in those schools where weapons had recently been found or gang violence was feared; random searches were banned. The Detroit police were forbidden to administer the searches, and women were to be hired as security personnel. Most significant, the board said that students were entitled to advance warning of any impending searches, and the metal detectors were taken out of the schools. Judge Cohn was pleased and gave the authorities the right to proceed.

The ACLU, after having succeeded in blunting the deterrent effect of the searches, was still not satisfied: it was opposed to any kind of random search. While the board was contemplating what to do with the ACLU's new complaints, a highly regarded student-athlete was killed in the parking lot of Murray-Wright High School in April 1987. At the behest of Mayor Coleman Young, the school board quickly reinstalled metal detectors in the schools. The advance warning problem was solved by simply posting signs saying that students are subject to weapons searches without stating which day the "sweeps" would take place.[56]

The result was a stalemate: the ACLU had lost in the courts in its attempt to get the metal detectors banned from the school but had succeeded in stopping random searches. Somewhat chastened by public opinion and the courts, the local affiliate made a move to build better relations with the school board. Early in 1988, the Metropolitan Detroit Branch of the ACLU of Michigan made a fairly novel decision: instead of working against the school board, it decided to work with it, suggesting tactics that might at once help control crime in the schools and protect civil liberties as well. So out of character was this ACLU gambit that it merited front page coverage in several of the nation's leading newspapers and was cited in many journals of opinion as a breakthrough. In the end, however, there was little to cheer about, because substantively there was little that was new in the ACLU's strategy.

The Detroit CLU established two task forces to address the problems of crime and education and eventually combined both to form the Task Force on Violence in the Schools. It developed thirteen recommendations, all of which were offered to the school board. Unfortunately, most of them had little to do with directly addressing the issue and much to do with furthering the ACLU's own agenda. For example, there were recommendations on creating a speaker's bureau to disseminate information on the Constitution, suggestions on creating an internship for students whereby they can work in law offices, proposals to establish public forums to discuss current local interests, ideas about periodic seminars on the Constitution, and the like. And guess who volunteered to supply the speakers and law offices as well as sponsor the forums and seminars? The ACLU.

Despite the self-serving nature of these proposals, there were some that did merit further consideration. The Detroit CLU's idea of using police cadets, parent patrols, and other volunteers to assist with security was as unusual (for the ACLU) as it was serious (it did have some potential to curb crime). Its support for a crackdown on truancy was also admirable and completely at odds with the thinking of most ACLU affiliates. But as for its recommendations on searching for weapons, the best it was prepared to do was to suggest individualized searches based on "reasonable suspicion," hardly a breakthrough. In any event, the credit for these modest gains goes to Leonard Grossman, the president of the Detroit affiliate, and not to the national office of the ACLU.[57]

What Does the ACLU Recommend?

There have been two major school reform proposals that have surfaced in recent years: school choice and the establishment of all-male public schools in the inner cities (home schooling, which the ACLU does not oppose,[58] has not attracted large support). Though both measures enjoy widespread support, especially among blacks, the ACLU has worked tirelessly to ensure their defeat. The Union has been successful in maintaining the status quo in most instances, with the result that most black parents have been denied the opportunity to send their children to the school of their choice.

School choice is hardly a new idea, but it is one that has caught fire only recently. Based on the free-market approach of the Nobel Prize-winning economist Milton Friedman, school choice has come to mean any plan that offers a meaningful alternative to the public school system. One variant is the voucher plan, a program whereby parents submit their voucher to whatever school they choose for their children, public or private. Another approach is a tuition tax credit, whereby parents are reimbursed for a portion of their private school fees. In other instances, as in the case of the Golden Rule Insurance Company of Indiana, private sources pay part of the cost of private education for needy families, thus circumventing the problems of the educational bureaucracy and the ACLU altogether.

The principal reason that school choice has taken on a new level of seriousness across the country is the efforts of local black leaders. Polly Williams, for instance, led a successful fight to establish parental choice in education in Milwaukee and has been instrumental in igniting the fires of change elsewhere. Starting in the 1990–91 school year, up to 1,000 students in Milwaukee could claim $2,500 worth of tuition vouchers to help defray the cost of private education. The waiting list now extends to the hundreds, as poor families await their chance at exercising choice. Williams knows that 62 percent of the teachers and administrators in the public school system send their kids to private schools, and she wants poor blacks to be given the same options. "Choice," Williams says, "empowers parents. It allows them to choose the best school for their children. It doesn't say, as the educrats do, that poor people are too dumb (they use the word 'uninformed') to make choices."[59]

The ACLU is officially on record opposing all school choice plans[60] and has filed suit after suit trying to stop reform, whether it be in the form of a voucher or tax credit. There are two major reasons why the ACLU opposes choice in education: it argues that choice would violate separation of church and state by subsidizing parochial schools and it maintains that choice would foster segregation in the public schools. Critics reply that the GI Bill has long allowed recipients to choose sectarian colleges and universities without any apparent violation of the Constitution. And the charge that school choice furthers segregation is somewhat disingenuous, given the sharp increase in urban segregated schools that has occurred in response to busing (it causes "white flight"), a proposal ironically sponsored by the ACLU.

Though the ACLU cites legal arguments against school choice, its public statements on this issue indicate that social policy considerations, and not civil liberties concerns, play a strong role in determining its position. For example, the ACLU has done what it could to stop school choice in Alabama, working on the basis that private schools might attract too many students, thus undercutting, it says, the public schools. It also complains that the school choice plans are not generous enough to cover all expenses for poor families, thus inaccurately leaving the impression that it might not object if all fees were covered.[61]

The establishment of all-male public schools in the inner cities has been opposed by the ACLU because of its segregating effect; in this instance, the Union fears sex segregation more than racial segregation. But the reason why so many black fathers and mothers want all-male schools is because young black males are in the most dire straits of any segment of the population. It has been reported many times that black young men today are more likely to die from homicide than it was likely for a U.S. soldier to be killed on a tour of duty in Vietnam. Indeed, the homicide rate among young black men in Harlem is so high that these men are less likely to reach the age of 40 than a person born in Bangladesh. While the specific statistics may not be known to most people, blacks in the inner city can certainly verify the veracity of the claim.

Because Detroit has been especially hard hit by a wave of violence and failing schools, it was the residents of that city, where 70 percent of the students come from one-parent families, who led the movement for all-male public schools. And just as these reform-minded blacks had run up against the ACLU in their quest to stem school violence, they met up with the mostly white civil libertarians on this issue as well. The ACLU, along with the mostly white members of the National Organization for Women (NOW), committed its considerable resources to stopping poor blacks from getting what they wanted. The ACLU won, though it is less than certain that the cause of liberty did.

On August 5, 1991, the ACLU and NOW sued the Detroit public school system for its plan to set up three all-male academies on the grounds that girls would be illegally excluded. There is evidence, like that compiled by Harvard emeritus sociologist David Riesman, that single sex schools can be beneficial, but no amount of evidence was sufficient to dissuade the ACLU. Ten days after the suit was filed, Federal District Judge George E. Woods agreed with the ACLU and NOW by denying the school board from setting up the all-male academies.

Jacqueline Berrien, staff attorney with the Women's Rights Project, offered the following line of reasoning justifying the ACLU's action: "When both the boy and the girl are hurting, how can we focus our attention on one child over the other, solely on the basis of immutable characteristics of birth?"[62] Of course, no one was saying that all-female schools couldn't be established, only that all-male schools were highly desirable at the present time. More important, the reason why black parents wanted all-male schools had nothing to do with such fanciful ideas as "immutable characteristics of birth." It had everything to do with the need for proper role models and a structured environment: young black males, more than females, are the most likely segment in society to engage in high-risk behavior, and that is why inner-city communities have targeted their needs.

So having succeeded in blocking needed school reform, the ACLU is in a position to command the respect, if not the good will, of school officials. It is not clear, however, how an organization that is ostensibly sensitive to the rights of minorities can continue to alienate so many nonwhites, especially African Americans. Just what are principals to do, to take one issue, about the problem of school crime if every time they try to stop it, they are met with a letter, phone call, or lawsuit from the ACLU focusing on the rights of the offenders?

Official ACLU policy on the rights of students makes one wonder how the ACLU could reasonably expect order in the schools to be maintained if the authorities were to adhere exclusively to its advice. It opposes, in elementary school, the policy of prohibiting misbehaving students from voting or running for school office as a form of disciplinary action. The Union reasons that "participation in elections is both a means of sharing school government and a form of preparation for future citizenship."[63] While this reasoning is hardly exceptional, it is strange to see the ACLU therefore conclude that offending students should be given the same rights as those who they have offended. What lessons about citizenship does the ACLU expect that these students will learn? That rights cannot be withdrawn no matter how a student conducts himself or herself? That rights and responsibilities do not—indeed should not—go hand in hand?

When the ACLU recommends as official policy that no high school student "should suffer any hurt or penalty for any idea expressed in the course of participation in class or school activities," does it really mean that no student should be disciplined for vicious and intimidating remarks, designed solely to insult and degrade other students in the classroom? If not, then why does it write such open-ended policies? And if a student suffers a "hurt" by being told by his teacher that certain ideas are plain wrong—like the idea that the Holocaust didn't happen—then why should this be a matter of concern to the ACLU?[64]

ACLU policies on students' rights serve to highlight the atomistic approach it takes to the subject of liberty. The Union's steadfast allegiance to individual rights, but not to individual responsibilities, is clearly evident. So, too, is its desire to eclipse the authority of school officials, and the sentiments of parents, with the authority of the state. It used to be thought that the schools were the one remaining bastion of local control in the nation. But by pushing the authority of the state, via the federal district courts, onto neighborhood schools, the ACLU has succeeded in making inroads against even this arena of local control.

Perhaps the most distressing aspect of all this is that the ACLU pledges a commitment to free speech without thinking through what free speech is predicated on in a modern society. It does not mean much in a post-industrial society for a person to have free speech if he or she is illiterate. Free speech can be used to empower the literate but does little for those who cannot read. By making the school environment a less disciplined place than it needs to be, the ACLU helps to erode the schools of fulfilling their number one obligation, namely, the education of all students. Sadly, then, it helps to attenuate the very First Amendment right it so loudly claims to support.

Notes

1. Bruce C. Hafen, "Developing Student Expression Through Institutional Authority: Public Schools As Mediating Institutions," *Ohio State Law Journal*, (Volume 48, Number 3, 1987): 699–702.
2. Edward B. Fiske, "U.S. Schools Put New Stress On Teaching of Moral Values," *New York Times*, September 15, 1986, pp. A1, B8.
3. Quoted by Ellen Graham, "'Values' Lessons Return to the Classroom," *Wall Street Journal*, September 26, 1988, p. 25.
4. Ira Glasser, "Taboo No More?" *Civil Liberties*, Fall/Winter 1989, p. 12.
5. This is the position taken by the Pennsylvania affiliate of the ACLU. See the state affiliate's newsletter, *Quarterly Comments*, Summer 1989, p. 2.
6. James Dao, "Critics Decry as Censorship the New York Schools' New Policy on AIDS Instruction," *New York Times*, May 29, 1992, p. A16.
7. Richard Vigilante, "Agreeing to Disagree," *City Journal*, Summer 1992, p. 82.
8. Mark O'Keefe, "Chesapeake May Be Sued On Sex-Ed," *Virginia Pilot*, April 6, 1990, p. A-1.
9. This program was eliminated after angry parents protested. See the *Pennsylvania Health Curriculum Guide*, published by the Pennsylvania Department of Education, 1984, p. 34, question #89, for the admonition that abstinence is not beneficial. For the statement that was quoted, see the booklet "I Deserve Love" that was distributed with this series.
10. Quoted in "Teen Chastity Programs Attacked as Breach of School-Religion Rules," *Pittsburgh Press*, February 18, 1991, p. A6.
11. Most of the material concerning the AFLA is taken from my article, "Anti-Catholic Liberties Union," *Crisis*, January 1988, pp. 34–37.
12. *Bowen v. Kendrick*, 487 U.S. 589 (1988).
13. Copies of the actual letter were widely distributed and are part of the records of the California Legislative Office of the ACLU. See the letter by Marjorie C. Swartz and Francisco Lobaco that was addressed to the members of the Assembly Education Committee in Sacramento, California, May 26, 1988.
14. Nat Hentoff, "The Enemy Within the ACLU," *Washington Post*, November 27, 1988, p. D7.
15. O'Connor's letter to the *Washington Post* was excerpted in a *New York Post* editorial, "The ACLU agenda (cont.)," December 7, 1988, p. 28.
16. The debate between Glasser and Prager took place in California on April 21, 1991. Glasser's comments can be heard on the tape, "The ACLU: Dialogue and Debate," available from Ultimate Issues, 6020 Washington Blvd., Culver City, CA 90232. Glasser misrepresented the ACLU's various positions on so many occasions that I was asked to provide a written rebuttal to his remarks. My remarks are distributed with the tape of the debate.
17. The *New York Post* editorial "The ACLU agenda (cont.)" appeared on December 7, 1988, p. 28. The letter by Ripston and Ehrlich was published December 20, 1988, p. 32.

18. For information on the success of *Sex Respect*, see the "Final Report, Office of the Adolescent Pregnancy Programs, #000816, Title XX, 1985–1990, Performance Report Summary," submitted by Project Respect. For information on the failure of the Planned Parenthood approach, see chapter 9 of my book, *The New Freedom: Individualism and Collectivism in the Social Lives of Americans* (New Brunswick, New Jersey: Transaction Press, 1985).

19. The ACLU of Wisconsin made its remarks in a media release, dated May 2, 1991.

20. Samuel Francis, "The Birds, the Bees and the ACLU," *Washington Times*, June 11, 1991, p. B1.

21. The ACLU of Wisconsin made its remarks in a media release, dated May 2, 1991.

22. "A Battle Over Teaching Sex Ed," *Newsweek*, June 17, 1991, p. 69.

23. Quoted by Samuel Walker, *In Defense of American Liberties: A History of the ACLU* (New York: Oxford University Press, 1990), 306.

24. Howard L. Hurwitz, *The Last Angry Principal* (New York: Halcyon House, 1988), 107.

25. Ibid., 51.

26. Ibid., 127.

27. Ibid., 122.

28. Ibid., 108. Hurwitz spells only the first letter of the obscene word, stating that the NYCLU Handbook spells the word in its entirety.

29. Janet R. Price, Alan H. Levine, and Eve Cary, eds., *The Rights of Students: The Basic ACLU Guide to a Student's Rights* (Carbondale and Edwardsville: Southern Illinois University Press), ix.

30. Ibid., 56.

31. Ibid., 55.

32. Ibid., 50.

33. "Asides," *Wall Street Journal*, April 27, 1989, p. A16.

34. See chapter seven, "Children's Rights," of my book, *The New Freedom*, especially pp. 85–86.

35. This is the characterization of Beatrice and Ronald Gross in their edited work, *The Children's Rights Movement* (Garden City, N.Y.: Anchor Press/Doubleday, 1977), p. 1

36. *Tinker v. Des Moines Independent Community School District*, 393 U.S. 503 (1968).

37. *Bethel School District No. 403 v. Fraser*, 478 U.S. 675 (1986).

38. *Kuhlmeier v. Hazelwood School District*, 484 U.S. 260 (1988).

39. Rosemary Herbert, "Vulgar Satirists Secure Freedom of Press, but Serious Students Lose Theirs," *Civil Liberties*, Winter 1988, p. 5.

40. *The Rights of Students*, 29, and the addendum to Chapter Two that was inserted in the 1988 handbook.

41. "ACLU Locks Horns with Principal Over Students' 'Obscene' T-shirts," *Washington Times*, October 6, 1988, p. B1.

42. "The ACLU Zoo," *Wall Street Journal*, September 24, 1990, p. A14.

43. "Great Moments in Free Speech," *Fortune*, March 9, 1992, p. 164.

44. Ira Glasser, *Visions of Liberty* (New York: Arcade Publishing, 1991), 264–65.

45. Quoted by Katherine Bishop, "As Violence Grows, Schools Order Pupils to Dress for Safety," *New York Times*, January 22, 1992, p. A13.

46. Kirkland's statement and the data cited in this paragraph were reported in "Deadly Lessons," *Newsweek*, March 9, 1992, pp. 22–30.

47. Felicia R. Lee, "Undercover Police Inquiry at 9 Schools Is Assailed," *New York Times*, February 15, 1990, p. B3.

48. Deanna Hodgin, "For Children, the Beep May Not Go On," *Insight*, July 29, 1991, pp. 24–26.
49. Policy #270, "Metal Detectors."
50. Quoted by Michel Marriott, "Detection Methods Raise Issue of Student Rights," *New York Times*, January 10, 1990, p. B9.
51. Policy #77, "Elementary School Students' Civil Liberties," passed April 10–11, 1987.
52. *The Rights of Students*, 89.
53. Ibid., 80.
54. Ibid., 47.
55. Ibid., 54.
56. Paul Glastris, ". . . One That Should Be the Best, But Isn't, *Washington Monthly*, March 1988, pp. 29–30.
57. The Detroit proposals are contained in a letter written by Grossman to the Detroit Board of Education, dated August 21, 1989.
58. Policy #78, "Selection of School and Library Materials and Pressure Group Attacks."
59. Polly Williams, "Inner City Kids: Why Choice Is Their Only Hope," *Imprimis*, March 1992, pp. 3–4.
60. Policy #80, "Separation of Church and State."
61. "As Our Public Schools Die, 'Parental Choice' Would Put Several Nails in the Coffin," *Civil Liberties*, Spring/Summer 1991, p. 11.
62. Jacqueline Berrien, "A Civil Liberties Must: High Quality Education for *All* Black Children," *Civil Liberties*, Fall 1991, p. 7.
63. Policy #77, "Elementary School Students' Civil Liberties."
64. Policy #76, "Secondary School Students' Civil Liberties."

3

The Churches

Church and State

Those who embrace a social idea of liberty understand the functional relationship that exists between religion and freedom. They understand that the churches, as mediating institutions, provide individuals with answers to ontological questions, place duties and obligations on them, and offer a sense of identity and roots. Those are three good reasons why religion should merit the attention of all those who profess a commitment to liberty. Moreover, it is in fluid societies like the United States that the need for social anchors is most needed, and that is why religion can justly be seen as a vital attribute in the constitution of liberty.

To those who entertain an atomistic conception of liberty, the role that religion plays in the development of a free society is not only unappreciated, it is seen as having little if anything to do with the cause of freedom. On the wings of this school of thought are those who are downright hostile to religion, maintaining that the relationship between freedom and religion is essentially inimical. The logical consequence of this belief is to emphasize freedom from religion rather than freedom of religion.

The atomistic approach is also dismissive of the mediating function of religion in a free society. In this view, freedom is best served by having the state award the individual with rights, rights that can be used against the authority of social institutions. The gradual encroachment of the state on society is not seen as a problem even if it means that by extending the reach of the state, public expressions of religion are minimized. The increased privatization of religion is seen as a good precisely because religion and freedom are seen as opposites.

The conflict between the social and atomistic conceptions of liberty, as it applies to religion, is generally not ventilated by way of sociological argument but via opposing interpretations of the Constitution. To those aligned with the social school of thought, a preference for basing constitutional decisions on the original intent of the Framers is favored. The atomistic perspective opts for judicial activism, with an emphasis on the need to update the Constitution according to modern needs and conditions. What this means today is that the increasing pluralism of American society argues for a strict separationist position regarding church and state. The ACLU, it can be safely said, is representative of this brand of thinking.

When the Constitution was written, crèches were permitted on public property and blasphemy was punishable by death. Now we've banned the crèches and provided public funding for blasphemy (the National Endowment of the Arts's funding of Andre Serrano's "Piss Christ" exhibit is a case in point). The inversion has much to do with a profound shift in the tastes of the cultural elite and with the tenor of contemporary legal arguments. According to Rev. Richard John Neuhaus, president of the Institute on Religion and Public Life, the single most important change to occur has been the reinterpretation of the establishment clause of the First Amendment; it is quite different from what was originally intended.

The First Amendment begins, "Congress shall pass no law respecting an establishment of religion, or prohibiting the free exercise thereof." Both of the clauses, Neuhaus contends, "are in service of religious freedom." It might even be said, he adds, that "there is really only one religion clause or provision, made up of two parts, each related to the other as the end is related to the means. The free exercise of religion is the end, and nonestablishment of religion is an important means instrumental to that end."[1] If this is the case, then there is no inherent conflict between free exercise and no-establishment, no need to "balance" one against the other.

Neuhaus' complaint is that the two parts of the religion clause have been inverted by constitutional scholars and, to a lesser extent, by the courts. He cites Harvard Law professor Laurence Tribe as an example. Tribe holds that there is a "zone which the free exercise clause carves out of the establishment clause for permissible accommodation of religious interests. This carved-out area might be characterized as the zone of permissible accommodation." Neuhaus calls Tribe's inversion both "astonishing" and a good illustration of the problem: "Professor Tribe allows—almost reluctantly, it seems—that within carefully prescribed limits, the *means* that is no-establishment might permissibly accommodate the *end* that is free exercise."[2]

The gravamen of Neuhaus's charge is this: freedom of religion has been jeopardized by inverting the religion clause to mean that the establishment provision should be given primacy. Why? Increasing statism has weakened the autonomy of religious institutions, as well as other mediating associations, thus creating the perverse condition that "wherever government goes, religion must retreat." In the minds of many people, Neuhaus instructs, "the religion clause is essentially a protection *against* religion rather than *for* religion."[3] It is a matter of some concern that there are those who would seize on this idea to deny many expressions of religious freedom, all in the name of servicing the First Amendment.

"The price of liberty is eternal vigilance." That is one of the ACLU's favorite mottoes. It is also one of the more revealing statements of the ACLU's attitude toward religion, as the original wording of John P. Curran's famous aphorism reads, "The condition upon which God has given liberty to man is eternal vigilance."[4] As the ACLU's record demonstrates, the excision of religion from the context of liberty is evident in more places than in its sloganeering about freedom.

To the ACLU, the First Amendment speaks more directly to freedom from religion than it does to freedom of religion. Its position is due largely to its reading of the original intent of the Framers and to its disposition toward a judicially active interpretation of the First Amendment. To get an idea just how far from mainstream thought the ACLU is in its reading of the original intent of the religion clause, consider Ira Glasser's contention that a voucher system in education would have been resisted by the Founders.

Glasser believes that to the "early Americans," a voucher system would have been seen as "a glaring departure from the principle of separation of church and state."[5] But it is not easy to understand why the "early Americans" would have so objected. It was they, after all, who approved of state churches, prayer in the schools, and federal funding of Congressional chaplains. Even Thomas Jefferson, who is often cited as the great proponent of separation of church and state, approved as

President a treaty that provided $300 in federal funds for the purpose of building a Catholic church for the Kaskaskia Indians.[6]

Part of Glasser's problem is his misreading of history. He cites three historical reasons why a strict separationist position was favored by the Founders. First, he says that Madison opposed a 1784 tax bill that would have subsidized religion "without preference."[7] But if what Glasser is referring to is Madison's "Memorial and Remonstrance Against Religious Assessments," written in 1785, it was nothing more than an argument against the government's granting tax support for only one religion.

Second, Glasser says that when the Senate was originally considering the First Amendment, it rejected three motions that would have put it on record as favoring the prohibition of laws that established "one religious sect or society in preference to others."[8] But Glasser does not say why. The historical record, however, offers sustenance to the point of view most clearly rejected by Glasser.

Madison's first draft of the establishment clause actually read as follows: "The Civil rights of none shall be abridged on account of religious belief or worship, nor shall any national religion be established." It was changed after Congressional deliberation because Congress, and especially the anti-Federalists among them, had a deep-seated aversion toward the use of the word "national" in the Constitution. After the so-called establishment clause was approved, Madison, who authored it, stated quite clearly that he believed it to mean "that Congress should not establish a religion, and enforce the legal observation of it by law, nor compel men to worship God in any manner contrary to their conscience."[9] That is why most students of the First Amendment, at least until the 1947 decision in *Everson v. Board of Education*,[10] have regarded the establishment clause to mean that (a) there could be no national church and (b) government could not show favoritism of one religion over another.

Glasser's last point is most erroneous. He contends that when the First Amendment was enacted "*no* state had an established church or supported one religion over another."[11] In fact, the Congregational Church in Massachusetts was not disestablished until 1833. In addition, it is worth noting that Fisher Ames of Massachusetts, and other New Englanders, favored the adoption of the First Amendment on the grounds that it would bar a national church, thereby assuring that the state church of Massachusetts would remain protected (it was almost certain that a national church would not be Congregational).[12]

In one sense, it matters little what Glasser sees as the original intent of the First Amendment, for the plain fact is that the ACLU has little regard for the original intent of any constitutional provision. Not even Glasser, for instance, would suggest that the Framers desired a complete separation of church and state, but according to one of its own board members, Samuel Walker, this is exactly the position the Union now favors: "In the Supreme Court, the ACLU gradually moved toward an 'absolutist' position on the First Amendment, eventually insisting... [on] a complete separation of church and state."[13]

Walker is correct to note that the ACLU was not always an advocate of complete separation of church and state. He is negligent, however, in not noting how an absolutist position works to undermine religious freedom. With regards to the ACLU, it is the organization's preference for freedom from religion, rather than freedom of religion, that has been the most obvious consequence of its strict separationist approach to the First Amendment. Lawrence Freedman, former legal counsel for the ACLU of northern Virginia, recalls that in the late 1960s and early 1970s, the Union was still hospitable to freedom of religion issues. But, he says, all that changed, as the ACLU grew increasingly hostile to religious expression of any kind. "They cannot represent a small segment that doesn't believe in religion," Freedman offers, "and say that they're protecting the exercise of religion."[14]

The ACLU's positions on church and state have become so unbending that even strict separationists, like former board member and professed atheist Nat Hentoff, have been taken aback by the Union's extremism. Hentoff would like to see "In God We Trust" taken off our coins, but nonetheless he concedes that "when I was elected to the national board of the American Civil Liberties Union some years ago, I thought I would be the most anti-clerical kid on that block." He soon found out how wrong he was. After three years on the board, he left with the knowledge that "there are members of that board—and of the far-flung affiliates of the ACLU—who see the separation of church and state as so absolute that not a single religious word must be allowed to pass a schoolhouse door."

Hentoff cites by way of example the Union's opposition to a Bethel High School performance of the play "Jesus Christ Superstar." When he called the director of the complaining affiliate (in the state of

Washington) inquiring whether the ACLU was prepared to file suit against a public school concert featuring Beethoven's "Missa Solemnis" or Duke Ellington's "Sacred Concert," he got no reply.[15] Had Hentoff asked whether the affiliate director would have objected to a public school offering of "Oh! Calcutta!," complete with total nudity and simulated sex, he no doubt would have been told that that was purely a matter of freedom of expression.

To be sure, there are still occasions when the ACLU rises to the defense of freedom of religion. In a 1989 policy statement, for example, the ACLU agreed that freedom of religion protected privileged communications with the clergy.[16] And in a case that had real repercussions, the Connecticut CLU in 1986 defended the right of William P. Nichols, a painting contractor, to hold prayer meetings in his home in Stratford, Connecticut. Stratford's anti-religious zoning ordinance required a permit for any religious purpose, even if the activity took place in the privacy of one's own home (Tupperware parties, the ACLU pointed out in court, required no such permit). The Union was successful in its bid to introduce the Constitution to Stratford and received a praiseworthy letter from Richard C. Halverson, Chaplain, U.S. Senate, for its role.[17]

Such examples, though frequently cited by the ACLU as demonstrative of its balanced approach to the subject, represent the exception, not the rule, to its basic position. More typical is its opposition to granting the churches a tax exemption, something almost all judges have been wont to do.

ACLU founder Roger Baldwin once told me that the ACLU's desire to strip the churches of their tax exempt status was "very foolish."[18] But in 1969, some nineteen years after Baldwin stepped down as executive director, the Union adopted its first policy opposing "tax exemption for church property which is used exclusively for religious purposes."[19] In the latest policy on this subject, it makes no difference to the Union whether church property is not used exclusively for religious purposes, all are denied: "The ACLU opposes tax benefits for religious bodies"; seven examples are listed for clarification, including the benefit of tax exemption.[20] It is fair to say that it is the application of this policy, more than its mere content, that has generated the most controversy.

The ACLU publishes many "Briefing Papers," in the form of a flyer, on many civil liberties topics, discussing some of the most often asked questions about its policies. In the Briefing Paper on "Church and State," it asks, "Should the Catholic Church lose its tax exempt status because its officials are involved in lobbying against abortion and birth control?" To which it responds, "No. The ACLU believes that clergy of any denomination who express their views on political and social issues are exercising their constitutional rights."[21] This answer is deceitful on two counts: (a) the ACLU opposes tax exemption for all churches, independent of whether the charge of political lobbying can be sustained and (b) as already discussed in the Foreward, the ACLU has assisted in an effort to strip the Catholic Church of its tax exemption.

In 1970, the year after the ACLU issued its first policy opposing the tax exempt status for churches, it accepted the advice of church and state extremist Leo Pfeffer and drafted a brief opposing tax exemptions in *Walz v. Tax Commission*.[22] In 1987, the American Civil Liberties Union Foundation and the New York Civil Liberties Union filed an amicus brief in support of Abortion Rights Mobilization *et al.* to secure standing in a suit challenging the tax exempt status of the Catholic Church. The Catholic Church was charged with violating its tax-exempt status by taking a stand against abortion. The brief contended that by granting the Catholic Church a tax exempt status, "it is no different than a direct federal subsidy limited to antiabortion candidates." The ACLU maintained that those engaged in the abortion rights coalition were stuck "fighting their political battle on an uneven playing field," the result of which was a dilution of their political clout.[23]

While the ACLU was taking aim at the Catholic Church's tax exempt status, the Union affiliate in Providence, Rhode Island, came out in favor of a tax exemption for Satanists. Following the logic of Barry Lynn of the Washington office,[24] the local affiliate got a tax administrator to rule that a coven of witches was entitled to the same tax-exempt treatment as accorded churches and synagogues. The high priestess of Rosegate Coven was delighted with the 1989 decision, exclaiming that "with this ruling, we witches will definitely be able to come out of the closet and take our place in society."[25] The ACLU's involvement in this case shows how accommodating it can be to the interests of Satanists. Many Christians, as we shall see, wonder why it is not as accommodating to their interests.

Religion and the Schools

There are millions of public school students who, at the end of the school day, are dismissed early so that they can partake of religious instruction in a sectarian school. There are also millions of students in sectarian schools who, during normal school hours—and on their own grounds—want to avail themselves of special state granted instructional support. The ACLU opposes both arrangements, known respectively as release time and shared time. Although the Supreme Court upheld the concept of release time in 1952, in the late 1980s the ACLU was still seeking to challenge its constitutionality, this time by objecting to a public school district's decision in Tecumseh, Nebraska, to cancel an after-school athletic program so that students could attend religious instruction at a local church.[26] The Union had better luck in getting the courts to strike down shared time programs, an accomplishment it celebrated in its amicus role.

In 1985, twin 5–4 decisions of the U.S. Supreme Court struck down shared time programs in Grand Rapids and New York City. From the mid-1960s to the mid-1980s, the federal government, through its Title I program, had allowed public school teachers to offer supplemental classes, most of which were remedial in nature, to underprepared parochial students on parochial school premises during regular school hours. The students who were served were mostly inner-city minority children, those who were in need of extra help in reading, math, English as a second language, and other subjects. In practice, what happened was that students in need of assistance would be excused from their regularly scheduled class so that they could avail themselves of the help they needed. The public school teachers would then take the students to a classroom, void of religious symbols, and provide the remedial instruction. That was it.

In the almost two decades of the program's existence, there was not one complaint filed in the entire nation, by any teacher, student, or parent, alleging any attempt at religious indoctrination. But that didn't matter in the end. In *Grand Rapids v. Ball*, the high court concluded that public school teachers "influenced by the pervasively sectarian nature of the religious schools in which they work, may subtly or overtly indoctrinate the students in particular religious tenets at public expense." It also held that the programs might convey public support for religion and in any event had the effect of "subsidizing the religious functions of the parochial schools by taking over a substantial portion of their responsibility for teaching secular subjects."[27]

What is striking about this conclusion is that it was based more on conjecture than experience. As Justice Rehnquist said in dissent, "Contrary to the law and the teachers' promises, they are assumed to be eager inculcators of religious dogma requiring, in the Court's words, 'ongoing supervision.'"[28] It was certainly contentious, to say the least, to assert that it was the religious function of the parochial schools that was being subsidized, when in fact students were given remedial lessons in academic subjects. Indeed, one of the classes that these students were typically excused from was religion, meaning that, if anything, the Title I programs worked against the religious function of the parochial schools.[29]

The related case, *Aguilar v. Felton*, shared many of the same attitudes toward the parochial schools. Unlike the Grand Rapids school district, the City of New York had adopted a system of monitoring the religious content of the Title I classes. But instead of appeasing the court, it was held that the supervisory aspect of the New York program actually furthered the breach of church and state lines, a judgment some dissenters said was "greatly exaggerated." Chief Justice Burger was particularly harsh in his criticism of the majority decision: "Under the guise of protecting Americans from the evils of an Established Church such as those of the Eighteenth Century and earlier times, today's decision will deny countless schoolchildren desperately needed remedial teaching services funded under Title I." He went on to say that many children who suffer from dyslexia "now will not receive the special training they need, simply because their parents desire that they attend religiously affiliated schools."[30]

Justice O'Connor, joined by Justice Rehnquist, declared the court's decision to be "tragic" for the nation's disadvantaged students. The ruling deprives these students "of a meaningful chance at success in life, and it does so on the untenable theory that public schoolteachers (most of whom are of different faiths than their students) are likely to start teaching religion merely because they have walked across the threshold of a parochial school." Not once, in the nearly two decades since the program had started, O'Connor added, was there an attempt to inculcate religion.[31]

It may not matter to some—it certainly does not matter to those who favor an atomistic conception of liberty—that as a consequence of these two decisions, many poor minority children have been deprived of the same kinds of government services that are afforded public school students. That is the price, the ACLU likes to say, of upholding constitutional law. But there is another price as well: some students from the parochial schools still participate in the remedial programs, but they do so in vans parked across the street from their school. The reigning logic has it that the public school teachers who still work in the program are now believed to be sufficiently distanced from the "pervasively sectarian nature" of the parochial schools.

More than twenty years before the Supreme Court banned shared time programs, it banned prayer in the schools, a case in which the ACLU was also active. In response to this, there was a movement to allow for a period of meditation, a silent moment at the start of the school day. It, too, was struck down with the help of the ACLU. When I asked Roger Baldwin what the ACLU had against meditation, he replied that "the implication is that you're meditating about the hereafter or God or something."[32] And that, apparently, is not something a free society can be expected to tolerate. But can it tolerate a prayer at a graduation ceremony? That became the new battleground of the late 1980s and early 1990s.

On December 3, 1987, the National Capital area affiliate and the Union's affiliate in Maryland sued the University of Maryland over the University's long-standing tradition of including a religious invocation and benediction as part of its graduation ceremonies. One student, Matthew J. Barry, said that he was "greatly upset and offended" by the prayer and contended that by allowing the invocation and benediction, the government was sending a message that his religious beliefs were "incorrect and unacceptable."[33] Unfortunately for Barry, U.S. District Court Judge Norman Ramsey refused to issue a preliminary injunction forbidding the traditional ceremony.[34] But that didn't mean the issue would go away. A few years later, the ACLU was successful in stopping two Philadelphia-area public schools from including prayers in their graduation ceremonies.[35] More such suits soon followed.

The response of ACLU affiliates to this issue, and the degree of success they have had, has varied considerably. For example, in the spring of 1990, the Utah affiliate sent a letter to all forty school districts threatening legal action if denominational prayers were offered at high school graduations, leaving the door open for nondenominational prayers.[36] At about the same time, the Southern California affiliate sued to stop a 50-year tradition in San Bernardino of opening and closing the district's high-school graduation ceremonies with non-sectarian prayers.[37] The case that won the most notoriety, however, was the challenge the ACLU brought to the graduation ceremonies at a public junior high school in Providence, Rhode Island.

In 1989, Rabbi Leslie Gutterman was invited to deliver the invocation and benediction at Nathan Bishop Middle School for the graduating eighth-graders. Rabbi Gutterman faithfully followed the strictures as outlined in "Guidelines for Civic Occasions," a pamphlet published by the National Conference of Christians and Jews, and delivered a decidedly nonsectarian prayer, void of any fire and brimstone. But that wasn't enough to satisfy Deborah Weisman and her parents, or the ACLU. The Union sued on their behalf, and in a highly controversial 5–4 decision the Supreme Court, in *Lee v. Weisman*, gave the ACLU what it wanted.[38] In 1993, however, the high court let stand a lower court ruling that upheld student-initiated prayers at graduation.

It happens that some of the most revealing statements about the ACLU's true beliefs are the cases it refuses to take. One such instance is the case of Angela Kaye Guidry, a straight-A student at Sam Houston High School in Moss Bluff, Louisiana. In 1987, Guidry was chosen co-valedictorian and was asked to prepare some remarks for the graduation exercises. When it was discovered that Guidry was planning to deliver a speech that had religious overtones, school authorities got worried and requested the student to drop all religious references from her speech. Officials said that someone might be offended by the Christian content of her remarks and that in any case it could not be allowed because it might be read as school endorsement of religion. Guidry replied that she could not in good conscience delete the "offensive" material (it was a brief tribute to Jesus), holding that if she were censored, she would not speak at all. She never did get a chance to give her speech.

Nat Hentoff, who broke the story, took the ACLU to task for absenting itself from the case. Guidry, as Hentoff pointed out, was a private person offering her own thoughts, not an agent of the state celebrating religion. The fact that the setting was a state-sponsored event did not mean that the First Amendment had become meaningless: Guidry was only speaking her mind. Represented by the Rutherford Institute, Guidry sued for damages for having her constitutional rights violated and for the mental and emotional distress she incurred. "It would be educational, all around, if the American Civil Liberties Union were to come in as an amicus in this case," wrote Hentoff, "since many religious people—and others— believe the ACLU is hostile to religion."[39] The suspicion still lingers: the ACLU never entered the case.

The Guidry case signifies just how murky the field of constitutional law has become with respect to the religious clause of the First Amendment. Principals are not sure what might or might not constitute a violation of church and state, so to play it safe, and to save the school district a lot of legal fees, they prefer censorship to the risk of freedom of expression or association. This has led to the absurd situation where a handicapped student was once told that she could not read her Bible on a school bus simply because the bus was state-funded.[40]

Those who have tried to distribute copies of the Bible on school grounds, as Gideons International has, have also found an unreceptive welcome, usually triggered by the ACLU. On occasion, however, some affiliates have taken a different stand, as when the Minnesota CLU filed an amicus in support of a student who was banned from distributing copies of a religious newspaper at Hopkins High School in Minneapolis.[41] More typical, however, has been the inaction of the ACLU. The ACLU has declined to intervene even in cases where teachers have been ordered to hide their Bibles at school; it has also chosen to remain on the sidelines when books like *The Bible in Pictures* and *The Story of Jesus* have been banned from school libraries.[42]

Should students be allowed to voluntarily meet after school hours for the purpose of forming a club dedicated to the advocacy of terrorism? The ACLU has no objection. What about genocide? The ACLU has no objection. What about religion? The ACLU's initial response was negative, but it later reversed its position.

The controversy began in 1984 after a proposed constitutional amendment allowing school prayer failed to garner the support of the Congress. In the wake of that defeat, a "Religious Speech Protection Act" was introduced, the purpose of which was to grant students the right to voluntarily engage in religious speech. Some liberals, like Massachusetts Congressman Barney Frank (he opposed the constitutional amendment), had no problems with the new bill. "I don't understand why anyone would want to tell high school students that they can't meet before school and pray," Frank said. He then chided some of his colleagues, saying, "Liberals can get in a reflexive position, where they just say no to anything." One of those liberals was Rev. Barry Lynn of the ACLU's Washington office. Lynn, a United Church of Christ minister, told the House Education and Labor Committee that the bill was "clearly unconstitutional," claiming that "it would be hard to tell the classroom from the Sunday school room."[43]

Lynn had further objections. He charged that the bill did not protect all nonreligious meetings and therefore had the effect of giving preferential status to religious meetings. In the end, the bill fell 11 votes short of the two-thirds majority necessary under the special procedure chosen for passage. But because a majority voted in favor of it, interest in the subject did not die; renewed efforts were made that were inclusive of many of the recommendations that critics of the original bill had made. After considerable negotiations, in which the ACLU was closely involved, an "Equal Access" bill was produced. The bill made it clear that if a school permitted even one noncurriculum-related student-initiated meeting to occur before or after school, it could not deny other student groups the right to hold meetings, regardless of how controversial or offensive the group might be to others. This was a way of supposedly appeasing everyone from fundamentalists to Marxists.

The "Equal Access" bill passed the Senate by a vote of 88-11, and won in the House by a margin of 337-77. The ACLU, which had every reason to endorse the bill, remained neutral. The Union feared that granting any permission for a religious club to meet was going too far, even if the bill contained a number of detailed restrictions. The bill clearly stated that the meetings had to be voluntary, student-initiated, and without school sponsorship. But the ACLU, which raised no objection to the right of extremist political groups from meeting on school premises, was still wary of granting equal access to religious groups.

Barry Lynn's preference for ACLU neutrality on the question of equal access proved not to be determinative. The national board of the ACLU overruled him, saying that monitoring possible abuses was not good enough: the Union had to come out squarely against the bill. It was this decision that led Nat Hentoff to charge that the ACLU "has become a relentless opponent of student religious groups trying to secure their First Amendment rights under the Equal Access Act."[44] It appears that Hentoff's criticisms had an impact: in 1993 the ACLU supported a

Supreme Court decision that allowed religious groups to use public school facilities after school hours.

A related issue is allowing school teachings and activities that are objected to on religious grounds. To be specific, if it is acceptable to deprive students of organized prayer in the schools, is it proper that they be required to study materials that conflict with their religious beliefs? In 1986, a federal district judge ruled that the school system of Hawkins County, Tennessee, had to accommodate parents' objections to textbooks. The teaching of certain ideas, such as supernaturalism and humanism, were seen as offensive by fundamentalist Christians, and the court ruled that the children did not have to attend reading classes in which these ideas were taught. But the Sixth Circuit Court of Appeals disagreed, sustaining ACLU arguments that exposing children to ideas that were inconsistent with their religious beliefs did not interfere with the children's right to choose.[45]

Is there a civil liberties issue involved when a college teaches ideas that run counter to accepted pedagogy? In the 1980s, the ACLU, in an unprecedented move, sought the denial of accreditation to a college merely because the religious views of its faculty and students ran counter to the accepted wisdom in science. Liberty Baptist College in Virginia teaches its students both the evolutionist and creationist perspectives in its biology classes, thus preparing students for teaching in the public schools without sacrificing intellectual nourishment in their faith. The Virginia affiliate of the ACLU challenged the accreditation of Liberty Baptist on the grounds that by teaching creationism, the college was preparing its students to teach a religious doctrine in the schools, thus violating what is today understood as "the establishment clause."

What made the issue so contentious was the presence of Rev. Jerry Falwell on the board of directors of Liberty Baptist. Falwell, founder of the now-defunct Moral Majority, had long been an adversary of the ACLU's and was an outspoken advocate of the creationist school of thought. But he held no executive position in the college, and in any event he was not in a position to determine what the school's graduates would teach in a public-school biology class. Chan Kedrick, the head of the Virginia CLU, was unpersuaded, holding that Falwell's association with the college, and the school's fundamentalist posture, raised serious questions about the preparedness of Liberty Baptist students to teach the state-approved curriculum in biology.

There are two interesting issues here. Is it consistent with civil liberties principles to penalize people because they might violate a law sometime in the future? That is what the ACLU would do: it would bar students from a career in teaching on the presumption that they might teach religious doctrine in the schools. Another issue is the propriety of the ACLU seeking to determine the accreditation status of a college. Is this the job of a civil liberties organization? With regard to the first question, Richard and Susan Vigilante comment that "the ACLU's position presumes without evidence that fundamentalists would violate state law and sneak creationism into the schools. It seeks, therefore, to punish fundamentalists not for any wrongdoing but for their privately held religious beliefs." As for the propriety of the issue, even Ira Glasser had his doubts about the wisdom of the case, stating that it was an unusual move for the Virginia affiliate to make.[46]

In another questionable call, the Kansas and Western Missouri affiliate sued the school district of Purdy, Missouri, for prohibiting dances on school property. The alleged constitutional issue? The ACLU believed that the ban reflected the thinking of the dominant religious group in the community and therefore unconstitutionally advanced a particular religion. The Union won in district court, lost in the Court of Appeals for the Eighth Circuit, and lost in its bid in 1990 to have the Supreme Court accept the case. The appeals court said that dancing was a "secular" activity and that its prohibition could be defended as appropriately neutral policy. "We simply do not believe elected government officials are required to check at the door whatever religious background they carry with them before they act on rules that are otherwise objectionable," the appellate panel said.[47] Had the ACLU won, many school rules, including prohibitions against swearing and fighting, would no doubt have come under court challenge on the grounds that such prohibitions reflect Judaic and Christian teachings.

Foster Care

The relationship between government and religion has not always been inimical, and indeed to the present day there are many examples of constructive church-state partnership, free of rancor and division. Unfortunately, ACLU activism has often resulted in an adversarial mode, particularly in instances of public policy. Perhaps nothing illustrates this better than the history of foster-care programs in New York City.

Since the nineteenth century, New York has had a program that allows for public funding of religious foster care agencies. In 1959, the state legislature passed a resolution, affirmed by voters two years later, that provided for child placement "when practicable, in an institution or agency governed by persons, or in the custody of a person, of the same religious persuasion as the child."[48] In doing so, the lawmakers and the voters were affirming the right of religious agencies to stand *in loco parentis*, holding that the "religion-matching" provision was in the best interests of the children and the agencies. Even the ACLU didn't object. But all that changed in 1973 when the re-radicalized ACLU (the change took place in the late 1960s) filed the first of several suits in federal district court challenging, on strict separationist grounds, the constitutionality of pertinent provisions of New York State's constitution, its Social Services Law and its Family Court Act.

The ACLU lost the first round when a three judge panel unanimously found that the constitutional and statutory provisions under question were indeed constitutional. The decision, which was never appealed, cited the need to balance the establishment clause with the free exercise clause and concluded that existing policy struck a workable compromise. But the ACLU didn't give up; it just changed strategies. It switched its argument from one of challenging the constitutionality of the "religion-matching" provision of the law to the contention that such a provision had a discriminatory effect: black Protestant children, the ACLU alleged, were screened away from receiving the superior treatment (another allegation) of Catholic and Jewish foster-care agencies. Ten years of discovery proceedings failed to settle the issue, though all parties tried several times to reach a mutually agreed-upon conclusion. Requests by the agencies for a speedy trial were denied.

In March 1984, a settlement was announced between the ACLU's Children's Rights Project and New York City. In the ACLU's lawsuit, *Wilder v. Bernstein*, it was charged that New York's child welfare system discriminated on the basis of race and religion, with the result that black Protestant children were placed in the lowest quality programs. The suit also challenged, on First Amendment grounds, the public funding of religiously affiliated child welfare agencies. The settlement was a split victory for the ACLU but a net loss for the agencies: funding of religiously affiliated foster care agencies was maintained, but their autonomy was severely restricted (for example, the role of religion in the child welfare system was gutted).

Under the terms of the settlement, New York's Special Services for Children was given control of all placement decisions, denying to the religious agencies any knowledge of the race or religion of the children placed in their program. The first-come, first-served basis of the new program not only prohibited "religion-matching," it denied the religiously affiliated agencies from imposing religious practices on children. In addition, the settlement guaranteed meaningful access to birth-control and abortion services, a provision that effectively targeted the doctrinal teachings of Catholicism. "The decision has broad national impact," offered Marcia Robinson Lowry, lead counsel in the *Wilder* case, and director of the Children's Rights Project, "because so many publicly funded social services are provided by religious agencies across the country."[49]

While it was clear that New York City and the ACLU had reached a settlement, it was anything but clear that the Catholic and Jewish agencies would accept the ruling. For example, in its lawsuit, the ACLU had charged that the Catholic and Jewish agencies discriminated in favor of their own religion and against black Protestant children. That Catholic agencies should prefer Catholics and that Jewish agencies should prefer Jews should come as no surprise: it was part of their mission to serve their own people. Even so, had the ACLU checked the statistics, at least for the Catholic agencies, it would have found its charge wanting. In 1986, after another "settlement" proved unsettling, the rolls of the Catholic foster-care agencies read as follows: Of the 5,137 children in the program, 43.2 percent were black; 31.6 percent were Hispanic; 16.4 percent were white; and 8.8 percent were classified as "other." As to religion, 45.9 percent were Catholic and 54.1 percent were classified as Protestant or other religions or having no known religion.[50] These figures are hardly supportive of the charge of discrimination, yet they proved to be insufficient evidence to convince the ACLU otherwise.

In the end, it didn't matter that no figures were brought to demonstrate the charge of discrimination, nor did it matter that no trial of the facts ever occurred, because New York City and the plaintiffs entered into a "Stipulation of Settlement," on terms that the city had previously found unacceptable. On April 28, 1987, the district court issued a judgment approving the stipulation over the objections of the Catholic and Jewish agencies, who then appealed the decision.

The stipulation contained many of the previous provisions of earlier settlements, plus some new ones. The stipulation said that the placement of children would occur on a first-come, first-served basis and that their race and religion would not be disclosed to the agencies. Thus, parental choice for religious placement was denied, as was the autonomy of the agencies. In addition to placing restrictions on teaching religious values, the agencies were prohibited from displaying "excessive religious symbols." As Msgr. Harry J. Byrne of New York's Epiphany Church put it, "Who is to count the crucifixes and Stars of David? Who is to decide what is excessive?" Incredibly, as Byrne points out, the court awarded that responsibility to the ACLU.[51]

Even more incredible was the fact that the city agreed to a stipulation that actually granted one exception: the terms apply to everyone but Orthodox Jews. According to the stipulation, an exemption to the agreement may be granted to those children whose religious beliefs "pervade and determine the entire mode of their lives" and "whose parents, for sincere religious reasons, believe it imperative that their children continue to practice the extensive religious customs and rituals that have been part of the child's life." The sole group designated for exemption were Orthodox Jewish children.[52]

Msgr. Byrne agrees that such religious beliefs and practices should be protected by the First Amendment. He just wants to know why those who are not Orthodox Jews are summarily excluded. "It seems singularly discriminatory to accord a privileged position to persons holding particular religious beliefs simply because of a set of external observances flowing from those beliefs, while at the same time denying such specially designated categories to persons who have equally deep and compelling religious beliefs that do not require certain dietary, culinary and other external practices. Are certain religious beliefs more worthy of governmental acceptance than others simply because certain external symbols are attached to them?" Msgr. Byrne wants to know why Catholic children, who customarily say the Sign of the Cross and a prayer before eating, are somehow considered insufficiently religious in their orientation to merit an exemption from the stipulation. And on what basis is the government supposed to make these decisions?[53]

There is also a provision that requires all agencies to afford "meaningful access to the full range of family-planning information, services or both." What this means in reality is that Catholic agencies must violate the professed moral teachings of the Catholic Church and provide their female clients with access to the services of an abortionist. This requirement appears in the same section of the stipulation that authorizes kosher dietary practices.[54] So much for equal treatment.

John Cardinal O'Connor, the Roman Catholic archbishop of New York, threatened to discontinue the foster care provided by Catholic agencies if the city refused to reconsider its actions. But Federal District Court Judge Robert J. Ward offered no relief, ruling that the Catholic agencies must begin providing contraceptive and abortion services. The decision was then appealed to the state court of appeals, by both Catholic and Jewish groups (the latter objected to the provision that would deny their agencies from giving preference to Jewish children). Again, the agencies lost. However, because full compliance with the consent decree was not forthcoming, the ACLU had to return to court in 1990 to press its case once again.[55]

The experiences that the ACLU had with the New York foster-care program motivated the national office to redo its policy in this area. In language that did not appear in its previous policy of 1974, the new 1988 policy begins, "Government funding of religious organizations *prima facie* violates the Establishment Clause." It then says that in exceptional circumstances, funding of services offered by religious organizations can take place, provided certain stipulations are followed. Among the stipulations is the requirement that the services be rendered "in a secular atmosphere"; six criteria of what constitutes a "secular atmosphere" are offered, just in case there is any doubt.[56]

The New York foster-care issue represents a fair characterization of the atomistic view of liberty. According to this perspective, freedom from religion is valued more highly than religious liberty, and that is why state encroachment on religious institutions is not interpreted as a threat. If anything, the atomistic view holds that the prospects of liberty are advanced by weakening the influence of religiously sponsored institutions. What else would explain the ACLU's willingness to litigate for nearly two decades on this issue? After all, the Union's charge of racial discrimination was developed after it had lost on a straight First Amendment case and was, in any event, never proven. It was the fear of public expressions of religion that drove the ACLU lawsuit in the first place, and it was the same fear that pushed it to pursue the matter to the end.

Day Care

The same mindset is evident in the ACLU's approach to day-care legislation. For some time now, feminists within the ranks of the ACLU have been successful in making federally funded day care a civil libertarian issue, so it was hardly surprising to see the Union take on the issue when it emerged during the 1988 election. The ACLU heartily endorsed day-care legislation, with one proviso: no monies should be awarded to religiously sponsored day-care centers. Democratic members in Congress thought they had resolved this matter when they agreed to change the wording of the proposed legislation in a way that negated the role of religion in religiously sponsored institutions. Unfortunately, the issue wouldn't rest.

Rep. Dale E. Kildee and Senator Christopher Dodd each sponsored versions of a day care bill, known as the Act for Better Child Care Services (the "ABC Bill"), that would accommodate working parents; the cost was an estimated $2.5 billion. The language of the bills made it clear that although religious institutions could participate in the program, there could be no religious instruction, worship, or other sectarian activities in the day-care program. But that still wasn't enough to placate the ACLU. When the House Education and Labor subcommittee headed by Congressman Kildee approved the ABC bill, Barry Lynn of the Washington Office of the ACLU "condemned" the vote, calling the proposal "a massive infusion of federal funds into sectarian day care which will *inevitably be used to indoctrinate impressionable young children*" (emphasis mine). When the committee rejected amendments by Rep. James Jeffords to bar religiously based hiring of child-care workers, Lynn characterized the rejection as "dangerous backsliding in the civil rights arena and a scandalous invitation to have tax dollars support job discrimination."[57]

It is interesting to note that the ACLU never calls young people "impressionable" when considering the social effects of pornography. But somehow when it comes to religion, another set of rules apply, and the ACLU gets worried. Notice, too, the Union's belief that it is inevitable that young people will be indoctrinated when exposed to a religiously sponsored day-care institution. Why is it not inevitable that they will be indoctrinated when exposed to obscene movies? The Union does not say. Equally troublesome is the ACLU's portrayal of religiously based hiring as a violation of civil rights. Is the cause of liberty advanced by denying Catholics, Protestants, and Jews the right to hire their own people in religiously sponsored centers?

As a result of ACLU efforts, the bill sponsored by Rep. Kildee, H.R.3660, made it illegal for religiously based hiring to take place; other restrictions were also incorporated. But again, the ACLU was not satisfied, and again it cited the effects of exposure to religious influences. "It is hard to imagine a child-care program in a religious setting," the Union exclaimed, "where there would not be either an intentional or inadvertent indoctrination of religious beliefs." It also played its Catch-22 card: Because the government would have to monitor the facilities for the absence of sectarian influences, it would be forced to violate church and state lines in the process.[58] These and other objections led to a new round of bills.

The "ABC Bill" took new life in the form of S.5 and H.R.30. But this time, the prohibition against religiously based hiring was lifted. As with the other bills, the legislation provided for grants and vouchers for the purpose of promoting "the availability and diversity of quality child-care services." Included in this arrangement were nonresidential "center-based" providers, group homes, and family providers who meet certain legal requirements. An estimated one-third of the providers were to be churches, synagogues, parochial schools, and other religious institutions.

Section 19(a) of the bill dealt with the familiar First Amendment objections: "No financial assistance provided under this Act shall be expended for any sectarian purpose or activity, including sectarian worship and instruction." Again, the ACLU was dissatisfied: "This general prohibition, however, simply does not solve the constitutional problem which arises from federal funds going for early childhood educational efforts in 'pervasively sectarian' institutions.'"[59]

It is noteworthy that in the New York foster-care program, the ACLU agreed to exempt Orthodox Jews (but no one else) from the stipulation agreement on the grounds that their religious beliefs "pervade and determine the entire mode of their lives." The clear message from the ACLU was that Catholics, Protestants, and most Jews do not share a "pervasively sectarian" experience. But when the federal day-care program surfaced, the ACLU sought to bar all religiously based institutions from participation on the grounds that all Christian and Jewish institutions are "pervasively sectarian." This kind of inconsistency raises serious questions about the ACLU's understanding of religion, its treatment of religious organizations, and its motives for doing so.

On March 29, 1990, an amendment prohibiting the use of federal funds for church-based child care and the hiring of religiously based personnel lost by a vote of 125–297. While the ACLU did not succeed, it certainly made its presence felt, and, more important, helped to shape the contours of future debates. By seeking to halt all federal funds to any religiously affiliated institution, the status of hospitals and social service agencies that are in any way connected with a religion is open to challenge.

Public Expressions of Religion

Perhaps no church-state issue rankles as many people each year as much as ACLU objections to crèches and menorahs on public property. As much as any issue, this one shows just how much First Amendment interpretations have changed. Throughout most of U.S. history, crèches and menorahs were placed on public property without court challenge and were never considered to be in violation of the Bill of Rights. But now not a December passes without the ACLU going into federal district court filing a lawsuit against a municipality for allegedly breaching church-state lines.

Congress has long declared Christmas to be a national holiday, so it was not unusual when the Christians in Pawtucket, Rhode Island, decided to honor the holiday by placing a crèche in a public square. Rhode Island, which was founded by Roger Williams in 1636 on the principle of religious freedom, has a long tradition of erecting Nativity scenes and has encountered little, if any, resistance for doing so. But in 1980 a woman phoned Steven Brown, director of the ACLU in Providence, saying she was offended by the placement of a crèche—one that had been routinely installed for forty years—on a parkland near the Seekonk River in Pawtucket. Her complaint wound up in the Supreme Court four years later.

The Reagan Administration supported the pro-crèche forces by arguing before the Supreme Court that any prohibition on the crèche would be tantamount to "cultural censorship." The ACLU countered by claiming that the crèche violated the establishment clause. The Union lost in a 5–4 decision. The ruling, formally known as *Lynch v. Donnelly*, but which has come to be known as "the reindeer decision," said that the crèche passed constitutional muster because it was surrounded by Santa and his reindeer, "a clown, an elephant, and a teddy bear." Though the pro-crèche side one, few were happy with this line of reasoning. But there were other statements made by the majority that did cut to the heart of the issue.

Chief Justice Warren Burger, writing for the majority, restated the high court's position in *Lemon v. Kurtzman* by saying that "total separation [of church and state] is not possible in the absolute sense." The Chief Justice further noted that the metaphor of a "wall" existing between church and state, though a useful figure of speech, "[was] not a wholly accurate description of the practical aspects of the relationship that in fact exists between church and state." But it was the majority's full embrace of a social conception of liberty that really defined its position: "No significant segment of our society and no institution within it can exist in a vacuum or in total or absolute isolation from all the other parts, much less from government. Nor does the Constitution require complete separation of church and state; it affirmatively mandates accommodation, not merely tolerance, of all religions, and forbids hostility toward any." ACLU fears that the crèche's religious symbols might beckon the day of an established church were labeled as "farfetched indeed."[60]

In the wake of the Pawtucket decision came more controversy, this time in New York. After two menorahs appeared on city property in December 1984, the Catholic League for Religious and Civil Rights petitioned the city to allow a Nativity scene at the Columbus Circle entrance to Central Park. It was permitted, with the proviso that a display sign designating sponsorship be affixed (the same conditions as the menorah display). Lawyers on both sides agreed that the fate of the menorahs and Nativity scene would turn on a Supreme Court ruling that was soon to be decided regarding the placement of a crèche on public property in Scarsdale, New York.

In 1981, the Scarsdale Village Board voted to withdraw permission to allow a private group to erect a Nativity scene in the local park, thus reversing a 25-year-old tradition. The sponsoring Crèche Committee sued and lost in district court. It appealed the case and won in the second circuit. In 1985, the Supreme Court, in a 4–4 decision, voted to sustain the appeals court ruling, holding that Scarsdale could not ban the privately owned crèche even though it was not surrounded by secular symbols.

Why? A tie vote leaves many unanswered questions, and while it affirms the lower court ruling, it does not serve as precedent. Some maintained that the existence of a disclaimer sign displayed next to the creche, indicating private ownership, was critical. Others saw it as sustaining freedom of expression.

To add to the confusion, in 1986 the Supreme Court denied review to a 2–1 ruling of a federal appeals court that a crèche could not be displayed on the front lawn of the city hall in Birmingham, Michigan. The court ruled that the display did not have the redeeming features found in the Pawtucket and Scarsdale situations: neither secular figures nor a disclaimer sign accompanied the Nativity scene.[61]

Pittsburgh was the site of the most controversial ruling on this subject. In 1989, the Supreme Court held that a Nativity scene inside the Allegheny County Courthouse was unconstitutional, but a menorah on display outside the City-County Building was acceptable; the menorah was surrounded by secular figures, but the crèche was not. The courthouse Nativity scene was placed on the grand staircase of the building and was adorned with a banner reading "Glory to God in the Highest." The 18-foot-high menorah, however, was placed on the steps of the building, next to a 45-foot-high Christmas tree and a sign saluting liberty. These were the kinds of distinctions the high court found meaningful.

The ACLU, which opposed both displays, found Justice Harry Blackmun's majority decision unpersuasive but was nonetheless "delighted" with a split victory. "The display of the menorah is not an endorsement of religious faith but simply a recognition of cultural diversity," wrote Blackmun, but "the crèche in this lawsuit uses words, as well as the picture of the Nativity scene, to make its religious meaning unmistakably clear." Interestingly, Justice Sandra Day O'Connor, while conceding the secular context of the menorah, nonetheless called it a "religious symbol," and not an icon of "cultural diversity," thus indicating that we have not heard the last word on this issue.[62]

Columnist George F. Will, adhering to a social conception of liberty, accused Justice Blackmun of wielding a "theological micrometer" and ridiculed the ACLU for rescuing Pittsburgh "from a seasonal menace that must be slain annually." Will then raised the larger issue: "This is the sort of howitzer-against-gnat nonsense that consumes a society that is convinced that every grievance should be cast as a conflict of individual rights and every such conflict should be adjudicated." But that is exactly how the ACLU perceives its mission. It firmly believes that it must intervene to save liberty by extending the reach of the law, interpreted civil libertarian style, into every crevice of society. When Will charges that the ACLU did not act to protect its members from injury but "to force the community into behaving the way the ACLU likes,"[63] he affirms the thesis being made here: it is not liberty that really drives the ACLU, it is power—the power to bring mediating institutions under the aegis of the state.

The whole issue of a crèche or menorah on public property got a new twist when the ACLU began to see degrees of difference between a religious symbol placed in a city park and one located on or near a city building. In 1989 the ACLU was successful in getting the Court of Appeals for the Second Circuit to accept its argument that it would be unconstitutional to allow the display of a menorah in a park in Burlington, Vermont. What was unusual about the ACLU's position was its reasoning. It found the display unconstitutional "mainly because of its position [the menorah's] with City Hall in the background."[64] The following year in Pittsburgh the local affiliate made the same qualification. Explaining why the ACLU is less tolerant of religious displays in city-owned buildings than in parks, attorney Robert Whitehill offered, "The City-County building is the seat of government. If I want to pay my taxes, I go there."[65] Parks, he held, were public forums. While the ACLU may find merit in such distinctions, it is less than certain that the courts—never mind the Founders—would. Moreover, the ACLU's ability to draw distinctions between city-owned buildings and public parks is demonstrative of its custom of seeing the world through the lens of power. In the end, however, the debate is all but academic: the ACLU sues no matter what public property a religious symbol is placed on.

Even when a city displays religious ornaments made by senior citizens, the ACLU gets enraged. In 1990, in the Capitol rotunda in Harrisburg, Pennsylvania, a Christmas tree was put on display, adorned with about 1,000 ornaments made by senior citizens. Three of the ornaments were made in the shape of a cross, and that was enough to send the ACLU into federal district court. It lost in its bid for a temporary restraining order, as the presiding judge found no basis for the Union's complaint. Now had the senior citizens decided to immerse their crosses in a jar of their own urine—much the way the celebrated artist Andres Serrano did—perhaps the ACLU would have defended their action as freedom of expression (they might even have qualified for a federal grant). Apparently the ACLU feels that the only religious symbols that should be allowed on public property are ones that have been sufficiently defaced and blasphemed.[66]

On occasion, ACLU activists rush to judgment in ways that prove embarrassing. This happened in 1991 when ACLU attorneys in Pittsburgh hurried to protest the display of a 40-foot-tall figure of Jesus Christ in the same City-County building involved in the earlier Supreme Court case. "The statue was so enormous, so unbelievably big, I concluded it wasn't possible the city would put it up," commented Union attorney Robert Whitehill. He was right. The statue of Christ was displayed as part of a Hollywood movie filmed in Pittsburgh, "Lorenzo's Oil." City officials agreed to put the matter to rest by erecting a sign informing citizens of this fact.[67]

It is because the ACLU has assumed the role as First Amendment police that it is drawn to answering false alarms. Its overall record suggests an organization far more concerned about erecting an impregnable wall between church and state than anything else, and that is why there are virtually no instances where the ACLU has responded to false alarms regarding freedom of religion. The following are indicative of its freedom-from-religion approach to the First Amendment. In addition to many of the issues already discussed, the ACLU has opposed as unconstitutional

- the right of Congress to maintain its chaplains
- the right of prisons to employ chaplains
- the right of the armed services to employ chaplains
- a city employees' Christmas pageant at the local zoo
- the right of private schools to have access to publicly funded counselors
- all blue law statutes
- the singing of "Silent Night" in the classroom
- the right of Christian anti-drug groups to cite their belief in Jesus before public school students
- public expenditures for bus transportation for parochial students
- all voucher plans and tuition tax credits
- the inscription "In God We Trust" on coins and postage
- the words "under God" in the pledge of allegiance

- the words "In God We Trust" on the city seal of Zion, Illinois
- a commemorative Christmas postmark, offered by the community of Nazareth, Texas, with an inscription depicting a Nativity scene
- government census questions on religious affiliations
- the building of a wooden platform by the city of Philadelphia for an address by Pope John Paul II
- formal diplomatic relations with the Vatican
- kosher inspectors on the payroll of Miami Beach
- a nine-foot underwater statue of Jesus Christ placed three miles off the coast of Key Largo
- a custom in Milwaukee County whereby delinquent tenants could not be evicted during the two weeks around Christmas
- a "Motorists Prayer" printed on the back of a state highway map in North Carolina
- the word "Christianity" in the town seal of Milledgeville, Georgia
- a plaque with the Ten Commandments in the courthouse in Cobb County, Georgia
- the right of a state district judge in North Carolina to open his court session each morning with a prayer
- the right of public school coaches to lead their teams in a prayer before a game
- the right of the *Christian Science Monitor* to fire a lesbian
- the right of the sheriff in Pierce County, Washington, to hire volunteer chaplains to provide crisis intervention services
- legislation that would criminalize damage to religious buildings and artifacts
- the right of two campus singing groups from Washington State University to perform in area churches
- the right of a nun to wear a habit while teaching in a public school
- the right of a school board to prohibit an Islamic public school teacher from wearing her turban while teaching
- the right of the armed services to prohibit the wearing of a yarmulke while in uniform
- the right of Catholic schools not to hire homosexuals
- the right of the Salvation Army not to hire homosexuals

- the right of a judge to order a person found guilty of drunk driving to attend meetings of Alcoholics Anonymous[68]

In short, there is hardly a public expression of religion that the ACLU has not sought to censor, and in the few cases where it has risen to the defense of religious liberty (for example, the Jewish soldier and the Islamic teacher), it has shown itself to be considerably inconsistent (for example, the nun schoolteacher). Just as exasperating is the ACLU's willingness to overlook clear violations of the First Amendment. During the presidential campaign of 1988, Rev. Jesse Jackson held fund-raisers in the black churches of Chicago, but the ACLU did nothing about it.[69] Perhaps nothing demonstrates the ACLU's inconsistencies better than its selective concern for the religious traditions of the American Indian.

Discovering Religious Freedom

When it comes to the American Indian, and to a lesser extent the Amish,[70] the ACLU exercises a sensitivity and appreciation for religious practices that is extraordinary. For example, official ACLU policy states that it supports the rights of Indian peoples to "retention of their cultural and religious heritage." It goes further by saying that "the ACLU is committed to the survival of American Indians as a native people," explaining further that it recognizes as paramount the hunting, fishing, and water rights of Indians. It even maintains that the government cannot interfere with those rights "on the ground of conservation or resource management" unless certain exacting criteria are met.[71]

Now no such sensitivity for the customs and traditions of Christians and Jews has ever been forthcoming from the ACLU. Indeed, the ACLU continually makes exceptions for American Indians that it refuses to make for others. Take the case of Little Bird of the Snow.

In 1985, the ACLU came to the rescue of a two-year-old Abenaki Indian girl who was denied public assistance because her father refused to use a social security number for her. The father contended that such an impersonal practice might endanger his daughter spiritually, so for reasons of religious conviction, he could not cooperate with federal and state law. What was most unusual about the case was the way the ACLU approached the subject of religion. The ACLU said the case "pits the purity of a religion that was close to the land and nature long before the European settlers arrived against the awesome power of the bureaucracy those settlers spawned." The girl, Little Bird of the Snow, was held by the ACLU to belong to a "religion of natural order" and was thus deserving of preferential treatment.[72]

It is beyond dispute that the ACLU would never show such empathy for those who belong to mainline religions. Is it because "more modern types" are considered to be less deserving than "people like them"? Such chauvinism, or anti-modernist bias, may explain the sentimentalism of the ACLU, but it has little if anything to do with providing a legitimate legal basis upon which First Amendment cases can be decided.

Does the government have the right to build a road on land that it owns? What if the land is regarded as sacred by the adherents of some religion? For the ACLU, it would make a difference if it were American Indians that were involved. But it didn't matter to the government, and that is why the ACLU complained when in *Lyng v. Northwest Indian Cemetery Protective Association*, it was ruled that the religious protestations of American Indians were not sufficient to stop the government from building the road. The Indians had used the land for centuries for religious ceremonies, and that is why the ACLU took their side.[73] Once again, it is not the Union's well-meaning position that is in question, it is its selective application of the free exercise clause that is troublesome.

If there ever was a contentious case affecting the religious liberties of American Indians—and in principle, the religious liberties of everyone else as well—it was the 1990 Supreme Court decision in *Employment Division v. Smith*. At issue was whether Oregon could bar the religious use of peyote as part of its general drug prohibition, without inquiring into the effects of the prohibition on the religious rituals of American Indians. The Supreme Court upheld the right of the states to do so because the prohibition was neutral; that is, it was not specifically directed at the religious practices of the American Indian.[74] What made this case so controversial was that it broke with previous interpretations of the First Amendment: in the past, restrictions on the free exercise of religion had to be justified by a compelling state interest.

Balancing religious liberty with legitimate public welfare interests has long been a challenge to the Supreme Court. In 1879, the high court ruled that polygamy statutes were constitutional, even though practicing Mormons (at that time polygamy was accepted by the Mormon Church) said the law violated their free exercise of religion. In 1972, the court granted the Amish an exception to a law requiring children to stay in school until age 16, on the grounds that to do otherwise would violate the Amish's religious objections to school attendance after the eighth grade. So why not let the American Indians use peyote in their religious rituals? Is there a compelling governmental interest in prohibiting the practice? That was the question the Supreme Court in the pre-*Smith* era would have answered. But now the court was saying that all that mattered was that the law was "generally applicable" and did not target a particular religion.

Serious questions about *Smith* were quickly raised, with the strangest of political bedfellows lining up on both sides. Some said religious liberty was the winner in *Smith*, while others said it was a big loser. Did *Smith* mean that those religions that reserve to men the right to be clergy now run afoul of sex discrimination laws? Could homosexuals claim discrimination if not ordained, citing prohibitions against sexual orientation? Could Catholic hospitals refuse to perform abortions? The jury was out, but the political battle was anything but absent.

In response to *Smith*, Democratic Representative Stephen Solarz of New York introduced the Religious Freedom Restoration Act (RFRA). The bill seeks to restore the compelling interest test as the basis of adjudication, holding that a person's free exercise of religion could not be overriden by the state unless there was a compelling governmental interest for doing so. The ACLU signed on to Solarz's bill, as did the National Council of Churches, the Christian Legal Society, National Association of Evangelicals, National Conference of Catholic Bishops, Concerned Women for America, National Sikh Center, Church of Scientology, Presbyterian Church (U.S.A.), American Jewish Congress, and Agudath Israel.

In opposition to RFRA stood the National Right to Life Committee, Americans United for Life, and the Lutheran Church-Missouri Synod, all of whom expressed fears that abortion rights could be sustained on the basis of freedom of religion if RFRA became law. What made this especially troublesome, the opponents said, was that after years of working to overturn *Roe v. Wade*, the pro-life community risked having their anticipated victory in the courts negated by a piece of new congressional legislation. The split among legal scholars was also evident, especially among those in the conservative camp.[75]

Whether *Smith* or RFRA is a worse omen for religious liberty is debatable, but what is not in doubt is the perception that any bill endorsed by the ACLU on matters of church and state is immediately rendered suspect. It is a backhanded tribute to the ACLU's strict separationist positions, and to its strong preference for abortion on demand, that some religious groups cannot bring themselves to be on the Union's side. Hidden agendas are expected in many places, and the ACLU is surely no exception.

Religion and Freedom

In 1952, Justice William O. Douglas wrote that "we find no constitutional requirement which makes it necessary for government to be hostile to religion and to throw its weight against efforts to widen the effective scope of religious influence." A fairly unexceptional line, even for today. But not for the ACLU. ACLU historian Samuel Walker recalls Douglas's statement as "a passage that years later came back to haunt him and other separationists."[76] Walker does not explain why the comment should haunt anyone. Is he implying that the government ought to be hostile to religion? Or does he mean that the state should attempt to thwart the influence of religion on society? Both courses of action, it hardly needs to be said, would violate the free exercise provision of the First Amendment.

Skepticism about the ACLU's real interest in religious liberty has also been entertained by William Scopes, son of John Scopes of the famous "monkey trial." According to Dr. Lawrence Cranberg, former ACLU activist and now searing critic of the Union, William Scopes objects to the way his father's memory is being treated by the ACLU. While John Scopes is remembered for his 1925 role in challenging the Tennessee law that banned the teaching of evolution (he was represented by the ACLU), it is not well known that Scopes later married a Catholic and converted to Catholicism himself; both his sons are Catholic as well. William Scopes told Cranberg that his father would be quite unhappy with the way the ACLU has exploited his name for radical causes.[77]

If the ACLU's only interest were to see that the government remain neutral in the affairs of church and state, it could take positions other than the ones it does without sacrificing principle. It could, for instance, insist that all socially recognized and bona fide religions should have an equal opportunity to display their religious symbols on public property. That would be the tolerant approach to neutrality. But, no, the ACLU settles the issue by recommending that all religious symbols be equally banned from the public square.

Some of these controversies could be defused if a voucher program for the schools were adopted. But the ACLU is resolutely opposed to allowing the taxpayers to send their children to schools of their choice. Indeed, it has sided with the extremists on this issue. In 1990 in Oregon, for example, the ACLU joined a coalition to defeat a voucher initiative, citing the threat of public funding for "cult" schools and the prospect of Christians receiving vouchers for home-schooling. "The Oregon ACLU did not let out a peep of protest against such tactics," observed attorney David Bernstein, "despite the ACLU's once-proud history of defending religious minorities from legislative campaigns based on intolerance."[78]

A social conception of liberty is contextual in nature and does not conceive of freedom as a force to be reckoned with. It sees religion the way deTocqueville saw it: "Freedom sees religion as the companion of its struggles and triumphs, the cradle of its infancy, and the divine source of its rights."[79] To be sure, religious extremism is no friend of liberty. But the same is true of any value, including individual rights: pushing an otherwise worthy value to extremes corrupts its essence.

Now it is not likely that the ACLU would ever be associated with deTocqueville's vision of liberty. No, the ACLU sees religion as something to be guarded against, at least in terms of its public manifestations. That is why it takes a position that effectively marginalizes the public role of religion in society.

It is partly because, as Nat Hentoff puts it, the ACLU ascribes "extraordinary powers to religious speech"[80] that it is so nervous about religion. But it is also due to the atomistic vision of the ACLU. It sees freedom as emanating from the state, in the form of individual rights, finding it difficult to conceive of an alternative conception of liberty. Religion, to the ACLU, is seen quite rightly as an obstacle to the reach of government. And by casting government as the basis of freedom, religion must surely be seen as a problem. Unless there is a change in the way liberty is interpreted, it is not likely that the ACLU will change its animus against all public expressions of religion. The record, thus far, suggests little likelihood of a change, thus ensuring future battles over the religious clause of the First Amendment.

Notes

1. Richard John Neuhaus, "The Upside-down Freedom," *Christianity Today*, December 9, 1988, p. 24.

2. Richard John Neuhaus, "A New Order of Religious Freedom," *First Things*, February 1992, pp. 15–16.
3. Neuhaus, "The Upside-down Freedom," p. 24.
4. Curran's statement on liberty appears in *Bartlett's Familiar Quotations* (Boston: Little, Brown and Company, 1949), 277. I am indebted to Dr. Lawrence Cranberg for bringing this to my attention.
5. Ira Glasser, *Visions of Liberty* (New York: Arcade Publishing, 1991), 98.
6. For a good treatment of how the Founders viewed religion, see Robert Cord, *Separation of Church and State: Historical Fact and Current Fiction* (New York: Lambeth Press, 1982).
7. Ira Glasser, *Visions of Liberty*, p. 75.
8. Ibid.
9. See the analysis of Hon. Kenneth W. Starr, "The Religion Clauses of the Constitution," *The Heritage Lectures*, #142, November 16, 1987.
10. It was the *Everson* decision that laid the groundwork for a more expansive interpretation of the establishment clause. *Everson* affirmed the right of parochial students to receive free bus transportation to school, but in the majority opinion, written by Justice Hugo Black, it stated that this aid was permissible because the aid went directly to the students and parents, not to the schools; it was also conceded that there was a public interest in the safety of transporting all students. The critical point came when Black said that the establishment clause meant that government could not "pass laws that aid one religion, *aid all religions*, or prefer one religion to another" (italics added). Beginning in the 1960s, the courts began to apply this newly-arrived at interpretation of the establishment clause. See *Everson v. Board of Education*, 330 U.S. 1 (1947).
11. Glasser, *Visions of Liberty*, 75.
12. Ames's concerns are explained by Russell Kirk, "The First Clause of the First Amendment: Politics and Religion," *The Heritage Lectures*, #146, December 9, 1987.
13. Samuel Walker, *In Defense of American Liberties: A History of the ACLU* (New York: Oxford University Press, 1990), 218.
14. Freedman's comment was taken from the transcript of an interview he had with Jerry Newcombe of Coral Ridge Ministries in 1990. Freedman appeared on the Dr. D. James Kennedy documentary, "Taking Liberties: The Case Against the ACLU," which first aired in April 1991 on the Christian Broadcast Network.
15. Nat Hentoff, "Even in High School," *Progressive*, August 1989, p. 13.
16. Policy #89a, "Privileged Communications with the Clergy," passed January 21–22, 1989.
17. The Summer/Fall 1986 edition of *Civil Liberties* reprinted a *Washington Post* column by Nat Hentoff, "Praying by Permit" that discussed the Stratford case. Also on p. 9 of that edition can be found a reprint of Chaplain Halverson's letter to the ACLU of Connecticut.
18. Interview with Baldwin in his home in New York City, June 2, 1978.
19. Policy #82, "Religious Bodies' Tax Exemption," passed October 4–5, 1969, and recorded in the 1976 Policy Guide.
20. Policy #92, "Religious Bodies' Tax Exemption," passed October 15–16, 1983, and listed in the 1986 Policy Guide.
21. ACLU Briefing Paper, No. 3, "Church and State." No date is listed, but it was still being circulated in the 1990s.
22. *Walz v. Tax Commission*, 397 U.S. 664 (1969).

23. The ACLU amicus brief was filed in *United States Catholic Conference and National Conference of Catholic Bishops v. Abortion Rights Mobilization, et al*, 487 U.S. 72 (1988).
24. Barry Lynn, "Memo on Witchcraft Amendment to the Appropriations Bill," ACLU Washington Office, October 10, 1985. It was cited in George Grant, *Trial and Error: The American Civil Liberties Union and Its Impact on Your Family* (Brentwood, Tennessee: Wolgemuth and Hyatt, 1989), 45.
25. Quoted in "Asides," *Wall Street Journal*, August 9, 1989, p. A10.
26. "Affiliate Notes," *Civil Liberties*, Winter 1989, p. 10.
27. *Grand Rapids School District v. Ball*, 473 U.S. 373 (1985).
28. Ibid.
29. That was clearly my experience. In the 1970s, I taught at St. Lucy's, a Catholic elementary school in Spanish Harlem.
30. *Aguilar v. Felton*, 473 U. S. 402 (1985).
31. Ibid.
32. Interview with Baldwin, June 2, 1978.
33. Quoted in "ACLU Challenges Graduation Prayer," *Capital Liberties*, newsletter of the National Capital Area CLU, Fall/Winter 1987, p. 7.
34. "ACLU Seeks Ban on U. of Md. Prayers," *Capital Liberties*, Winter 1988, p. 3.
35. "ACLU Halts Illegal Religious Ceremonies in PA Public Schools," *Civil Liberties Record*, newsletter of the Pennsylvania ACLU, Summer 1990, p. 1.
36. "Graduation Prayers Ignite Church/State Debate," *Sunstone*, October 1990, p. 59.
37. "Affiliate Notes," *Civil Liberties*, Winter 1990-1991, p. 14.
38. *Lee v. Weisman*, 112 S.Ct. 2649 (1992).
39. Nat Hentoff, "The Censored Valedictorian," *Washington Post*, July 2, 1988, p. A23.
40. See the Dr. D. James Kennedy documentary, "Taking Liberties: The Case Against the ACLU," which first aired in April 1991 on Christian Broadcast Network and is available through Coral Ridge Ministries.
41. Nat Hentoff, "Religion in School Still Has a Prayer," *Pittsburgh Press*, August 29, 1984, p. B3.
42. There are many instances when occurrences like these have been cited. The *Civil Liberties Record* of Pennsylvania has recorded some examples of ACLU activism undertaken to stop Bible distribution; see the Summer editions of 1990 and 1991. For the information on the teacher who was ordered to hide his Bible, and the banning of religious books in the libraries, see Phyllis Schlafly, "In the Spirit of Salem Witch Hunts, ACLU Is Busy Banning the Bible," *New York City Tribune*, December 22, 1988, p. 8.
43. Steven V. Roberts, "House Studies Bill on Student-Run School Prayer," *New York Times*, April 1, 1984, p. 17.
44. Nat Hentoff, "Even in High School," *Progressive*, August 1989, p. 14.
45. "Victory, Victory Is Our Cry!" *Capital Liberties*, the newsletter of the National Capital Area, Fall/Winter 1987, p. 3.
46. Richard and Susan Vigilante, "Taking Liberties: The ACLU Strays from its Mission," *Policy Review*, Fall 1984, pp. 30-31. See also Michael L. Bentley, "Report: Creationism through the Back Door—The Case of Liberty Baptist College," *Science, Technology and Human Values*, Fall 1984, pp. 49-53.
47. *Clayton v. Place*, 889 F.2d 192 (1989).
48. Quoted by Msgr. Harry J. Byrne, "Church, State and Foster-Care Children," *America*, July 25, 1987, p. 39.

49. See "New York Agrees to Unbiased Foster Care Placements," *Civil Liberties*, Spring 1984, p. 8. Lowry's quote is listed in "New York's Foster Care Case Settled," *Civil Liberties*, Summer/Fall 1986, p. 11.

50. These were the official figures as of July 1, 1986, for the Roman Catholic Archdiocese of New York's foster care agencies.

51. Byrne, "Church, State and Foster-Care Children," p. 40.

52. Ibid.

53. Ibid.

54. Ibid.

55. See Joyce Purnick, "Koch Sees Diocese Foster-Care Curb," *New York Times*, February 3, 1987, p. B3; Ari Goldman, "Foster Agencies Lose a Decision Over Abortions," *New York Times*, May 8, 1987, p. B3; Josh Barbanel, "New York Foster-Care Rules Upheld," *New York Times*, June 9, 1988, p. B3; Suzanne Daley, "Foster Placement by Skin Shade Is Charged," *New York Times*, January 18, 1990, p. B5; Jeff Gracer, "Saving the Children," *Civil Liberties*, Spring 1990, p. 10.

56. Policy #98, "Government Funding of Social Service Programs of Religious Bodies," passed January 23–24, 1988.

57. Barry Lynn, "ACLU Condemns Religious Indoctrination in Child Care Bill," *ACLU News*, 1988.

58. "Child Care Funding Will 'Advance,' Subsidize Religious Groups," *Civil Liberties Alert*, May 1988, p. 3.

59. "Church-State Problems Taint Child Care Bills," *Civil Liberties Alert*, April 1989, pp. 1–2.

60. *Lynch v. Donnelly*, 465 U.S. 668 (1984)

61. For a brief review of these cases, see Robert F. Drinan, "Is a Christmas Creche Legal in 1986?" *America*, December 13, 1986, pp. 375–76.

62. *County of Allegheny v. American Civil Liberties Union*, 488 U.S. _____ (1989). ACLU comments can be found in Jack Torry, "Nativity Scene Blocked, Menorah Approved," *Pittsburgh Post-Gazette*, July 4, 1989, pp. 1, 5. See also the Union's 1988 annual report, p. 4.

63. George F. Will, "Nonsense About Church and State," *Washington Post*, July 9, 1989, p. B7.

64. That was the reasoning of Mark A. Kaplan, a lawyer on the board of the Vermont CLU. See "Menorah Display Is Ruled Unconstitutional," *New York Times*, December 13, 1989, p. 18.

65. Quoted by Jeffrey Fraser, "Tree, Menorah Are in at Point, Out at City Hall," *Pittsburgh Press*, December 12, 1990, p. B4.

66. See my article, "How the ACLU Stole Christmas," *Pittsburgh Post-Gazette*, December 19, 1990, p. 11.

67. Tom Barnes, "Church, State Mix But Only for Movie," *Pittsburgh Post-Gazette*, October 18, 1991, p. 1.

68. The examples cited are culled from the ACLU's policy guide and newsletters as well as from many news stories. See also my article, "Anti-Catholic Liberties Union," *Crisis*, January 1988, pp. 34–37.

69. In a radio debate I had with Diane Geraghty, executive director of the Illinois CLU, she claimed not even to know about Jackson's tactic. The debate took place on WEPO Peoria, Illinois, April 29, 1988.

70. See Policy #86, "State Educational Standards," for a description of the ACLU's readiness to endorse special considerations for the Amish.

71. Policy #313, "American Indians."

72. "Toddler's Religious Freedom Upheld," *Civil Liberties Record*, of Pennsylvania, March 1985, p. 6.

73. *Lyng v. Northwest Indian Cemetery Protective Association*, 485 U.S. 439 (1988).

74. *Employment Division v. Smith*, 110 S.Ct. 1595 (1990).

75. See especially "For the Religious Freedom Restoration Act," *First Things*, March 1992, pp. 42–44; and "How to Restore Religious Freedom: A Debate," *First Things*, April 1992, pp. 37–51. Several authors take varying positions on this controversial issue.

76. Walker, *In Defense of American Liberties*, 221.

77. Private correspondence with Dr. Lawrence Cranberg. See also Cranberg's piece, "The ACLU and Its Continuous Struggle Against Religious Freedom," *New York City Tribune* January 29, 1990, p. 12.

78. David Bernstein, "Religion in School: A Role for Vouchers," *Current*, May 1992, p. 15. This was a reprint of an article that appeared in the February 1992 edition of *Reason*.

79. Alexis de Tocqueville, *Democracy in America*, J.P. Mayer, ed. (Garden City, New York: Anchor Books, 1969), 47.

80. As quoted by the Vigilantes in "Taking Liberties," p. 29.

4

The Private Sector

The ACLU Preference for Statism

"The basic insight of the American Founders was sound: freedom requires many law-free spaces, where social life is left to the regulation of norms other than those of state-guaranteed law."[1] It is the need to maintain "law-free spaces," as Mary Ann Glendon puts it, that is currently under attack, most especially by those who share an atomistic vision of liberty. The ACLU, to take the leading exponent of this perspective, wants to extend the power of government into areas traditionally seen as "law-free," usually to support some egalitarian or collectivist program. The record will show that the ACLU does not hesitate to call on the federal government to subordinate the authority of private associations whenever the prospective outcome promises more in the way of equality.

Though the ACLU likes to see itself as the living embodiment of the Founders' dream, in reality the civil libertarians have less in common with Madison than they do with Rousseau. The Founders wanted a democratic system that allowed for considerable diversity and autonomy, and that is why they deliberately did not seek to blanket the states with federal mandates. They also treasured the right of private institutions to exercise considerable authority, taking, in effect, a social perspective on the meaning of liberty.

Unlike the ACLU, the Founders were not radical egalitarians, constantly blurring the boundaries of state and society. "Egalitarians," writes Berkeley professor Aaron Wildavsky, "reject authority as illegitimate—immoral, wrong, and improper—unless it increases equality."[2] That not only explains the ACLU's thinking, it also explains why the ACLU invariably works to inflate the powers of the state: If the contemporary

ACLU perspective on liberty is to be realized, the power of the state to level the playing field among competing and clearly unequal private associations has to be enhanced. The Founders, it can be safely said, had no such aspirations and no such grandiose designs for the state.

The case of Grove City College is a good illustration of how the ACLU interprets liberty these days. Grove City, a small Presbyterian-affiliated college north of Pittsburgh, is proud of its reputation as one of the last truly private colleges left in the United States; its policy of accepting no federal monies fits its mission as a college dedicated to the merits of free enterprise. Given the nature of the school, it came as no surprise that when the federal government requested the College to sign a form pledging its allegiance to a policy of nondiscrimination, school officials felt no need to oblige the meddling bureaucrats. After all, no one had ever maintained that Grove City discriminated against anyone. But the government pressed forward nonetheless, demanding compliance with its strictures. Grove City pressed back, refusing to cooperate. The fight ended in the Supreme Court, but that didn't end the case.

The matter went before the courts because of the finding that some Grove City students received federal monies in the form of student loans, and that, it was argued, was sufficient to bring the entire college under federal statutes barring discrimination on the basis of sex. But the 1984 decision in *Grove City College v. Bell*, while presumedly favoring the college, was proclaimed unsatisfactory by nearly everyone. The Supreme Court ruled that since the student financial aid office was the only part of Grove City College receiving direct federal funds, that office alone was subject to the antidiscrimination provisions of Title IX of the Education Amendments of 1972. The rest of the college, the court determined, was not covered by these provisions.[3] The ACLU, along with a host of other egalitarian organizations, moved to counter the high court's ruling by pushing for a new, more complete, federal statute.

After years of sustained effort, the ACLU got what it wanted: in March 1988, the Congress mustered the two-thirds vote it needed to defeat a presidential veto of the Civil Rights Restoration Act. It was concluded that the receipt of federal money by any part of an institution of higher learning mandated that observance of federal antidiscrimination laws applied throughout.

The ACLU was undisturbed by charges of callous indifference to the discretionary authority of a private, religiously-affiliated college. Indeed,

Samuel Walker of the ACLU interpreted the Union's effort at passage of the Civil Rights Restoration Act as "one of the ACLU's most important victories" of recent years. But Cornell professor Jeremy Rabkin saw it differently: "It does not strike Walker at all incongruous that the organization counts it an 'important victory' when it succeeds in passing legislation designed to punish a small religious college—which is what Grove City is—for declining to pledge support for bureaucratic definitions of sex discrimination—which is what the *Grove City* case was about."[4]

If the ACLU prized the role of mediating institutions in the cause of liberty, it would not have taken aim at Grove City College. Instead, it would have come to its defense, seeking to push back the heavy hand of government. But to those who hold an atomized view of society, what passes as liberty is the volume of rights held by individuals. It is the state, of course, that distributes rights to individuals, and that is why the ACLU's vision of society is dubbed atomistic: there is room for the state and the individual, but not much else. And that means that the liberty of private associations to determine their own destiny is given short shrift by the ACLU.

The current ACLU policy guide lists as official policy a decision made by the board of directors in 1952 that the owners of private facilities are free to deny access to any group they want.[5] This is one of the ACLU's few remaining policies addressing support for the rights of private associations, and in reality the Union's statement is more nominal than honored. This policy didn't stop the ACLU chapter in Scranton, Pennsylvania, from suing the Catholic Youth Center in 1983 for its decision not to open its doors to rock singer Ozzy Osbourne.[6] Nor did it stop the Vermont affiliate in 1990 from suing the privately-owned Regal Arts Press Inc. for its decision to refuse service to an official from Catholics for Free Choice.[7]

Another instance where ACLU policy is more nominal than adhered to is its policy on "Private Organizations." Formulated in 1972 and never revised since, the policy says that "private associations and organizations, as such, lie beyond the legitimate concern of the state and are constitutionally protected against governmental interference. The freedom of association . . . guaranteed by the First Amendment, insulates individuals in these private activities."[8] But no more. It would be more accurate to say that private associations have lost much of their insularity, due in large measure to the success of the neo-civil libertarian perspective in the courts. The court-ordered integration of women into the Jaycees and Rotary Clubs in the 1980s is just one illustration of how this perspective has triumphed in the judiciary. Associational rights have clearly been trumped by an interest in fostering gender equality.

It is important to note that there are still occasions when the ACLU rallies to defend freedom of association. One of the most notable examples occurred in 1992 and 1993 when the New York CLU supported the right of the Ancient Order of Hibernians not to include a contingency from the Irish Lesbian and Gay Organization in its St. Patrick's Day Parade. Norm Siegel of the New York affiliate accused the city of unnecessarily interfering with the rights of a private organization, holding that "political correctness cannot nullify the right of association under the U.S. Constitution."[9]

Though Siegel could have made a First Amendment argument citing freedom of religion (the Hibernians are an Irish Catholic fraternal order), he chose to make his case on straight associational grounds. In any event, the willingness of the New York affiliate, and of Norm Siegel in particular, to fight Mayor David Dinkins on this matter (he sided with gay activists on this issue) is proof that the ACLU has not abandoned principle altogether. In 1993, a federal judge ruled that the city had no right to bar a permit to the Ancient Order of Hibernians; Judge Kevin Thomas Duffy ruled that the city's action violated the free speech rights of the parade's sponsors.

The Boy Scouts wish they were as fortunate as the Ancient Order of Hibernians. They have been sued by atheists, homosexuals, and eight-year-old girls on the grounds that they discriminate on the basis of religion, sexual orientation, and sex. The ACLU, active in some of these cases, and supportive of all, has been at the forefront of the movement to challenge the associational liberty of the Boy Scouts. It is not hard to understand why. Freedom of religion, as we have seen, has never been viewed by the ACLU as a paramount right. But the rights of homosexuals and women have. Put this together with the Union's penchant for challenging traditional values, and there is not much mystery left in why the ACLU would want to sue the Boy Scouts.

The Boy Scout Oath requires members "to do my best to do my duty to God and my country." In 1991, this pledge was found unacceptable to the families of two young boys and so they sued, represented by the ACLU, claiming religious discrimination. The Boy Scouts accept as a member any person who proclaims a belief in God, be he Hindu or Rastafarian, and even accepts religious persons like Buddhists who do not believe in a Supreme Being. But they will not accept agnostics or atheists. The Oath also says that members commit themselves to being "physically strong, mentally awake and morally straight." Being "morally straight," the Boy Scouts declare, excludes homosexuals, and that is because homosexuality is regarded as immoral behavior, a stance the organization has consistently taken since it was incorporated in 1910. The reason for excluding girls is evidenced by the name of the organization and is further justified on the basis of the various needs of boys and girls in their developing years.

None of these reasons was found persuasive to the ACLU. The legal basis of the Union's position was grounded in its conviction that the Boy Scouts was not really a private organization, and therefore it should not be immune from antidiscrimination statutes. The Boy Scouts point out that they receive no federal support whatsoever. But the ACLU counters by saying that the Scouts receive indirect public subsidies, in the form of space that is allotted in the public schools, and also receive what are in effect public funds from the United Way. According to this interpretation, virtually every private organization could be seen as a public institution, which, it seems plain, is exactly the point the ACLU wants to make.

What is most interesting about the ACLU's approach to the Boy Scouts is its determination to contract the private sphere and expand the public domain. With few exceptions, the ACLU seeks to lengthen the arm of government by narrowing what constitutes the private orbit, often by reinterpreting the criteria on which private associations are based. It took State Superior Court Judge Sally G. Disco to redirect the ACLU's thinking back to basics. In rebuffing ACLU claims that the Boy Scouts should be forced to accept homosexuals as Scoutmasters, Judge Disco ruled in 1991 that "the Supreme Court has long recognized a right to 'engage in association for the advancement of beliefs and ideas.' The converse, a right not to associate, or the right of the group to exclude unwanted members, is also recognized."[10]

These cases, which first began in 1980 and have traveled well into the 1990s, show that even private organizations whose membership is entirely voluntary are not free from the scrutiny of the ACLU or the state. Those who, like Midge Decter, view freedom from a social perspective are concerned that if the ACLU ultimately succeeds in this area, it will be at a price to the social order that no distribution of rights will ever make up for: "If civil liberties are ever destroyed in this country, it won't be by boys taking oaths but rather by people intent on stretching the delicate and complex social fabric of this free society beyond its breaking point."[11] Decter's trenchant observation was directed at Ira Glasser.

The ACLU's disinterest in protecting the private sphere from state encroachment is at one with its long history of neglect, if not disregard, for property rights. Since its founding in 1920, the ACLU has never been receptive to free market principles and has in fact been openly hostile— especially in its founding period—to a market economy.

In its first annual report, it charged that the American people lived under a "dictatorship of property" but were so "drugged by propaganda and blinded by a press necessarily subservient to property interests" that few realized it.[12] "Economic or political power," it said, "is necessary to assert and maintain all rights."[13] Unionomics was so radical that mainstream labor leaders, John L. Lewis and Samuel Gompers among them, openly criticized the ACLU for aiding and abetting revolutionary movements.[14] The Union earned its radical stripes most earnestly in its effort to kill the Wagner Act, the bill designed to afford rights to working men and women. The government, the ACLU reasoned, was so thoroughly fascist that it could never be trusted to really distribute rights to labor.[15]

In the 1930s, ACLU founder Roger Baldwin described his thinking as "anti-capitalist and pro-revolutionary,"[16] admitting that he was "sympathetic [to] the economic system being worked out in Soviet Russia."[17] Indeed, he did not hesitate to say, "I believe in the economic goal of communism, namely sharing in common the world's wealth."[18] It was only fitting, then, that fully eighteen years after the ACLU was founded, a major debate ensued within the organization over the question of free-speech rights for employers. Though the Union had already defended communists and fascists, most board members—as late as 1938—were still of the conviction that employers should not have free speech rights; in that same year, after much deliberation, the board finally endorsed free speech for employers.[19]

Unionomics, then, has a rich history of anti-market positions. To this day, virtually the only ACLU policies that address property rights are those that touch on such issues as due process rights in government seizure cases and the equitable treatment of property rights for all citizens. When it comes to filing suit protecting property interests, the

Union's record is dismal. As *Barron's* contributor David Kelley notes, there were several landmark Supreme Court cases in the 1980s that sharply limited the power of government to take property by regulation, and the ACLU was active in none of them.[20]

Rights in the Workplace

In the 1950s, the ACLU could say something it couldn't say today, namely, that freedom of access to jobs and freedom of business contract "lie outside the scope of civil liberties."[21] Now the ACLU believes that the private sector should lose its traditional immunities from government policing and is determined to place the rights of employees at the center of its agenda. In 1978, Ira Glasser, before leaving the New York affiliate to head the national organization, argued the case for extending the reach of constitutional protections to the workplace. He did not disagree then with the idea that the Bill of Rights was designed to protect a large sphere of private activity from the reach of government, but he nonetheless concluded that corporations had grown so large, they had in effect become "minigovernments," necessitating updating of our understanding of constitutional rights.[22]

It is significant that Glasser made no attempt then—and he makes no attempt now—to square his thinking with the intent of the Framers of the U.S. Constitution. Were he to do so, he might feel obliged to wonder why, if it were sheer size (or even power) the Founders were alarmed about, they didn't want government to police the churches as well. The answer, of course, is that it was government, not corporations or churches, that the Framers were interested in taming. And for good reason. Only the state, as Max Weber put it, has a monopoly on the legitimate use of violence.

Unexpectedly, Glasser's ambitions were derailed temporarily as the ACLU's defense of Nazis to march in Skokie, Illinois, led to the resignation of 75,000 members, putting all new issues on the back burner. But by the mid-1980s, the Union had rebounded, and with a conservative in the White House, Glasser was successful in reinvigorating the organization. As the 1985 Biennial Conference demonstrated, the rights of private sector employees were not going to go away. At the conference in Boulder, Colorado, Ed Asner, president of the Screen Actor's Guild, implored the ACLU to include the rights of private employees in its mission. All the traditional civil liberties concerns, he said, were present in the private workplace: free speech, due process, equal protection, and privacy. "Like privacy rights established through other fundamental rights," Asner contended, "there is a fundamental right to decent employment."[23]

At the same Biennial Conference, strategies to bring civil liberties into the workplace were discussed. It was decided that the ACLU should start with some fairly innocuous issue, one that was certain to garner widespread support. The need for whistle-blowing statutes (since adopted by federal law) was given priority. Why? Because such statutes would prepare the way to further weaken employer sovereignty. Such a strategy, it was stated in no uncertain terms, would necessarily open the door for an attack on the concept of termination-at-will, which, in turn, would grease the slopes for the ultimate ACLU objective of having right to a job encoded in law.[24]

As of the spring of 1986, the ACLU was still prepared to admit that the Constitution did not apply to private employees.[25] But the annual report of 1986-87 made it clear that the traditional view was about to be officially discarded. The report noted what it called "the growing problem of workers' rights in the private sector" and pledged the resources of the ACLU to doing something about it. Given this cast of mind, it was only logical that it would declare that "the Constitution's principles must be extended to the private sector."[26]

But what was particularly revealing—revealing in that it evinced a preference for an atomistic conception of liberty—was the way in which the ACLU framed the argument: "Each day the institutions entrusted with power over people must be watched closely to guard against abuses."[27] But who will do the policing? Is the interest of liberty advanced by granting government the right to police private institutions for violations of civil liberties? Is this not a prescription for despotism? The very fact that the ACLU does not address this issue is cause for concern.

In addition to ideological reasons for extending civil liberties into the workplace, the Union was motivated by the promise of new business and a new base for attracting donations. In the summer of 1987, Glasser told PBS host Bill Moyers that the ACLU gets more employment-related complaints than any other kind.[28] That alone wouldn't have been sufficient to nudge the ACLU, but put together with the Union's affection for inflating the power of government in the cause of equality, it explains why the temptation to seize new turf proved irresistible.

In 1988, the ACLU affirmed its new mission by releasing a major report entitled "Liberty at Work: Expanding the Rights of Employees in America." In his introductory remarks, Glasser opines, "We should not have to hang up our Bill of Rights at the time clock or the office door." Making clear his perspective on the Bill of Rights, Glasser held that "it does not make sense to say we live in a free country unless we're free at work."[29] He did not say why claims of freedom were not similarly bogus unless we were free in our homes and in our churches. Why, it could be asked, should we hang up our Bill of Rights as we enter our homes, or at the church door? Freedom, Glasser seems to assert, means, in part, the right of the federal government to police private institutions to assure compliance with its mandates.

The issue of "genetic discrimination" is an example of the problems in the workplace that the ACLU seeks to correct. The Union thinks it should be illegal for private employers not to hire people with a genetic abnormality, even when there is good reason to believe that the nature of the job would expose the worker to great risk. What should employers do about the likelihood of catastrophic insurance coverage in such instances? Here the ACLU calls on government to provide the right tonic. It wants the government to provide "adequate health care to everyone, regardless of employment status," thereby relieving employers of having to pay for health insurance.[30] In 1990, the ACLU strengthened its position by passing a policy on genetic testing in the workplace. Interestingly, the policy's pronouncement that "employment decisions should be made on the basis of individual ability and character, not on the basis of stereotypes and generalizations about the groups to which an individual belongs,"[31] put it at odds with the Union's reasoning in support of affirmative action.

"'Have you ever done anything you are ashamed of?' . . . 'Not counting masturbation and sexual intercourse with a willing partner, what was your most unusual sex act ever?' . . . 'When was the last time you unintentionally exposed yourself after drinking?'" According to Ira Glasser, questions like these are routinely asked of prospective employees, and the use of a polygraph is commonly used to test for lying.[32] Why the market wouldn't be an adequate safeguard to such extremely rare cases (for example, people can refuse to answer), Glasser doesn't say. ACLU privacy expert Janlori Goldman thinks the best way to solve this problem is to give the government more authority to prohibit employers from asking such questions in the first place. But as *Reason* contributor Jacob Sullum sees it, "Contracts only work if they bind both parties. Unfortunately, the ACLU, which is very concerned about informational privacy in the abstract, is chipping away at the most practical means for protecting it."[33]

The ACLU objects to polygraphs and to video display terminals (mechanisms that monitor the work of employees)[34] for another reason: they are used to punish minorities. The Union contends that "there is no reason to believe that polygraph examiners are free of the racial biases that permeate the rest of society."[35] Nowhere does the ACLU allow that in some contexts, such monitoring may be necessary. For example, no distinction is made between indiscriminately subjecting janitors to a polygraph and requiring pilots suspected of drug abuse to undergo testing. Similarly, the ACLU believes that even in the area of government intelligence and counterintelligence work, polygraphs should be barred.[36]

The ACLU is opposed to discrimination against smokers in the hiring and retention of employees, but it does not object to government regulation of smoking in public places.[37] Drug testing is also condemned, regardless of the nature of the job, on the grounds that such tests invade the privacy of employees. The ACLU recommends performance testing as a way to defend against substance abusers on the job.[38] Such tests measure impairment, which may or may not be due to drug use, and thus get around the civil liberties problems of a urinalysis. The problem, however, is that performance tests exact a price in terms of time, manpower, and money, and are thus ill-suited to many types of employment.

Personal appearance should no longer be a criterion by which private employees are judged, unless it can be said to be "reasonably related to job performance."[39] According to the ACLU, fat people are particularly prone to victimization in this area. Expressing its solidarity with the National Association to Aid Fat Americans (NAAFA), the ACLU went on record in 1991 opposing what it calls the "lifestyle discrimination" of fat people (the NAAFA rejects the term "obese"). The Union joined the NAAFA and other "victims' advocacy groups" in pushing for more legislation in this area.[40]

The most serious aspect of the ACLU's new position on rights in the workplace concerns the termination of unsatisfactory employees. The right to fire is now labeled as "an embarrassing relic"[41] and "an unfortunate anachronism."[42] Offering nothing but anecdotal evidence, the ACLU claims that "the magnitude of the problem is enormous."[43] The rule it wants to substitute would state that "employees have a right to keep their job unless their performance or workplace conduct is deficient."[44] So as not to be misunderstood, the ACLU believes that infractions like lateness or absenteeism should not (in most instances) be cause for termination. A hearing should be required before a dismissal can take place, and that, the ACLU readily admits, may mean arbitration, possibly even a full-blown trial.[45]

What is most unusual about all this is the ACLU's frank admission that it arrived at its conclusions before it developed a legal theory upon which to base its judgments. That is why, in an official policy passed in 1986, it called upon the board to "develop the legal theories and a policy in support of the concept of due process of employees in private employment situations."[46] For the ACLU, then, it is not its theoretical orientation that drives its decisions; rather, it is its preferences that determine its theoretical content.

The ACLU knows that if any of these proposals are going to be sustained in law, it will mean an uphill battle with public opinion. In the concluding section of the report "Liberty At Work," Lewis L. Maltby openly admits that the American people "would not support it [the ACLU's position] because they would see it as interfering with free enterprise." Maltby thinks it regrettable that "the idea of free enterprise is near and dear to us," arguing that notions like the pioneering entrepreneur are "part of our emotional heritage."[47] It is a sign of just how antiquated Maltby's ideas are that the new Russian Constitution gives far more emphasis to property rights than either he or the ACLU is willing to do.

As libertarian Charles Oliver puts it, "because the ACLU does not distinguish between economic power and physical force, it ends up calling for more government involvement—more coercion—to restrict the power, or freedom, of business managers and owners."[48] It can also be said that the ACLU's penchant for egalitarianism has something to do with its failure to appreciate the difference between economic liberty and unadulterated statism.

Discrimination

The ACLU's record on racial equality is commendable, for its having pushed for better relations between whites and blacks throughout most of its history. It is one thing to speak in favor of racial harmony in the 1990s, but the ACLU took that stand long before it became culturally acceptable to do so. However, the Union's approach to race relations has changed markedly over the years, and it is a fair question as to whether its latest strategies abet or hinder the cause of liberty in the long run.

The racial bigotry that led to the 1986 beating and death of Michael Griffith in Howard Beach, New York, resulted in the creation of a New York City Civil Rights Coalition, dedicated to the advancement of racial equality and harmony. Among the organizers were Norman Siegel and Michael Myers of the ACLU. Shortly thereafter, when a demonstration calling for racial justice took place in Forsyth County, Georgia, the ACLU sent a delegation. When Yusuf Hawkins, a black teenager, was killed by white youths in Bensonhurst, Brooklyn, Ira Glasser took the occasion to condemn the act and blame Ronald Reagan for nourishing "the disease of racial separation."[49] But when a band of black youths beat, sodomized, and left for dead a white woman in Central Park, the ACLU had nothing to say. As will become evident, the unevenness of the ACLU's response was not out of step with its more general approach to racial issues.

Political equality for minorities is high on the list of ACLU priorities. It supports statehood for the District of Columbia,[50] a move that would clearly benefit blacks (they represent 80 percent of the District's population). Where this issue gets complicated is when the need for equitable treatment of minorities clashes with the democratic principle of majority rule. The ACLU has challenged the direct election of state judges, claiming that the result is often discriminatory, that is, it results in too few minorities being elected. Some Union officials favor the limited or cumulative voting system that makes it easier for minorities who unite behind a candidate to win.[51] The ACLU's results-oriented tactic may indeed increase minority representation, but it is not at all clear how this issue involves the Bill of Rights.

The ACLU has also filed suit in Nassau County, Long Island, challenging the weighted voting system designed for the election of the Board of Supervisors. It has filed suit against the runoff election system in Georgia on the grounds that it prevents the election of minority candidates. But does the ACLU want more minority representation in government or more minorities elected to office who hold politically liberal views? To Sarah Flores, the Hispanic woman who had her first-place primary showing invalidated in 1990 as a result of an ACLU lawsuit, there is little doubt that the Union favors the latter position.

Flores, who competed in the primary that preceded the election of the Los Angeles County Board of Supervisors, had her victory upended by Federal Judge David Kenyon on the grounds that the way district lines were drawn, "an Hispanic is unable to be elected to the board." Amazingly, Judge Kenyon's ruling occurred the day before Mrs. Flores won 68 percent of the Hispanic vote, finished first among Anglo voters, and carried 29 out of 31 cities. So why did the ACLU move to overturn district lines? As the editors of the *Wall Street Journal* pointed out, Flores may be Hispanic, but she is a Republican, and her election would have continued the 3-2 conservative majority on the Board of Supervisors.[52] The ACLU, which is strongly opposed to "English-Only" laws[53] and is generally protective of Hispanic interests, apparently felt that in this instance there was something more at stake than minority representation.

It is widely acknowledged that although racial discrimination still exists in the United States, the civil rights laws of the past several decades have had a meliorating effect. The ACLU, however, does not concur with this judgment, holding that "race discrimination is alive and well," resulting in "the loss of brilliant minds of people of color, through hopelessness, anger, and negative involvement in the criminal justice system."[54] The ACLU's dour assessment may have something to do with its penchant for finding racism in places few others have noticed. Indeed, it sometimes trivializes racism, as when it labels the installation of a garbage incinerator in a black neighborhood as "environmental racism."[55]

If a disproportionate number of black motorists are stopped on turnpikes in search of drugs, is that a violation of civil liberties? The ACLU of New Jersey thinks so.[56] If schools adopt an Indian nickname, are they disparaging of Indian traditions? The Minnesota CLU thinks so, and that is why it threatened to go into federal district court against 50 school districts. Never mind that the Minnesota Chippewa saw it differently. "We are opposed to the action of the MCLU, and we question their authority to speak on our behalf," said Myron Ellis, the tribe's representative. Also targeted by the ACLU was Pipestone High School, chosen for its allegedly racist nickname "Arrows." However, Pipestone was quickly dropped from the list when it was discovered that the nickname referred to Robin Hood, not Sitting Bull.[57]

Sex discrimination has always been a problem, and the ACLU has been right to fight it where it exists. But sometimes it finds sexism in rather strange places, and in cases where there is no governmental abridgment of rights. For example, in 1989 the state affiliate in Washington found sex discrimination in a laundry service's practice of charging more to launder women's shirts than men's. The ACLU dropped the case when the privately owned establishment agreed to base its charges on the size and not the gender of the shirt (the latter was apparently indicated by the label).[58] In the same year, the ACLU won a case in its challenge to New York State's exclusive reliance on Scholastic Aptitude Test (SAT) scores in awarding Empire and Regents scholarships. The Union's complaint stemmed from the fact that boys do better than girls on the test, and therefore the state's method was held to be discriminatory under Title IX and the Fourteenth Amendment's equal protection clause.[59]

The Union was less successful in its bid to prohibit Virginia Military Institute's practice of denying admission to women. The 1991 decision by Federal Judge Jackson L. Kiser was partly based on research that demonstrated the merits of single-sex education,[60] a fact deemed irrelevant by the ACLU. Ironically, it was something the Union fervently believes in—namely diversity—that was the gravamen of Judge Kiser's decision to permit the exclusion of women from V.M.I.

On appeal, the Union lost again in 1992.[61] What is most interesting about this second round of challenges is that the ACLU actually admitted that while publicly-funded single-sex education was impermissible for men, such schools could be defended under a "compensatory" (read: affirmative-action) rationale for women. But as Notre Dame law professor Douglas W. Kmiec put it, "The equal protection guarantee should not mean one thing when applied to one individual and something else when applied to another."[62] Kmiec's logic notwithstanding, this is a case that refuses to die. Not only do new charges continue to be brought against V.M.I., the institution's corps of cadets was unofficially reprimanded when they were deliberately uninvited to march in President Clinton's inaugural parade, thus breaking a tradition that began with the inauguration of President Truman.

The ACLU is living testimony to the charge that the cure of routing out discrimination can occasionally become a worse problem than the disease. Consider the following: A homeowner, interested in supplementing his income, decides to rent his basement to a tenant. He has a wife and two teenage daughters and wants to screen the applicants carefully. He refuses a lease to the first applicant when he discovers that he is a drug addict, alcoholic, former mental patient, and convicted rapist presently out on parole. Is there anyone who would find this decision unreasonable? Yes, the ACLU would. Indeed it would find the decision a violation of the rapist's "basic civil rights." This is the official housing policy of the ACLU, rendered in January 1988: "Discrimination in the rental, sale, or mortgaging of housing, public or private, based on race, color, sex, religion, national origin, political affiliation, alienage, illegitimacy, sexual orientation, marital status, presence of children in the family or household, age, physical or mental disability, status as a recipient of public assistance, an alcoholic, or drug addict, or ex-offender, including a parolee, is a denial of basic civil rights."[63]

The Union's commitment to ending housing discrimination took a new turn in 1989 when it decided to excise from its existing housing policy the exemption it had traditionally granted to fraternal orders.[64] Previous policy held that with respect to private housing, "groups established in good faith for non-housing purposes—e.g., religious bodies or fraternal orders—should be permitted in good faith to limit to their members the sale or rental of housing accommodations provided specifically for their members."[65] But due to the ACLU's war on sexism, the exception for fraternal orders could no longer be tolerated. It cannot go unnoticed that current ACLU policy contains a clause recognizing "the special needs" of alcoholics and drug addicts; it is permissible, the Union says, to grant them residences "established in good faith."[66]

Much as the ACLU claims to hate housing discrimination, especially when the victims are minorities, it does not find objectionable discrimination against individual blacks if the net effect is to foster integration. The Union says that "race-conscious measures to achieve racially diversified housing may reflect laudable good faith efforts to eliminate discrimination." It specifically supports racial quotas in instances where "the purpose of the ceiling quotas is to achieve or maintain integration or to prevent rapid resegregation, rather than to maintain a permanent white majority."[67] This policy was written to give ACLU support to the kind of social engineering experiment carried out in Brooklyn's Starrett City, an experiment declared illegal in the late 1980s.

Starrett City is a federally subsidized housing complex in the East New York section of Brooklyn. Built in the mid-1970s, Starrett City was designed as a planned integrated middle-class community, modeled after sociological research on the subject. Previous research on neighborhoods in the midst of integration had indicated that integration can proceed without much difficulty up to a point. That point usually comes when the neighborhood becomes approximately 20 percent black; after that point "tipping" occurs, with the result that white flight soon leaves the neighborhood almost all black. Knowing this, some urban experts suggested that a racial ceiling be imposed, limiting the number of whites and blacks who could live in Starrett City; this would then prevent "tipping" from occurring. After certain quotas were experimented with, it was decided that integration could still be maintained if the complex were 65 percent white and 35 percent nonwhite. What this policy meant was that prospective black tenants were often turned aside while management looked for white families willing to move into the integrated project.[68]

Did Starrett City work? Yes and no. Those who lived in the complex, both white and black, liked living there: neighbors got along well, racial incidents were few, and drugs and crime were uncommon. The problem came from those who wanted to live in Starrett City, most of whom were black, but were denied entry because of the color of their skin. That is why the Reagan Justice Department sued and eventually won in 1988.

For those whose priority it is to foster integration, the Starrett City scheme may make sense. But for those committed to the principle of individual rights, there can be no justification for racial discrimination. That is why the ACLU's position on this issue is so revealing. By endorsing racial discrimination as a means toward racial integration, the Union shows that its true interest is not individual rights, but group equality.

The ACLU's conception of liberty not only allows it to endorse race-based ceiling quotas in housing, it permits it to defend the right of judges to raise taxes so as to further integration. In 1987, in a highly unusual move, Federal District Judge Russell G. Clark of Kansas City, Missouri, ordered the doubling of property taxes (on residences, business property, cars, and such) in the Kansas City school district. He took the action after the Kansas City school board was unable to pay its share of a major desegregation plan approved by the judge. Judge Clark also imposed a surcharge on the Missouri income tax, raising the levy by 25 percent for those who lived in the school district, and ordered major capital improvements for existing schools, as well as the construction of new "magnet" schools. The total estimated cost in 1989 was in excess of $700 million.

In *Missouri v. Jenkins*, the Supreme Court in 1990 held that Judge Clark had indeed abused his authority. The court majority did not say that there were never grounds for a court to constitutionally order a local government to increase its taxes (it was okay when necessary to "vindicate constitutional guarantees"), only that in this instance Judge Clark's reach extended far beyond any reasonable limit; the four dissenting judges thought any power of a judge to tax was impermissible.[69] Startling as Judge Clark's ruling was, it paled next to the ACLU's reaction.

The ACLU, which is presumedly not against the concept of separation of powers, found nothing wrong with Judge Clark's order. Before the Supreme Court had a chance to rule on the case, ACLU legal director John Powell warned that if the high court overturned the judge's decision, it would "essentially cripple the Judiciary from executing its role protecting constitutional rights."[70] That would seem to imply that the unelected judiciary has greater constitutional authority to raise taxes than the constitutionally charged and democratically elected Congress. The way the ACLU sees it, the cause of desegregation is too important not to matter: "How far is the United States prepared to go, and how far will this Court go, to ensure equality? Is racial justice a principle worth achieving at all costs, or only when the costs are not too high?"[71] But if the cost is ignoring a plain reading of the Constitution, then some might reasonably argue that that indeed is too high a price to pay.

Affirmative Action

"A central concept of civil liberties is that all individuals have the right to be judged on the basis of their individual capabilities, not the characteristics and capabilities that are supposedly shared by any group or class to which they may belong." That is the lead sentence in the ACLU's official policy on "Rights of Persons with Disabilities." A little later in the policy, the Union endorses affirmative action in employment.[72] The apparent contradiction—in theory supporting individual merit, and in practice advocating the primacy of group characteristics—is not something that catches the eye of civil libertarians. But no matter how they want to frame the issue, equal opportunity and equal outcome are diametrically opposed principles, and the ACLU's preference for the latter, as demonstrated in court, makes superfluous its nominal statements to the contrary.

The ACLU was not always in favor of judging people on the basis of group criteria. Prior the 1970s, the ACLU opposed racial quotas in hiring and the Equal Rights Amendment (ERA) for women, taking the position that the Fourteenth Amendment provided all the relief that blacks and women needed; racial quotas had the additional liability of being anti-civil libertarian, since they inexorably collided with the individual's right not to be discriminated against on the basis of race. But as the march for equality quickened, the ACLU reversed its positions and became a rabid enthusiast of equal results and a proponent of the ERA.

With regard to women, the ACLU supports "the use of narrowly drawn, temporary, sex-specific remedies when the factual record establishes that the implementation of gender-neutral policies cannot eliminate identified sex-based discrimination. In these circumstances, the concept of equality of opportunity can only be satisfied by such an affirmative action approach."[73] The ACLU does not say how long "temporary" is supposed to mean, but since this policy was framed in 1985, we can assume that it doesn't mean "for a few years." The idea of satisfying equal opportunity by rejecting equal opportunity raises additional questions about the logic of the policy.

The ACLU says that affirmative action is needed when a gender-blind approach cannot end "identified sex-based discrimination," suggesting that such discrimination must first be established before a gender-conscious method can be adopted. But in reality, all that it takes to satisfy the ACLU is the absence of women in a given line of work. For example, in the 1980s, in the case of Santa Clara dispatcher Diane Joyce, the Union defended, in an amicus role, a voluntary affirmative-action plan designed to correct gender imbalance on the job. Joyce was hired over Paul Johnson, a white male who scored higher than Joyce on a qualifying test, simply because she was a woman. It did not matter to the ACLU, nor to the Supreme Court, that there was not one case of discrimination ever recorded by the transportation agency; gender imbalance was sufficient grounds to discriminate against white men.[74]

The ACLU has repeatedly challenged the merits of qualifying exams used to select police officers, firefighters, truck drivers, electricians, et al., arguing that women and minorities fail the tests at a higher rate than white males because the tests discriminate against them. Here are a few examples of the ACLU's reasoning.

On a test for firefighters, is it fair that women (as well as men) are asked to discuss the operation of a rotary engine? Some civil libertarians say no, maintaining that such a question involves knowledge traditionally more familiar to men than women (solving the problem by making that knowledge more familiar to women was evidently not acceptable). Tests that measure physical strength, something reasonably related to firefighting, are also deemed to be suspect. As Isabelle Katz Pinzler sees it, such tests are analogous to literacy tests for blacks.[75] It seems clear that what concerns the ACLU in these instances is less the validity of the tests than the gender distributions they yield.

There are some occasions when ACLU victories in behalf of women leave even women to wonder what they've won. For instance, in 1989 the ACLU relied on the Equal Rights Amendment to the Pennsylvania Constitution to challenge a state law that authorized the setting of auto insurance rates by sex.[76] Though the Union won, it proved to be a costly victory in the end, as the rates for women were hiked to match the rates for men.

In recent years, there have been any number of ACLU lawsuits filed in behalf of female athletes, usually aimed at opening school and community athletic competition to girls as well as boys. Equal treatment has been demanded with regard to quality of coaches, facilities, and resources. On occasion, the quest for equality gets into some pretty bizarre issues. In Montana, for example, what fired the ACLU into action was the practice of high-school girls playing basketball in the fall and volleyball in the winter. Because boys usually play basketball in the winter and volleyball in the fall, ACLU Executive Director Diane Benjamin charged that the girls were being harmed psychologically. But besides the fact that Benjamin's charge would be difficult to prove, the larger question is why the ACLU finds it necessary to consider matters like these as worthy of its resources. In the end, a settlement led to greater overall equality, but it didn't resolve the civil libertarian problem of off-season sports.[77]

The ACLU's defense of affirmative action even extends to free speech issues. The Union calls on government to ensure a fair voice for women and minorities on radio and television. Speaking of the role of the Federal Communications Commission (FCC), the ACLU says that "equal representation of the viewpoints of minorities and women on the airwaves is no less important than equal opportunity for those groups in all other sectors of the national life."[78] Besides the contentiousness of assuming that there is such a monolithic thing as a minority or female point of view, it is striking that the ACLU, which sees itself as absolutist in free-speech matters, would call on government to police the broadcasting industry.

Even when it comes to television technology, such as cable and direct-broadcast satellite, the Union sees an egalitarian role for government. It calls upon the FCC and Congress to make new technologies available for "minorities, women and other hitherto disenfranchised groups," noting that only two percent of all broadcast properties are minority owned, most of which are in radio. The ACLU also favors "a preference for an expedited consideration of applications for licenses supported by the tribal government in question where broadcast areas include an Indian reservation."[79] These positions can be argued on their own merit, but they are rather strange coming from an organization supposedly dedicated to limited government.

Limited government was also not the ACLU's goal when it pressed for the passage of the Civil Rights Act of 1991. In a series of Supreme Court decisions in the 1989-90 term, the high court sharply cut back on the scope of federal laws by making it harder for minorities and women to challenge workplace discrimination and easier for white males to challenge affirmative action plans. In essence, the court said that the burden of proof should fall on the alleged victim and not on the accused employer. Outraged, the ACLU clamored for the need for specific Congressional legislation that would overturn the effect of these decisions.

The heart of the controversy was the Supreme Court's ruling in *Wards Cove Packing Co. v. Antonio*. In that decision, the court effectively overturned its own 18-year-old landmark ruling in *Griggs v. Power Duke Co.*, which had required employers to justify, as a "business necessity," practices that had an adverse impact on minority workers. Under *Wards Cove*, the court held that an employer could defend a discriminatory impact if it met a legitimate business objective, a relatively low standard.

Further, it was up to the employee to show that each challenged employment practice that had a disparate impact on the employee's racial, ethnic, or gender classification was not justified by business necessity.[80] Enter the Civil Rights Act of 1990, which President Bush successfully vetoed, and its successor in 1991, which Bush did not challenge.

The Civil Rights Act of 1991 explicitly shifted the burden of proof back to the employer by requiring that practices be "job related for the position in question and consistent with business necessity." Though it was not touted as a quota bill, the implementation of the bill made the use of quotas likely. When organizations are required to legitimize statistical disparities that are inconsistent with the area's demographic profile, many prefer the easy way out and simply use quotas to settle the matter. This is more well known than admitted by those in business, law, and government.

Given the ACLU's atomistic leanings, it is not hard to understand why it would side with the government, and not private organizations, in workplace issues. But what is surprising is the ACLU's readiness to abandon its traditional interest in due process. The ACLU prefers an "effects test" to prove discrimination, that is, a showing of discriminatory effect, as opposed to a demonstration of intent. Why? Because, as it readily admits, the standard of intent is more difficult to prove than the "effects test."[81] But imagine what the ACLU would do if someone were to suggest that we jettison due process in favor of an effects test when addressing the rights of the accused. As Cornell scholar Jeremy Rabkin has noted, "civil libertarians are obsessed with due process, except when it comes to civil rights litigation, where they want no due process for the other side. They say, 'Let's impose quotas, without requiring any standards of proof and with no defenses. The deck should be stacked in our favor.'"[82]

It is also blatantly inconsistent for the ACLU to bemoan the lack of finality in lawsuits charging reverse discrimination, while simultaneously opposing any limits on the number of appeals that inmates on death row can file. For example, in a complaint registered against the Supreme Court in 1990, it was charged that "the Court set the stage for endless legal assaults on affirmative action plans by allowing some white municipal employees to file a new lawsuit that, in effect, reopened a case settled many years ago." Ironically, in the same issue of the Union's newsletter where this remark appeared, the case is made supporting the "unrestricted right" of death row inmates to file as many habeas corpus petitions as they want.[83] For an organization ostensibly committed to procedural rights, these contrary opinions are hard to square.

The ACLU's public pronouncements regarding fairness in employment often differ with the standards it sets for itself. A case in point is the ACLU's internal policy on the rights of the disabled. It calls upon the national office and the affiliates to "make every reasonable effort" to accommodate people with physical disabilities; it allowed three years to accomplish this task, beginning in 1990.[84] However, the Union's litmus test for public buildings is not so generous. There is no "reasonable effort" clause; rather, there is the flat assertion that public buildings, accommodations, and services are "to be accessible to persons with disabilities." The same goes for public transportation, with the caveat that alternative transportation may be substituted "until such time as transportation systems are made accessible within an appropriately developed timetable."[85]

When it comes to affirmative action, the ACLU's internal policies are quite consistent with its expectations for other employers. It's just that it doesn't honor them. Not only has it given itself waivers when it has been unable to find a qualified minority to serve as a staff attorney,[86] its practices have alienated many of its black board members. In 1985, after John Shattuck left as director of the ACLU's Washington office, Ira Glasser authorized the merging of Shattuck's old job with the directorship of the Union's Center for National Security Studies, also located in Washington. Morton Halperin, who directed the latter post, was named as acting director of the newly merged office. That raised suspicions that Halperin, a white male, was being groomed for the job, and led to an outcry among board members.

Michael Myers, one of the black board members, publicly charged the ACLU with violating its own affirmative action policy in its search for the new director of the Washington office. He called it "a power grab" and accused "some of the people at the top of the organization" of trying to "centralize power." Roger Wilkins was so incensed that he resigned as chairman of a nine-member committee established to offer advice about the new hire. He said Glasser's move to install Halperin as acting director had rendered "a true affirmative action search impossible," contending that the executive director had subtly discouraged several promising minority persons from applying for the job. "I'm not going to be part of an organization that ignores its own bylaws," Wilkins said.[87]

In the end, Halperin got the job. Was it a setup? In one sense it doesn't matter. What matters is the ACLU's willingness to make claims on other organizations regarding minority hiring that it refuses to make for itself. In 1977, the ACLU set explicit quotas for itself, but as late as 1990, the ACLU had no Asians or Arabs on its board of directors, and out of a total of 81 members, only 11 were from minority groups. Such figures led Chicano board member Antonio R. Villaraigosa to complain that the ACLU uses the same excuses as corporations when it comes to minority hiring, offering the refrain that there are few qualified candidates available. "The Reagan administration had more racial diversity than the national ACLU," Villaraigosa observed.[88] Even worse is the gratuitous way in which the ACLU has gone about the selection of its board members. "Some people were elected *because* they were women and *because* they were minorities," charges former board member Alan Dershowitz. "And they were told that they were there to represent women and minorities."[89]

Economic Justice

The ACLU accepts the Rawlsian view that justice can be understood as equality, and it is that conviction—not any civil libertarian principle—that colors its thinking on matters of economic rights. True to its roots, the ACLU is committed to state engineering and collectivist programs, not the autonomy of private organizations. This explains the Union's embrace of comparable worth, the policy that purports to establish pay equity for women and minorities by using a rating system based on the alleged comparable worth of each job at the workplace; the state is expected to enforce the system. It is a scheme no skeptic of big government has ever endorsed, explaining why even the editors of the *New York Times* and the *New Republic*, two bastions of liberalism, have refrained from defending it.

In 1986, the ACLU adopted the policy of comparable worth as "the essential next step in achieving full equality for women and minorities." The board did not hesitate to say that market-based reasons that explained the pay differential between the races and sexes were unacceptable.[90] According to Isabelle Katz Pinzler, the discussions that led to this conclusion revolved around Union policies on discrimination. Those policies, it was observed, "generally recognize and support the use of statistics, disparate impact, or the so-called 'effects test,' as being sufficient to prove a *prima facie* case of discrimination. Wage discrimination should be treated no differently."[91] What matters, then, is the mere appearance of inequality and not any intentional violation of civil liberties.

Welfare rights is another cause for civil libertarians. For ACLU activist Shirley Pedler, welfare rights are a proper focus for the organization because "decency and dignity are civil rights."[92] If that is indeed the case, then it could be argued that the decent and dignified thing to do about able-bodied people on welfare is to have them work in return for public assistance. But that is not what Ms. Pedler, or the ACLU, has in mind. Quite the opposite.

It was due to the leadership of radical activist Frances Fox Piven that the ACLU reversed its long-standing position that workfare requirements were not, in principle, objectionable. In 1971, Piven co-authored a book on the poor wherein it was declared, "We are opposed to work-enforcing reforms."[93] Ten years later she headed an ACLU Task Force on this issue, with the result that in 1982 the Union accepted her logic. "The ACLU rejects any presumption that welfare recipients do not want to work or receive income," the policy said. But it then concluded by saying that the Union "opposes work requirements at government-assigned tasks as a condition of eligibility for welfare benefits or for any transfer payments designed to compensate for insufficient income."[94] For the record, Piven even manages to find fault with the goal of full employment, arguing that it is nothing less than "emancipation" that should be the goal: "There's nothing particularly ennobling about making cigarettes, or serving fast food, or about most wage work."[95]

The Union's policy is no academic matter. It has challenged, albeit unsuccessfully, workfare plans for the able-bodied in Pennsylvania[96] and workfare requirements in federal legislation. Thus, when in 1988 the House and Senate voted on a major welfare reform bill (it passed in the Senate 93-0) mandating workfare for welfare recipients, it did so over protests from the ACLU. The ACLU even went on record as opposing the withholding of wages for child support.[97] Affiliates of the ACLU have taken various strategies to protect welfare rights, ranging from filing suit over a welfare motel owner's practice of charging blind persons a dollar a day for a Seeing Eye dog[98] to suits that challenge the right of welfare authorities to establish the paternity of children by asking welfare mothers questions about their sex lives.[99]

In the early 1990s, welfare reform took place in the states at a faster rate than at any time since the 1960s. Most of the reforms were aimed at curtailing abuses and the problems associated with dependency. Polls showed the public strongly supportive of laws requiring the able-bodied to work as a condition of assistance, and the nation's governors listened attentively. In New Jersey, a law was passed in 1992 denying additional welfare benefits to women if they had more children. Wisconsin, Pennsylvania, California, Kansas, Maryland, and Ohio weighed in with similar initiatives, motivating the ACLU to take action against them. "These proposals demonstrate the continued vitality of myths about why recipients are on welfare and specifically penalize single women for being mothers," offered Gretchen Miller, legal director of the Wisconsin affiliate.[100]

The ACLU's defense of welfare rights is only a piece of its larger agenda based on the concept of economic justice. It is not without significance that the ACLU prefers to speak of economic justice rather than economic liberty. The latter term refers to constitutionally protected rights, such as property rights,[101] while the former encompasses anything that one wants to ascribe to it. What the ACLU does not mean by economic justice are the rights of the individual against the state; it flatly rejects the constitutionally understood meaning of economic rights and prefers to cast the issue in terms of entitlements, or what the state owes the individual. This is necessary, of course, if collectivist economic programs are to be achieved.

Beginning in 1966,[102] virtually every Biennial Conference of the ACLU has entertained the idea of a guaranteed annual income. In 1971, ACLU President Norman Dorsen urged his colleagues to declare "minimal economic security" a civil liberties issue.[103] But thus far, the Union has held back, fearful of taking the plunge into uncharted waters. So it is that the ACLU's current policy on poverty and civil liberties[104] stops short of proclaiming poverty to be a violation of constitutional rights per se and does not yet hold the state responsible for the economic well-being of its citizens. However, as we shall see, it has already taken a much more aggressive stand in this area, rendering moot its official position on economic rights.

"Poverty," says the ACLU, "cannot be explained as resulting from 'natural' economic differences." Unionomics sees discrimination as the cause of poverty, blaming unequal treatment on the basis of "race, sex, ethnic background, religion and physical defect or condition."[105] It does not find it necessary to quote a single source of empirical evidence that would support this extraordinary claim, being content to present such a conclusion as though it were an uncontested fact of life. Asians, to take one obvious example, are a nonwhite people who have experienced their share of discrimination, yet that hasn't stood in the way of remarkable progress.

There are two major reasons why the ACLU has yet to declare poverty to be a violation of civil liberties. To begin with, there are still members on the national board of directors who are principled civil libertarians. They have been quite adamant in their belief that the ACLU would seriously undermine its credibility as a civil liberties organization if it were to go any deeper into the area of economic rights.[106] They realize that such adventurism would make the ACLU indistinguishable from a host of other liberal activist organizations, thereby undercutting its unique role. The other objection, though principled on its face, is politically inspired.

There are some in the ACLU who oppose declaring poverty a civil liberties issue for purely tactical reasons. They believe that the crusade for a full panoply of economic rights will be difficult to achieve through the courts, holding that the best prospects for doing so lie with the legislature. What motivates these activists, some are frank to admit, is their commitment to socialism.[107] They have no principled objection to departing from the original intent of the Framers, but they think it's a mistake to cast the issue in terms of constitutionalism versus majoritarianism.

Here's how an avowed socialist, and one of the authors of the ACLU's policy on poverty, explained her opposition to declaring poverty a violation of constitutional rights: "I don't think it's a satisfactory answer to say because it's not in the Constitution or because we've never defined them as civil liberties before—because that's not a principled answer. The Constitution is a living document, our society is a living society, its conditions change and the history of this organization is a history of innovation, a history of change as well."[108] Having said this much, the activist remained firm in her position that the best way to resolve the poverty issue was to cast it as a political one, focusing all attention on securing a victory in the halls of Congress.

Regardless of which strategy is used, it is likely that the ACLU will continue to broaden its interpretation of its own policy on poverty. Current policy authorizes ACLU action only when "there is a direct and substantial connection between poverty and particular deprivations of civil liberties and civil rights."[109]

It was the cutbacks in the entitlement programs by the Reagan administration that ignited the ACLU to reconsider economic rights, and it was the Union's modest recovery from the fallout of Skokie that allowed it to regroup. In 1983, Burt Neuborne, a senior ACLU official and New York University law professor, argued that food, medicine, and shelter should be seen as civil liberties interests, deserving of constitutional protection.[110] The following year, John Shattuck stated that a constitutional right to a shelter was "very much the perspective of the civil liberties advocates."[111] But the person who has had the greatest impact on ACLU thinking is Sylvia A. Law. Law is an ACLU supporter and a colleague of Neuborne and Dorsen at NYU, and a person who worked on the historic 1970 welfare rights case *Goldberg v. Kelly.*

Law's 1984 essay, "Economic Justice" (published as part of an ACLU Report),[112] has been the most widely cited source of ACLU thinking on this issue. Like others in the ACLU, Law does not find it necessary to square her notion of constitutional law with that of the Framers. There is a paragraph acknowledging that "the founders understood that civil liberties and economic arrangements are closely related,"[113] but there is no attempt by Law to show how this has anything to do with her socialist conception of "economic justice." She prefers to quote Pope John Paul II[114] and Karl Marx,[115] neither of whom is known as an expert in constitutional law (or, for that matter, economics), at least outside the ranks of the ACLU.

"The core social issue of our time," says Law, "is whether liberal civil liberties will serve values of human self-realization, community, and equality or whether these liberal rights will rather legitimate the entrenched power of bureaucratic and market institutions that deny those values."[116] This statement is truly revealing of what motivates the ACLU today. Law is not concerned with civil liberties but with using civil liberties as an instrument to obtain certain social objectives. It is not the Bill of Rights that charges the ACLU, but notions of human self-realization, community, and equality, values that are evidently denied under a market economy.

Law finds it regrettable that "the public/private distinction persists in constitutional doctrine," holding that in the real world "the distinction between public and private is not sharp; it may indeed have no coherent meaning."[117] This is, of course, a reflection of the atomistic hue in Law's thinking, and it represents the traditional politics of the left as well: war on everything that is private and bring it under the aegis of the state. And the reason that this must be done is to advance the goal of equality-as-community, the perennial ideological signature of radical politics.

For Law, there is no private action that exists *sui generis*, whether it be in the form of an activity, exchange, relationship, or institution. All that is private is *granted* by the state.[118] "Corporations," she believes, "are the creation of the state," adding that it was the government that decided "to leave profitable activities to private enterprise."[119] Now, she insists, it is time to start thinking about "democratic control of accumulation,"[120] a concept she does not define but that is suggestive of her socialist vision of economic life. "Because individual material support is a prerequisite to the exercise of all rights," Law argues, "civil libertarian values support individual claims against the state for subsistence."[121]

What is striking about Law's position is that she is not even content to settle for a right to work. No, it is the right to subsistence that she wants to establish. Indeed, she speaks alternatively about how the state must "assure individual economic support" or provide "opportunities for work."[122] And with regard to work, she does not mean the provision of just any job. Concurring with Norman Dorsen, Law maintains that a "fundamental" right that should be made available to all Americans is "the right to useful work at a decent wage."[123] She gives us no idea as to what might constitute useless work and similarly offers no clue as to what an indecent wage might be.

Law also believes that in addition to financing the cost of subsistence, government should pay for day care and health care as well (only the upper class, she contends, can presently obtain these services for themselves).[124] She recommends that her plan be financed through changes in the tax law (close the loopholes) and from cuts in military spending. Law contends that "our commitment to militarism," by which she means the Defense Department budget, "precludes economic justice."[125] She is concerned, however, that the social movement necessary to achieve these ends may not materialize, finding it "distressing" that there are "few signs of rebellion" among the public.[126]

Law's essay has had a significant impact on ACLU activists. Indeed, in 1985 the Biennial passed the following resolution (vetoed by the national board): "The ACLU recognizes that constitutional guarantees of equal protection and due process are meaningless when people are without sufficient money to provide themselves with a minimum standard of living. Recognizing that what is needed is money, the ACLU calls on the federal government to enact laws guaranteeing every individual a minimum standard of living as a matter of constitutional right."[127] Notice that once again the goal is a right to a guaranteed income, not a right to work.

It is clear that most ACLU activists are committed to entering the economic arena, but the question of means has not yet been resolved. There are those, like Sylvia Law[128] and the contributors to "Liberty At Work,"[129] who favor the legislative track. There are others who want to make economic entitlements a constitutional issue, though their argument appears to be losing ground. The 1989 Biennial Conference voted down a resolution similar to the one that passed in 1985.[130] It may be that as a result of all the persons appointed to the federal bench under Presidents Reagan and Bush, the ACLU sees few options. In any event, to a large extent what official ACLU policy says may not be as important as the work that is already being done in the affiliates and by those in the national office responsible for the selection of cases.

The actual text of panel discussions on economic rights offers a glimpse into ACLU thinking not found in its policy guide.[131] What is sometimes revealed is an agenda, and the means to affect it, that is less than principled. For instance, ACLU operatives freely admit that they have "spent hours" trying to "find a hook" by which they could justify their political objectives. The "hook" they are looking for, of course, is a constitutional pretext for pursuing their politics. Here are a few documented example's of how it works.

In the 1980s, Boston adopted a housing program that targeted both the working poor and the nonworking poor. For every nonworking family that was accommodated, the program allotted two places for working families. The theory behind this idea was that working families can be expected to take better care of their quarters than their nonworking counterparts, hence the greater likelihood of public support for the program. Though there are good sociological reasons to buttress this idea, some might reasonably question its veracity. Even if granted that such a policy is debatable, it is hard to see how it can seriously be viewed as a constitutional matter, and on first reflection, that is the way the ACLU saw it as well. Then the search for a "hook" began.

When the program was announced ACLU activists scheduled a meeting with the Greater Boston Legal Services Corporation to map out a strategy for opposing the housing venture. After "spending hours" trying to "find a hook," it was finally agreed upon that the housing policy would have a disproportionate impact on minorities (they had the highest unemployment rate in Boston) and single-parent families headed by women. The response by ACLU attorney Laura B. Monroe said it all: "So you've got sex and race and you're in, you're into ACLU territory and now we were able to get involved."[132] So in the end, it may not really matter what the national board says, as long as there are always activists like Monroe ready to find a "hook."

Sometimes even the most creative ACLU activist has a hard time "finding a hook" in the United States Constitution. On occasions like these, the most common practice is to scour the state constitutions in hopes of finding a hook in some ambiguously worded clause like "the welfare of the people." This is what Robert Hayes, a lawyer for the homeless, did to establish shelter rights for his clients; he used the New York State Constitution to his advantage, finding more expansive protection there than in the federal Constitution. When an ACLU attorney from Massachusetts read about Hayes' strategy, she repaired to her state's Constitution, looking, she said, "for a hook." To her chagrin, she was unable to find one. "We struggle constantly to still find a hook," she said, adding, "we try desperately to find a hook."[133]

Apparently, not everyone is equally gifted in their hook finding abilities. There are some, in fact, who think it needless even to bother with state constitutions, maintaining that there is enough slack in the Fourteenth Amendment to handle any political issue. "The due process handle can be used much more creatively in this area than we tend to use it—whatever the existing or nonexisting laws." This is how some in the ACLU see things, contending, for example, that whenever the homeless occupy a government-funded vacant building there is a due process violation. And what exactly is the source of the violation? The condition constitutes "an arbitrary risking of life by the government." As one activist conceded, "it's not all that hard to find a hook on many of these issues."[134] True enough. All it takes is a little imagination and a determination to make an end-run around the legislative process.

Some ACLU operatives come right out and say that the Constitution can mean anything we want it to mean. Like their deconstructionist colleagues in the humanities, they believe that it is the contemporary reader, and not a deceased author, who should properly determine the meaning of a text. It was with this frame of mind that an ACLU activist and constitutional law professor was able to say that "everything that we know about constitutional interpretation in 200 years worth proves that there is virtually nothing that cannot be written into that Constitution." She then explained that one of her favorite classroom exercises is to "dare" her students to show that the Constitution is a capitalist document. After all attempts fail, "then I show them, starting with TVA, the way you can build a socialist society here without changing anything in the Constitution at all."[135]

Ramona Ripston is one ACLU official who sees much of the bickering over what "hook" to use, and whether the national board ought to be more "progressive," as simply passè. Under the tutelage of Ms. Ripston, the Southern California affiliate has become the vanguard of the economic rights movement within the ACLU. Since the late 1970s, it has been affiliate policy to declare not only that "everyone has a right to a job" but that "everyone is entitled to a decent standard of living" as well.[136] It matters little that the high court decided in 1947 that there was no *ipso facto* constitutional right to work for the government, much less a right to "a decent standard of living."[137] What matters is that such rights are being proclaimed.

Ms. Ripston says candidly that she is "having difficulty getting it through to the ACLU" that it would be wise for the national organization to fall in line with her affiliate's position. It may be that the New York office is slow to respond, but this certainly has not deterred Ms. Ripston. She gets away with her policies not because of a supposed policy of affiliate autonomy (the national office would never remain passive if an affiliate head were to proclaim a pro-life position on abortion) but because her affiliate's ideas on economic rights are no longer outside the mainstream of Unionomics.

Given Ms. Ripston's vision of what constitutes economic justice, it was only to be expected that in the aftermath of the Los Angeles riot of

1992, the Southern California affiliate would file suit in federal court to compel the U.S. Department of Agriculture to provide emergency short-term food relief for those affected by the riot. Officials from the USDA had investigated the area and concluded that under the terms of the law, conditions were such that emergency food stamps were not warranted.[138] Now from a strictly humanitarian perspective, it is easy to side with the ACLU. But what any of this has to do with an organization that is supposedly in the business of protecting the rights of the individual from government abuse is not at all clear. If the ACLU had evidence that the law was not being followed because of racism, then filing suit would have been appropriate. But it didn't. The point is, we don't look to the United Way to defend freedom of speech, so why does the ACLU think it necessary to monitor the distribution of food stamps? The answer provided here, of course, is that the ACLU is more interested in social and economic equality than it is civil liberties, which is precisely why it does what it does.

Given the ACLU's long list of policies and lawsuits filed in behalf of social engineering, it is remarkable that Samuel Walker continues to claim that the ACLU can be distinguished from mainstream liberals by its "skepticism of government power and a willingness to challenge extensions of that power justified in the name of social betterment."[139] In fact, there is hardly an egalitarian program that the ACLU has not supported. Its defense of comparable worth, affirmative action, busing, scatter-site housing, government policing of the private workplace, and entitlements programs are not the kinds of positions associated with organizations skeptical of government power.

More important is the ACLU's atomistic vision of liberty. The need for mediating institutions that are relatively free of the reach of government is not a priority for the ACLU. In most instances, it would rather see the state sit in judgment and render an outcome consistent with egalitarian principles before it would defend the autonomy of private associations. Similarly, the Union's entitlement approach to economic rights, complete with an aversion to property rights, makes dubious any statement regarding its alleged "skepticism of government power." No, what the ACLU wants more than anything else is leveling, and most especially economic and moral leveling. That is why it takes the positions it does, and that is why so much of its work bears little relationship to the concerns of those who wrote and ratified the Bill of Rights.

Notes

1. Mary Ann Glendon, *Rights Talk*, (New York: Free Press, 1991), 104.
2. Aaron Wildavsky, *The Rise of Radical Egalitarianism* (Washington, D.C.: American University Press, 1991), 11.
3. *Grove City College v. Bell*, 465 U.S. 555 (1984).
4. Rabkin made his comment in a book review of Walker's *In Defense of American Liberties*. It appeared in the winter 1991 edition of *Constitutional Commentary*, p. 305.
5. Policy #45, "Private Facilities for Public Meetings."
6. William A. Donohue, *The Politics of the American Civil Liberties Union* (New Brunswick, New Jersey: Transaction Press, 1985), 228.
7. "Affiliate Notes," *Civil Liberties*, Winter 1990-91, p. 14.
8. Policy #303, "Private Organizations."
9. Quoted by Rita Delfiner, "St. Pat's Parade Heads for Court," *New York Post*, January 25, 1992, p. 7.
10. Quoted by Michael deCourcy Hinds, "In Tests of Who Can Join, Scouts Confront Identity," *New York Times*, June 23, 1991, pp. 1, 12.
11. Decter's comment was a reply to Glasser's response to her article, "The ACLU's Next Target," *National Review*, June 24, 1991, pp. 29-39. The exchange of letters occurred in the August 12 edition of the magazine, p. 4.
12. Annual Report for 1920, p. 4.
13. Ibid., p. 18.
14. Annual Report #3, p. 23.
15. Cletus Daniel, *The ACLU and the Wagner Act* (Ithaca, New York: Cornell University, New York State School of Industrial and Labor Relations, 1980), 73.
16. Roger Baldwin, "Freedom in the U.S.A. and the U.S.S.R.," *Soviet Russia Today*, September 1934, p. 11.
17. Quoted by Daniel, *The ACLU and the Wagner Act*, 129-30.
18. Ibid.
19. See Donohue, *The Politics of the American Civil Liberties Union*, 47-50, for a discussion of this matter.
20. David Kelley, "Those Card Carriers: Civil Liberties, Argues the ACLU, Don't Include Economic Freedom," *Barron's*, October 17, 1988, p. 9.
21. Annual Report #31, p. 100.
22. Glasser registered his comments in a book review of David Ewing's *Freedom Inside the Organization*. See "Civil Liberties in the Private Sector," *Social Policy*, March/April 1978, pp. 58-60.
23. Quoted in "Rights in Conflict," *Civil Liberties*, Summer 1985, p. 1.
24. See the tape of the session on "Poverty and Civil Liberties" that took place at the 1985 Biennial Conference.
25. See the discussion on drug testing in the workplace that appeared in the Spring 1986 edition of *Civil Liberties*, p. 6.
26. Annual Report for 1986-87, p. 29.
27. Ibid.
28. The Moyers interview was a part of the PBS series "In Search of the Constitution." The portion alluded to is transcribed in the Summer 1987 edition of *Civil Liberties*, p. 3.
29. ACLU Public Policy Report, "Liberty at Work: Expanding the Rights of Employees in America," 1988, p. 3.

30. Lewis L. Maltby, "Future Issues: Genetic Testing," in the ACLU Report "Liberty at Work," p. 38.
31. Policy #320a, "Genetic Testing in the Workplace."
32. Solicitation letter sent by Ira Glasser in March 1988, p. 3.
33. Jacob Sullum, "Secrets for Sale: Do Strangers With Computers Know Too Much About You?" *Reason*, April 1992, p. 33.
34. Karen B. Ringen, "Privacy: Electronic Monitoring," in "Liberty At Work," pp. 9-11.
35. Judy Crockett Goldberg, "Privacy: Polygraphs," in "Liberty At Work," p. 14.
36. Ibid.
37. Policy #271b, "Smoking."
38. Policy #55a, "Privacy Rights of Private Sector Employees."
39. Ibid.
40. Lewis L. Maltby and John Rosenthal, "Lifestyle Discrimination Threatens Employees' Private Lives," *Civil Liberties*, Spring/Summer 1991, p. 8.
41. Lewis Maltby, "Due Process: An Unjust Workplace," in "Liberty At Work," p. 18.
42. Loren Siegel, "ACLU Launches New Task Force On Rights in the Workplace," *Civil Liberties*, Spring 1989, p. 3.
43. Maltby, "Due Process: An Unjust Workplace," in "Liberty At Work," p. 17.
44. Ibid., p. 19.
45. Ibid.
46. Policy #55, "Due Process Rights of Private Employees."
47. Maltby, "Conclusion: Free Enterprise and Workers' Rights," in "Liberty At Work," p. 45.
48. Charles Oliver, "The First Shall Be Last?" *Reason*, October 1990, p. 27.
49. Ira Glasser, "How Long, America?" *Civil Liberties*, Summer 1989, p. 10.
50. Policy #324b "Self-Governance for the District of Columbia."
51. Laughlin McDonald, "High Court Will Rule On Free and Fair Judgeship Elections," *Civil Liberties*, Spring/Summer 1991, p. 4.
52. "Republican Hispanics, Keep Out," *Wall Street Journal*, August 7, 1990, p. A16.
53. Policy #312a, "English-Only Amendment or Legislation."
54. Policy #312b, "Race Discrimination."
55. This was the assessment of Deidre S. Janney, executive director of the Mississippi Civil Liberties Union. See Frances Frank Marcus, "Medical Waste Divides Mississippi Cities," *New York Times*, June 24, 1992, p. A13.
56. Peter Kerr, "Florio Appoints New Head of State Police," *New York Times*, February 6, 1990, pp. B1, B6.
57. Quoted by Katherine Dalton, "ACLU Watch," *Chronicles*, June 1989, p. 18.
58. "Affiliate Notes," *Civil Liberties*, Spring 1989, p. 10.
59. Isabelle Katz Pinzler, "Awards Favor Boys, Court Rules," *Civil Liberties*, Winter 1989, p. 6.
60. *U.S. v. Commonwealth of Virginia*, 766 F.Supp 1407 (1991).
61. *U.S. v. Commonwealth of Virginia*, 976 F.2d 890 (1992).
62. Douglas W. Kmiec, "Single-Sex Schools Aren't Unconstitutional," *Wall Street Journal*, October 14, 1992, p. A17.
63. Policy #301, "Housing Discrimination."
64. Policy #301, "Housing Discrimination," as revised in October 1989.
65. Policy #301, "Housing Discrimination," as first passed in 1959, remaining extant until 1989.
66. Policy #301, "Housing Discrimination," passed January 23-24, 1988.
67. Policy #301, "Housing Discrimination," passed June 14, 1989.

68. For a good discussion of Starrett City's experiment, see Howard Husock, "Subsidizing Discrimination at Starrett City," *City Journal*, Winter 1992, pp. 48-53.
69. *Missouri v. Jenkins*, 490 U.S. 1034 (1990).
70. Quoted by Stephen Wermiel, "Test of Power: Can a Federal Judge Raise Property Taxes?" *Wall Street Journal*, October 2, 1989, pp. 1, 9.
71. See Victor Bolden, "The Question Is Whether Court Values Equality Goals—And If So, How Much?" *Civil Liberties*, Spring 1990, p. 13.
72. Policy #317, "Rights of Persons with Disabilities."
73. Policy #315, "Employment and Education."
74. "The Court Refuses to Play Follow the Leader . . . so far," *Civil Liberties*, Summer 1987, p. 6.
75. See Susan Blank, "Women Firefighters: Can They Do the Job?" *Civil Liberties*, Summer 1984, pp. 7-8.
76. Deborah A. Ellis, "Insurance Stereotyping Robs Women—and Men," *Civil Liberties*, Summer 1989, p. 7.
77. Daniel Jussim, "Girls in High School Sports Gain Equality with Boys," *Civil Liberties*, Winter 1985, p. 10.
78. Victor Bolden, "The Question Is Whether Court Values Equality Goals—And If So, How Much?" *Civil Liberties*, Spring 1990, p. 13.
79. Policy #25, "Fairness Doctrine."
80. *Wards Cove v. Antonio*, 109 S.Ct. 2115 (1989).
81. See the ACLU Report, "In Contempt of Congress and the Courts: The Reagan Civil Rights Record," February 27, 1984, p. 7.
82. Quoted by Daniel J. Popeo, *Not OUR America: The ACLU Exposed!* (Washington, D.C.: Washington Legal Foundation, 1989), 71.
83. See Victor Bolden, "The Question Is Whether Court Values Equality Goals—And If So, How Much?" and Sherrille Ismail, "Spotlight on Crime, Choice and Civil Rights," in *Civil Liberties*, Spring 1990, pp. 12-13.
84. Policy #522a, "Organizational Policy on Access for People With Disabilities."
85. Policy #317, "Rights of Persons with Disabilities."
86. Donohue, *The Politics of the American Civil Liberties Union*, 80.
87. David Burnham, "Civil Liberties Group Embroiled in Hiring Dispute," *New York Times*, January 24, 1985, p. A19.
88. Quoted by Bill Blum and Gina Lobaco, "Fighting Words at the ACLU," *California Lawyer*, February 1990, p. 45.
89. Quoted by Charles Oliver, "The First Shall Be Last?" p. 24. On the previous page mention is made of the absence of Asians and Arabs on the board.
90. Policy #315, section b, "Employment and Education."
91. Isabelle Katz Pinzler, "Comparable Worth is the Next Step Toward Full Equality," *Civil Liberties*, Spring 1986, p. 9.
92. Quoted by Ken Wells, "ACLU Chief in Utah Makes Liberal Waves in Sea of Conservatism," *Wall Street Journal*, December 10, 1986, p. 1.
93. Frances Fox Piven and Richard Cloward, *Regulating the Poor* (New York: Vintage Books, 1971), p. 347.
94. Policy #318, "Poverty and Civil Liberties."
95. Piven, along with three other leftists, made this comment in a letter to the editor, *Nation*, August 2/9 1986, p. 82.
96. Susan Blank, "The Homeless: ACLU Responds to the Emergency," *Civil Liberties*, Winter 1986, p. 3.

97. See "Setbacks for the ACLU," *Civil Liberties Alert*, November 1988, p. 11, and Sherrille Ismail, "Victories, Victories: In Congress" *Civil Liberties*, Spring/Summer 1988, p. 3.
98. Ted Gest, "The Aging Bulldog of Civil Liberties," *U.S. News and World Report*, February 18, 1991, p. 57.
99. "Affiliate Notes," *Civil Liberties*, Spring/Summer 1991, p. 14.
100. Quoted by Maya Wiley, "ACLU Tackles Abuse of Welfare Recipients," *Civil Liberties*, Winter 1991-92, p. 8.
101. The best discussion of this issue is Bernard H. Siegan, *Economic Liberties and the Constitution* (Chicago: University of Chicago Press, 1980).
102. Annual Report #42, p. 64.
103. Norman Dorsen, ed., *The Rights of Americans XV* (New York: Pantheon Books, 1971.
104. Policy #318, "Poverty and Civil Liberties."
105. Ibid.
106. See my book *The Politics of the ACLU*, chapter two. In conversations I have had with many former ACLU members over the past several years, many expressed despair over the ACLU's increasing politicization.
107. This information was taken from a tape of the 1985 Biennial Conference (session on Poverty and Civil Liberties). Because there is no transrcipt of the proceedings, and because the names of all the participants either were not announced or were occasionally inaudible, it was not possible to reveal the identity of all the persons quoted in the remainder of this chapter.
108. Ibid.
109. Policy #318, "Poverty and Civil Liberties."
110. Burt Neuborne, "The ACLU and Poverty," *Civil Liberties*, June 1983, p. 5.
111. Interview with John Shattuck, "The Main Civil Liberty: A Right Not to Starve," *New York Times*, July 18, 1984, p. A14.
112. Sylvia A. Law, "Economic Justice," in Norman Dorsen, ed., *Our Endangered Rights* (New York: Pantheon Books, 1984).
113. Ibid., 136.
114. Ibid., 147.
115. Ibid., 148.
116. Ibid., 135.
117. Ibid., 146-47.
118. Ibid., 147.
119. Ibid., 149.
120. Ibid., 151.
121. Ibid., 154.
122. Ibid., 155.
123. Ibid., 135.
124. Ibid., 149.
125. Ibid.
126. Ibid., 144.
127. The Resolution was passed at the 1985 Biennial Conference.
128. Law, "Economic Justice," 155.
129. See Lewis Maltby, "Conclusion," in the ACLU Report "Liberty At Work," p. 45.
130. See John N. Rosenthal, "Biennial, Reitman's Last, Rated a Big Success," *Civil Liberties*, Summer 1989, p. 3.

131. Tapes of various Biennial conferences can be purchased. While what is said is technically part of a public discussion of the issues, the milieu is conducive to an open dialogue, thus allowing for a more revealing look at what really motivates ACLU activists.

132. Tape of the 1985 Biennial Conference session on "Poverty and Civil Liberties."

133. Ibid.

134. Ibid.

135. Ibid.

136. Ibid.

137. *United Public Workers v. Mitchell*, 330 U.S. 75 (1947).

138. Christopher J. Herrera, "ACLU Goes To Court To Get Food For L.A. Riot Victims," *Civil Liberties*, Summer-Fall 1992, p. 6.

139. Samuel Walker, *In Defense of American Liberties* (New York: Oxford University Press, 1990), 5.

PART II

The Public Weal

5

Freedom of Expression

The Purpose of Free Speech

It is often said that no freedom is more important than freedom of expression, and that is why the Framers chose to list it in the First Amendment. This is wrong on three counts. The first freedom is freedom of conscience, a liberty inseparable from freedom of religion; victims of religious persecution and mindcontrol—both staples of totalitarian rule—know this better than anyone. Mistake number two is simply a matter of bad history: the First Amendment was initially chosen as the Third but was elevated to the First after the first two amendments failed to achieve ratification by the states. Perhaps the most important mistake is the reference to freedom of expression. There is no mention of such a right in the First Amendment or anywhere else in the Constitution: the First Amendment guarantees freedom of speech, meaning, it is generally conceded, the freedom to engage in political discourse.

On occasion, the ACLU has recognized the limited purpose of the First Amendment, as envisioned by the Framers. In 1982, the board of directors stated that "the purpose of free speech, particularly speech expressing a minority view, is to help in the formation of a wise decision by a majority."[1] Speech, then, is functional to the ends of good government, and that is why it is deserving of protection from those who would stifle it. This view, however, is more scorned than praised these days, and in its place has come the expansive doctrine of freedom of expression. Under this new understanding of the First Amendment, there is hardly a form of expression—from tobacco advertisement to nude dancing—that the ACLU isn't willing to defend, regardless of its relationship to the process of self-government.[2]

Norman Dorsen, past president of the ACLU, provides good insight into the thinking of civil libertarians on the meaning of the First Amendment. It is Dorsen's belief that there are four purposes to freedom of speech. He lists as fourth the goal of advancing knowledge and revealing truth. No problem there, nor with his third choice, namely the "checking value" of free speech against possible government abuse. It is with the ordering of Dorsen's first two choices that questions can be raised: he says the first purpose of freedom of speech is "individual fulfillment through self-expression" and the second purpose is "upholding the concept of democratic self-government," that is, the commitment to robust political discourse.[3]

What Dorsen lists as a secondary purpose of free speech has typically been viewed as its primary purpose, and what he lists as primary has typically not been mentioned at all. More to the point, "individual fulfillment through self-expression" is the lingo of self-actualization therapists—straight out of the human potential movement—and not constitutional law professors. Dorsen's vision of liberty is more than novel, it has virtually nothing to do with the stated purpose of the First Amendment as understood by the Framers. That individuals could be free even if they lacked fulfillment in their personal lives was well understood by the Framers, and that is why they spoke about the pursuit of happiness, not its fulfillment.

It is striking that Dorsen sees freedom of speech as servicing the needs of individuals more than society. This is exactly what an atomistic conception of liberty does: it gives priority to individual pursuits over the social interest in self-government. Cast this way, it is not hard to understand why civil libertarians are typically so indifferent to issues affecting the common good. The way they see liberty, if the individual attains a measure of uninhibited self-expression, that's what really counts. The strain on the social fabric might be acknowledged, but that is all. And any damage done to social cohesion, or for that matter to the security of the nation, is quickly dismissed as the price one pays for liberty.

Doctrinaire though the ACLU is on the First Amendment, it nonetheless recognizes certain exceptions to freedom of speech. For example, the Union does not defend the wrongful appropriation of person's name,[4] false advertisement, or resistance to full and truthful disclosure of finances.[5] Also out-of-bounds is the right of newspapers to print sex-specific ads; the Union sued the *Pittsburgh Press* in a landmark case to stop "Girl/Friday" types of ads.[6] The ACLU supports anti-blockbusting statutes as well, that is, it supports laws that prohibit "false and deceptive statements" regarding the changing racial composition of a neighborhood.[7] The Union finds no problem with the "fairness doctrine," the legal requirement that broadcasters afford a "reasonable opportunity" for contrasting viewpoints to be heard.[8] Nor does it oppose laws that prohibit speech to captive audiences.[9] Support for cloture, the rule that limits Congressional debate, is another instance of the ACLU's willingness to endorse exceptions to freedom of expression.[10]

These examples to the contrary, the ACLU naturally inclines toward the most latitudinal interpretation of the First Amendment to be found anywhere. In fairness to the Union, it is only right that an organization dedicated to civil liberties should give priority to freedom of expression. But that is not the issue. The issue is whether liberty is best advanced when individual rights are pushed to extremes. The reason that the ACLU's record is outside the mainstream of constitutional thought has much to do with its outright rejection of a social conception of liberty. It appreciates little in the way of "balancing," something most constitutional experts see as vital and natural. And without a willingness to balance individual rights and the public weal, the prospects for liberty are seriously impaired.

National Security

Most constitutional scholars, and most Supreme Court decisions, have wrestled with the delicate issues involved when civil liberties conflict with national security. To be sure, the ACLU understands the danger of tipping the scales too heavily in favor of national security. But it does not seem to recognize the reverse danger. Consider the following, taken from the testimony of Morton Halperin, who at that time was director of the Washington Office of the ACLU, before the Senate Select Committee on Intelligence, July 12, 1990: "The ACLU is deeply troubled by the notion that there is a national security exception to the Fourth Amendment or any part of the Bill of Rights. We regard those rights as fundamental and absolute."[11]

Now contrast Halperin's vision of liberty with that of Jefferson's: "A strict observance of the written laws is doubtless *one* of the high duties of a good citizen, but it is not *the highest*. The laws of necessity, of self-preservation, of saving our country when in danger, are of higher obligation. To lose our country by a scrupulous adherence to written law, would be to lose the law itself, with life, liberty, property and all those who are enjoying them with us: thus absurdly sacrificing the end to the means."[12]

There is no doubting the ACLU's concern that there are untrustworthy public officials who will invoke national security as a cloak to cover their own wrongdoings; the pages of history are full of them. But does that mean that the only proper response is to make absolute the Bill of Rights, even in those clear-cut instances when the nation's viability is seriously called into question? It is fair to say that most who have studied the question would prefer to side with Jefferson on this matter.

The Pentagon Papers case shows how extremist the ACLU can be. In that suit, the Supreme Court ruled against the efforts of the Nixon Administration to suppress documents that were a veritable history of U.S. involvement in the Vietnam War. The ACLU, which filed an amicus, was happy with the immediate outcome—the newspapers could run copies of the Pentagon Papers—but was less than pleased with the high court's reasoning. The Union was disturbed that the Supreme Court gave life to the idea that the president and the Congress had a right to restrain the press in bona fide instances of national security. It wanted nothing less than an absolute ban on prior restraint. Alexander Bickel, the brilliant constitutional scholar who argued the case against the government, criticized the unreasonableness of the ACLU stand. He accused the Union of being too ideological, labeling the absolutist position "foolish to the point of being almost unprofessional." Like most students of the Constitution, Bickel was generally opposed to prior restraint but nonetheless conceded that there may be times when not to invoke prior restraint may be disastrous to the well-being of the republic. This is something the ACLU has not acknowledged and will not acknowledge.[13]

There was a time, mostly in the 1940s and 1950s, when the ACLU was quite serious about balancing the need for civil liberties with the interests of national security. Indeed, up until the 1990s, the ACLU's policies on security clearances for employees were fairly reasonable. In 1957, the board adopted a policy that said it was legitimate to inquire into a person's political behavior when application for private employment in sensitive security positions was being made.[14] In 1966, the board gave the okay to inquiries regarding past or present affiliations when a sensitive position in government was being sought.[15] Both policies remained on the books until 1990, when they were excised.

The new standard says that a person's political affiliations should not be an area of investigation for employment in either the private or public sector, regardless of how sensitive the nature of the job.[16] To show how determined the ACLU is on this issue, it was still not satisfied when in 1991 the government dropped questions about affiliation with the Communist party on its Standard Form 86. The Union was upset because of inclusion of questions designed to uncover whether the applicant believed, or in any way participated in organizations that believed, in the overthrow of the government.[17] The logic that argues that only democrats can be expected to uphold a democracy seems not to be accepted by the ACLU.

What to do about the enemies of democracy functioning within its midst is another serious issue. It is acknowledged by most that freedom of expression and national security interests routinely collide when intelligence agencies make inquiries into the allegiances and behavior of extremist political organizations. One of the more celebrated cases in recent times was the FBI's investigation of the Committee in Solidarity with the People of El Salvador (CISPES).

CISPES was formed in 1980 as a result of an organized tour by Farid Handal, an agent for the Salvadoran guerrilla group FMLN (Faribundo Marti National Liberation Front). Handal, brother of Salvadoran Communist leader Shafik Handal, wasted no time garnering assistance from a host of far-leftist groups, including the Cuban Mission to the U.N., the Institute for Policy Studies, and the Central Committee of the Communist Party, USA. It didn't take long before the U.S. Peace Council (the American affiliate of the World Peace Council, formerly a well-known Soviet front group) became a member of the CISPES steering committee.

Now it must be conceded that there are organizations that take an anti-intelligence stance on the basis of a principled objection to government surveillance. But when the network of associations resemble those of CISPES, it is not unreasonable to think that there may be other motives involved. Was it working illegally to subvert U.S. foreign policy by covertly assisting terrorist organizations? After all, it wouldn't be the first time that foreign forces had targeted domestic groups to do their bidding. These were the kinds of concerns that some journalists began to have about CISPES. So did the FBI.[18]

The FBI conducted two investigations of CISPES. The first, begun in September 1981, tried to ascertain whether CISPES was violating the Foreign Agents Registration Act by failing to register as an agent of a foreign entity, namely the FMLN. After six months, the Bureau concluded its investigation without finding CISPES at fault. Just over a year later, a second investigation was triggered, this time directed at the issue of international support for terrorism. Twenty-seven months of investigatory work resulted in another "not guilty" verdict. To the ACLU, and to many organizations generally associated with opposition to intelligence work, the CISPES investigations were not only unjustified, they represented a disrespect for the First Amendment right of freedom of expression. But this is not as clear as the ACLU would have it.

It is true that from the beginning, the FBI knew that "the great majority" of CISPES members did not support violence or crime and that "many" members were unaware that CISPES officials may have been supporting terrorism.[19] But if some were guilty, especially those at the top, then that was not something that could be ignored. It is the job of the FBI to investigate. Not all investigations turn up wrongdoing. The central issue is whether there was enough reason to launch an investigation of CISPES in the first place. Even Morton Halperin, who objected to the second investigation, acknowledged that there may have been a sufficient basis to conduct an "initial limited investigation" of CISPES.[20] In any event, no one was rounded up or subjected to third-degree measures. Indeed, the initial FBI instructions warned field agents that "this investigation is not concerned with the exercise of rights guaranteed by the United States Constitution."[21] And in an Interim Report, FBI Headquarters directed that "should it be determined the group [CISPES] was not engaged in support of terrorism, the investigation should immediately be closed."[22]

The CISPES case would hardly be worth mentioning were it not for the ACLU's proposed reforms of the FBI. Though the ACLU did not charge the FBI with wrongdoing (disputes over judgment are not synonymous with charges of illegality), it nevertheless took the occasion to propose a comprehensive statutory FBI charter, complete with suggestions as to its content. At present, FBI Guidelines authorize investigations of international terrorism, defining an "international terrorist" as "an individual or group that knowingly engages in international terrorism or activities." The ACLU objects to the investigation of groups on the basis that not all members may be suspected of breaking the law.[23] But if some have been kept in the dark, intentionally or as a result of self-deception, it surely counts for something that the leaders, and the organization's resources, might be contributing to terrorism. And if it counts for something, shouldn't it count for the FBI?

On what grounds, then, should the FBI investigate? Must it await violence? Apparently so. "The ACLU recommends the enactment of a statute that authorizes 'criminal intelligence investigations' only where two or more persons are engaged in a pattern of activities for the purpose of furthering political or social goals wholly or in part through activities that involve force or violence and a violation of the federal criminal law." Even this is not fully satisfactory to the ACLU. It maintains that "the FBI may not infiltrate someone into a leadership or decision making capacity without disclosing that person's identity to the appropriate official of the organization."[24] The effect of the ACLU's position, however, would be to cripple the FBI from infiltrating suspected terrorist organizations. If that is its goal, then it should say so explicitly. If not, then the ACLU needs to say how it expects the FBI to do its job while living with strictures like these.

If there is one organization that would like to see the ACLU's ideas implemented, it is the Palestine Liberation Organization (PLO). No stranger to the ACLU, or to terrorism, the PLO was ordered at the end of 1987 to close its offices in New York and Washington. The ACLU quickly protested, citing freedom of speech violations. But to those who crafted the legislation (it was actually a rider to the State Department Authorization Bill), the ordered shutdown sought to affect the conduct, not the speech, of the PLO. What drove the decision were the killing of Leon Klinghoffer on the hijacked Achille Lauro and the unrelenting episodes of violence against other noncombatants. When PLO henchman Abu Mustafa called for a war against the United States as a form of retaliation against the statute, he was acting in the grand tradition of the PLO. The law, it should be noted, never barred an American citizen from joining the PLO or from receiving any of its literature. It was aimed at stopping citizens from acting as paid agents of the PLO in the United States and at shutting down its offices.

To Morton Halperin, however, closing the offices of the PLO was seen as a "grave threat" to the First Amendment, proving that "once again we are permitting claims of national security to erode our freedoms."[25]

Legal analyst Bruce Fein put it differently: "Closing PLO offices no more violates the First Amendment than does excluding Austrian President Kurt Waldheim from the United States under immigration laws because of past associations with Nazis in the persecution of Jews and Yugoslav partisans."[26] In the end, a federal district court allowed the PLO offices to remain open, though the decision turned on grounds other than the First Amendment grounds the ACLU wanted (for example, the terms of the U.S.-U.N. Headquarters Agreement). In fact, with respect to the First Amendment challenge, the court refused to enjoin the Justice Department from enforcing the law authorizing the closing of the PLO's offices.[27]

At about the same time the ACLU was defending the PLO, it was litigating the case of Samuel Loring Morison, a former naval intelligence analyst charged with espionage and theft of government property. Morison was charged and convicted of giving three photographs, taken by satellite and classified as secret, to the British publication *Jane's Defence Weekly*. He was also found guilty of keeping secret military documents pertaining to the Soviet Union in his home. The ACLU maintained that the general espionage statute and theft of government property statute were not intended "to apply to the provision of information to the press."[28] Besides the issue of the ACLU's selective interest in original intent, there is the matter of treating Morison's actions as just another example of a government leak, something the ACLU tried hard to do ("framing leakers as spies").[29] That spies can also be leakers seems not to be acknowledged.

The clash between national security and civil liberties is nowhere more apparent than in wartime. Unusual responses are called for during times of war, oftentimes requiring a suspension of certain liberties. To be sure, war gives governments, including the democracies, opportunities for abuse, and that is why organizations like the ACLU are right to watch for them. But context in this area, more than in others, matters greatly. There is not an equal playing field when a war breaks out between the democracies and the dictatorships, and that is why what might pass as unexceptional in the latter (for example, censorship) is greeted with alarm in the former. The central dilemma for the democracies is how best to win a war without unduly burdening civil liberties in the process.

Owing to its absolutist, and therefore atomistic, perception of freedom, the ACLU worries about one side of the ledger only: civil liberties. This in not something new. The ACLU grew out of an organized effort to protest U.S. involvement in World War I.[30] Therefore, its anger and lawsuits directed at more recent U.S. initiatives in Grenada, Libya, Panama, and the Gulf are in keeping with its historical interest in challenging U.S. wartime policies (the exception being Union support for World War II). ACLU policies passed prior to the Persian Gulf war are particularly noteworthy, as they all but ensured that there would be much to litigate about when the United States sought to stem Iraqi aggression.

In support of a lawsuit brought by the radical Center for Constitutional Rights, the ACLU charged that the Pentagon's press restrictions on coverage of the war in the Persian Gulf violated the First Amendment. In another case, the Union itself brought suit against the Pentagon's decision to close Dover Air Force Base to the press when bodies were being returned.[31] These actions reflect, in part, the new absolutism of the ACLU's approach to free speech during wartime.

In 1984, the ACLU added a new policy on the rights of the media during wartime, one that was updated just four years later. In 1984, the Union called for the government to allow the media access to combat zones and combat personnel once the fighting began.[32] In 1988, stronger language was added: "The government has an *absolute* obligation not to impede the media's use of its own resources." (My emphasis.) In fact, the ACLU was now calling on the government to "provide the [press] pool with transportation to the scene of any military operation, so that the press can witness and report hostilities from the onset." Not satisfied, the ACLU demanded that the press pool "should be as large and diverse as possible, including ideological diversity." But curiously omitted from the revised policy is the statement that "the government may appropriately require members of the press to assume the risk of death or injury from normal combat operations."[33]

Perhaps the most revealing commentary on the ACLU's new posture on national security was the action the board of directors took at its October 1989 meeting: It dropped section (a) from its policy entitled "Wartime Sedition Act." From 1942 to 1989, the ACLU flatly stated that it would not participate (save for fundamental due process violations) in the defense of any person believed to be "cooperating with or acting on behalf of the enemy." This policy was based on the recognition that "our military enemies are now using techniques of propaganda which may involve an attempt to pervert the Bill of Rights to serve the enemy rather than the people of the United States." In making its determination as to whether someone were cooperating with the enemy, "the Union will consider such matters as past activities and associations, sources of financial support, relations with enemy agents, the particular words and conduct involved, and all other relevant factors for informed judgment." All this is now omitted from official ACLU policy on the subject.[34]

As these new policies indicate, balancing national security interests with a respect for civil liberties is increasingly not the goal of the ACLU. Its goal is the absolute pursuit of civil liberties, without concern for its consequences. Gone are the nuanced and carefully crafted policies that guided Union thinking during World War II. Gone, too, is any talk about the enemies of the United States. It is hard to imagine a person vile enough—or a crisis serious enough—to shake the ACLU from its absolutist position during wartime. The tragedy is it is not just the nation's security that stands to lose as a result, it is the cause of liberty itself.

Libel Law

In the 1980s, former Israeli defense minister Ariel Sharon and General William Westmoreland brought libel suits against *Time* magazine and CBS News, respectively. Both cases demonstrated how irresponsible some in the media can be and how difficult it is for public officials to win a libel suit.

The Sharon case centered around the events of the aftermath of the assassination of Lebanese President-elect Bashir Gemayel. Following the assassination, Sharon visited with the Gemayel family to express his condolences. According to *Time*, Sharon also discussed the need for the Christian Phalangists to take revenge (the article cited an appendix to a secret Israeli commission report as evidence of this discussion).

Now it is true that two days after the assassination, revenge was taken, as the Phalangists killed hundreds of unarmed civilians in a Palestinian refugee camp. It is also true that Sharon had been cited by his own government as bearing "indirect responsibility" for the massacre; a commission report explained that Sharon allowed the Phalangists to enter the camp. What was in contention was whether Sharon had actually discussed the propriety of the revenge with the Gemayel family.

David Halevy was the *Time* correspondent in Jerusalem who wrote the article that incensed Sharon. At the trial, it was revealed that Halevy had initially written that Sharon "gave them [the Gemayel family] the feeling" that he understood the need for revenge. The article was later revised in New York as saying that Sharon had "discussed" the need for revenge. Halevy testified that "gave the feeling" could have included "a body movement," "silence," or "indifference." Incredibly, when the article was read back to him, Halevy made no objection to the fact that his initial subjective impression of Sharon's body language had now transpired into an actual "discussion" of the need for revenge. Even more incredible is the fact that Halevy never read the secret appendix to the Israeli commission report that allegedly mentioned the "discussion" in question. To top it off, the appendix bears no mention of any discussion of revenge![35]

The Westmoreland case centered on a 1982 CBS documentary, "The Uncounted Enemy: A Vietnam Deception." It charged that General Westmoreland deliberately underreported the number of enemy soldiers in Vietnam, leading President Lyndon Johnson and others to believe that the United States was winning the war. The documentary included an interview with General Westmoreland, who had initially agreed to be interviewed by Mike Wallace; Westmoreland was told that the interview would center on "the role of American intelligence in the Vietnam War." He had no idea that CBS had laid a trap for him, carefully orchestrating a series of events designed to embarrass him.

What Westmoreland did not know when he agreed to the interview was that one of his leading critics, Sam Adams, was working as a paid consultant to CBS on the Vietnam documentary. For 13 years Adams had pursued his cause against Westmoreland and was now in a position to discredit the General once and for all. In addition, Adams was the chief witness against Westmoreland and, more important, was portrayed in the documentary as being a *friendly* witness. Here's what happened.

To make sure that the interview produced the desired results, Mike Wallace rehearsed Sam Adams in his role as a "friendly witness" before the actual footage was run; Adams was never questioned or challenged by Wallace. After the interview was completed, CBS producer George Crile sent a note to Wallace congratulating him for setting Westmoreland up: "The Adams interview was not only a terrific interview. It looks beautiful. Now all you have to do is break General Westmoreland and we have the whole thing aced."[36]

In the end, the jury in the Sharon case berated *Time* for acting "negligently and carelessly." It also found *Time* guilty of defamation and inaccurate reporting, albeit without malicious intent. Since Sharon had failed to prove that *Time* had acted with a reckless disregard for the truth, he lost the legal battle. In the Westmoreland case, the General dropped his suit against CBS just a few days before the case was scheduled to go to trial; the mounting legal fees were a major factor. Even so, even Westmoreland's severest critics knew he had been wronged. Left-wing writer Alexander Cockburn, no friend of Westmoreland's (the General should have been tried for genocide!) commented that the portrayal of Westmoreland as being "unpatriotic and disloyal" was "exactly what George Crile's documentary implied," leaving little room for any alternative conclusion.[37]

And what was the ACLU's reaction to all of this? Ira Glasser said it best. Referring to the Sharon and Westmoreland trials, he said, "Irrespective of their merits, the two giant libel trials going on in New York City should be immediately dismissed because of their chilling effect on the press. In addition, Federal steps should be taken to ensure that no such trials are ever permitted again."[38] Glasser could have offered that steps should be taken by the media to ensure that no such trials are ever necessary again. But he didn't. He could have suggested alternative means of redress for those who claim they have been libeled. But he didn't. His objective was to deny public officials the right to sue for libel.

Glasser's position squares with official ACLU policy, though the Union was not always so absolutist. It was not until October 1982 that the ACLU abandoned the *New York Times* rule. From 1965, the year after *New York Times v. Sullivan* was decided, until 1982, the ACLU held that in order for public persons to win a libel suit, they had to demonstrate malice. "By malice," the ACLU said, "is meant actual knowledge of the falsity of the statement or a reckless disregard of whether or not it is false."[39] This, and much more, is now deleted from the ACLU's policy on libel.

What is most striking about the ACLU's new policy on libel is that it reaches an entirely different conclusion based on the identical predicate of its previous policy. Both the old and the new policy on libel begin the same way: "A free society is one in which there is freedom of speech and of the press—where a marketplace of ideas exists in which all points of view compete for recognition. Whatever viewpoints or ideas are wrong or right, obnoxious or acceptable, should not be the criterion.

Speech cannot be restricted without the danger of making the government the arbiter of truth."[40] This is what followed in the old policy: "But defamatory attacks on individuals have little relation, if any at all, to the purposes for which freedom of speech is safeguarded. False statements regarding character assassination do not forward the process of a marketplace of ideas. In the absence of an overriding interest, therefore, the right to sue for libel has not in itself been regarded as a violation of civil liberties."[41] This is what follows in the new policy: "Therefore, the ACLU regards the existence of the right of action for defamation to be violative of the First Amendment" (in cases involving public persons).[42]

What changed? Are defamatory attacks on public persons now seen as inextricably tied to the purposes for which freedom of speech is safeguarded? Do false statements regarding character assassination now forward the process of a marketplace of ideas? If so, how? If not, then why the change in conclusions? According to Gilbert Cranberg, professor of journalism and communications at the University of Iowa, what triggered the change in thinking was the rejection of the idea that the libel issue represented a conflict between freedom of speech and the right of an individual to protect his reputation. At the October 1982 board meeting that reversed this assumption, it was argued that "protection of reputation is a property interest; in a conflict between property rights and First Amendment rights, they said, the choice for a civil liberties organization was clear."[43] No doubt it was. Having redefined out of existence the clear conflict involved in libel cases, the Union was prepared to graciously accept its own verdict.

Is It "Speech"

The ACLU's highly individualistic vision of liberty can also be seen in its approach to matters that bear directly on the political process. Should those who have been privy to the inner workings of government have the right to profit from their experience by engaging in lobbying activities after they have left government service? On this issue, President Reagan and the ACLU took the same position in opposing the Ethics in Government Act that was designed to stop such activity. The ACLU opposed legislation aimed at preventing top Reagan officials such as Michael Deaver, the former deputy chief of staff, from lobbying on behalf of foreign governments. The Union even came to the defense of Lyn

Nofziger, former White House political director, when he was charged (and later convicted) of improperly lobbying former colleagues.

Given the ACLU's absolutist approach to free speech, there is a certain consistency to its position. Indeed, because Deaver and Nofziger were Reagan insiders, there is an admirable nonpartisanship about the Union's stance as well. Nonetheless, there are still some questions left outstanding. When do concerns about the integrity of the political process enter the picture? To be more exact, when, if ever, should such concerns override free speech interests? Unfortunately, the ACLU sheds little light on such questions. Its policy on campaign financing is similarly posed.

The ACLU opposes limitations on "contributions or expenditures made for the purpose of advocating causes or candidates in the public forum." The Union does not accept the reasoning of the Supreme Court on this issue. The Court recognizes the legitimacy of putting limits on contributions but not on what a candidate chooses to spend. The high court reasons that everyone should be allowed to spend as much money as deemed desirable to distribute his or her political beliefs; contributions are different, as they may corrupt the integrity of the electoral process by allowing influence to be purchased. But for the ACLU, the principle of equal protection argues against drawing any distinction.[44] In keeping with its policy, the Union adamantly opposes putting any restrictions on campaign spending, including funds spent by political action committees (PACs).[45] The only alternative to the present system favored by the ACLU is public financing of campaigns.

Political persuasion is integral to a democracy. In the past, much of it occurred on the street corner, as pedestrians were cornered by activists of every stripe. Today, however, the mall has become the chief venue of pedestrian traffic—but with a noticeable difference: the absence of political punditry. Private malls maintain they have the right to limit speech and have done so with increasing frequency, over the objections of the ACLU. Comparing the mall to the village green in colonial America, civil libertarians maintain that the future of the First Amendment is at stake. ACLU board member Martin Margulies explains it this way: "Freedom of speech is useless unless the speaker has access to an audience—and the audiences today are at the malls, not in the publicly owned urban downtowns and village greens of old." But as Charles Oliver astutely notes, "The ACLU's position is tantamount to a requirement for *listening*." He ruefully suggests that "Catholic churches are full of potential audiences. Why not force them to accept speakers for abortion rights?"[46]

Thought Police on Campus

Political speech of a "politically correct" kind became the rage of the college campuses in the 1990s, as one school after another attempted to muzzle offensive speech aimed at politically protected groups, namely women, minorities, and homosexuals. For example, in 1987 the law school faculty at the State University of New York at Buffalo unanimously adopted a speech code that carried lifelong penalties. It targeted "racist, sexist, homophobic and anti-lesbian, ageist and ethnically derogatory statements," holding that if such speech occurs "the school can and will make appropriate communications to the character and fitness committees of any bar to which such a student applies, including, where appropriate, its conclusion that the student should not be admitted to practice law." It also pledged that it might notify state and federal law enforcement agencies of the student's misbehavior.[47]

In 1990, while Smith College was railing against "lookism" (the sin of constructing a standard for "beauty/attractiveness"), the University of Connecticut was banning "inappropriately directed laughter" and "conspicuous exclusion of students from conversation." Brown University matched Connecticut by outlawing "inappropriate verbal attention" and expelled a student for getting drunk and shouting racial epithets. But most of the attention focused on the University of Michigan and the University of Wisconsin.

Michigan and Wisconsin both adopted elaborate speech codes, and both lost in court. Michigan sought to ban speech that stigmatized or victimized an individual "on the basis of race, ethnicity, religion, sex, sexual orientation, creed, national origin, ancestry, age, marital status, handicap, or Vietnam-era veteran status." Wisconsin's code was similar; it also penalized students for slurs that created a "hostile learning environment."[48] In both instances, it was the ACLU that brought suit. These were bold moves for the ACLU, for it pitted the Union against its ideological friends in the academy. Both of these cases show the readiness of some civil libertarians to fight for principle; however, an examination of the ACLU's overall record on campus free speech issues yields mixed results.

In April 1987, student leftists at Harvard prevented a South African official from speaking on campus. Coming to their defense was Randall Kennedy, board member of the Massachusetts CLU and professor of law at Harvard. "There comes a point where a speech is so far apart" from the community's values, Kennedy said, that "it shouldn't be tolerated." South African officials "represent an advocacy that is beyond the pale," said the civil libertarian. When someone asked him whether he thought it okay to beat or kill the speaker, Kennedy replied, "It's a close call, something I'd have to think deeply about."[49] While Kennedy's comments did not represent the official position of the ACLU, it is worth noting that no sanctions were taken against him, even though the organization's rules require that officials be "unequivocally committed" to free speech.[50]

The ACLU's professed belief in a more inclusive society does not seem to extend to the role of the military on college campuses. In the 1980s, to cite one example, the ACLU tried to suppress the free-speech rights of military recruiters to speak to students at Temple University. The Union charged that "these were actually employment interviews and that the employment discrimination laws would be left a mockery if employers could claim that their discriminatory actions were protected by the First Amendment of free speech."[51] In another case, the ACLU defended Amy Carter and Abbie Hoffman in 1987 after they were arrested for trespassing during a protest against CIA recruitment at the University of Massachusetts.[52] Instead of protecting the free-speech rights of CIA recruiters, the Union chose instead to defend the rights of the trespassing censors. And at the University of Connecticut, the ACLU went into the Supreme Court to get an injunction lifted against students charged with disrupting on-campus appearances by recruiters from several defense contractors.[53]

Unfortunately, there are many in the ACLU these days who are not at all troubled by such decisions. Take the case at the University of Massachusetts that was just mentioned. According to Alan Dershowitz, political leftists in the ACLU who oppose the CIA have become a strong force, thus accounting for the outcome. "Unless principle prevails over politics," Dershowitz says, "the credibility of the ACLU—as a neutral advocate of all free speech—will suffer. More importantly, a ban on the CIA will be another step on the road to erosion of the very rights that the

ACLU was founded to protect."[54] It is this last point that seems so very hard for many in the ACLU to understand. Students who write for the *Dartmouth Review*, a conservative, independent campus paper, know full well not to count on the ACLU. In a much publicized incident in the late 1980s, student writers for the controversial publication were suspended from Dartmouth for engaging in "vexatious oral exchange." Actually, they were disciplined for confronting a black music professor, William Cole, who assaulted the students after the "vexatious oral exchange" took place (Cole's violence went unpunished). When the suspended students went to the ACLU for help, the New Hampshire affiliate duly studied the case and did nothing. To his credit, Morton Halperin of the Washington office openly accused the national office of also sitting on its hands.[55] Norman Dorsen provided the biggest surprise when he commented on John Sutter, the student who sought the ACLU's help: "Sooner or later, everybody seems to come to us for help. And when they do, we will be here."[56] But not for Sutter, they weren't.

John Powell, national legal director of the ACLU, defended the organization's refusal to help the Dartmouth students by citing an overriding allegiance to the equal protection clause of the Fourteenth Amendment. "To the degree that a university does not support an environment where blacks can feel welcome, then maybe a university could be subject to attack on equal protection grounds."[57] Powell did not waffle on the issue: "My concern is less with the strength of the First Amendment than with the wave of racial harassment that has swept the country . . . . The campus is not under the threat of being silenced."[58] Justifying speech codes in general, Powell insists that "sometimes we get confused and say that if something is a verbal utterance, then it's protected, but that's not what the First Amendment is about."[59] The same John Powell, however, finds no problem defending the sale of child pornography as a First Amendment right. On this issue, he invokes the slippery slope: "This year, it's pornography; the next year, it's literature."[60]

Powell's views on speech codes are not, however, representative of most ACLU board members. Nadine Strossen of the New York office and Morton Halperin and Anthony Califa of the Washington office (Halperin has since left) have been particularly outspoken about free-speech rights on campus. Official Union policy opposes speech codes and recommends the utilization of other corrective measures to deal with the problems of bigotry on campus.

Commendable though the ACLU has been in fighting speech codes, the alternatives it recommends are not without problems. It supports "new-student orientation programs and continuing counselling programs" that promote mutual understanding, and it calls upon colleges "to pursue vigorously efforts to attract enough minorities, women and members of other historically disadvantaged groups as students, faculty and administrators." Also endorsed are curricula reform, with an emphasis on consideration of required courses on "the history and meaning of prejudice," as well as restructuring existing courses with an eye toward inclusion of the works of those who have been "insufficiently reflected" in traditional courses of study.[61]

While none of these proposals are inherently problematic, in practice they often are. For example, "counselling programs" have been used in a manner that often resembles thought reform. In 1990, at the State University of New York at Binghamton, student editors of a conservative newspaper were sentenced to attend "sensitivity training sessions"; they were found guilty of criticizing a newly proposed major in homosexuality.[62] ACLU demands that more minorities be recruited as students, faculty, and administrators are fine, provided that standards are not lowered in the process, as they undeniably have been in the past.[63] As for tampering with the curriculum, surely all authors who have made substantive contributions to their field should be included, without concern for ancestry or anatomy. There is a good risk, however, that "politically correct" works will be used, creating a problem that itself has free speech dimensions. The ACLU, of course, is responsible for none of these problems and must overall be given high marks for its steadfast approach to campus speech codes.

Unfortunately, not all of the ACLU's affiliates have a good record on this issue. In Michigan, a policy condemning speech codes was easily passed, but it only narrowly got by in Massachusetts; all three affiliates in California went on record endorsing speech codes. The situation in California is particularly interesting because just prior to the adoption of a speech code, the Southern California affiliate had successfully defended James Taranto, a former student at California State University at Northridge. Taranto had written a column in the student newspaper criticizing officials at UCLA who had suspended a student editor for printing a cartoon making fun of affirmative action; Taranto was removed from his editorial position for two weeks without pay because he published "controversial material" without the permission of his faculty advisor.[64] Taranto, who has since gone on to work for The Heritage Foundation and the Manhattan Institute, was appreciative of the ACLU's help.

Morton Halperin has consistently opposed speech codes, maintaining that "the ACLU's position is absolute, all kinds of speech are permissible."[65] However, the national policy does say that "threatening telephone calls to a minority student's dormitory room, for example, would be proscribable conduct under the terms of this policy."[66] From the perspective of a social conception of liberty—one that recognizes the purpose of free speech—this caveat makes eminently good sense. Not to carp, but why does the ACLU pretend that an intimidating phone call is conduct? It is clearly speech, though not the kind having anything to do with what is meant by the free circulation of ideas. But were the ACLU to admit this, it would then have to explain why it doesn't take a less-than-absolute stand when considering issues like pornography. Better to redefine speech as conduct.

There are three elements to part one of the Southern California affiliate's speech code. The first two parts are not particularly controversial since they stipulate, following the "fighting words" doctrine approved by the Supreme Court, that the harassing statements must be intentionally directed at specific individuals. It is the third part that is troublesome. Punishing speech for creating "a hostile and intimidating environment"[67] is specious and, above all, dangerous to any elementary definition of liberty. This does not mean, however, that every form of harassment is acceptable. Surely a case can be made for punishing students even when no intimidating remarks are made. If white students were to follow a black student around campus, encircling him everywhere he went—constantly chanting his name—that should be sufficient grounds for punishment. The racists should be punished not for chanting the student's name but for their conduct.

The problem of left-wing extremism on the campus, in the form of political correctness, is serious. But some cures may be worse than the illness. In 1991, Congressman Henry Hyde introduced legislation that would amend Title VI of the Civil Rights Act of 1964 to provide a civil lawsuit for students at nonreligious private schools similar to that available under the Constitution to students at public schools. Hyde's objective is to protect the free-speech rights of college students at private schools where political correctness reigns. That is an admirable goal, but it is one that would be done at an excessively high cost: it would give the federal government new police powers over private schools.

It is not for nothing that the ACLU, which is an ideological foe of Hyde's, dispatched Nadine Strossen to stand with the Illinois Congressman when he introduced the bill. As previously mentioned, Strossen has consistently fought against campus speech codes, so there was nothing incongruous about her support for Hyde's bill. But it is also true that the Union favors more encroachment of the state on the autonomy of private institutions. Put the two interests together and it is clear that the ACLU saw a grand "nonpartisan" opportunity to pursue its mission by endorsing the Hyde bill.[68]

The future of all speech codes, however, was largely mooted by the Supreme Court in 1992 when it struck down a St. Paul ordinance that singled out certain kinds of hate speech for prosecution.[69] But in 1993, the high court drew a line between proscribing a class of "fighting words" and the right of a state to impose harsher sentences on criminals who choose their victims on the basis of race, religion or other characteristics. The latter, it was unanimously decided, was acceptable because it was directed at conduct, not expression. Interestingly, the national ACLU, along with the three affiliates in California and the Oregon affiliate, supported the Supreme Court decision while the Ohio affiliate filed a brief on the other side. The Ohio affiliate, which supported the suit brought by Alan Dershowitz, Nat Hentoff et al., argued that such laws threatened freedom of expression.[70]

Trivializing Free Speech

The ACLU's open-ended approach to freedom of expression has led it to take some bizarre cases. Consider the "frivolous" income tax return case of Emily Kahn, filed in the mid-1980s. Kahn's request for a refund would have been unusual even on "civil disobedience" grounds, but it was the ACLU's defense of Kahn on the basis of freedom of expression that was really innovative. The ploy didn't succeed, even though Circuit Court Judge Leon Higginbotham couldn't resist comparing Kahn to Gandhi and Martin Luther King.[71]

Then there is the Union's defense of the right of the North American Man-Boy Love Association (NAMBLA) to use a public library to strategize on ways to molest little boys. In 1992, a chapter of NAMBLA met regularly at the Potrero Branch of the San Francisco Public Library. It met to exchange seduction tips, including how to discourage children from talking about sexual exploitation and statutory rape. When the child molesters were barred from using the public facility, the ACLU went to work, citing freedom of speech and association. It had nothing to say regarding the planning of pederasty at a public library.[72]

The government has the right to ban public nudity, but what if a First Amendment right is being exercised in the nude? Does that change matters? The ACLU thinks so, but the Supreme Court thinks not. In 1991, the Supreme Court ruled that while erotic nude dancing was a form of expression entitled to First Amendment protection (but only "marginally so"), states may ban it in the interest of "protecting order and morality." The case involved the right of Indiana to prohibit nude dancing. In writing a plurality decision, Chief Justice William Rehnquist said that "the perceived evil that Indiana seeks to address is not erotic dancing, but public nudity."[73] The ACLU, which filed an amicus in the case, saw the matter as a violation of free speech. Marjorie Heins called into question the state's right to ban public nudity,[74] and Ira Glasser warned that "the beast of censorship, once unleashed, is impossible to control."[75]

Other examples of the ACLU's understanding of the First Amendment include its defense of dwarf-tossing, mud wrestling, sleeping in parks, and the right of demonstrators to stop traffic on bridges. In 1989, the Union opposed a bill in Florida that would have prohibited dwarf-tossing in bars. What the Little People of America saw as abusive, the ACLU saw as a "liberty issue."[76] When in 1986 the administrators at the University of Pittsburgh tried to ban mud wrestling as "sexually exploitative," the ACLU rushed to the defense of the Phi Gamma Delta fraternity. According to the ACLU, the specter of young women and men wallowing in the mud in bikinis and briefs was a straight freedom of speech issue.[77] Expressing its views on sleeping in public parks, the Union once chided Judge Antonin Scalia for not defending such behavior as a First Amendment right.[78] And in 1991, the ACLU noted its objections to regulations imposing fines on demonstrators who stop traffic on San Francisco's Golden Gate Bridge; this was another free speech right.[79]

What these cases suggest is that the ACLU will interpret as speech virtually every form of conduct that has an element of expression in it. This is not something altogether new. In the 1960s, the Union successfully defended flag burning as freedom of speech, and, of course, did so again in 1989 in the *Texas v. Johnson* case. The idea that flag burning is conduct, not speech (the position of First Amendment "absolutist" Hugo Black), has never been popular with the ACLU.

The Union even sees the burning of draft cards as freedom of speech, something the Supreme Court has been reluctant to approve. Samuel Walker regards the Union's loss in that case (*United States v. O'Brien*) as "a serious setback for free speech."[80] And in keeping with this sort of reaction, it was quite expected that the ACLU would take offense at a Senate action to bar the display of the American flag "on the floor or ground." The bill was inspired by an exhibit in the late 1980s at the Chicago Art Institute in which an artist displayed a flag on the floor in a way that encouraged people to walk on it. The 97–0 vote in the Senate making such action illegal was greeted by the ACLU as "another warning signal that civil liberties are in constant threat of being violated in the name of 'patriotism'."[81]

Obscenity

On July 1, 1988, the state legislature in Louisiana passed a bill regulating the size of vulgarities on bumper stickers . The bill, which passed the House by a vote of 96–0, limited to one-eighth of an inch high and wide the letters used to spell six specific words describing bodily functions, women's body parts, and sex acts. The ACLU threatened to sue.[82] Three-and-a-half years later, Governor Robert Casey of Pennsylvania signed a similar bill. The ACLU threatened to sue. Marion Damick of the Pittsburgh chapter of the ACLU offered the following advice to motorists caught behind a car with a vulgar bumper sticker: "You can look at traffic, the trees, the cars around you."[83]

In 1987, some fans of the Detroit Tigers, known commonly as the "bleacher creatures," got into the habit of taking umpires to task whenever they detected a bad call. Their response was to chant "Fuck you! Eat shit!" to the beat of the Miller Lite beer commercial. Not all the fans appreciated this (including those who listened to the game on radio and TV), and that is why a sign was posted in the ballpark saying "No chanting." The ACLU, as George Will put it, "went ballistic, saying that chanting is a cherished right." When the Tigers had the sign amended to read "No obscene chanting," the ACLU was still not satisfied, this time claiming the restriction was "overbroad."[84]

What these cases reveal is a mindset that understands no need to balance freedom of expression with the social interest in protecting the public weal. The ACLU's atomistic picture of society portrays individuals as going about their business unencumbered (ideally unencumbered) by the expressed sentiments of others. That is why the Union prescribes avoidance as a means of coping with assaultive speech. This may satisfy as philosophy, but it is poor sociology. A vision of liberty grounded in sociological insight understands that intentional assaults on the sensibilities of others are not likely to be received as demonstrations of liberty. On the contrary, they will be seen as liberty's abuse, namely license.

George Will understands what a social conception of liberty entails. "The First Amendment," Will notes, "is not itself the entire Constitution. It is a portion of a political document. What are the values and objectives that document seeks to secure?"[85] These are not the kinds of remarks ACLU officials are likely to make; quite the opposite. To them, freedom of expression is an absolute right. That being the case, there is no need for balancing, no need for intellectually difficult decisions. To the ACLU, the First Amendment *is* the entire Constitution, or close to it. What values and objectives that document seeks to secure is without meaning to civil libertarians. Freedom of expression is a good unto itself, requiring no purpose, no legitimating goal.

"When other values are injured by the exercise of the right of expression," writes Will, "restriction of expression is reasonable if the expression involved is utterly unconnected with the civic values that are the core concerns of the First Amendment."[86] What Will is enunciating is the instrumentalist interpretation of free speech, that is, the doctrine that speech ought to be freely expressed because it is instrumental to the ends of good government. This perspective is perhaps most cogently argued by the Jesuit scholar, Francis Canavan. For Canavan, the central reason that freedom of speech is guaranteed by the Constitution is "to protect and facilitate the achievement of rational ends by communication among free and ordinarily intelligent people. Chief among these ends is the successful functioning of the democratic political process."[87]

If freedom of speech is to be valued because it serves the ends of good government, then there must be limits to that right. As Canavan instructs, "end or purpose is also a limiting principle, regulating and restricting the uses of means to those which in some way contribute to the end." It would make no sense, for instance, to justify a right that would sunder liberty. "If a freedom is guaranteed for the sake of a certain end," writes Canavan, "those uses of the freedom which make no contribution to that end, or are positive hindrances to its achievement, are abuses of the freedom and cease to enjoy the protection of the guarantee, *unless the effort to suppress the abuses would be an even greater hindrance to the end.*"[88]

Though Canavan's view is foreign to the ACLU, it historically represents the thinking of most students of the Constitution, until, arguably, recent times. Surely the Supreme Court has not accepted the ACLU's absolutist doctrines. In 1942, the high court laid down a standard that is still valid today:

> There are certain well-defined and narrowly limited classes of speech, the prevention and punishment of which have never been thought to raise any constitutional problems. These include the lewd and obscene, the profane, the libelous, and the insulting or 'fighting' words—those which by their very utterance inflict injury or tend to incite an immediate breach of the peace. It has been well observed that such utterances are no essential part of any exposition of ideas and are of such slight social value as a step to truth that any benefit that may be derived from them is clearly outweighed by the social interest in order and morality.[89]

As Canavan has said of this decision, it "says that the First Amendment has a purpose—the search for truth—against which one can weigh a particular utterance; and also that if one finds this utterance has little or no role in this search, or in the exposition of ideas, then it can be clearly outweighed by the social interest in morality."[90]

In the latter half of the twentieth century, the Supreme Court has issued three major rulings on obscenity, none of which departs from the principal constitutional insights as depicted by Canavan. In 1957, the Court ruled in *Roth v. U.S.* that a work is legally obscene if the dominant theme, taken as a whole, appeals to the prurient interest.[91] In 1973, in *Miller v. California*, the Court extended the *Roth* standard by adding to it the test of whether the material portrays sexual conduct "in a patently offensive way," lacking in serious "literary, artistic, political or scientific value."[92] *Miller* said that determinations of obscenity should be based on community standards, and in 1987, in *Pope v. Illinois*, the Supreme Court added that such judgments must assess the social value of the material from the standpoint of a "reasonable person."[93]

The ACLU dissents from all three decisions. It wants absolutely no limits placed on the sale or distribution of obscenity and says all laws that prohibit pornographic literature should be stricken, including child pornography. Official policy reads, "The ACLU opposes any restraint on the right to create, publish or distribute materials to adults, or the right of adults to choose the materials they read or view, on the basis of obscenity, pornography or indecency."[94] In this everything-goes world of the ACLU, nothing is more precious than the right of the people to access whatever material they want, even if the contents include actual portrays of the abject sexploitation of infants. For the ACLU, everything from dismemberment to bestiality qualifies as freedom of speech. Its position is not only at odds with over 200 years' worth of constitutional law—and with the purpose of free speech—it is at odds with the cause of liberty as well.

According to Samuel Walker, it was Arthur Garfield Hays and Morris Ernst, active during the Union's first few decades, who were most responsible for pressing the absolutist position. "Thoroughly secularized Jews," says Walker, "they shared none of the puritanism of the ACLU Protestants."[95] But this is not exactly true. Baldwin, the ACLU founder, was no puritan—he was a nudist. In any event, in 1962 the ACLU became officially doctrinaire, endorsing the idea that obscenity should be fully protected by the First Amendment.[96] Today it takes an even bolder stand. It receives funding from the Playboy Foundation, as well as leadership: Christie Hefner, daughter of *Playboy* magnet Hugh Hefner, has served on the Illinois CLU board of directors; Burton Joseph, president of the Playboy Foundation, has served on the national board of the ACLU. In addition, some affiliates have even raised funds by showing hard-core pornographic movies: the San Diego affiliate aired "Deep Throat" and "Behind the Green Door" as a fund-raising gimmick.[97]

If, as the Supreme Court has consistently said, there is a legitimate government interest in order and morality, then it follows that no right—not even freedom of speech—can be exercised absolutely. But the ACLU does not speak to issues like this. Its abstract, and profoundly atomistic, ideas about liberty, and about society in general, have no place for such considerations. It ascribes to what Ronald Dworkin calls the "constitutive" justification of free speech (as opposed to the instrumentalist position).[98] From this perspective, nothing is more important than the right of people to express themselves.

The extreme libertarian position makes no distinction between the printed and pictorial media. It also treats as equals political discourse and obscene literature. But is there not a difference between the right to circulate pamphlets of protest and the right to circulate pictures of perversion? Dworkin and the ACLU to the contrary, a society interested in freedom must be prepared to defend its moral order as much as it is prepared to defend freedom of speech. If that is true, it follows that in a collision between the two, the latter cannot always be expected to win.

On those rare occasions when the ACLU does talk about quality-of-life issues, it does so in a highly reductionist manner. For example, Barry W. Lynn contends that the ACLU is interested in "the quality of the life of our democracy." "For us," he argues, "one of the bedrock principles which will enhance the quality and vitality of our nation is its unfailing committment [sic] to the full and open expression of ideas."[99] Lynn has just fingered the problem with the ACLU, unintentionally, to be sure: The ACLU cannot conceive of quality-of-life issues in terms other than individual rights. That the quality-of-life in a democracy might have something to do with issues of civility and community—not just civil liberties—is beyond the vision of freedom as sported by the ACLU.

It is no wonder that Lynn sees as important the defense of "sexual minorities" (he cites masochists as an example), holding that "material which depicts or affirms their life-style can be a means of self-affirmation."[100] Much the same could be said of those who practice bestiality or incest. Is this what is meant by taking a "quality-of-life" stand? Referring to civil libertarians, Jean Bethke Elshtain has said that "their notion of freedom precludes consideration of substantive morality and disconnects at the base reflections on how pornography may be symptomatic of wider features of American society." This is certainly true of the ACLU. "They cannot get beyond a picture of essential isolates," the Vanderbilt professor adds, "bound up in their rights and their 'freedom from,' going through the world *en grande* against possible constraints from aroused and potentially 'repressive' communities."[101]

The ACLU's subjectivist approach to obscenity is perhaps best stated by Ira Glasser. "No one knows," he says, "what obscenity is, or precisely how to define it. Like 'false speech,' obscenity often lies in the eye of the beholder."[102] It would be more accurate to say that obscenity is always partly but never fully in the eye of the beholder. There are cultural standards, and understandings, as to what is considered obscene. It does not matter, for example, that some utterly bizarre people think it acceptable for men to expose themselves to children. The reason it doesn't matter is because *most* everyone else considers it to be obscene. Moral standards are social constructs; they are not a matter of personal whim. Furthermore, we have laws against "false speech" (for example, false advertising) that, though inexact, are found acceptable even by the ACLU. Why should obscene speech be treated any differently?

In an effort to legitimatize pornography, the ACLU prefers not to address the viciousness of much that is sold in adult bookstores and video shops. Glasser, for instance, wonders why "the image of two people making love tenderly is considered obscene,"[103] suggesting that tender love-making is the stuff of "Deep Throat." Similarly, the on-stage simulation of sex performed by naked men and women in "Oh! Calcutta!" is labeled by the ACLU's Marjorie Heins as "merely" an example of "the unclothed human body."[104] Was this the reason that the Israeli Censorship Board initially banned "Oh! Calcutta!" as "pornographic and vulgar"?[105] Because that is how the Israelis see "the unclothed human body"?

The Meese Commission

On May 20, 1985, Attorney General Edwin Meese announced the names of those who were appointed to serve on the Attorney General's Commission on Pornography. Minutes later, Barry Lynn, legislative counsel to the ACLU, accused the panel of "dreaming up new ways to curtail speech about human sexuality" and complained that a train marked "censorship" had just left the station.[106] The fact that the panel had yet to meet was apparently without significance to Mr. Lynn.

Actually, Lynn took aim at the Commission before the panelists were even selected. Lynn criticized President Reagan in May 1984 when the first announcement of the Commission was made, stating that the ACLU took issue with the President's characterization of pornography as a "problem." As Lynn saw it, such a choice of words "appeared to leave little room for alternative conceptions or for a careful examination of possible values of permitting the unfettered distribution of sexually explicit material."[107] It was clear from the start, then, that the ACLU would monitor the Meese Commission right to the end. Lynn not only testified before the Commission in Washington, he followed it around the country, traveling to Chicago, Los Angeles, Houston, and Miami.[108]

One of the things that bothered Lynn right away was President Reagan's call for a study that would take a fresh look at how pornography had changed since 1970, the last year that a presidential commission on the subject had addressed the issue. The 1970 Commission, Lynn said, "would have shunned" labeling pornography a "serious national problem."[109] Lynn was not contesting the growth and availability of pornography, just the idea that it has bad effects. Indeed, he said, it may have good effects: "Although we are far from a sexually enlightened society today, our greater openness about sex should be viewed as a reasonable explanation for much of the growth in sexually explicit materials."[110]

From the beginning, the ACLU constantly portrayed the Meese Commission unfavorably to its predecessor. The 1970 Commission, which recommended decriminalization of all forms of pornography, was touted by the ACLU as objective, nonpartisan, scholarly, and so forth. The Meese Commission was said to imbue just the opposite values.[111] But the 1970 Commission was not as flawless as the ACLU would have us believe. In the Hill-Link Minority Report of the Presidential Commission on Obscenity and Pornography, Morton A. Hill and Winfrey C. Link charged that "the Commission's majority report is a Magna Carta for the pornographer." Calling the majority report "slanted and biased," Hill and Link accused their colleagues of engaging in a "shoddy piece of scholarship that will be quoted ad nauseam by cultural polluters and their attorneys within society."[112]

Perhaps the most serious charge filed by Hill and Link against the 1970 Presidential Commission Report was its ties to the ACLU. The chairman of the 1970 Commission on Obscenity and Pornography was William B. Lockhart, long-time member of the ACLU; Paul Bender, an executive of the Philadelphia CLU, was chosen as general counsel. Curiously, Lockhart's selection as chairman was "announced" by the White House and not voted on by the Commission from among the members; this was a procedural violation of public law. For Hill and Link, the ACLU tandem of Lockhart and Bender meant that "the conclusions and recommendations of the Commission majority represent the preconceived views of the Chairman and his appointed counsel that the Commission should arrive at those conclusions most compatible with the viewpoint of the American Civil Liberties Union. Both men singlemindedly steered the

Commission to this objective."[113] This makes explicable the ACLU's continuous praise of the 1970 Commission: it delivered on the ACLU agenda.

Selective Perception

Criticism of the Meese Report came from all quarters. Hendrik Hertzberg of the *New Republic* began by congratulating the 1970 Commission for approaching their duties "with an open mind" and charged the Meese Commission with encouraging censorship.[114] In the pages of the *Nation*, Carol S. Vance expressed her fears that "sexual modernization" might be rollbacked.[115] It was Christie Hefner, however, who provided the most memorable lines. She started her piece by finding fault with the term—but not the contents—of pornography (it is "a very derogatory term") and ended her article with a call "to recapture our confidence in our ability to shape the morals of our families," including "religious training."[116] All this from the president and chief operating officer of *Playboy Enterprises, Inc.*

When the Meese Commission Report surfaced in 1986, the ACLU issued its own critique of the Report, authored by Barry Lynn. In it, Lynn expressed the standard ACLU position that "the entire concept of 'obscenity' is inherently subjective"[117] and suffers from a problem of "vagueness." The Union's insistence that determinations of obscenity cannot rely on judgments of the "average person" (there is no such thing) is similarly designed to strengthen its argument. However, a look at some of the ACLU's most cherished policies suggests that it has no problem calling for law enforcement in matters that are also "inherently subjective"; vague laws apparently come to the ACLU's attention rather selectively.

In the same ACLU policy that says "all definitions of obscenity are meaningless because this type of judgment is inevitably subjective and personal," it calls for "strengthening the rape laws including elimination of the 'spousal rape' exception under which husbands may not be prosecuted for raping their wives."[118] But are not determinations of spousal rape "inevitably subjective and personal"? Indeed, in the Union's policy that addresses spousal rape, it states that "sexual assault laws" may properly "distinguish degrees of force and coercion—threats with a deadly weapon, verbal threats, etc."[119] But what constitutes a "verbal threat" between a married couple in bed? The ACLU does not say.

In the ACLU's policy on "Private Pressure Groups," it cites the Union's willingness to defend such groups but notes that the ACLU will not refrain from objecting "when the likely consequences of private pressure group activities would be inimical to civil liberties."[120] This is not an unreasonable stance, but it requires a tough call. How will the ACLU decide when the "likely consequences" may prove to be "inimical" to liberty? Is this not a "vague" standard? On another matter, consider the Union's ideas about when the fairness doctrine ought to apply. It says that if a particular product commercial gives rise to controversy, it should be subject to the fairness doctrine in the same way as any other controversial airing. But who will decide when controversy has arisen? The ACLU cites "interest reflected by substantial numbers of people or by responsible experts on the subject" as being sufficient.[121] But what does "substantial numbers" mean? And how do we tell the "responsible" experts from the "irresponsible" ones?

The ACLU's policy on "Captive Audiences" says that "the First Amendment is not inconsistent with reasonable regulations designed to restrict sensory intrusions so intense as to be assaultive." But how do we know when such intrusions have become assaultive? "Assaultive sensory intrusions," the policy reads, "are those that are objectionable to the average person because of an excessive degree of intensity, e.g., volume or brightness, and which cannot be avoided."[122] So now we have the ACLU on record as endorsing the concept of "the average person," a being said not to exist when determinations of obscenity are called for. And what does an "excessive degree of intensity" mean? Sounds awfully subjective and personal.

The ACLU's policy on heckling is quite interesting. It defends heckling save when it becomes so extreme that it prevents communication. At that point, "it must be deemed a form of action that is not covered by the First Amendment. The speaker is as entitled to protection from this form of interference as from any other physical obstruction."[123] We now have a true novelty: the ACLU has redefined speech as conduct. Why, then, does it squarely resist interpretations of pornography that deny it the status of speech? Surely heckling is more clearly speech than is pornography. Moreover, a case against heckling could be made on the same grounds as opposition to cloture: when obstructionist speech stops the free circulation of other speech, it loses its constitutional protection. Or, alternatively, the Union could have said that "a statement which is demonstrated to be part of a campaign of intimidation may be proscribed." That is its exact policy regarding the free-speech rights of employers,[124] a policy that is itself plagued with vagueness.

The Union's policy supporting "antiblockbusting statutes which prohibit false or deceptive statements concerning changes in racial, religious, or national origin character of a neighborhood" has been taken to task by Charles Oliver. "Although the ACLU does limit its support to laws against 'false or deceptive' statements," notes Oliver, "'deceptive' is in the eye of the beholder, and an absolutist position on the First Amendment should lead one to oppose such laws."[125] But owing to the ACLU's commitment to racial equality, it cannot countenance antiblock-busting activities.

So as not to be misunderstood, it is not the Union's commitment to racial equality that is being questioned (it is a noble commitment). Nor is it the Union's equally admirable opposition to bigoted "expression" that is at issue. It is the organization's lack of consistency regarding what constitutes "inherently subjective" determinations.

If there is one policy that shows the ACLU's ability and eagerness to engage in an "inherently subjective and personal" judgment, it is its policy on sexual harassment. But what is sexual harassment? "The behavior," says official ACLU policy, "is that which, because of its pervasiveness or intensity, creates a situation for the employee which a reasonable person in the employee's situation would experience as harassment."[126] Now if the ACLU feels comfortable with this kind of subjectivity, why does it object to determinations of obscenity? In addition, notice that once again the Union has discovered the existence of the "reasonable person," the exact creature deemed worthy of judging obscenity in *Pope*, but not by the ACLU.

What kinds of situations constitute sexual harassment? Among them is "where an employee is subjected to intentional unwanted physical contact of a sexual nature which is clearly offensive."[127] But in some circumstances the line between an intentional and an unintentional contact is surely in the eye of the beholder. And are there not instances when someone has intentionally coaxed a fellow employee? When is flirting not flirting? Is this not an "inherently subjective and personal" call? And can we really be sure when such contact is "clearly offensive"? Some might see a hug as an expression of affection.

The ACLU's policy on sexual harassment is so vague that even its officers can't agree on what it is. For example, the ACLU's national office and its Florida office came down on two different sides on *Robinson v. Jacksonville Shipyards*. In that 1991 case, U.S. Judge Howell Melton ruled that male shipyard workers harassed a female welder with lewd comments and photos of nude women.[128] The national office agreed with the verdict (the females are a "captive audience"), but the Florida affiliate interpreted the matter as a free-speech violation. Robyn Blumner, executive director of the Florida CLU, said that "just as the ACLU defended Nazis in Skokie, we're going to do the constitutionally proper thing by representing an unpopular cause: sexist speech."[129] Which side is right is academic. What this case shows is that determinations of sexual harassment are subjective and often difficult to render. But that hasn't stopped—and shouldn't stop—the ACLU from considering the subject. Nor should it serve as an adequate excuse to walk away from determinations of obscenity.

The Absolutist Position

The real difference between the ACLU's policy on obscenity and the Meese Commission's understanding of the issue has less to do with quarrels over subjectivity than with quarrels over the meaning of the First Amendment. The Meese Report explicitly held that the First Amendment ought to cover "a wide range of sexually explicit material conveying unpopular ideas about sex in a manner that is offensive to most people," but it also said that there was some hard-core material that fell below a "minimal threshold." Admitting that lines "are of course not always easy to draw," the Report contended that there is some pornographic material that "is so far removed from any of the central purposes of the First Amendment, and so close to so much of the rest of the sex industry, that including such material within the coverage of the First Amendment seems highly attenuated." It emphasized that lines must be drawn if the plausibility of the First Amendment is to be protected.[130]

The ACLU's approach is quite different. The Union maintains that "sexually explicit material fulfills the traditional functions of speech: transmitting ideas, promoting self-realization, and serving as a 'safety valve' for both the speaker and audience." Furthermore, such material is "clearly considered socially useful by many consumers," for example, they "spend billions of dollars each year on the material."[131] The same is true, of course, of guns and drugs. But what exactly are the ideas that pornography transmits?

According to the ACLU, pornography has an instructional aspect to it that should not be overlooked. "To the extent that pornography depicts sexual activity in nearly clinical detail, it can be educational. It shows what people can do and how to do it. It can also suggest that the kind of sexual activity depicted is worth doing, or at least worth watching." Are these the virtues of S&M? Even more revealing is the ACLU's opinion on the attitudes that pornography fosters. Echoing the opinions of other commentators, it attributes to pornography "a vision of 'pornotopia,' a view of sexual conduct implying 'easy freedom without consequences, a fantasy of timelessly repetitive indulgence.'" Also noted are "'the joys of passivity, of helpless abandon, of response without responsibility.'" Finally, "to the extent that pornography presents adults engaging in sexual conduct without 'benefit' of marriage, privacy or anything resembling romance, it asserts the moral appropriateness of such behavior."[132]

The ACLU is quite right that these are attitudes fostered by pornography. Promoting a sense of liberty without responsibility is indeed what pornography does. It also sells the idea of enjoying sex without the "benefit" (the quotation marks are telling) of marriage, privacy, or romance. But only those who ascribe to a highly atomistic conception of liberty would regard this as freedom. From a social perspective, these attributes are the very attributes that war on liberty. If it is to be sustained, liberty needs a moral basis, lest it devolve to libertinism. The effect of pornography is to enervate that basis, and that is why its distribution deserves to be stymied.

The Union does not duck the issue of pornography's effects on women. It admits that much of it "represent[s] male anger towards women and seeks to humiliate women by portraying them as submissive and unprotected." However, the ACLU reasons that that kind of message is "quintessentially political" and therefore deserving of full constitutional protection.[133] Now if the sexual brutalization of women qualifies as political speech, it is not certain what type of conduct the ACLU would find void of political import.

Following the logic of Norman Dorsen, the ACLU regards pornography as deserving free speech protection on the basis of its "self-actualization" merits. The Union hails the progress that pornography has made over the years, moving well beyond its early fixation on "young women's breasts." As proof that all of us are now "sexual beings," the ACLU offers the following observation: "Contemporary sexually explicit publications include portrayals of pregnant women and grandmothers, as well as once-shunned images of male genitalia. This should not be seen as an entirely negative development. Acknowledgment of the sexual diversity of our society can be an important step toward a healthier overall understanding of human sexuality."[134]

Not everyone might agree that we are a better society for freely circulating pictures of naked old ladies and frontal male nudity. But if this is an unsatisfactory reason, there is always the "safety valve" explanation. The gist of this argument is that for some persons pornography may have a cathartic effect, thus channeling sexual fantasies in a way that is not destructive to others. To be sure, to the extent that sick persons masturbate their fantasies away and not try to practice them on unconsenting persons, society is better served. It is also true that there are drugs—otherwise dangerous—which may have a meliorating effect on certain kinds of maladies. That is why doctors can prescribe them for those in need. Treatment is available (including pornography) for those who suffer from sexual problems as well, making unnecessary the wholesale elimination of the obscenity laws.

Part of the reason that the ACLU takes such an absolutist stand on pornography has to do with its professed respect for sex between "consensual adults." But even when women are forced to submit, the ACLU refuses to budge. For proof, consider the testimony of Barry Lynn before the Senate Judiciary Committee, commenting on the "Pornography Victims Protection Act." The bill Lynn testified against would, in Lynn's words, "criminalize the conduct of any person who 'coerces, intimidates, or fraudulently induces an individual 18 years or older to engage in any sexually explicit conduct for the purpose of producing any visual depiction of such conduct' if interstate transportation of the material is anticipated." Other aspects of the bill also targeted the element of coercion. And what was Lynn's response? He said such cases were few in number and it was unclear what "intimidation" and "fraudulent inducement" meant. At bottom, Lynn said, the bill was "an unduly paternalistic approach to dealing with adults."[135]

In the ACLU's critique of the Meese Commission Report on Pornography, the Union takes strong exception to social science data that show the negative effects of pornography. For example, the ACLU says that there is no satisfactory way that the legal concept of "harms" can be used to deal with pornography; it takes issue with the Meese Commission's definition of "causation"; it downplays the independent role that pornography may play in causing antisocial behavior (such conduct is due to "broken homes" and such); and it holds that sex offenders caught with extensive amounts of pornography in their homes may not be any different from everyone else since we don't know how much pornography is held by non-offenders.[136] But in the end none of this really matters. Official ACLU policy says quite explicitly that "scientific proof" showing a causal relationship between pornography and antisocial behavior is irrelevant, as "no different test of the effects of speech is applicable in this area as in any other area."[137]

The quest to determine a unicausal relationship between pornography and antisocial behavior is a fruitless one, but not because pornography has no effect on conduct: behavior is a function of multiple causation, not just one variable. Reading Shakespeare doesn't make the reader noble, but that isn't to say that an environment nurtured by noble experiences doesn't matter. It matters also when a person's environment is laced with the kind of ignoble experiences that pornography delivers. And there is no doubting that many women have been victimized in and with pornography, a fact reported on by several witnesses to the Meese Commission. What does the ACLU have to say about this? "These were quite frankly not cases where *but* for pornography, life would have been a bed of roses."[138] In other words, the victims of pornography were losers anyway. Imagine commenting on AIDS victims the same way: These are quite frankly not cases where *but* for AIDS, life would have been a bed of roses.

In 1992, victims of pornography found an ally in Senator Mitch McConnell, the sponsor of "The Pornography Victims Compensation Act." The bill said that victims of sex crimes should be allowed to sue for damages if they can prove that reading or viewing obscene material or child pornography caused the attack. Branded as an instrument of "censorship" by the ACLU's Marjorie Heins,[139] the bill contained no censorial powers whatsoever and made it difficult to extract compensation. For example, the plaintiff had to prove that exposure to obscenity or child pornography was a substantial cause of the crime, and that the producer, dealer, or exhibitor responsible for the exposure should have reasonably foreseen that his role would create an unreasonable risk of the crime that caused the injury. As Bruce Fein saw it, "the bill hits only material subject to criminal penalties; to the extent it deters such criminality, the bill should be applauded, not deplored. If opponents wish to argue against any pornography restrictions, they should make their case directly, not use the bill to camouflage their ultimate goal."[140]

If one were to read only the comments of the critics of the Meese Commission Report, and not the Report itself, the conclusion that the Commission recommended a new wave of censorship would be inescapable. But nowhere in the Report is such a recommendation made. What the Meese Commission recommended was the enforcement of the law *as it already exists*. In point of fact, a majority of the Meese Commission explicitly said that it did not "desire to restrict materials not currently subject to restriction under *Miller*." To this the ACLU replies that the *Miller* standard gives law enforcement enormous power, offering by way of example "cities with vigorous *Miller*-based obscenity enforcement have virtually eliminated all sexually explicit materials."[141] This seems to suggest that cities like Cincinnati and Atlanta are less free than New York and Los Angeles because they enforce the obscenity statutes and the latter do not. At the very least, this is a dubious proposition to make.

Just about every method of regulating pornography is resisted by the ACLU. Even when citizens assert their First Amendment right to protest pornography, they are occasionally met with ACLU opposition. In 1987, when the citizens in Kansas City organized to combat pornography, they were accused of "false advertising" by Dick Kurtenbach, regional head of the ACLU. Their offense, said Kurtenbach, was in stating that pornography caused violence and abusive behavior.[142] The issue, of course, remains unsettled. But to say that there is a causal link between one variable and the other is not the same as saying that A causes B. There is a causal link between smoking and lung cancer, notwithstanding the fact that most smokers do not die of cancer. There is also some link between today's brand of pornography and antisocial behavior. In any event, to say that there might be such a link is hardly the equivalent of "false advertising," which is, after all, advertising known to be false.

The ACLU refuses to give any quarter even when steps are taken to shield children from obscenity. It objects to any rating system, whether it be the movie rating system or labels on records;[143] in doing so, it confuses society's right to censure with the government's right to censor.

Though almost everyone else agrees that profanity should not be aired during the hours children are most likely to listen, the Union continues to criticize the *Pacifica* decision, which barred the radio stations from doing so.[144] And in Nashville, Tennessee, the ACLU brought suit in 1991 challenging the constitutionality of a state statute that restricted the sale of publications and videos deemed "harmful to minors." The law targeted material containing "excess violence" and "nudity" and required that such items be packaged in protective wrapping and kept out of reach of those under 18. The ACLU's suit claimed that the law should be stricken as it might ban *King Lear*.[145]

Some towns have decided that the best way to handle the spread of pornography is to limit adult theaters to one zoned area. The ACLU says they should have no right to do so and has fought, unsuccessfully, to ban all zoning ordinances aimed at pornography. The Union also objects to the banning of billboards that depict copulation and claims that laws that require adult magazines be shielded in covers are "highly dangerous to First Amendment interests."[146] Even more stunning is the ACLU's defense of unsolicited sexually-oriented advertisement sent in the mails. It says that if we allow people to tell the postman which mail they don't want coming into their homes, we will be permitting "precensorship."[147] The ACLU concedes that an all-out ban on unsolicited pornography might prevent children from seeing such material, but, it reasons, "this minimal degree of protection for children [would be] achieved at an unacceptable expense—by purging all mailboxes of unsolicited material that is entirely suitable for adults."[148]

In an effort to track convicted pornographers, the Meese Commission urged the creation of an obscenity law enforcement data base housed within the Department of Justice. The ACLU called the proposal "Orwellian," claiming that the data bank could be misused. Indeed, it said there was "no better evidence" of why such a proposal was unwise than an incident in which a documented mishap occurred. It cited a case where a keypunch error resulted in the merging of a list of persons charged (but never found guilty) with violating federal obscenity laws with a list of persons found guilty.[149] What is striking about this line of reasoning is that just five pages earlier, in the same ACLU report, the Union treated as merely "anecdotal" reports of the "Playboy Channel" inadvertently showing up on the "Disney Channel" and adult channels becoming visible to nonsubscribers.[150] Apparently, what passes as "no better evidence" or the merely "anecdotal" is in the eyes of the ACLU.

In an effort to thwart the production of pornography, the Meese Commission called for the enactment of legislation making it an unfair labor practice for any employer to hire individuals to participate in commercial sexual performances. Incredibly, the same ACLU that routinely complains of exploitation on the job, in this instance cited its allegiance to the principle of "freedom of contract." The Union also found fault with the Commission's request that some pornographic studios be abolished due to their extraordinarily wretched working conditions; the civil libertarians chastised the Commission for not making recommendations to improve those conditions.[151] But would the ACLU defend a sweatshop owner from government regulators trying to shut him down on the grounds that he be given the opportunity to make some home improvements? Or on the basis of "freedom of contract"?

Some of the Meese Commission's proposals were rejected by the ACLU out of allegiance to gay rights. For example, it was proposed that the Mann Act be updated to make its provisions gender-neutral. At present, the Mann Act makes it illegal to transport "any woman or girl" in interstate or foreign commerce for the purpose of prostitution or any other immoral purpose. The Meese Commission would like the legislation to include men and boys as well, but the ACLU objects on the grounds that the proposal "would simply give prosecutors a new weapon against gay lifestyles."[152] The ACLU seems to be suggesting that the illegal transportation of boys across state lines for prostitution and other debaucheries is an ongoing affair in the gay community. If that is indeed happening, then the ACLU has unwittingly made the Commission's case for them. In any event, this is one of those rare occurrences where the ACLU has taken a position against the crafting of gender-neutral laws.

Homosexuals figured heavily in the ACLU's rejection of several Meese Commission recommendations regarding peep show booths as well. It is well known, and was well reported to the Commission, that adult peep show booths have long been the center of illicit sexual activities. Such facilities are typically equipped with doors and are dotted with holes designed to facilitate fellatio between men in adjoining booths. The Commission took note of this and recommended the elimination of both doors and holes in peep-show booths. It also suggested greater enforcement of public health laws in these establishments. "These all appear," said the ACLU Report on the Meese Commission, "to be transparent efforts to find new ways to criminalize or regulate consensual (albeit dangerous in some cases) behavior, largely of gay or bisexual men."[153] But there was more to the ACLU's position than this: it did not want to criticize what was happening in the booths.

The ACLU derided the Commission for recommending the prosecution of "consensual sexual activity which simply happens to occur in places where pornography is sold." Simply happens to occur? It's okay for men to have sex in a store? The Union then said that if the adult stores are made to follow the Commission's proposals, "anonymous encounters will simply [occur] elsewhere, whether in a park, a public restroom, or someone else's bedroom."[154] This is quite a commentary on how the ACLU sees gay men: they are so compulsive that we had better let them practice sodomy in the local adult bookstore lest we chase them down the block to the nearest park.

It does not surprise to learn that the ACLU opposed the recommendation that more money be spent on enforcing the obscenity statutes.[155] Or that it opposed the incarceration of convicted porn kings. Of the latter, the Union recommended "community service," but it did not say what kind of service these gentlemen should be required to perform, only that it be "creative."[156] And although the RICO statute (Racketeer Influenced Corrupt Organizations) was intentionally designed to stop the kind of racketeering that exists in the pornography industry, and although the Union affiliates have used RICO against antiabortion protesters, the ACLU Report recommended against using RICO in the war on pornography.[157]

Child Pornography

Students of liberty, from John Stuart Mill to Thomas Emerson, have all intentionally excluded children from their formula for freedom. The ACLU does not—not even when the subject is pornography. In 1982, the ACLU, in an amicus role, lost in a unanimous decision in the Supreme Court to legalize the sale and distribution of child pornography.[158] It may consider the nation less free as a result, but few of the children who have been beaten, tortured, held prisoner, gang raped, and drugged would be inclined to agree.

The ACLU's position is this: criminalize the production but legalize the sale and distribution of child pornography. This is the kind of lawyerly distinction than no one on the Supreme Court found convincing. And with good reason: as long as a free market in child pornography exists, there will always be some producers willing to risk prosecution. Beyond this, there is also the matter of how the sale of child pornography relates either to free speech or the ends of good government. But most important, the central issue is whether a free society should legalize transactions that involve the wholesale sexploitation of children for profit.

The Meese Commission held that "child pornography *is* child abuse" and labeled such depictions as "inherently nonconsensual."[159] It favorably quoted from the Supreme Court decision in *New York v. Ferber* that "[t]he value of permitting live performances and photographic reproductions of children engaged in lewd sexual conduct is exceedingly modest, if not de minimus. We consider it unlikely that visual depictions of children performing sexual acts or lewdly exhibiting their genitals would often constitute an important and necessary part of a literary performance or scientific or educational work."[160] The ACLU found this logic unpersuasive and maintained that lest we allow these "expressions," we risk hanging the First Amendment in balance. Indeed, in its Report on the Meese Commission, the ACLU even went so far as to label as an "assumption" and a "premise" the high court's statement that child pornography was nonconsensual.[161]

Of the 49 recommendations the Meese Commission made on the subject of child pornography, the ACLU passed no judgment on four of them, found 19 acceptable, found 15 as posing "substantial threats to civil liberties," and declared 11 to be an "inappropriate focus on the fruits of coercion and abuse," as opposed to coercion itself.[162] A sampling of ACLU objections reveals a desire to crush the effective enforcement of the child pornography laws.

The ACLU objects to the idea that porn movie producers be required to maintain records of the ages of its performers; this would be "a gross violation of privacy."[163] Lynn's reasoning on this issue is even more remarkable than the ACLU's privacy argument: "If there is no federal record-keeping requirement for the people portrayed in *Road and Track* or "Star Wars" there can be no such requirement for *Hustler* or "Debbie Does Dallas."[164] With this characterization, Lynn has given new meaning to the term *moral equivalency.*

The Meese Commission was concerned about the use of computer networks to exchange information concerning child pornography, and to that end, it proposed that it be illegal to pass on information about a minor "for purpose of facilitating, encouraging, offering, or soliciting sexually explicit conduct of or with any minor, or the visual depiction of such conduct." To which the ACLU replied: the terms "facilitating" and "encouraging" are too vague. It even said that these were not "the levels of causation which our Constitution recognizes as sufficient to justify the suppression of speech,"[165] not indicating what level of causation would satisfy. Yet as was earlier demonstrated, the ACLU itself found no qualms about suppressing the speech of private pressure groups when the "likely consequences of private pressure group activities would be inimical to civil liberties." Can it really be said that "likely consequences" is at a higher level of causation than "facilitating" and "encouraging"? Is not the determination itself not hopelessly "vague"?

Since the ACLU thinks that child pornography should be legal, it is not surprising to read that it is against making it a felony to advertise, sell, purchase, barter, exchange, give, or receive child pornography. It is particularly distressed about the prohibition on advertisement, arguing that "the law cannot expect every publisher to decode every advertisement for some hidden or even sinister meaning," as if it took a technician—armed with a special decoding device—to ferret out pictures of children lewdly exhibiting their genitals. It should be noted that although the Union objected to the penalties for possession, it did not participate in *Osborne v. Ohio*, the case that criminalized the possession of child pornography.[166] The ACLU's absence, due probably to concerns about its increasingly tainted image in this area, did not sit well with Alan Dershowitz: he blasted the organization for not fighting for this great liberty.[167]

Other objections center on data bases used to track those involved in the child porn industry, the use of search warrants to apprehend suspected child porn kings, and the like.[168] The familiar ACLU retort is that these measures could be misused, which, of course, is true, but not exceptionally so; all law enforcement tactics—from fingerprinting to wiretapping—could be misused. What are we to do, then, ban all law enforcement on the theory that any of the measures could be misused? Why not simply punish those guilty of misuse?

The most telling statement on the ACLU's attitude toward the crime of child pornography concerns its position on what should be done about convicted child pornographers. It adamantly rejects the Meese Commission recommendation that judges should be permitted to impose a sentence of lifetime probation on those found guilty of trafficking in the child pornography industry. The ACLU complains that lifetime probation "may be a disproportionate sentence even for many child abusers," which, even if it were true, doesn't justify opposition to the recommendation; all that is being called for is the right of judges to impose such a sentence. The Union even admits that the recidivism rate for child molesters is high but still thinks they shouldn't be placed on lifetime probation. Why? Those on probation face "heavy discrimination in employment." This is the best the ACLU can do: child pornographers should not be punished because it may hurt their future career opportunities.[169]

The Real Censors

Before the Meese Commission's final report was released, it was sued by the ACLU, *Playboy*, *Penthouse*, and the American Booksellers Association. The ACLU suit, which charged that the Meese Commission violated federal law by withholding from the public all drafts and working papers, was dropped after a week when the Justice Department acceded to the Union's request.[170] The other three parties accused the Meese panel of attempting to suppress sexually explicit books and magazines.[171]

Perhaps the most significant reaction came from the publishing industry: no one was interested in publishing the final report. The reasoning had nothing to do with money and everything to do with ideology. Michael J. McManus was able to round up promises of advance sales that would have guaranteed the book's profitability, but the New York publishing houses wouldn't have anything to do with it. "It is interesting, isn't it," said McManus, "that the publishers who are most loudly opposed to censorship won't publish a document they don't agree with."[172] Even after the book was eventually published by Rutledge Hill (a small Nashville firm), the book was faced with a blackout: 8 of the nation's 10 largest bookstore chains refused to buy it, and one, Waldenbooks, bought only 250 copies for its 1,000 stores.[173]

New Frontiers of Sex and Violence

There has always been an audience for sex and violence, but not until recently have appetites grown so huge and the media for expression become so varied. From dial-a-porn to snuff movies, the level of sex and violence has reached new lows, even as the ability to distribute the new recklessness has grown to new heights. It is difficult to measure exactly what the effect of this onslaught has been, but it is undeniably true that the index of the nation's social pathologies has kept pace with the new frontiers of sex and violence.

As the ACLU sees it, there is nothing "magical" about dial-a-porn. Barry Lynn contends that dial-a-porn doesn't replace "the values taught before a young person encounters them," nor does it prevent "parents, schools, churches, and other institutions from successfully combatting" values they disapprove of.[174] Now it is certainly true that exposure to negative values does not diminish the right of parents, teachers, and clergy to counteract them. But it is also true that children are in the process of catching their values, and the question most parents want asked is this: what is the nature of the values they are catching and what can be done to inhibit exposure to values found objectionable?

Most parents, it is fair to say, approve of, and make good use of, the movie rating system. The G, PG, PG-13, R, and NC-17 ratings are useful guideposts that facilitate judgments about what movies are appropriate for young people. The ACLU wants it abolished.[175] Worse, it has misled the public about its position. During the presidential campaign of 1988, many commentators, including George Bush, drew attention to the Union's opposition to the movie rating system. For example, L. Gordon Crovitz of the *Wall Street Journal* made mention of the ACLU's concern that the rating system deters the airlines from showing porn movies. Ira Glasser got angry at both Bush and Crovitz.

Commenting on what Bush said, Glasser argued that the issue is not about "whether 'Debbie Does Dallas' should be shown on TWA flights to California."[176] In his other reply, Glasser opined: "Mr. Crovitz cites our objections to the current film industry's rating system, and implies that we advocate showing X-rated porn films on transcontinental flights. That is nonsense."[177] But the official policy of the ACLU on this subject lists several reasons the movie rating system should be abolished and explicitly notes as a problem the fact that "some subsidiary markets for films (hotels, *airlines*, pay television) frequently refuse to accept X-rated films."[178] (Emphasis added.) It is just as dishonest for Glasser to complain, as he has in debates, that government bureaucrats shouldn't be in the business of deciding what the ratings should be.[179] He knows as well as anyone that the movie rating system is an entirely voluntary effort, having nothing to do with government bureaucrats or censorship. Violence is another theme objected to by many parents. The degree of television violence is particularly troublesome, given its near-ubiquitous presence. Here again, the ACLU's role has been uniformly obstructionist. In 1989, bowing to public pressure, the House and Senate passed bills to grant the television industry an antitrust exemption to discuss programming restrictions. It initially focused on the prevalence of violence and then added illegal drug use and sexually explicit material. The ACLU opposed the bills on the grounds that "Congress should not be signalling its view of the preferred content of television through granting antitrust exemptions,"[180] a charge that was wide of the mark. The legislation simply gave the networks the right to talk about restrictions they might jointly agree to place on themselves.

The recording industry has also been active in the promotion of violence, especially against the police. The ACLU has opposed labeling of records, a kind of buyer-beware notification, on the grounds that it chills speech. Parents, the police, and lawmakers, however, have voiced support for this type of legislation, having become alarmed over songs like "Fuck tha' Police," a rap number sung by "Niggers With Attitude." When this song was identified as the type that necessitated labeling, the Pennsylvania affiliate said that "though offensive to some, [it] has a clear political message." Ergo, there should be no labeling. Similarly, when Time Warner was asked in 1992 to withdraw its album "Body Count" because of Ice-T's song "Cop Killer," the ACLU advised the company not to yield. The lyrics, which galvanized the police nationwide, included "I've got my 12-gauge sawed off . . . I'm 'bout to dust some cops off . . . die, pig, die."[181]

ACLU activism in behalf of vulgarity in the recording industry has occasionally been cost efficient. After Florida attorney Jack Thompson tried to use the obscenity laws against "2 Live Crew," the rap group held a fund-raising concert for its counsel, the ACLU.[182] Thompson, it should be noted, was the object of a vicious and wholly contrived campaign to discredit his authority, simply because he challenged the legality of "2 Live Crew's" work; it was an attack that had the participation of some prominent ACLU members.[183] Due to groups like "2 Live Crew," several bills to include a rating system were introduced in Florida. Led by Robyn Blumner, the Florida CLU fought all such attempts, going so far as to say that we should be cognizant of "the walls of oppression crumbling in Eastern Europe" and ought therefore be mindful of "how fragile are our own American freedoms."[184]

Artist Andres Serrano places a crucifix in a jar of his own urine and Ira Glasser calls it "a work thought to defame the Christian religion."[185] In other words, he's not sure. Robert Mapplethorpe's contribution to high culture includes picturing a black man urinating into the mouth of a white man. Both of these projects were funded by the public, all in the name of art. It didn't take long until public accountability was asked for, and as soon as it was, the artistic community and the ACLU screamed and fought back.

The National Endowment for the Arts (NEA) began to feel the heat in the late 1980s. Senator Jesse Helms pushed for legislation that barred offensive displays from public funding. Then conservative commentator and presidential hopeful Pat Buchanan made the NEA an issue in his bid for the Republican nomination. No one felt the heat more than John E. Frohnmayer, the head of the NEA: he was dismissed in the spring of 1992. As a direct result of the public outcry over the NEA, some of the more outrageous artists had their grants denied. They sued, claiming that they were denied grants on political grounds, not on the basis of aesthetics. The ACLU was there to help them.

John Fleck is an artist known for his simulations of masturbation while "performing." Tim Miller says his work explores his identity as a gay person. Karen Finley calls herself the "Queen of Dung," and with good reason: she is best known for smearing her naked body with chocolate and bean sprouts and inserting yams into her vagina. Holly Hughes's specialty is lesbian themes. In *World Without End*, Hughes is reported to say that she saw "Jesus between my mother's legs"; she is also known to put her hand up her vagina "to show how her mother imparted the secret meaning of life."[186] All of these artists had received funding from the NEA in the past but were denied new grants in 1990.

It is interesting to note that if an institution like Grove City College is 99.9 parts private and .1 part public, the ACLU deems it public and demands that it comply with federal law. But when it comes to the NEA, a federally funded organization, the ACLU seeks to fully immunize it from public scrutiny. In the end, there is no anomaly: its hostility to Grove City is an expression of its statist leanings—to bring virtually every private institution under the aegis of the state; its support for the NEA is the result of the Union's advocacy of unbridled expression, without respect for the public weal. That the ACLU would conclude that not only should there be no law against obscenity, but the public should be obligated to pay for it, is in keeping with its approach to liberty.

Students of free speech like Francis Canavan look in vain for the ACLU to define a social purpose for freedom of expression. True to its atomistic vision of liberty, the ACLU sees freedom of expression solely in terms of individual rights. It does not seem to matter what is being expressed or how, only that it be expressed. There is no sense of balancing, no appreciation for the fact that rights can be enjoyed only in a social context. To be sure, the First Amendment must be protected from those who would silence dissent or otherwise stifle the meaning of free speech. But it is just as important that liberty be differentiated from license. If it isn't, society might well reconsider what purpose is served by having it in the first place.

Notes

1. Minutes of the board of directors, January 23–24, 1982, p. 1.
2. The ACLU's animus against free enterprise might suggest a position opposing the right of tobacco advertisement. But the Union's policies on freedom of speech are so thoroughly absolute—more so than in any other area—that it would be difficult to justify a different response to this issue. See Testimony of Barry W. Lynn before the Subcommittee on Health and Environment, House Committee on Energy and Commerce, regarding Efforts to Ban Advertising or Promotion of Tobacco Products, July 27, 1987.
3. Norman Dorsen made his remarks at the Liberty Conference on July 5, 1986, in New York City. Parts of the address were printed in his article "Liberty or License: Can Free Speech Become Too Costly?" *Civil Liberties*, Summer/Fall 1986, p. 4.
4. Policy #6, "Libel and Invasions of Privacy through Speech."
5. Policy #16, "Commercial Advertising."
6. Ibid.
7. Policy #301, "Housing."
8. Policy #25, "Fairness Doctrine." The ACLU's initial interest in this issue can be traced to its protestations in 1964 of television broadcasters who snubbed the viewpoint of the Communist Party. See Norman Dorsen, *Frontiers of Civil Liberties* (New York: Pantheon Books, 1968), 141–48.
9. Policy #43, "Captive Audiences."
10. For some recent examples see "Congressional Voting Records," *Civil Liberties Alert*, November/Decemeber 1990, p. 9.
11. Testimony of Morton H. Halperin on S. 2726, "The Counterintelligence Improvements Act of 1990" and "The Jacobs' Panel Recommendations For The Enhancement of U.S. Counterintelligence Capabilities Before The Senate Select Committee on Intelligence," July 12, 1990, p. 35.

12. Letter to J.B. Colvin, September 20, 1810, *The Life and Selected Writings of Thomas Jefferson*, Koch and Peden, eds. (New York: Random House, 1944), 606–607.
13. Samuel Walker, *In Defense of American Liberties: A History of the ACLU* (New York: Oxford University Press, 1990), 289–90.
14. Policy #111, "Private Employment Security."
15. Policy #115, "Loyalty Oaths."
16. See Policies #110 and #111, "Federal Employee Security" and "Private Employment Security," both of which were passed in 1990.
17. Leslie Harris, "Intrusive Background Questionnaires for Government Employees Revised," *First Principles*, June 1991, pp. 6, 10.
18. W. Raymond Wannall, "The FBI: Perennial Target of the Left," *Nightwatch Special Report*, August 1988, pp. 9–10. The Report is a publication of the Security and Intelligence Foundation.
19. Gary M. Stern, "The FBI's Misguided Probe of CISPES," a publication of The Center for National Security Studies, June 1988, pp. 8n–9n.
20. Ibid., p. 10.
21. Ibid., p. 13n.
22. Ibid., p. 22.
23. Ibid., pp. 27–28.
24. Ibid., pp. 31–33.
25. Morton Halperin, "All Lose if the Hatred and the Feared Are Denied Liberty," *First Principles*, May 1988, p. 2.
26. Bruce Fein, "Laudable Move Against the PLO?" *Washington Times*, January 19, 1988, p. F3.
27. For a short analysis of this case, see Michael Carvin, "Booting the PLO," *Legal Backgrounder* of the Washington Legal Foundation, September 30, 1988.
28. See Halperin's prepared testimony and statement before the Senate Select Committee on Intelligence, July 12, 1990, pp. 23–25.
29. "Framing Leakers as Spies After *Morison*," *First Principles*, May 1988, pp. 3–4.
30. William A. Donohue, *The Politics of the American Civil Liberties Union* (New Brunswick, New Jersey: Transaction Press, 1985), 123–28.
31. For an account of the ACLU's position, see Gary M. Stern, "Persian Gulf Crisis Sees Rise in Civil Liberties Violations," *First Principles*, March 1991, pp. 1, 4.
32. Policy #8, "Press Coverage of Military Hostilities."
33. Ibid.
34. Policy #106, "Wartime Sedition Act." See the Policy Guide of 1986 for the inclusion of the policy passed in 1942. The new policy was passed October 14–15, 1989.
35. For a good discussion of this issue, as well as media abuse in general, see Robert F. Nagel, "How to Stop Libel Suits and Still Protect Individual Reputation, *Washington Monthly*, November 1985.
36. See *AIM Report* (Accuracy in Media), March 1985.
37. Alexander Cockburn, "CBS Surrenders," *Nation*, March 2, 1985, p. 228.
38. Ira Glasser, "The Punitive Libel Trials," *New York Times*, December 10, 1984, p. A23.
39. Policy #6, "Libel and Invasions of Privacy through Speech," passed by the board of directors on April 4, 1965. It is published in the ACLU's 1976 Policy Guide.
40. Policy #6, "Libel," passed April 4, 1965, and Policy #6, Libel and Invasions of Privacy through Speech," passed October 9–10, 1982.
41. Policy #6, "Libel," passed April 4, 1965.

42. Policy #6, "Libel and Invasions of Privacy through Speech," passed October 9-10, 1982.
43. Gilbert Cranberg, "ACLU: Second Thoughts on Libel," *Columbia Journalism Review*, p. 43.
44. Policy #35, "Contributions and Expenditures for Election Campaigns."
45. Letter from Morton Halperin and Barry Lynn to Senator Claiborne Pell, March 6, 1990.
46. Charles Oliver, "The First Shall Be Last?" *Reason*, October 1990, p. 27.
47. "Faculty Statement Regarding Intellectual Freedom, Tolerance, and Prohibited Harassment," unanimously signed by the Law School Faculty at the University of Buffalo, October 2, 1987.
48. See, among many other sources, Brian Mitchell, "Radicals Intimidate Christians on Campus," *Focus on the Family Citizen*, October 21, 1991, p. 14, and Michele N-K Collison, "Hate Speech Code at U. of Wisconsin Voided by Court," *Chronicle of Higher Education*, October 23, 1991, p. A1.
49. Quoted in "The Week," *National Review*, June 5, 1987, p. 10.
50. Policy #515, "Qualifications for Governing Boards and Staff."
51. "Gay Rights Threatened," *Civil Liberties Record* (of Pennsylvania), September 1985, p. 4.
52. Alan Dershowitz, "Freedom of Speech for CIA," in Alan Dershowitz, *Taking Liberties* (Chicago: Contemporary Books, 1988), 263-65.
53. Daniel J. Popeo, *Not OUR America . . . The ACLU Exposed* (Washington: Washington Legal Foundation, 1989), p. 74.
54. Alan Dershowitz, "Freedom of Speech for the CIA."
55. Carol Innerst, "ACLU Is Divided Over Support for Dartmouth Rebels," *Washington Times*, July 29, 1988, p. A3.
56. Quoted by Jeffrey T. Leeds, "The A.C.L.U.: Impeccable Judgments or Tainted Policies," *New York Times Magazine*, September 10, 1989, p. 78.
57. Ibid., p. 76.
58. Quoted by Jonathan D. Karl, "Hey Hey, Ho Ho, Free Speech Has Gotta Go," *Freedom at Issue*, September-October 1990, p. 22.
59. Charles Oliver, "The First Shall Be Last?" p. 22.
60. Quoted by Charlotte Low, "Defending the Constitution for a More Perfect Union," *Insight*, March 21, 1988, p. 16.
61. Policy #72a, "Free Speech and Bias on College Campuses."
62. Kathryn Doherty, "Speech Police Aim to Destroy Diversity," *Human Events*, November 24, 1990, p. 20.
63. See Dinesh D'Souza, *Illiberal Education* (New York: Free Press, 1991).
64. Carol Innerst, "ACLU, Meese Condemn Colleges' Anti-Conservatism," *Washington Times*, May 17, 1989, p. A1.
65. Jonathan D. Karl, "Hey Hey, Ho Ho, Free Speech Has Gotta Go," p. 22.
66. Policy #72a, "Free Speech and Bias on College Campuses."
67. "ACLU/SC Policy Concerning Harassment on College Campuses." This policy statement can be accessed from the Southern California affiliate of the ACLU.
68. There is another bill, introduced by Senator Larry Craig, that attempts to mitigate the weaknesses in Hyde's bill, though it too extends to private schools. See Thomas L. Jipping, "Education vs. Indoctrination: Does Washington Have a Role in Fighting 'PC' on Campus?" *Heritage Lectures*, #336. Jipping made his remarks at The Heritage Foundation on June 27, 1991. For a good criticism of the Hyde bill, see L.

Gordon Crovitz, "Henry Hyde and the ACLU Propose a Fate Worse Than PCness," *Wall Street Journal*, May 1, 1991, p. A15.
69. *R.A.V. v. St. Paul*, 112 S.Ct. 2538 (1992).
70. Linda Greenhouse, "Justices Uphold Stiffer Sentences for Hate Crimes," *New York Times*, June 12, 1993, p. A1.
71. "Frivolous Tax Return," *Civil Liberties Record* (of Pennsylvania), March 1985, p. 6.
72. "Pederasty at the Public Library," *Rights and Responsibilities* (newsletter of the American Alliance for Rights and Responsibilities), May/June 1992, p. 2.
73. *Barnes v. Glen Theater*, 111 S.Ct. 2456 (1991).
74. Marjorie Heins, "The Supreme Court Dances in the Dark," *Civil Liberties*, Fall 1991, p. 3.
75. Ira Glasser, *Visions of Liberty* (New York: Arcade Publishing Co., 1991), 151.
76. "Dwarf-toss a Right, ACLU Says," *Pittsburgh Press*, April 26, 1989, p. 19.
77. Cristina Rouvalis, "ACLU Dives into Muddy Issue at Pitt," *Pittsburgh Post-Gazette*, December 3, 1986, pp. 1, 13.
78. See "Report on the Civil Liberties Record of Judge Antonin Scalia," September 8, 1986, pp. 2-3.
79. "The Box Score on Bloody Nonsense," *Fortune*, February 25, 1991, p. 150. The ACLU's position in this case appears to be in violation of it own policy ruling on this subject. See Policy #51, "Picketing in Labor-Management Disputes."
80. Walker, *In Defense of American Liberties*, 280.
81. Sherille Ismail, "The First 100 Days: The Flag, Family and Ethics," *Civil Liberties*, Spring 1989, p. 8.
82. "Bumper Sticker Bill Approved," *Lake Charles American Press*, July 2, 1988, p. 5.
83. "Obscenity Law Doesn't Cover Offensive Bumper Stickers," *Pittsburgh Press*, January 6, 1991, p. A14.
84. George Will, "Who Are the 'Moderates'?" *Newsweek*, October 12, 1987, p. 100.
85. Ibid.
86. Ibid.
87. Francis Canavan, *Freedom of Expression: Purpose as Limit* (Durham, North Carolina: Carolina Academic Press, 1984), 6.
88. Ibid., 6-7.
89. *Chaplinsky v. New Hampshire*.
90. Francis Canavan, "The First Amendment and Pornography," *Proposition*, May 1989, p. 2. This was a published account of a speech sponsored by the Claremont Institute's Bicentennial and Golden State Projects in Sacramento on April 20, 1989.
91. *Roth v. U.S.* and *Alberts v. California*, 354 U.S. 476 (1957).
92. *Miller v. California*, 413 U.S. 15 (1973).
93. *Pope v. Illinois*, 481 U.S. 497 (1987).
94. Policy #4, "Censorship of Obscenity, Pornography and Indecency."
95. Walker, *In Defense of American Liberties*, 83.
96. Ibid., 235.
97. Ann Hibbard, "The Unbelievable Beliefs of the ACLU," *Citizen*, March 1988, pp. 1-3.
98. Ronald Dworkin, "The Coming Battles Over Free Speech," *New York Review of Books*, June 11, 1992, pp. 56-58.
99. "Testimony of Barry W. Lynn, Legislative Counsel of the ACLU, Before the Attorney General's Commission on Pornography," Washington, D.C., June 20, 1985.

100. Ibid., p. 10.
101. Jean Bethke Elshtain, "The Victim Syndrome," *Society*, May/June 1991, p. 35.
102. Ira Glasser, *Visions of Liberty*, 145.
103. Ibid., 146.
104. Marjorie Heins, "The War on Nudity Continued," *Playboy*, November 1991, p. 53.
105. "Revised 'Oh! Calcutta!' Is Headed for Israel," *New York Times*, March 4, 1986, Section III, p. 17.
106. William A. Donohue, "Hysteria and the Pornography Panel," *Pittsburgh Post-Gazette*, May 31, 1986, p. 8. See also the comments by Barry Lynn, "The Meese Commission EXPOSED," proceedings of a National Coalition Against Censorship, January 16, 1986, pp. 11–12.
107. Public Policy Report of the ACLU, "Polluting the Censorship Debate," A Summary and Critique of the Final Report of the Attorney General's Commission on Pornography, July 1986, pp. 5–6. Hereafter this document will be referred to as simply "Polluting the Censorship Debate."
108. "The Meese Commission EXPOSED," p. 11.
109. "Polluting the Censorship Debate," p. 5.
110. Ibid., p. 24.
111. Ibid., p. 14.
112. Statements of Morton A. Hill and Winfrey C. Link, "The Report of the Commission on Obscenity and Pornography," a 1970 publication of the U.S. Government, p. 385.
113. Ibid., pp. 386–88.
114. Hendrik Hertzberg, "Big Boobs," *New Republic*, July 14 and 21, 1986, pp. 21–21
115. Carol S. Vance, "The Meese Commission on the Road," *Nation*, August 2/9, 1986, p. 82.
116. Christie Hefner, "The Meese Commission," *Humanist*, January/February 1987, pp. 25, 46.
117. "Polluting the Censorship Debate," p. 27.
118. Policy #4, "Censorship of Obscenity, Pornography and Indecency," sections "c" and "f."
119. Policy #231, "Sexual Assault Laws."
120. Policy #3, "Private Pressure Groups." The same caveat is found in Policy #18, "Rating Systems Sponsored by the Communications Industries," and Policy #24, "Cable Television."
121. Policy #16, "Commercial Advertising."
122. Policy #43, "Captive Audiences."
123. Policy #44, "Heckler's Veto."
124. Policy #52, "Free Speech for Employers."
125. Charles Oliver, "The First Shall Be Last?" p. 23.
126. Policy #316, "Sexual Harassment in the Workplace."
127. Ibid.
128. *Robinson v. Jacksonville Shipyards*, 760 F.Supp. 1486 (1991).
129. "Harassment, Free Speech Collide in Florida," *USA Today*, November 20, 1991, p. 9A.
130. "Attorney General's Commission on Pornography," Final Report, July 1986, pp. 264–67.
131. "Polluting the Censorship Debate," pp. 29–30.
132. Ibid., pp. 30–31.
133. Ibid., p. 31.

134. Ibid., pp. 32–33.
135. "Testimony of Barry W. Lynn, before the Senate Judiciary Committee, regarding S.703, 'The Pornography Victims Protection Act,'" June 8, 1988, pp. 28–30.
136. "Polluting the Censorship Debate," pp. 59–67.
137. Policy #4, "Censorship of Obscenity, Pornography and Indecency."
138. "Polluting the Censorship Debate," p. 161.
139. Marjorie Heins, "Punishing Sexual Crimes: A New and Dangerous Approach," *Civil Liberties*, Spring 1992, p. 10.
140. Bruce Fein, "Liberals Mask Truth About a Worthy Bill," *Insight*, May 18, 1992, pp. 22–23.
141. "Polluting the Censorship Debate," p. 93.
142. William Robbins, "Beachhead in a War on Pornography," *New York Times*, November 2, 1987, p. A16.
143. "Polluting the Censorship Debate," pp. 113–14.
144. Ibid., p. 101.
145. "Affiliate Notes," *Civil Liberties*, Spring/Summer 1991, p. 14.
146. "Polluting the Censorship Debate," pp. 97–99.
147. William A. Donohue, *The Politics of the American Civil Liberties Union*, 292–93.
148. "Testimony of Barry W. Lynn on Behalf of the ACLU Before the Subcommittee On Postal Personnel and Modernization of the Committee On Post Office and Civil Service Regarding Mailing Of Sexually Oriented Advertisements," September 21, 1989, p. 7.
149. "Polluting the Censorship Debate," p. 130.
150. Ibid., p. 125.
151. Ibid., pp. 119–21.
152. Ibid., pp. 122–23.
153. Ibid., p. 135.
154. Ibid., pp. 134–35.
155. Ibid., p. 155.
156. Ibid., p. 136.
157. Ibid., p. 129.
158. *New York v. Ferber*, 458 U.S. 747 (1982).
159. "Attorney General's Commission on Pornography," Final Report, July 1986, pp. 406, 411.
160. Ibid., p. 414.
161. "Polluting the Censorship Debate," pp. 151, 169.
162. The four recommendations it passed no judgment on were #68, 73, 74, and 76. The fifteen it most objected to were #37–40, 44, 45, 48, 52, 53, 56, 59, 64, 66, 70, and 75. The other eleven it found problems with were #41, 42, 47, 54, 55, 57, 58, 62, 63, 65 (incorrectly listed by the ACLU as #64), and 72.
163. Ibid., p. 137.
164. "Testimony of Barry W. Lynn, before the Senate Judiciary Committee, regarding S.2033 'The Child Protection and Obscenity Enforcement Act,'" June 8, 1988, pp. 10–11.
165. "Polluting the Censorship Debate," p. 140.
166. *Osborne v. Ohio*, 495 U.S. 103 (1990).
167. Charles Oliver, "The First Shall Be Last?" p. 21.
168. "Polluting the Censorship Debate," pp. 145–46.
169. Ibid., p. 144.

170. "A.C.L.U. Reports Settlement of Suit for Pornography Data," *New York Times*, April 11, 1986, p. A16.
171. Philip Shenon, "Playboy and Booksellers Suing Pornography Panel," *New York Times*, May 20, 1986, p. A17.
172. Edwin McDowell, "Some Say Mees Report Rates an 'X,'" *New York Times*, October 21, 1986, p. C13.
173. Michael J. McManus, "Report on Porn Turns Publishers Into Censors," *Wall Street Journal*, July 30, 1987, p. 18.
174. "Testimony of Barry W. Lynn, regarding Regulation of 'Cable Porn' and 'Dial-A-Porn' before the Senate Judiciary Subcommittee on Crime," July 31, 1985, p. 15.
175. Policy #18, "Rating System Sponsored by the Communications Industry."
176. Ira Glasser's remarks were made in an address before the National Press Club, October 6, 1988. His speech was entitled "Presidential Politics and the ACLU."
177. Ira Glasser, letter to the editor, *Wall Street Journal*, October 13, 1988, p. A17.
178. Policy #18, "Ratings Systems Sponsored by the Communications Industry."
179. Glasser made that charge in a debate with Dennis Prager that is available on cassette from *Ultimate Issues*. The tape is entitled "The ACLU: Dialogue and Debate." The debate occurred on April 21, 1991. See, too, my comments "Reflections on the Prager-Glasser Dialogue" that accompany the tape.
180. "Clash on T.V. Violence?" *Civil Liberties Alert*, September 1989, p. 7.
181. Sheila Rule, "Police Plan to Expand Time Warner Protest," *New York Times*, July 8, 1992, p. B1.
182. "ACLU Affiliates on Front Lines Against Censorship," *Civil Liberties*, Fall 1990, p. 3.
183. Private correspondence with Jack Thompson.
184. Robyn Blumner and Christopher Hosford, "Hear No Evil," *Civil Liberties*, Spring 1990, p. 5.
185. Ira Glasser, "Artistic Freedom: A Gathering Storm," *Civil Liberties*, Spring 1990, p. 11.
186. Robert H. Knight, "The National Endowment for the Arts: Misusing Taxpayers' Money," *Heritage Backgrounder*, January 18, 1991.

6

The Homeless

The Making of Homelessness

When rights mania hit in the 1960s, most of those who jammed the courts in search of rights stood to gain at least something. But it's never been clear what the mentally disabled were supposed to win. If freedom means that people should be allowed to live as they wish, respectful of the rights of others and community norms, it is not certain how the mentally ill homeless are supposed to experience liberty. Unfortunately, such persons are too often disrespectful, albeit not willfully, of the rights of others and the normative order of society. The net result is an absolute degradation of human liberty for everyone.

The mentally ill are only a part of the homeless population, but they are a major part of it. Two major studies put the number of homeless who are mentally ill at close to 50 percent.[1] A Johns Hopkins study of the homeless in Baltimore found that 80 percent of the women and 91 percent of the men had mental problems.[2] And after looking at the various studies conducted in the nation's cities, psychiatrist E. Fuller Torrey concluded that a minimum of one-third of the homeless in the United States were seriously mentally ill, mostly with schizophrenia.[3]

In addition to the mentally ill, the homeless are populated by drug addicts, alcoholics and ex-cons. Many researchers put the number of drug addicts and alcoholics at about 35 to 40 percent of the nation's total homeless population. In the South Bronx, Philadelphia, and Washington, D.C., the figures are estimated at 75, 80, and 90 percent, respectively;[4] in Baltimore, the Johns Hopkins study found that 69 percent of the men and 38 percent of the women were probable or definite alcoholics.[5] When one adds to these figures the more than one-fifth of the homeless who

221

have served time in a penal institution,[6] the inescapable conclusion is that the average homeless person is a very troubled individual, in desperate need of help.

If there is one common denominator among the homeless, it is family status: they do not live in intact families. Up to 90 percent of the homeless are single men; the rest are single women or women with children. When some say that there has been a rise in homeless families, what they mean is that there has been a rise in the number of homeless women and children. They certainly do not mean—could not mean—that there has been a rise in homeless intact families, for the fact is that families of father, mother, and children are so rare that they are hard to find in any city.[7] According to Richard W. White, Jr., author of a book on the homeless and research scholar at The Institute for Contemporary Studies, there is "a very strong relationship between the weakening of the family through a variety of forces and an increase in homelessness."[8]

How many homeless are there? The three million figure bandied about by homeless advocates has been totally discredited by every serious study of the problem. Indeed, the late Mitch Snyder, the homeless advocate and ex-con who refused to support his own family,[9] admitted before a Congressional committee that he simply made up the fantastic figure of three million.[10] Sociologist Peter Rossi estimates there are 250,000 to 350,000 homeless nationwide, the same figure that the Department of Housing and Urban Development arrived at in 1984. In 1986, the National Bureau of Economic Research found 343,000 to 363,000 homeless. Two years later, the Urban Institute said there were up to 600,000 homeless.[11] It is fair to say, then, that between 250,000 and 600,000 are homeless. That is a big problem, but it is still not as bad as some homeless advocates have made it out to be.

Homelessness is not a new phenomenon, though the composition of the group has changed. A little over a century ago, Jacob Riis vividly described the masses of humanity found homeless in New York, estimating their numbers to be far in excess of even the most exaggerated figures we have today. Most of the homeless congregated in the Bowery, an area Riis called "the great democratic highway in the city." Noting there were more than 4,000 saloons below 14th Street alone (the area of the Bowery), Riis intimated that there was a symbiotic relationship between alcoholism and homelessness.[12] Alcoholism, along with mental illness, was a staple among the Bowery homeless in the 1960s as well. As far as

Michael Harrington could tell, the majority of the street people were Irish.[13]

The homeless today are a different lot. There are more young people and more women and children among the homeless today than ever before.[14] However, drugs and alcohol, as well as mental illness, remain a problem. "Substance abuse is one of the major issues causing people to be homeless and keeping them homeless," comments Irving Shandler, head of the Diagnostic and Rehabilitation Center in Philadelphia. Similarly, Ernest Drucker of the Albert Einstein College of Medicine in New York labels alcohol and drug abuse "the nasty little secret of the homeless." Even homeless advocate Robert Hayes admits that he has intentionally downplayed the significance of addiction, hoping to divert public attention away from this side of homeless life.[15]

Perhaps what has changed most about the homeless is the way society treats them. Bad as conditions were in the days of Jacob Riis, notes New York chronicler Roger Starr, "the police managed at least a touch of humanity with these helpless people." In those days, the police would allow the mentally ill to sleep on the floor of police stations, giving shelter on cold winter nights. Not so today: "They [the homeless] sleep in doorways and at municipal shelters, disturb and frighten fellow citizens, and constitute a living reproach to those ideologues who think freedom gives its beneficiaries the right to live in destitution on the streets." And just who are the "ideologues" Starr has in mind? The ACLU.[16]

The mentally ill, as Starr implies, did not wind up on the streets wholly of their own accord. They are the human legacy of deinstitutionalization, the massive exiting of mental hospitals that took place over a period of decades, beginning in the 1960s. Generally seen now as a failure, deinstitutionalization began with the promise of treating the mentally ill in local communities. It was preferable to treat the mentally ill in community mental health centers, the experts reasoned, because the hospitals were actually contributing to—if not actually causing—mental illness. In the 1960s it was also popular to think that poverty caused mental illness, thus giving further support to the policy of deinstitutionalization.

What went wrong? A combination of poor planning and flawed ideas assured the failure of deinstitutionalization. Those who were to blame include psychiatrists, lawyers, intellectuals, policy administrators, and public officials. "Wonder drugs" such as Thorazine were oversold, and a lack of planning killed the prospects for community-based treatment. The idea that poverty caused mental illness was, like much of the social analysis of the 1960s, wholly without empirical support.[17] So was the notion that mental hospitals caused mental illness.

In 1984, the American Psychiatric Association, which was an early advocate of deinstitutionalization, labeled the practice of discharging mentally ill patients from state hospitals into local communities "a major societal tragedy."[18] Dr. John A. Talbot, president of the American Psychiatric Association, said that the policies "were based partly on wishful thinking, partly on the enormousness of the problem and the lack of a silver bullet to resolve it, then as now."[19] In a 313-page report on the homeless mentally ill, the Association blamed not only its own oversold ideas, but also "patients' rights" lawyers for being more interested in getting patients released than in ensuring that they are properly cared for in local communities. There is little doubt that the report was fingering the ACLU.

There were two books published in 1961 that effectively sold the idea that mental hospitals were dangerous to the mental health of its patients: Erving Goffman's *Asylums* and Thomas Szasz's *Myth of Mental Illness*. Goffman, the late University of Pennsylvania sociologist, maintained that asylums were "total institutions," places oriented to the total control of patients' lives. He believed that most of the problems suffered by the mentally ill were the result of institutionalization, and would be "cured" by simply letting them go.[20] Szasz, the anti-psychiatrist-psychiatrist, argued then, as he does now, that there is no such thing as mental illness. There are maladjusted individuals, Szasz contends, but this is not the same as saying they are mentally ill.[21] As for the deinstitutionalized homeless who live on the streets of urban America, Szasz says they are merely "losers"; they are not "sick."[22]

In the late 1960s, it was Szasz's ideas that hit a resonant chord with a young ACLU lawyer named Bruce Ennis. Though the ACLU had done some earlier work on the mentally ill, it is fair to say that Ennis firmly put the cause of the mentally ill on the ACLU agenda. While indebted to Szasz, Ennis held to the more conventional belief that mental illness was real, and not an intellectual construct. But in the end it didn't matter, reasoned Ennis, because Szasz's conclusion was correct: people should not be hospitalized against their will. Stating that the abolition of involuntary confinement was a "personal goal," Ennis pledged that at the very least he would "set up so many procedural roadblocks and hurdles that it will be difficult, if not impossible, for the state to commit people against their will."[23]

To this day, Ennis believes that it is no more acceptable to involuntarily hospitalize the mentally ill than someone suffering from a heart problem. "The problem, which Ennis blithely ignores," charges Rael Jean Isaac and Virginia C. Armat, "is that when the diseased organ is the brain, the afflicted individual cannot make the reasoned decisions regarding treatment that a cardiac patient can be expected to make. Nor does heart disease produce the disordered, sometimes dangerous behavior characteristic of mental illness."[24] But consequences, including consequences to liberty, matter little to those who see freedom through atomistic eyes. It is rights that matter, and no one can doubt that the mentally ill have won their share of rights, including the right to be homeless.

In 1972, Ennis got what he wanted: In *Lessard v. Schmidt*, a federal court held that it was illegal to involuntarily commit someone unless it could be shown that the person was a danger to himself or others. Soon after, Ennis and his colleagues at the ACLU adopted a strategy that included filing class-action lawsuits against state mental hospitals that either were overcrowded or lacked adequate care. The Union found the right target in Willowbrook, a poorly run mental institution on Staten Island. With help from journalist Geraldo Rivera, the ACLU brought to light some of the worst abuses in state mental hospitals. Its lawsuit, which was joined by the Legal Aid Society, resulted in the depopulation of Willowbrook and a better life for the former patients.[25]

W. Robert Curtis, who served as director of the Consent Decree Office for the State of New York during the Willowbrook litigation, credits the ACLU for improving the conditions in the nation's state mental institutions, but he also finds reasons to fault the Union. Too many individuals, he contends, were released from mental facilities without themselves being competent to make such judgments; they were simply discharged without adequate attention being given to their future needs. Curtis, with the American Psychiatric Association, says civil libertarian lawyers see their duty as extending only to the release stage, professing no interest in what happens next. Making the case for institutionalizing the most disabled of the mentally ill, Curtis charges that "civil-liberties lawyers misunderstand the human dynamics that make for quality care in any setting. Effective workers must carry out their hands-on work in an environment that respects and supports them."[26]

Curtis' point is well taken: the ACLU has taken a broad brush to the rights of the mentally ill, not always having the salutary effect of its Willowbrook effort. For example, in 1973, the year after the Union brought suit against Willowbrook, Ennis and the New York affiliate took aim at the City Council of Long Beach, Long Island, challenging a recently passed ordinance. The law was directed at the newly released mental patients who were taking up residence in the town's hotels. It stated that if a discharged mental patient was a danger to either himself or others, and he did not take his prescribed medication, he could be evicted from the hotel. The City Council acted after a local Catholic church reported instances of former mental patients urinating on the floor during Mass and eating the altar flowers. The New York CLU was not impressed and filed suit maintaining that the ordinance was unconstitutional. It won.[27]

The late Seymour Kaplan, the psychiatrist who pioneered deinstitutionalization in New York State, often said that his contribution to emptying the mental wards was the gravest mistake of his life.[28] Kaplan's admission is by now commonplace among those who had a hand in the deinstitutionalization movement. The noticeable exception is the ACLU. It not only defends its initial involvement, it considers itself the strongest advocate of rights for the mentally ill homeless that exists today. That is because ACLU policy sees the problem as having more to do with political economics than with the mentally acuity of the homeless.

The argument that homelessness is primarily due to economic factors, though widely entertained, is without empirical support. Virtually every study of the homeless has recorded the extent to which behavioral problems drive their condition, and common sense informs that most poor people are not now—nor ever were—homeless. Most of those who are homeless come from dysfunctional families and suffer from untreated mental illness, alcoholism, or drug abuse. Giving them money, or a home, may temporarily advance their lifestyle, but it will do nothing to prevent a recurrence of the maladies that afflict them.

"The dearth of affordable housing is not attributable to the unpredictable, free play of market forces as is commonly thought," opines Ira Glasser. "It's a direct result of government action and inaction."[29]

Glasser's position squares with ACLU policy on the issue; it blames government policy for the condition of the homeless.[30] The ACLU's decision to blame government, and not the free market, is no accident. If it were the free market that were accountable, then the ACLU would have a much harder time trying to justify its intervention. But if government causes homelessness, civil liberties kicks in, and so does the ACLU.

As it turns out, the ACLU is not wrong to finger government as a culprit. The government's contribution to homelessness (aside from deinstitutionalization, a policy that the ACLU had something to do with), lay in the area of rent control. Rent control has clearly retarded the growth of low-income housing wherever it has been tried, the result being that cities with rent-control policies have a higher homeless rate than cities that do not.[31] And what does the ACLU have to say about this? It says that it "opposes any government policy that has a substantial likelihood of causing homelessness,"[32] but strangely enough it never mentions rent control.

One reason the ACLU doesn't mention rent control is because it doesn't count property rights as one of its concerns. Perhaps that is why Norm Siegel of the New York affiliate thinks rent control is irrelevant: "That's a social issue, not a civil liberties issue."[33] It may be for Siegel, but not for others in the ACLU. John Powell has defended rent control in San Diego,[34] and in 1989 the Massachusetts CLU successfully opposed a ballot initiative that would have reduced the number of rent-controlled apartments in Cambridge by allowing landlords to sell the apartments to tenants after two years.[35]

By blaming the government for not building enough housing for the poor, the ACLU is poised to file suit on many fronts. And no affiliate provides greater testimony to this approach than the Southern California CLU. According to affiliate director Ramona Ripston, there is "a constitutional right, under the California Constitution, to a home."[36] While this may be a surprise to many Californians, apparently some judges agree with Ms. Ripston. When, for example, in the 1980s a number of homeless people in California experienced delay in obtaining shelter from the state government, the ACLU stepped in and demanded same-day placement in a welfare hotel. When government officials replied that it took time to process the applications of those lacking any form of identification, the ACLU countered that this requirement was unfair because the homeless were often victims of robbery. A judge agreed with the ACLU and instant shelter was provided.

But this wasn't the end of it, not by a long shot. Still not satisfied, the ACLU filed suit once again, this time claiming that the application forms were "very complicated" and therefore a deterrent to the exercise of one's constitutional right to a home. Score another victory. The ACLU's next complaint centered on the policy of providing an $8-a-day stipend, per homeless person, to cover the cost of shelter in a welfare hotel. The ACLU demanded, and won, a stipend of $16 a day.

The ACLU wasn't finished yet. It then sued for blankets. When blankets were provided, it sued for a court order mandating that the temperature in all rooms be set at sixty-eight degrees. It won. Still not happy, the Union sued over the rule that said that no visitors were allowed (the government wanted to assure that only authorized persons were living in the shelters). Again, the ACLU won. Finally, the ACLU challenged the rule that said that if any homeless recipient of aid misses two successive appointments for a job, he is denied relief for sixty days. The Union argued that missing two appointments is "something that can happen" and then took the opportunity to blame inadequate public transportation (another civil liberties violation?) as the reason why its clients were often late for appointments. The judge sided with the ACLU.[37]

The Assault on Public Order

The New York CLU also believes there is a fundamental "right to housing," a position not endorsed by the national office. Thus, according to the NYCLU, local governments are obligated to provide facilities to house the homeless. While the taxpayers are obliged to pick up the tab for this expense, they are not, according to the Union, permitted to require the recipients of social services to behave in a responsible and orderly fashion. Indeed, as the NYCLU made graphically clear in the Tompkins Square Park case, society should not only tolerate but subsidize antisocial behavior.

During the 1980s, Tompkins Square Park, a park below 14th Street on New York's Lower East Side, became a gathering place for a motley crew of anarchists, skinheads, squatters, and other belligerents, as well as a camp for homeless people. On the hot Saturday night of August 6, 1988, a "squatters' concert" was held at the park, featuring local rock bands such as Public Nuisance and Letch Patrol. Things got out of hand, and a riot erupted between protesters and police who had been called in to keep the peace. Fifty people were injured, 31 were arrested, and 121 filed complaints of police brutality.

The following Monday, some four hundred Lower East Side residents met at St. Brigid's Church on Avenue B and East Seventh Street. Norm Siegel was there, bringing tempers to a boil by denouncing the "police riot" and urging his audiences to find out "who gave the order to send the cops into the crowd to beat" the demonstrators. Siegel's call for a march on the Ninth Precinct occurred two days later and, according to *Newsday*, drew about four hundred "yippies, hippies, punk rockers, anarchists, communists, a few homeless people, and members of the sizable squatters movement." Siegel led the marchers in the chant "Free the Park," although some improvised their own slogans: "Kill Cops!"[38]

The police, subject to such unrelenting criticism, were unable to quell the disorder and sporadic violence that plagued the park during the next three years. Finally, in June 1991 the administration of David Dinkins closed the park for a renovation that had been planned for some time. Siegel was outraged. "The closing of the park represents the visible failure of the Dinkins administration to address serious urban problems," he said.[39] In an interview, he elaborated, saying that he believed the park could have been cleared by improving social services for the homeless: "People would leave voluntarily if [the city provided] even one floor of a shelter, and let the homeless people, in association with the Human Resources Administration, manage it."[40]

The battle to close the park left Robert Rohn, Lower East Side community leader, furious with Siegel. "We can't make a move down here on the Lower East Side without first clearing it with him," Rohn said. "He's not an elected official, yet he has managed to thwart the city's plans with his ridiculous lawsuits on behalf of the city's lowlifes."[41]

Although the NYCLU never actually went to court over Tompkins Square Park, Siegel's position on the matter reflects a familiar pattern. What most people regard as social disorder, civil libertarians frequently construe as expressions of individual freedom; society, in their view, may enforce standards of public behavior only extremely sparingly and with layer upon layer of safeguards against potential abuse. "What's out of control or out of hand for one person may not necessarily mean that for the other," says Siegel.[42] It is this kind of extreme relativism that colors the atomistic view of liberty; it explains why rights and freedom are not always positively correlated.

One of the reasons why it is so difficult to maintain civility in urban public spaces is due to court rulings on loitering laws. In 1988, New York's highest court struck down the state's anti-loitering law, ruling that the 23 year-old law (an earlier one had been passed at the time of the 1939 New York World's Fair) gave the police arbitrary power to pick up and charge suspects. In doing so, the Court of Appeals followed U.S. Supreme Court precedence in this area. In 1972, the high court found a vagrancy ordinance in Jacksonville, Florida, to be too vague, and in 1983 it struck down a California law that made it a crime not to show identification to police when asked.

Now it is one thing to say that laws prohibiting loitering must be narrowly drawn, quite another to say that there is an absolute right to loiter. Some in the ACLU actually go further than this, trumpeting the nobility of loitering. But the attempt to portray loitering as some kind of cultural treasure only reveals that there is something else at work beyond the mere scrutiny of the law. Laughlin McDonald, director of the ACLU's Southern Regional Office, believes that "wanderers and loafers" have "an honored place in our culture." When fighting an Atlanta effort to "take back the streets," McDonald made clear his position: "Loafing and loitering, like privacy and many other rights we take for granted, are not specifically mentioned in the Constitution, but they are protected by it. They give value and meaning to life and nurture our sense of independence, self-confidence and creativity."[43]

McDonald's characterization of loitering as a social good signifies the adversarial relationship the ACLU has with the social order itself. Yet if standards of civility and community are to be maintained, there must be some willingness on the part of all citizens to abide by the settled norms and values of society. Tragically, this maxim matters less and less to the ACLU.

Abuses of the court's rulings on anti-loitering laws was to be expected. It is fair to say that no one exploited those rulings more than Richard Kreimer, an able-bodied white man who used to live in the Morristown, New Jersey, public library. His counsel: the ACLU.

Beginning in 1989, Richard Kreimer, along with about two dozen other "homeless" persons, began camping out in the Morristown public library. Patrons, especially females, soon started complaining about the constant staring, body odor, and disheveled appearance of people like Kreimer. "It's a very hard problem," said library director Barbara Rice. "We want to serve everyone in the community. But we're not social workers." Fearing more complaints, in July 1989 the library instituted new rules, banning "unnecessary staring" and requiring patrons to have dress and personal hygiene that conformed to the "standards of the community for public places." In stepped the Newark branch of the ACLU, intervening in Mr. Kreimer's behalf. The library was willing to compromise and rewrote its directive to ban staring with the "intent to annoy" another person; it banned offensive hygiene when it was a "nuisance."[44]

The ACLU didn't waste any time filing suit. This is how Elizabeth J. Miller, the ACLU lawyer who represented Kreimer, characterized the town's opposition to having the homeless live in their local library: "Morristown is a quiet middle-class community that, until recently, has been insulated from the problems of homelessness."[45] But insulated it would be no more, thanks to Ms. Miller, a nonresident of Morristown. "The issue is," as Miller's client saw it, "does a homeless person have the same right to read, to sit and think, as someone else. You can't discriminate. Just because a person doesn't look as good, smell as good or dress as good, you're not going to keep him out of the library."[46] Many patrons, however, felt that the issue centered more on the harassment of women and the creation of an unworkable environment for serious research and studying.

On May 22, 1991, a federal judge ruled that public libraries could not bar homeless people because of their staring or offensive bodily hygiene. "If we wish to shield our eyes and noses from the homeless, we should revoke their condition, not their library cards," ruled Judge H. Lee Sarokin. But what about Kreimer's stench? Judge Sarokin took a leaf out of the ACLU's book by concluding that "one person's hay fever is another person's ambrosia."[47] He added that "the First Amendment protects the right to express ideas and the right to receive ideas," thus casting the issue as a classic case over the free circulation of ideas. Kreimer's court-appointed lawyer on this round of challenges (the ACLU filed an amicus) was Bruce S. Rosen, who aptly called the decision "novel."[48] The library appealed the decision.

Two days after Judge Sarokin's ruling, the Morristown Headquarters Plaza hotel offered to enroll the 41-year-old Kreimer in its job program for the homeless. He refused the offer. He also refused to exit the library or to change his behavior. This was his "right." Not satisfied, Kreimer had another lawyer, Denise Reinhardt, file suit seeking monetary damages. Kreimer pledged that any out-of-court settlement would cost the town more. "Now that I've won the library suit," the jubilant Kreimer exclaimed, "my demands will go higher. To the victor belongs the spoils."[49]

In November 1991, the town council voted to give Kreimer $150,000 in exchange for dropping several lawsuits against town officials and the police. The Morristown authorities were faced with the prospect of having to defend a series of suits costing a million dollars or more; it had already spent a quarter of a million. Still outstanding, however, was the suit over the library's patron policy. For Lisa Glick Zucker, ACLU staff attorney from the Newark office, the case had to go forward. What was at stake was "a new class of persecuted people, the homeless," a group whose treatment she compared to African Americans.[50]

On March 24, 1992, the 3rd U.S. Circuit Court of Appeals in Philadelphia overturned Judge Sarokin's decision barring the library from prohibiting access to the homeless. The court held that the library's patron policy was grounded in "well-established constitutional principle" and did not violate the rights of Mr. Kreimer. The decision, which expressed a social conception of liberty, held that a library is a limited public forum, obligated only to permit the public to exercise rights "that are consistent with the nature of the library." Though Kreimer lost his case in the end, he did so after having received $80,000 for compensatory damages from Travelers Insurance Company, the library's carrier.[51] This brought Kreimer's total awards to almost a quarter-million dollars.

The ACLU's defense of the right to sleep in libraries antedated the Morristown case by at least five years. Things got so bad at the Ann Arbor public library in 1984 that 30 new guidelines had to be posted. The library prohibited fighting, drugs, weapons, gambling, alcoholic beverages, sleeping (for more than 10 minutes), and "extremely poor personal hygiene." In stepped the ACLU, focusing on the last two rules. Calling the ban on sleeping an "arbitrary standard," ACLU attorney Jean King worried that the rules were aimed at the homeless. As for the body odor problem, King said, "How will library personnel distinguish persons with poor personal hygiene from persons with extremely poor personal hygiene?"[52] The logic of King's argument suggests that librarians should be barred from ejecting noisy patrons as well. After all, what is noisy to one person may not be noisy to another.

Burt Neuborne of the ACLU thinks that sleeping overnight in public parks is a First Amendment right.[53] In 1984, the Supreme Court ruled 7-2 against Neuborne's wishes, declaring that barring people from sleeping in Lafayette Park across the street from the White House, or on the Mall in downtown Washington, was not a violation of the expressive conduct of the campers.[54] In the mid-1980s, the Atlanta affiliate sued, demanding public toilets,[55] and the Vermont branch sued over the right of people to sleep in malls.[56]

In 1989, the ACLU affiliate in Rhode Island argued that there is a constitutional right to sleep on beaches (it actually said that a law banning sleeping outside could be used against kids having a sleep-over in a neighbor's yard)[57] and two years later the ACLU went to court trying to stop the police in Miami from ejecting homeless persons from sleeping on sidewalks and in the street.[58] To top it off, after doing so much to get the mentally ill deinstitutionalized—many of whom subsequently engaged in violence and wound up in jail[59]—the ACLU in 1990 sued an Ohio prison on the grounds that the presence of mentally ill prisoners created a "dangerous and stressful environment."[60]

In 1989, the affiliate in Northern California proved to be especially successful in getting its way in San Francisco. It helped draft a "Homeless Bill of Rights," which is now official police policy, instructing officers to abide by newly invented rights: "All persons have the right to use the public streets and places so long as they are not engaged in specific criminal activity. Vagrancy . . . is not a crime . . . Factors such as . . . race, dress, unusual or disheveled or impoverished appearance do not alone justify even a brief detention." But what if someone takes a nap on the sidewalk? Don't pedestrians have rights as well? The ACLU explains that "with the new policy, which responds to specific ACLU concerns, the decision on whom to arrest is no longer left to the discretion of an individual officer; now a pedestrian must have been victimized in some way by the sidewalk-blocker, and a police report must be filed."[61]

Train stations and subways are places that are heavily traveled, making them difficult to keep clean. But until the last decade or so, they were at least tolerable. Now these public places are filthier than ever, owing in large part to the decline in civility that has marked urban areas. In New York, transit officials at the Metro-North Commuter Railroad Company have sought to address the problem by passing new proposals aimed at restoring a sense of decency. In the fall of 1989, Metro-North submitted two sets of proposals to the board of the Metropolitan Transportation Authority. One of the proposals barred sexual misconduct, but it was rejected by M.T.A. board chairman Robert Kiley on the grounds that such activity was already covered by state statute.[62]

The measure that passed muster was designed to keep places like Grand Central Station from further deterioration. It banned such acts as smoking, spitting, and littering; washing oneself at a drinking fountain; washing clothing or other personal belongings in a restroom; changing clothes or "remaining undressed"; lying on floors, platforms, stairs, or landings; occupying more than one seat, and creating "unreasonable noise."[63] Kiley explained why the rule was necessary: "People have a perception of rising disorder and a sense of a loss of control." Though he emphasized that "we're not proposing jackboots, whips and clubs,"[64] Norm Siegel labeled the action "mean-spirited" and possibly "discriminatory against the homeless."[65]

Being confronted with beggars in the subways is nothing new for New Yorkers, but by the late 1980s it was clear that the situation had gotten out of control. Eric Pooley of *New York* magazine wrote in 1988 that "even liberals are getting tired of navigating the sea of beggars."[66] Perhaps. But not the liberals at the NYCLU: they filed an amicus brief on behalf of William B. Young Jr., asserting the right of this homeless man to beg in the subways.[67]

Federal District Court Judge Leonard Sand agreed with the ACLU, proclaiming that begging in the subways was a constitutionally protected First Amendment right. ACLU'er Burt Neuborne concurred, saying that "to the extent subways are simply extensions of the streets, the same freedoms should apply in both places."[68] But in 1990 a federal appeals court overturned Judge Sand's opinion, holding that "Whether intended or not, begging in the subway often amounts to nothing less than assault, creating in the passengers the apprehension of imminent danger."[69] The Supreme Court let this decision stand.

Neuborne's inability, or unwillingness, to tell the difference between begging on a street corner and begging in a subway betrays an atomistic conception of reality. To Neuborne, and to most ACLU officials as well, there is this piece of paper called the Constitution that guarantees, among other things, free speech; because it doesn't make any exceptions, neither should we. But time, place, and manner are well-understood contexts in which speech may be required to conform. Leaving aside the question of whether begging is speech, and not conduct, it is nothing if not atomistic to close one's eyes to the reality of subway life. New York subways are dangerous and dirty places, places where the difference between a request and a demand for money is not easy to discern. In making his decision to overturn Judge Sand's ruling, Judge Frank X. Altimari quoted a 1988 study commissioned by the M.T.A. showing that a majority of subway riders perceive begging as "intimidating," "threatening," and "harassing."[70] By putting context back into the picture, Judge Altimari was able to see the captive nature of subway life, thus enabling him to render a decision that affirmed a social conception of liberty.

The homeless have tested New York more than most cities. Even when they are given jobs, many don't want them. For example, in 1988, Mayor Koch instructed Employment Commissioner Lilliam Barrios-Paoli to offer jobs to 30 homeless persons camped outside City Hall. Though 19 agreed to go to a job-referral appointment, only one showed up, and he quit his $9-an-hour janitor's job the first morning. Mayor Koch said his effort showed that "not one of them was willing to take the job. It demonstrates that many of these people who are complaining that the city isn't doing enough, that when they're offered jobs, they don't take 'em." Those who refused work replied that Koch was "lazy." Offering the ACLU view was Norm Siegel, who said that city officials had not spent enough time with the homeless trying to understand their motivations and ambitions.[71]

The Right to Freeze to Death

The right to shelter was first won in New York; the 1979 *Callahan v. Carey* consent decree, and the subsequent ruling in *McLain v. Koch*, gave the city no other choice. But those rulings didn't settle the issue. What should be done about those homeless persons who don't, but arguably should, seek shelter or hospitalization? Two years after *Callahan* was settled, the state legislature in Albany dealt directly with this question by seeking to amend the Adult Protective Services Act, a social services law. Specifically, it sought to allow a social worker or anyone working for the city to take someone who is endangering himself off the street and place him in an institution or hospital for 72 hours. The bill got nowhere because of opposition from the ACLU. Then a woman died in a cardboard box and the bill was quickly passed.[72]

Philadelphia was among the first cities in the nation to address the seriousness of the issue. At the start of the winter of 1985, Mayor Wilson Goode authorized the police to remove the homeless from the street whenever the temperature fell below freezing. Many of these persons, of course, did not possess the faculty of mind necessary to make informed consent. But that didn't stop the local ACLU from carping. Jane Edenbaum and Barry Steinhardt accused Mayor Goode of "cutting constitutional corners," maintaining that it was flatly wrong to assume that anyone who refused shelter was "mentally ill and incompetent."[73] But if cats and dogs know enough to get off the streets in freezing weather, why isn't it reasonable for Mayor Goode to conclude that humans who balk are probably incompetent? After all, the Animal Rescue League and similar organizations rescue homeless animals. Why shouldn't government rescue homeless men and women?

Even more incredible than the position of Edenbaum and Steinhardt was the one advanced by Elizabeth Symonds of the Washington, D.C., chapter of the ACLU. In January 1988, city council member John Wilson introduced legislation authorizing District police to pick up homeless persons when the temperature dipped below 25 degrees. Symonds saw this as an excuse for fascism: "They could take in you and me if we happened to be walking down the street at night."[74] In attempting to refute the charge that people who refuse shelter in sub-freezing temperature must be mentally ill, Symonds said that it was not uncommon for ACLU clients to demonstrate at round-the-clock vigils in cold weather.[75]

As usual, it was in New York where the ACLU got most involved. In January 1985, Mayor Koch, following the lead of Philadelphia's Mayor Goode, sought to empower the police to transfer the homeless from the streets to a hospital when the "effective temperature," including wind chill, dropped below 5 degrees. Koch's new proposal was designed to supersede his previous order—one that took considerable time to implement—which allowed the police to remove the homeless only after an examination by two psychiatrists.

Predictably, the New York CLU objected on due-process grounds. Commenting on the NYCLU, the *New York Times*, in a rare departure from its traditional defense of ACLU policies, editorialized that "it hardly helps the problem to defend, literally to the death, the rights of people often unaware of the finer points of due process. The Mayor and common sense are right."[76]

There was another showdown between the NYCLU and Mayor Koch the following winter. Koch sought to expand his policy (it was later dubbed "Project HELP") by permitting the police to remove the homeless whenever the temperature fell below 32 degrees; he also authorized mental health workers to hospitalize homeless people who were endangering themselves through self-neglect. In addition, the new policy allowed for psychiatric teams, including doctors, nurses, and social workers, to visit Grand Central and other terminals at night, for the purpose of treating the homeless and identifying those in need of hospitalization.[77]

The NYCLU's response was vitriolic. Director Norm Siegel and staff attorney Robert Levy lambasted Koch's policy for violating "the rights of countless homeless people who have competently refused to go to a shelter."[78] They offered no evidence of how they determined the competency of those who refused shelter. For Siegel and Levy, the problem of the homeless was simply an inadequate supply of low-income housing. They made no mention then, and they have made no mention since, of the complex behavioral problems that most homeless people experience. To do so, of course, would undermine their argument that the fundamental problem with the homeless is a lack of homes.

The NYCLU then went on the offensive: it instituted its own "freeze patrol."[79] When the temperature went below freezing, volunteers from the NYCLU, untrained in psychiatry, descended on stations like Grand Central and informed the homeless that they could either seek shelter or stay exactly where they were. Those who "preferred" the streets, sidewalks, and park benches—in the freezing cold—to the warmth of a hospital bed or shelter were advised by the patrol's leaflets to stick to their guns and refuse help. The way Siegel and Levy saw it, "The problem with the Mayor's directive is that it creates the presumption that anyone who chooses to remain on the streets in freezing weather is mentally ill and dangerous."[80] That such persons might be a danger to themselves was obviously not a persuasive point.

The radical individualism of the NYCLU is not shared by most professionals in the field of psychiatry. Dr. Alan Stone, a psychiatrist and lawyer at Harvard University, sees the ACLU as part of the problem: "The liberty of psychotic persons to sleep in the streets of America is hardly a cherished freedom, but a cruel and immoral consequence of failed libertarian reform."[81] Fellow psychiatrist E. Fuller Torrey agrees, complaining that the law prevents him from hospitalizing individuals desperately in need of care.[82] As a testimony to how bad conditions are living in the street, Torrey says that the rehospitalization rate for individuals released from mental hospitals is approximately 50 percent within one year. "What such figures do not tell, however, is that many of these individuals purposefully do such things as stopping their medicine or acting bizarre in public in order to get themselves rehospitalized. This fact may be the ultimate commentary on the quality of life for many mentally ill persons who have been deinstitutionalized."[83]

The issue that most galvanized New Yorkers against the ACLU was the "Billie Boggs" case, a case in which the NYCLU represented a mentally disturbed homeless woman seeking to avoid commitment to Bellevue Hospital. "When the Boggs case was going on, it was the prime topic of conversation for parents at my son's Little League games," says Fred Siegel (no relation to Norm Siegel of the NYCLU). "I heard comments like, 'This time they've gone off the deep end.' These were Little League games in Park Slope," a well-known liberal neighborhood in Brooklyn.[84]

In December 1986, Project HELP's professionals began receiving reports about Joyce Brown. The forty-year-old Brown, who used the pseudonym Billie Boggs (after a local radio-show talk host by that name), had made her home on a Second Avenue sidewalk between 65th and 66th streets in Manhattan. For a period of months, she was observed burning money, running into traffic, and urinating and defecating on the street. Brown, who is black, also shouted racial and sexual epithets at black male passers-by and refused all services offered by Project HELP.

Brown was not always down and out. Raised in a middle-class home in New Jersey, she had worked as a secretary for more than a decade. But in 1985 her sister had her committed to East Orange General Hospital, where she was restrained and medicated with Thorazine, an antipsychotic drug. Two weeks later she was released, certified as "not dangerous" and "not psychotic."

She soon migrated to New York, where on October 28, 1987, Project HELP staff picked her up and had her admitted to the psychiatric ward at Bellevue. She was examined by five psychiatrists, who diagnosed her as paranoid schizophrenic. Among other things, they said she was suicidal because she had run into oncoming traffic, and dangerous to herself because her hostility and obscene language might provoke others to cause her harm. They said she was delusional because she responded to questions about her use of the street as a toilet by telling an irrelevant story about events in Connecticut; they also noted that she had torn or burned money that was given by passers-by. For her part, Brown said she believed the passers-by were black males (some were not) who wanted to buy sex.

After arriving at Bellevue, Brown contacted the NYCLU. Robert Levy, who became her lawyer, disagreed sharply with the Bellevue diagnosis. Calling her "very intelligent" and "extremely lucid, extremely articulate,"[85] Levy said Brown not only wasn't sick, she was as mentally fit as his colleagues at the ACLU. "I didn't think I'd spoken to a mental patient," Levy said after his first meeting with Brown. "She sounded more like a board member of the civil liberties union."[86] The irony of this remark obviously escaped Levy.

Levy agreed to represent Brown and enlisted his own team of psychiatrists, headed by Dr. Robert Gould, professor of psychiatry at New York Medical College. Levy began in court by painting his client as fundamentally no different than most other citizens. Brown may have urinated on the sidewalk, Levy conceded, but every day in New York there are cab drivers and businessmen who do the same. What about burning the money she was given? This was a symbolic gesture similar to the protesters of the 1960s who burned draft cards.[87] Dr. Gould took the same approach.

Dr. Gould found Brown's judgment and insight "slightly impaired" but said she was generally coherent and logical, not delusional or psychotic. He rebutted each of the diagnoses of the hospital psychiatrists. Her obscene shoutings on the street, he said, were no different from the language he had heard in "every movie" he had seen recently.[88] Burning money, Dr. Gould said, was not an irrational reaction if Brown felt insulted by the manner in which it was offered. Moreover, he quipped, "I put a lot of money in the stock market, and I hope Ms. Boggs doesn't think I was crazy for getting a burn there." Brown herself denied running into traffic, and besides, Dr. Gould pointed out, jaywalking is common in New York. As for her toilet habits, the doctor noted that she was not allowed to use the restroom of the neighborhood restaurant and thus had no alternative but to use the street. "It's not nice, but it's not delusional," he said.[89]

In short, the NYCLU presented Brown's behavior as an alternative lifestyle. As Gould and Levy wrote in a *New York Times* op-ed essay, "It is quite possible to mistake homeless, unconventional, or unaesthetic behavior for serious pathology."[90]

Presented with the testimony of experts utterly at odds with each other, Judge Robert Lippmann threw up his hands and declared that the psychiatric evidence was inconclusive. He refused to hear testimony from Brown's sisters (who were furious at the ACLU) about her history of mental illness, relying instead on the testimony of Brown herself, whom he found to be "rational, logical, [and] coherent." Ironically, her credible performance on the witness stand may have been the result of two weeks of hospitalization, which had freed her from the stresses of life on the street. Dr. Albert Sabatini, then medical director of Bellevue's Department of Psychiatry, testified that it is common for schizophrenic patients to "stabilize" after undergoing treatment.

Judge Lippmann's ruling was appealed by the city and reversed by an appellate division panel. The NYCLU then appealed to the Court of Appeals, New York's highest court. Meanwhile, however, Bellevue psychiatrists determined that Brown, who remained hospitalized, needed immediate medication. The city petitioned another trial judge for permission to medicate her. A court-appointed psychiatrist agreed that Brown was ill and could be helped by medication but said that because she had displayed hostility toward the Bellevue doctors, it would be counterproductive for them to medicate her against her will. The judge accepted the recommendation and denied the city's request. At that point, the city gave up and released Brown. The Court of Appeals then dismissed the NYCLU's appeal, holding that the issue was moot since Brown was no longer in the hospital.

Legally, then, the case ended inconclusively. The highest court to rule on the matter upheld the city's standard for institutionalization, and Project HELP continued as it had in the past. Brown, meanwhile, worked briefly as a receptionist for the NYCLU but left, Siegel says, because she was unable to cope with the job. Brown then appeared on several talk shows. She went on *Donahue*, but not before the producers bought her $300 worth of clothes at Bloomingdales and paid $200 for a new hairdo (her stylists first had to get the lice out of her hair). Then Brown hit the lecture circuit, visiting many of the nation's top law schools. Sixteen days after she spoke at Harvard Law School, she wound up on the street again, panhandling and swearing at black people.[91] Was she now free at last, as the ACLU claimed? Let's put it this way: the week she won her reprieve from forced medication, three homeless men were found frozen dead in New York.[92]

City officials view the result as a tragedy for Brown. The fact that Brown led a fairly normal life in the past, says Dr. Sabatini, suggests there is a strong possibility she could be treated successfully with psychotropic drugs. Yet the NYCLU regards her personal autonomy— including her prerogative to live on the street—as sacrosanct, outweighing both the social costs of that decision and the cost to Brown herself. Moreover, it hardly helps to maintain that it was the city's lack of adequate resources that resulted in Brown's despair. After all, it was the NYCLU that fought hard not to accept the services the city offered. This can hardly be characterized as a failing of society.

There are significant social costs that inevitably result from extreme interpretations of individual rights. "In *Boggs*, one could not argue the case by saying Billie Boggs was offensive," says Paul Rephen of the New York City Law Department (he was part of the legal team that prepared the city's case). "Individuals have a constitutional right to be offensive. So, you can't go into court saying that part of the problem when we have homeless like this is that it affects the quality of life in New York City. That is not an issue that the City can argue."[93]

The legal system, which exists to resolve individual claims, is not well suited for weighing social costs and benefits. There is no public-interest law group that truly represents the public interest in a case like *Boggs*; even if there were, "society" would not have legal standing in the case. Because judges often end up serving as the final arbiters on important social issues, a court system receptive to reckless claims of individual freedom can do great social damage by unsettling the delicate balance between the rights of the individual and the needs of society.

Compounding the problem is the ACLU's conflation of social issues with civil liberties concerns. This was shown quite vividly in the NYCLU's 1985 class-action lawsuit, a case that lasted well into the 1990s. In part, the suit was clearly a civil liberties case: it challenged the use of allegedly excessive methods to restrain mental patients in city hospitals and demanded that adequate medical services be offered to patients who were committed or detained in hospital waiting rooms.

But in pursuing the case, the NYCLU was also acting as an advocate for expanded mental health services. City officials readily conceded that overcrowding was a problem in the city's mental hospitals and that the NYCLU's demands were a defensible policy position. To satisfy the NYCLU, however, the city would have to enter into a legally binding agreement committing itself to certain levels of service. "While it may seem reasonable," says Leonard Koerner, the city's chief assistant corporation counsel, "to the extent that you have to allocate additional resources in order to satisfy those demands, it means allocating less resources to other areas."[94]

Koerner likens the NYCLU and other advocacy groups to labor unions. "Their job is to demand as much as they can get, and there are judges here who will accommodate them."[95] The influence of these organizations on New York's political culture is pervasive: Even when advocacy groups do not involve themselves directly in an issue, city officials must anticipate and avoid policy decisions that might give rise to costly lawsuits.

Caught in the middle, of course, is the urban middle class, which must bear the burden of both expensive court-mandated social services and growing public disorder. The result, in the words of Charles Morris, New York's former director of welfare and Medicaid: "New York City's current social policy is based on the presumption that you can do whatever you please, and it is the City's job to pick up after you."[96] That line of thinking is unfortunately advanced by the actions of the ACLU.

Freedom or Slavery?

If there is an answer to the plight of the homeless, and especially to the large numbers who are mentally ill, it will take a change in policy along the lines suggested by Charles Krauthammer, the columnist who was trained as a psychiatrist. "The standard for the involuntary commitment of the homeless mentally ill is wrong," Krauthammer argues. "It should not be dangerousness but helplessness." But what prevents us from doing this, he notes, "is the misguided and pernicious civil libertarian impulse that holds liberty too sacred to be overridden for anything other than the preservation of life. For the severely mentally ill, however, liberty is not just an empty word but a cruel hoax. Free to do what? To defecate in one's pants? To wander around Grand Central Station begging for sustenance? To freeze to death in Central Park?"[97]

The ACLU remains steadfast in its belief, however, that it is the real champion of the homeless, and of the homeless mentally ill in particular. It is convinced that the problem is a matter of money: if the government would only build more housing, the problem would go away. What this position neglects is not just the behavioral problems of the homeless; it sorely underestimates the extent to which good housing, provided at public expense, becomes a magnet for the less-than-truly homeless or dispossessed. In the 1980s, Thomas J. Main, one of the early students of the homeless in New York, provided a cogent case outlining why better housing might abet an increase in demand, thus engendering not only fraudulent applications but a state of dependency as well.[98]

Main's thesis was shared by officials of the Koch administration, and in particular by William J. Grinker, head of the Human Resources Administration. Grinker issued explicit warnings that speeding up the placement of families in permanent housing could encourage more families to enter the system. The senior critic of this view, aside from the ACLU, was Nancy Wackstein, author of a 1987 report on the homeless. Wackstein dismissed the idea that people used shelters as a route to permanent housing, saying it was little more than cynical to even suggest it.

When David Dinkins became mayor, he appointed Wackstein his chief advisor on the homeless. She quit in frustration in September 1991, less than two years into Dinkins's rule. Her tenure provided the opportunity for a badly needed reality check: upon resigning, she acknowledged the veracity of the Koch position, admitting that the faster the city provided housing, the faster people applied. Commenting on her previous position, Wackstein offered, "I was a little more naive then."[99] Her husband, Victor Kovner, who spent two years with the Dinkins administration as the city's corporation counsel, had also rethought his views. "Victor and I were such good Upper West Side liberals," Wackstein confessed. "And look what's happened to us."[100]

Perhaps it is because ACLU officials have never had to struggle with the difficulties of implementing social programs that they have been spared the reality check of Wackstein and Kovner. One thing is for sure: New York's housing program has indeed turned into the magnet that people like Main feared. Since 1986, New York has been required to provide instant shelter to anyone who demands it and is under increasing pressure by the courts to update the accommodations. It is not uncommon now for the city to house able-bodied, well-educated families at the cost of $3,000 per month. Indeed New York, which has 7.3 million people, spends seven times as much on the homeless as Los Angeles, Chicago, Houston, and Philadelphia, which have a total of 9.7 million people.

Trying to screen the fraudulent from the truly needy requires questioning. Yet when government officials seek to place the homeless in decent housing, Norm Siegel still throws up roadblocks. Siegel raised objections when in 1989 Westchester County began screening applicants for shelter services. He demurred, asserting: "The homeless are a fragile and loner constituency that very often likes to be left alone. They value their anonymity and freedom and do not want to be assessed, surveyed, and studied."[101]

There is something terribly inconsistent about the ACLU's approach to mental illness. On the one hand, we hear how the homeless value their anonymity and how people like Joyce Brown are "rational," indeed "very intelligent," human beings. On the other hand, when it comes to the insanity defense, the ACLU is quick to assert its legitimacy, holding that there are felons, including serial killers, who should be found not guilty by reason of insanity. What explains these positions is an atomistic vision of liberty, one that maximizes individual rights and minimizes individual responsibilities. It is wrong, so we are told, to punish the Jeffrey Dahmers and the Ted Bundys of this world: they did not choose to kill their victims. In the meantime, we should depopulate the mental institutions, treat as rational people who defecate on the street, and at the same time refuse to hold them accountable for their behavior.

If the homeless are to be helped, then those among them who can help themselves will have to do so. That is the perspective of many of those who have actually been in, or worked in, their ranks. When Middle Tennessee State University sociologist Dan McMurry posed as a homeless person in the late 1980s, he said the most striking aspect of being homeless was the extent to which no one demanded any responsibility from him. McMurry's experience convinced him that unless we replace the "hand-out" and "care-giving" approach with a "hand-up" and "enabling" strategy, it is not likely that the conditions of the homeless will demonstratively change for the better.[102] Dr. Laurence Schiff, a psychiatrist who spent several years working with the homeless, agrees:

"The real solution to the homeless problem lies in a return to 'middle-class values,' and indeed to the promotion of them in the lower class."[103]

ACLU attorneys, safely ensconced in their law offices, are never to be heard demanding accountability from the homeless. Nor are they inclined to insist on the importation of middle-class values. Their view of liberty doesn't quite reach that far. But as W. Robert Curtis has put it, "The tragedy of deinstitutionalization stems not from the idea of liberty itself but from its extreme application to all disabled individuals irrespective of their disability."[104]

Rael Jean Isaac and Virginia C. Armat, after having written a splendid book on the homeless, ended their work with an indictment of the ACLU: "Groups like the ACLU become self-righteous spokesmen for the very people they have 'liberated' to the shame of the streets. The real torment of their victims is buried under the cant of 'homelessness' with its hypocritical indictment of the political system for mistreating the poor."[105] The ACLU no doubt disagrees, but it is remarkable nonetheless how many experts on the homeless have come to the same conclusion as Isaac and Armat. And that is an indictment not easily shaken, not even by the ACLU.

Notes

1. See D.J. Baumann, et al., *The Austin Homeless: Final Report Provided to the Hogg Foundation for Mental Health* (Austin, Texas: Hogg Foundation for Mental Health, 1985); and Peter Rossi, et al., "The Condition of the Homeless in Chicago," National Opinion Research Center, Chicago, Illinois, and Social and Demographic Research Institute, University of Massachusetts, Amherst, Massachusetts, 1986.
2. William R. Breakey, et al., "Health and Mental Health Problems of Homeless Men and Women in Baltimore," 262 *Journal of the American Medical Association* (September 8, 1989): 1352–57.
3. E. Fuller Torrey, *Nowhere To Go* (New York: Harper and Row, 1988), 8.
4. John Scanlon, "Homelessness: Describing The Symptoms, Prescribing A Cure," Heritage Foundation *Backgrounder*, October 2, 1989, p. 5.
5. William R. Breakey, et al., "Health and Mental Health Problems of Homeless Men and Women in Baltimore," pp. 1352–57.
6. Bryce J. Christensen, "On the Streets: Homeless in America," *Family in America*, June 1990, p. 2.
7. Ibid., p. 4.
8. Interview with Richard W. White, Jr., "The Homeless and the Confused," in *Family in America*, August 1992, p. 1.
9. For a revealing portrait of Snyder, see Howard Kurtz, "The Home He Left Behind," *Washington Post*, March 16, 1988, p. C1.

10. Snyder made his admission in testimony before the House Banking and Government Operations Committees, in a joint hearing on the HUD Report on Homelessness, May 24, 1984, p. 32. It is cited by Scanlon in his Heritage *Backgrounder* piece.
11. See Scanlon, "Homelessness: Describing the Symptoms, Prescribing a Cure,"; and Peter Rossi, *Down and Out in America: The Origins of Homelessness* (Chicago: University of Chicago Press, 1989).
12. Jacob A. Riis, *How the Other Half Lives*, (New York: Dover, 1971), 69–75, 165. The book was originally published in 1890.
13. Michael Harrington, *The Other America* (New York: Macmillan, 1963), 88–91.
14. Peter Rossi, *Down and Out in America*, 44.
15. The quotes were taken from Gina Kolata, "Twins of the Streets: Homelessness and Addiction," *New York Times*, May 22, 1988, p. A1.
16. Roger Starr, *The Rise and Fall of New York City* (New York: Basic Books, 1985), 155–56.
17. Torrey, *Nowhere to Go*, 120–22.
18. Quoted by Philip M. Boffey, "Failure Is Found In The Discharge of Mentally Ill," *New York Times*, September 13, 1984, p. A1.
19. Quoted by Richard D. Lyons, "How Release of Mental Patients Began," *New York Times*, October 30, 1984, p. C1.
20. Erving Goffman, *Asylums: Essays on the Social Situation of Mental Patients and Other Inmates* (New York: Doubleday, 1961).
21. Thomas Szasz, *The Myth of Mental Illness* (New York: Harper and Row, 1961).
22. Thomas Szasz, "New Ideas, Not Old Institutions, for the Homeless," *Wall Street Journal*, June 7, 1985, p. 12.
23. Quoted by Rael Jean Isaac and Virginia C. Armat, *Madness in the Streets* (New York: Free Press, 1990), 111.
24. Ibid.
25. Jeffrey T. Leeds, "The ACLU: Impeccable Judgments or Tainted Policies," *New York Times Magazine*, September 10, 1989, p. 78.
26. W. Robert Curtis, "The Deinstitutionalization Story," *Public Interest* (Fall 1986): 43.
27. Torrey, *Nowhere To Go*, 158.
28. Oliver Sacks, "Forsaking the Mentally Ill," *New York Times*, February 13, 1991, p. A19.
29. Quoted by David Rocah, "Homelessness and Civil Liberties," *Civil Liberties*, Fall/Winter, p. 5.
30. Policy #318, "Poverty and Civil Liberties."
31. William Tucker has done the best work on this subject. See his "Where Do The Homeless Come From?" *National Review*, September 25, 1987, pp. 32–43, and "America's Homeless: Victims of Rent Control," Heritage Foundation *Backgrounder*, January 12, 1989.
32. Policy #318, "Poverty and Civil Liberties."
33. Quoted by William A. Donohue and James Taranto, "The Assault on Public Order: How the Civil Liberties Union Goes Astray," *City Journal*, Winter 1992, p. 47.
34. This information was supplied to me by Charles Oliver of *Reason* magazine on May 9, 1990. Oliver was working on an article on the ACLU at the time, one that appeared in its October edition.
35. David Rocah, "Taking Liberty to the Streets," *Civil Liberties*, Spring 1990, p. 4.
36. See the tape recording of the 1985 Biennial Conference section on "Poverty and Civil Liberties."

37. Ibid.
38. Rita Giordano, "Protest Gives Way to a Sign of Hope: Clash Brings Unity to Tompkins Square," *Newsday*, August 14, 1988, p. 2.
39. Quoted by Curtis Taylor and Chapin Wright, "Tomkins Sq. Park Chain-Link Fence to Circle Former Haven for Homeless," *Newsday*, June 4, 1991, p. 5.
40. Quoted by Donohue and Taranto, "The Assault on Public Order," p. 42.
41. Robert Rohn, "Oh, Lucky Day," *Newsday*, June 12, 1991, p. 99. Rohn's Op-Ed piece appeared in the "Viewpoints" section of the newspaper.
42. Quoted by Robin Pogrebin, "Does Civil Libertarian Hinder City Order?" *New York Observer*, March 9, 1992, p. 1.
43. McDonald originally posted his remarks in an article he wrote for the *Atlanta Constitution*. Portions were republished in "A Song for Loafing," *Civil Liberties*, Spring/Summer 1988, p. 7.
44. Eric Schmitt, "Sssh! And Scram! Library Fights Homeless Invasion," *New York Times*, September 15, 1989, p. 24.
45. Ibid.
46. Robert Hanley, "Ruling Bars Libraries From Banning the Homeless as Offensive, *New York Times*, May 29, 1991, p. B1.
47. This part of Sarokin's ruling was mentioned in "Libraries and License," *Wall Street Journal*, June 12, 1991, p. A14.
48. Robert Hanley, "Ruling Bars Libraries From Banning the Homeless as Offensive," May 23, 1991, p. B1.
49. Robert Hanley, "Protection of Homeless Has Library in Quandary," *New York Times*, May 29, 1991, B1.
50. Lisa Glick Zucher registered her remarks in a letter to the editor, *Wall Street Journal*, December 2, 1991, P. A13.
51. Robert Hanley, "Library Wins in Homeless-Man Case," *New York Times*, March 25, 1992, p. A14.
52. "New Library Code Issue in Ann Arbor," *New York Times*, December 2, 1984, p. 36.
53. Burt Neuborne, "Supreme Court Falters, Alas," *New York Times*, July 22, 1984, p. E21.
54. *Clark v. Community for Creative Non-Violence*, 468 U.S. 288 (1984).
55. See the tape recording of the 1985 Biennial Conference section on "Poverty and Civil Liberties."
56. Susan Blank, "The Homeless," *Civil Liberties*, Winter 1986, p. 3.
57. "Affiliate Notes," *Civil Liberties*, Spring 1990, p. 14, and "Perhaps the Best Thing to Do Is To Enliven Westerly's Night Life," *Wall Street Journal*, June 29, 1989, p. B1.
58. "Miami Fined for Violating Homeless Rights," *New York Times*, March 20, 1991, p. A11.
59. Torrey, in *Nowhere to Go*, says that the deinstitutionalized mentally ill "are responsible for an increasing number of violent acts." See p. 17.
60. Eileen Hershenov, "Diverse Issues Confront Court; Souter Stance Remains Elusive," *Civil Liberties*, Winter 1990–91, p. 12. The case was *Wilson v. Seiter*.
61. David Rocah, "Homelessness and Civil Liberties," *Civil Liberties*, Fall/Winter 1989, p. 7.
62. David E. Pitt, "M.T.A. Rejects Sex-Act Curbs By Metro-North," *New York Times*, September 23, 1989, p. 27.

63. Michael Freitag, "Grand Central Barriers To Homeless at Station," *New York Times*, September 17, 1989, p. 25.
64. Sara Rimer, "Pressed on the Homeless, Subways Impose Rules," *New York Times*, October 25, 1989, p. B5.
65. Pitt, "M.T.A. Rejects Sex-Act Curbs By Metro-North."
66. Eric Pooley, "Beggars' Army," *New York*, August 29, 1988, p. 32.
67. David Rocah, "Taking Liberty to the Streets," *Civil Liberties*, Spring 1990, p. 4.
68. Quoted by Andrea Sachs, "Buddy Can You Spare a Dime?" *Time*, February 12, 1990, p. 55.
69. *Young v. New York City Transit Authority*, 729 F.Supp. 341 (1990).
70. *Young v. New York City Transit Authority*, 903 F.2d 146 (1990).
71. Kevin Flynn, "Homeless Outside City Hall Don't Want Jobs, Koch Says," *Newsday*, September 3, 1988, p. 3. 71.
72. See the interview with State Senator Frank Padavan, "Private Rights, Public Fears," *New York Times*, February 3, 1985, p. E9.
73. Jane Edenbaum and Barry Steinhardt, "Rounding Up the Homeless," *Civil Liberties Record* (of Pennsylvania), December 1985, p. 6.
74. Quoted by Charlotte Low, "A Rude Awakening from Civil Liberties," *Insight*, March 21, 1988, p. 9.
75. Liz Symonds, "Homeless Legislation," *Capital Liberties* (newsletter of the National Capital Area), Winter 1988, p. 4.
76. "In From the Cold," *New York Times*, January 24, 1985, p. A24.
77. Donohue and Taranto, "The Assault on Public Order," p. 43.
78. Norman Siegel and Robert Levy, "The Real Problem Is Housing," *New York Times*, December 17, 1985, p. A27.
79. Susan Blank, "The Homeless," *Civil Liberties*, Winter 1986, p. 1.
80. Siegel and Levy, "The Real Problem Is Housing."
81. Quoted by Daniel Goleman, "States Move To Ease Law Committing Mentally Ill," *New York Times*, December 9, 1986, p. C4.
82. Ibid.
83. Torrey, *Nowhere to Go*, 25.
84. Donohue and Taranto, "The Assault on Public Order." Much of the material on the Boggs case is taken from this article.
85. Quoted by Jeanie Kasindorf, "The Real Story of Billie Boggs," *New York*, May 2, 1988, p. 41.
86. Ibid. Levy's exact words were printed in the transcript of the *60 Minutes* television show of January 24, 1988.
87. Jeanie Kasindorf, "The Real Story of Billie Boggs," p. 42.
88. Ibid.
89. Donohue and Taranto, "The Assault on Public Order," p. 44. See also the discussion about the Boggs case in Isaac and Armet, *Madness in the Streets*, 256–60.
90. Robert E. Gould and Robert Levy, "Psychiatrists as Puppets of Koch's Roundup Policy," *New York Times*, November 27, 1987, p. A35.
91. Kasindorf, "The Real Story of Billie Boggs," p. 44.
92. Charles Krauthammer, "How to Save The Homeless Mentally Ill," *New Republic*, February 8, 1988, p. 24.
93. Donohue and Taranto, "The Assault on Public Order," p. 45.
94. Ibid., p. 47.
95. Ibid.
96. Ibid.

97. Krauthammer, "How to Save the Homeless Mentally Ill," p. 23–24.

98. See Thomas J. Main's two articles published in the *Public Interest*. The first, "The Homeless of New York," appeared in the Summer 1983 edition, pp. 3–28; the other, "The Homeless Families of New York," was published in the Fall 1986 edition, pp. 3–21.

99. Quoted by Celia W. Dugger, "Benefits of System Luring More Families to Shelters," *New York Times*, September 4, 1991, p. A1.

100. Quoted by Peter Hellman, "Sue City," *New York*, September 16, 1991, p. 60.

101. Quoted by Lisa Foderaro, "Queries First, Aid Later For a County's Homeless," *New York Times*, September 4, 1990, p. B3.

102. See the two articles by Daniel McMurry, "Hard Living on Easy Street," *Chronicles*, August 1988, pp. 15–19; and "Down and Out in America," *Crisis*, February 1989, pp. 27–31.

103. Laurence Schiff, "Would They Be Better Off in A Home?" *National Review*, March 5, 1990, p. 35.

104. W. Robert Curtis, "The Deinstitutionalization Story," p. 47.

105. Isaac and Armat, *Madness in the Streets*, 335.

7

Crime and Civil Liberties

The ACLU View of Crime

One of the purposes of the Constitution, as stated in the Preamble, is to ensure domestic tranquility. Due process, the Fifth Amendment right, is a procedural right, one that defines the methods that can properly be used to ensure domestic tranquility. Without both, there can be no liberty. Domestic tranquility can easily be achieved without respect for due process, as dictatorships throughout history have shown. It is also quite possible to have a society where due process is respected—even considered sacrosanct—and still lack for domestic tranquility. The latter predicament more closely resembles the situation in the United States today.

Owing to its atomistic vision of society, the ACLU disconnects due process from the ends that it was designed to serve. Civil libertarians maintain that it is their job to attend to due process and it is the job of the police to ensure domestic tranquility. But what if the situation were reversed? What if we said it was the police's job to attend to domestic tranquility and it was the job of civil libertarians to worry about due process? Would that not be a recipe for police misconduct, perhaps on a very wide scale? It seems to be generally understood that the exclusive concern for domestic tranquility is detrimental to the process of liberty. What is less often acknowledged is that the exclusive concern for due process can also disable liberty.

A social conception of liberty does not consider it a victory for freedom if due process systematically stands in the way of justice. All the rights in the first ten amendments are predicated on the ability of people to exercise them freely, and for this to be done, a modicum of civility must prevail. What good does it do if people have the freedom to speak, or to travel, if they are afraid to venture outside their homes? Life, liberty, and the pursuit of happiness are conditional properties, not realizable in an environment of lawlessness. The fact that this needs to be said at all is demonstrative of the problem. The only liberty worthy of its name is one that allows people to enjoy the fruits of their liberty, and this simply cannot be done in a society plagued with drugs and violence.

"According to the ACLU," writes Jeffrey Leeds, "there is no right to live in a quiet or pleasant society, but there is a right to speak, to seek to persuade, to have unpopular or even stupid views. Moreover, there is no right even to live in a safe society. The A.C.L.U. will work to vindicate a convicted criminal's rights to due process, even if it means setting a killer free."[1] Leeds does not exaggerate. The ACLU has a very selective view of what constitutes a right. Take, for example, the ACLU's perspective on the constitutional right to life.

The Fifth Amendment mentions that no one shall "be deprived of life, liberty, or property, without due process of law." Now consider what the ACLU has to say about the right to life that ordinary citizens seek to enjoy. Former Attorney General Edwin Meese, who once called the ACLU a "criminals lobby," explained to Meg Greenfield of the *Washington Post* that the ACLU was so preoccupied with the rights of criminals that it was in need of a counter organization, one that would oppose the Union "on the basis of the rights of the law-abiding citizen to be free from criminal activity." To this, ACLU official Dorothy Ehrlich replied that "the citizens' need to be 'free from criminal activity' . . . is not, in the legal sense, a 'right' at all (and thus is nowhere mentioned in the Bill of Rights) but, rather, an essential social good, like fire prevention, or adequate medical care, or the prevention of famine."[2]

Ehrlich's comment is revealing for several reasons. Here is an official of the ACLU stating that if a right is not mentioned in the Constitution, it is therefore not a right at all. This from an organization that defends such things as abortion-on-demand, the sale of child pornography, dwarf-tossing, and the right to sleep in public parks, though none of these alleged rights are anywhere mentioned in the Constitution. Even more telling is Ehrlich's conception of what constitutes a right. The first purpose of government is to provide for order. That all Americans have a right not to be molested is surely implicit in the concept of domestic tranquility. Just having to repeat this verity is demonstrative of the extent to which civil libertarians have embraced an atomistic vision of freedom.

That the ACLU's interest in criminal issues extends only to criminals can be seen quite clearly in the way it approaches the the rights of the victims of crime. Unlike the Washington Legal Foundation, which has made crime victims' rights a priority, the ACLU has shown little interest in the subject. Indeed, Washington Legal Foundation president Dan Popeo quotes an ACLU staffer as saying "Victims don't have rights."[3] Perhaps this explains why former ACLU executive director Aryeh Neier once exploded in anger when I asked him why the ACLU hadn't issued a handbook on the rights of crime victims. Since my exchange with Neier, which took place in 1978, the ACLU has released a book on the subject, though as Dr. Lawrence Cranberg has noted, it did so only after it had already released four editions of its handbook entitled *The Rights of Prisoners*; *The Rights of Crime Victims* has merited just one printing.[4]

Ed Martone, head of the New Jersey affiliate, has said that giving victims a role in parole decisions would violate prisoners' rights, and that is why he recommends that "the proper role for a victim's testimony is during a trial."[5] But the organization he works for thinks there should never be a place for a crime victim's testimony. The ACLU opposes the use of a crime victim impact statement in capital sentencing because it "unconstitutionally requires consideration of factors which have no bearing on the defendant's responsibility or guilt."[6] In 1991, the Supreme Court, in *Payne v. Tennessee*, ruled otherwise, holding that juries deciding whether to sentence convicted murderers to death may consider evidence relating to the victim's personal characteristics as well as the emotional impact of the murder on the victim's family. The court's ruling sustained the arguments put forth at the trial by the Washington Legal Foundation.[7]

Drugs

The nightmare of drugs, and the violence it spawns, is known everywhere in the United States, but nowhere is the problem more serious than in the nation's inner cities. So what does Harvard professor Alan Dershowitz recommend we do about it? He thinks we should decriminalize drugs and have mobile vans distribute heroin in the inner cities to "medically certified addicts."[8] His Ivy League colleague at Princeton, Ethan Nadelmann, goes even further by declaring that legalization is "probably the godsend in the minority, inner city communities."[9] But with the notable exception of former Washington mayor Marion S. Barry and Mayor Kurt Schmoke of Baltimore, virtually all those clamoring for drug legalization have been white. Indeed, most of those who live in the inner cities have been silent on the issue, making it seem curious why some well-educated white people think it is in the best interest of black people to legalize drugs.

Those pushing for drug legalization cross the political spectrum, ranging from William F. Buckley, Jr., and Milton Friedman on the right to the ACLU on the left. In general, those who call for legalization can be grouped into two camps: those who are driven by principle and those who are motivated by pragmatism.

Pragmatists like Mayor Schmoke favor drug legalization as a way of curbing violence. If the profit were taken out of drug trafficking, the drug wars, we are told, would stop, as would the recruitment of youngsters as runners. But no one knows for sure what would happen, and there is ample reason to question Schmoke's reasoning. Almost all advocates of drug legalization, Schmoke included, do not recommend that every conceivable drug be made available in unlimited amounts. That means there will still be a black market for drugs. And with the black market comes turf wars, hence the spuriousness of the claim that drug legalization would necessitate an end to gang warfare. Moreover, when the U.S. Justice Department estimates that 70 percent of criminals arrested for serious offenses regularly use drugs, it tells us something about the character of those engaged in antisocial behavior.

The hard reality is that drugs typically do not turn people into criminals; rather, it is criminals who typically turn to drugs. According to the reputed criminologists James Q. Wilson and Ricard Herrnstein, "it is a mistake to assume that all or even most [heroin] addicts turn to crime for the first time as a result of becoming dependent on an illegal drug. Most studies of addicts reveal, on the contrary, that they started committing crimes before they started using heroin."[10]

Buckley's position is similar. His stance is born of exasperation with a policy that seems to have failed; legalizing drugs, he thinks, might at least curb gang disputes over control of neighborhoods. But even Buckley admits that his proposal is fraught with danger: "I have the horrible feeling that addiction definitely will increase" if drugs are legalized.[11] Mr. Buckley's "feelings" are substantiated by the evidence.

During Prohibition there was a dramatic decline in alcohol-related mental and physical illnesses, a situation that reversed itself quickly once the Volstead Act was repealed. Other nations have had similar experiences. After Britain won the Opium Wars and forced China to rescind its drug ban in 1858, almost one-third of the nation became addicted by the turn of the century. In Franco's Spain, severe penalties for drug use resulted in few addictions. However, since the Socialists relaxed the penalties and decriminalized possession for personal use in 1982, addiction has soared. In Britain, during the years when heroin could be legally prescribed, addiction increased fortyfold. Zurich's experiment with decriminalization has been an absolute disaster: both addiction and crime have escalated. To cite another instance, it is well known that addiction is rampant among peasants involved in cocaine and opium production. And in this country, it is known that more than 40 percent of doctors in hospitals use illicit drugs.[12]

The principled argument in favor of drug decriminalization is based on a dubious conception of liberty. The ACLU calls drug use a "victimless crime" and thus opposes laws that prohibit "the introduction of substances into one's own body."[13] But using drugs is not a victimless crime, not when 60 to 70 percent of the children born in Washington, D.C., are born to mothers who use drugs. And when fully 30 percent of the babies born in New York City are crack babies, talk about drugs as a "victimless crime" seems almost criminal. The billions that are spent annually trying to prepare these children for kindergarten similarly casts doubt on the "victimless" nature of this behavior.

Even more troublesome is the ACLU's readiness to treat drug use as a principled right. Only a truly atomistic idea of liberty would cast drug use as nothing more than "the introduction of substances into one's own body." Accessing a needle at a shoot-up gallery is not on a par with accessing water from a fountain, yet the "body liberation" school of thought that motivates the ACLU seems unwilling to draw this distinction. Obsessed with the idea of rights, the ACLU cannot think beyond the level of the autonomous individual reflexively exercising his or her rights. But at some point, dysfunctional individuals make for a dysfunctional society, leaving no escape valve for anyone, not even for civil libertarians.

Prior to the mid-1960s, the ACLU had no policy on drugs. While Dr. Timothy Leary of Harvard University was telling youngsters to "turn on, tune in, and drop out," the ACLU was declaring drug addiction to be an illness, not a crime. However, the Union's first policy on drugs, framed in 1966, did not recommend the abolition of criminal penalties; that would not occur for another ten years. Then, beginning in 1976, the Union started taking an absolutist position—making no exceptions even for drugs like crack and angel dust— that every drug should be legalized, allowing only for what it calls "reasonable regulatory restraints."[14] Indeed, the ACLU's policy is so radical that Ira Glasser has a hard time trying to defend it in public, often leaving the impression that the Union isn't in favor of drug legalization.[15]

It could be argued that the ACLU's policy has no effect on the lives of ordinary Americans. But as public housing tenants have found out, this is not the case. In the 1980s, New York Mayor Edward Koch tried repeatedly to oust drugs from public housing projects, only to be met by opposition from the New York Civil Liberties Union. Jack Kemp ran into ACLU obstructionism as well.

One of the first acts that Kemp performed as Secretary of Housing and Urban Development in the Bush administration was to order a crackdown on drug dealers and abusers in public housing projects. After visiting housing projects in Baltimore and Philadelphia, and seeing the ease with which drug trafficking takes place, Kemp sent a memorandum to over 3,000 public housing authorities throughout the country informing them of his willingness to help rid the projects of drugs. He wanted to know what the local authorities were doing to oust drug dealers from the projects and how HUD could help. The immediate reaction of the ACLU, as expressed by housing specialist Wade Henderson, was predictable: "I'm concerned about the memo being misinterpreted as being a hunting license that encourages extrajudicial procedures that jeopardize constitutional rights." To which Kemp responded, "In some cases, the A.C.L.U. is part of the problem."[16]

As a priority, Kemp sought to do something about the outrageously long delays associated with the eviction of known drug dealers and abusers from the housing projects. It is well known that it takes more than a year to rid the projects of drug offenders, during which time they can continue to practice their trade. Hearings must be set, and both the tenant and the housing official must first agree on who the hearing officer should be. If they can't agree, they each appoint a member of a hearing panel, and those two members appoint a third hearing officer. That can take more than a year. Then the housing authority must show that the accused tenant has impaired the physical or social environment of the project. Many of the accused will admit they use drugs but claim not to interfere with the rights of others (thus offering the ACLU line, as expressed by Norm Siegel). If the accused loses, he can appeal to a local court, consuming even more time. This is the way justice is meted out in the nation's housing projects.[17]

In March 1989, after a policeman and his assailant were killed in a drug-related shootout at a public housing development in Alexandria, Virginia, Secretary Kemp began giving localities the authority to waive federal requirements for a grievance hearing before securing a court-ordered eviction. The ACLU screamed foul and sent Wade Henderson and Jacqueline Berrien to testify against Kemp's initiative before the Senate Subcommittee on Housing and Urban Affairs. Henderson and Berrien stressed the need for hearings and opposed the eviction of family members of convicted drug offenders. As to what should be done about the problem of drug-infested public housing units, the ACLU operatives recommended the expenditure of more money for modernization of the projects.[18] The fact that the presence of the drug runners made for deteriorating conditions was apparently lost on Henderson and Berrien.

One housing project that impressed Secretary Kemp was Chicago's Rockwell Gardens. Under the tutelage of Chicago Housing Authority chairman Vince Lane, the gang-controlled, drug-ridden Rockwell Gardens were made respectable once again. In the fall of 1988, after years of despair, the tenants at Rockwell Gardens were treated to a massive crackdown, led by Chairman Lane. A team of police and housing authority guards was sent in to clean house, searching apartments for weapons and drugs and chasing away anyone not authorized to be inside. Called "Operation Clean Sweep," it was quickly dubbed by Kemp as "a model for the rest of country." The tenants responded with enthusiasm to the sweeps. "Before the crackdown," said Mildred Wortham, "kids couldn't sit on the playground for 30 minutes without having to scatter because of the gunfire." Everyone seemed happy about the turn of events, except for the ACLU. It sued the housing authorities for violating the privacy rights of the tenants.[19]

Kemp questioned the residents of Rockwell Gardens to see if the crackdown on drug dealers and abusers led to a lessening of rights. One of the tenant leaders questioned by Kemp "indicated that she never had any rights prior to the sweep, as the elderly and single-parent mothers in the building lived in a state of perpetual fear and were forced to pay gangs 'for protection' when they used the elevators." Kemp added that "it is indeed ironic—and tragic—that legal-aid groups and the ACLU would deny the right of poor people to live in healthy communities free of thugs and dope fiends who threaten the lives of their children."[20]

To be sure, the war on drugs, if not tempered by a legitimate concern for due process, can lead to tyranny in the name of justice. But that is not the problem that those who live in the projects face. They are faced with a system that creeps along, serving the lawyers and the guilty more than the housing officials and the innocent. It is not for nothing that Vince Lane once remarked, "The ACLU and everyone else are going to have to recognize that the majority of residents in public housing have rights as well as the wrongdoers."[21]

Loren Siegel, the person in charge of the ACLU's public education programs on drugs and civil liberties, charges that Jack Kemp's war on "drug dealers and *users* has impacted disproportionately on people of color and victimized the innocent on a large scale." As proof, Siegel says that "the police are actually razing residential buildings in black communities to the ground, an act worthy of the Nazis." The net result is that "martial law has been declared in our inner cities."[22]

Siegel's characterization of Kemp's program highlights the ACLU's perspective on drugs. To begin with, there is the curious emphasis on cracking down on *users* as well as dealers. Siegel's emphasis, of course, is meant to suggest ACLU disapproval of arresting drug users, a position quite in step with the Union's advocacy of drug legalization. Siegel is correct to maintain that the war on drugs has "impacted disproportionately on people of color." But it is also true that the persons most likely to be victimized by drug offenders are also "people of color," and it is precisely those people who have been the strongest advocates of Kemp's program. And Siegel's excitable prose about "Nazis" and "martial law" is also misplaced: when the cops take a sledgehammer to a crack house, they are not greeted by community residents as storm troopers but as liberators.

One way to combat drug dealing in the inner cities is to have a tightly drawn antidrug loitering law. This is what the citizens in Alexandria, Virginia; Tacoma, Washington; and Tampa, Florida have done, all over the outcries of the ACLU. The trigger case was the one in Alexandria; it resulted in a showdown between the ACLU and the National Association for the Advancement of Colored People on one side and the American Alliance for Rights and Responsibilities and the Washington Legal Foundation on the other side.

In 1988, Alexandria passed an antiloitering ordinance designed to combat drug dealers. Mindful of the potential for abuses in such a law, local officials drew the ordinance very narrowly, making it quite difficult to break: In order to be in violation, one would have to stand on a corner for more than fifteen minutes *and* meet with more than two people in succession for less than two minutes each *and* exchange small parcels of money *and* attempt to hide such transactions from public view *and* have no other explanation for these actions. The law was supported by all civic association presidents in the affected neighborhoods, both African American members of the Alexandria City Council, the police, and Democratic Mayor Jim Moran. The ACLU sued, claiming that the law was so overbroad that it could lead to the arrest of lawyers handing out business cards.[23] It won.

In the end, the citizens of Alexandria managed to get a new law passed, one that the ACLU said it would not challenge. Though watered down, the law gave the police something to work with, and within six months it was evident that street drug activity had abated markedly. Maxine Clark, a public school teacher and civic leader in Alexandria, was not appreciative of the ACLU's contribution to her liberty. "The ACLU," commented Ms. Clark, "is stuck in a time warp. They don't see that drugs are a problem where the black community is being destroyed from within, not from Jim Crow or bigoted sheriffs."[24]

The ACLU not only misunderstands the sentiments of the black community regarding drugs, it is baffled by the widespread support that most Americans give to the war on drugs. After looking at the results of a 1989 poll taken by the *Washington Post*, Ira Glasser was moved to write another one of his EMERGENCY FUND-RAISING LETTERS (his third of the year), this time expressing his frustration with the American people. Because most Americans favor stricter measures than heretofore have been used and want stiffer penalties for both users and sellers, Glasser concluded that the people were "ready to give up fundamental rights to win the war on drugs." Indeed, in an emotional statement, Glasser said that the tough measures being advocated amounted to "public hysteria."[25]

If the American people love freedom, why are so many of them willing to support the war on drugs? That drugs deny liberty to those who don't use them (as well as to those who do) is not something Glasser or the ACLU wants to acknowledge. Matters might be different if drug users lived on their own island, engaged in acts of pure self-destruction. But the reality is that drug users unavoidably affect the liberties of those they come in contact with, beckoning many Americans to consider trading a diminution of their privacy rights for a safer environment. Now if the point ever came that the war on drugs was taking a higher toll on liberty than the current reign of unrestricted drug dealing is, it seems plain that most Americans would support a less aggressive drug-enforcement policy.

It comes as no surprise to learn that the ACLU opposes virtually all measures taken to curtail drug use. The Union opposes traffic checks in open-air drug markets, notwithstanding the fact that stopping cars to check for driver's licenses, insurance, and registration has reduced drug trafficking in these areas.[26] It has gone into court protesting the right of the police to fly over a man's backyard to check for marijuana plants;[27] the Union cited an abridgment of the man's privacy rights (it lost in the Supreme Court). When the Naval Research Lab reported that it had developed a new, inexpensive high-tech system to screen for drugs—one that takes just 45 seconds to detect for minuscule amounts of cocaine in blood, urine and saliva—the ACLU complained that this was "an alarming development."[28] The Union was similarly alarmed when it learned that a person can be searched at an airport if he matches a government profile of a drug courier.[29]

The ACLU opposes bans on the advertisement of products used in the distribution or transfer of illegal drugs.[30] In 1991, the Union criticized an Oklahoma law designed to curtail abuses in drug prescriptions. The law was aimed at flagging doctors who appear to be overprescribing controlled drugs and patients who "doctor shop" for multiple prescriptions. The "triple prescription" law, effective in many states, was labeled by the Oklahoma CLU as "just a vehicle for the government to further snoop and dig around in people's private lives."[31]

Also in 1991, Illinois Bell took steps to deter drug dealers by altering pay phones in two Chicago neighborhoods so they could no longer take coins after dark. If only collect calls or a calling card can be used to activate the phones, the phone company reasoned, drug dealers might well think twice about leaving a record of their calls. "We're willing to give up something to bring back dignity and respect to our community," said Sharon Benson-Lewis of Chicago's Westside Business Improvement Association. But to Jay Miller of the Illinois CLU, the new policy was seen as "terribly discriminatory." That it was: it discriminated against the drug runners, and that is why the residents of the two neighborhoods agreed with Ms. Benson-Lewis, and not with Mr. Miller.[32]

What penalty is appropriate for drug kingpins? Take the case of Ronald Harmelin, sentenced to life without parole for drug dealing. The ACLU, which was opposed by the Washington Legal Foundation in *Harmelin v. Michigan*, argued that Michigan's mandatory penalty of life without parole for large-scale drug dealing was "cruel and unusual punishment" that violated the Eighth Amendment. On June 27, 1991, the Supreme Court, by a 5-4 margin, upheld the Michigan law.[33] The facts of the case made the ACLU's argument hard to sustain.

Harmelin was arrested following a traffic stop in October 1986. At the time of his arrest, he was carrying on his person several marijuana cigarettes, four brass cocaine straws, a cocaine spoon, three individually packed vials of cocaine, twelve Percodan tablets, twenty-five tablets of phendimetrazine tartarate, a .38- caliber revolver, a Motorola beeper, and nearly $600 in cash. After his arrest, police searched the trunk of his car and found Harmelin's shaving kit. Inside it was $2,900 in cash and a bag of pure cocaine weighing 672 grams (approximately one-and-a-half pounds), enough for between 32,000 and 65,000 doses; the street value was estimated between $60,000 and $100,000. This is the guy the ACLU said shouldn't be sentenced to life without parole.

The ACLU has opposed virtually every bill allowing for tough penalties against drug offenders. It was highly critical of the "Zero Tolerance" policy of the Reagan administration and fought most of the initiatives of William Bennett, George Bush's drug czar. The Union worked against the Omnibus Drug Bill of 1988 (which passed the Senate by a vote of 87-3) and protested legislation introduced by Senator Phil Gramm aimed at yanking driver's licenses, student loans, and housing grants from those convicted of drug offenses. In addition, the ACLU opposes the denial of federal licenses and contracts to those convicted of two drug offenses, wants no penalties incurred for women convicted of child abuse for taking cocaine while pregnant, rejects the idea that the military should have a role in stopping drug trafficking, opposes boot camp for those who commit a crime while on drugs, and disapproves of invoking the death penalty in cases of drug-related murders.[34]

Drug testing is another taboo for the ACLU. It has done all it could to obstruct and halt drug testing wherever it occurs, typically citing the rights of privacy and bodily integrity. It is not just mandatory drug testing that the Union objects to: it even has qualms about voluntary testing. In some parts of Texas, for instance, high-school students are given discounts at local theaters, fast-food restaurants, bowling alleys, and the like if they agree to test for drugs. In Tyler Texas 93 percent of the students at Whitehouse High School voluntarily submitted to testing in 1990, leaving Joe Cook of the Dallas office of the ACLU "suspicious of the effect on civil liberties." Cook registered his complaint this way: "The occurrence of a false positive on a test could have a devastating effect on a child. We believe this kind of peer pressure can result in civil liberties violations." Billy Pricer, a retired minister who founded the program, reminded Mr. Cook that the testing was voluntary and added, "we have had negative peer pressure on kids for a long time and the ACLU never jumped on that."[35]

It is a popular ACLU argument, not central to its principled objection to drug testing, that drug tests can be flawed. No one, of course, doubts this to be true. Moreover, there may be good scientific reasons for employers not to rely too heavily on drug tests as a basis for making important personnel decisions. But it is peculiar, to say the least, for the ACLU to at once declare its opposition to all drug testing and then cite the validity of drug tests to buttress a point it wants to make.

In their 1990 testimony regarding the President's National Drug Abuse Strategy, Lynn Paltrow, Kary Moss, and Judy Crockett of the ACLU offered by way of example the case of a Michigan woman who had been unfairly accused of taking "illegal drugs" (their choice of quotes) during pregnancy. The three ACLU women said that the "drug screens to which she agreed were negative." Perhaps they were, but what of it? Just three pages later, in the same testimony, the authors contended that "false positives in drug tests are quite common and the prevalence is magnified by human error."[36] Now if this is true, then how can these women be sure that the test of the Michigan woman was really negative? Maybe it was a "false negative"?

When it comes to drug testing, the Union has been active on all fronts, ranging from the criminal justice system to the private workplace. With regard to convicted criminals, the ACLU opposes drug testing prior to sentencing and as a condition of federal parole, probation, or supervised release.[37] The Union also objects to drug testing in the workplace[38] and even goes so far as to say that if an employee is currently taking drugs, he should not be subject to disciplinary action by his employer unless he cannot perform his job or endangers the life of others.[39] Of course, demonstrations of incapacity may come too late to matter, especially in jobs affecting the health and safety of others. That is why in some jobs there are few practical alternatives to drug testing.

The ACLU may consider taking drugs a "lifestyle choice," but when innocent human lives are lost as a direct consequence of this choice, we are dealing with something that goes beyond a mere choice of lifestyles. "As we grope for what to do about hazards such as drunk driving and kids routinely toting pistols down school corridors," writes Paul Glastris, "and as we seek to stem drug and alcohol abuse by the people who operate our trains and aircraft, the ACLU puts up its dukes as if it were mixing it up with Bull Connor."[40] Glastris, a former editor of the *Washington Monthly*, is no conservative, but he recognizes a weak argument when he sees one.

From jockeys and horse trainers in Massachusetts to school bus attendants in the nation's capital, the ACLU has filed suit to stop drug testing.[41] But it has been its unrelenting opposition to drug testing in safety-sensitive jobs that has drawn the most fire. How much sense does it make for the ACLU to maintain that the nuclear weapons industry "has a shocking record of contamination, unsafe working conditions and nuclear accidents"[42] and then oppose drug testing for employees in that industry? And how much sense does it make for the ACLU to oppose drug testing *after* a major train wreck leaves 16 people dead and 178 injured? This is exactly what happened in 1987 in the Amtrak-Conrail collision.

The Amtrak-Conrail story is particularly disturbing. On January 4, 1987, the brakeman and engineer of a three-engine Conrail train smoked marijuana while on duty. Consequently, the engineer ignored several warnings and failed to slow the train, the end result of which was that the train drove through an intersection and onto a track in Chase, Maryland, just ahead of an Amtrak passenger train traveling at 105 miles per hour. The collision, and the ensuing fatalities, led the authorities to test the brakeman and engineer for drugs. The ACLU immediately filed suit. It was undismayed when the tests proved positive, still convinced that the privacy rights of its clients were of overriding importance.[43]

To this day, when Ira Glasser is questioned about the ACLU's role in the Amtrak-Conrail wreck, he tries to deflect attention away from the Union's opposition to drug testing by saying that the ACLU supports performance testing.[44] Performance testing means that each and every employee must be randomly tested on the job to see if he can demonstrate the kind of dexterity that the job demands. But it is hardly an economical operation. Imagine subjecting air traffic controllers and pilots to performance testing before they take to their job. The ACLU knows this but is unprepared to take the kinds of steps that really matter, owing, perhaps, to its professed interest in legalizing drugs altogether.

After the Amtrak-Conrail crash, there was a groundswell of support for testing employees in safety-sensitive jobs, leading almost all members of Congress to endorse tough measures. The ACLU did not read this reaction as cause for a policy change, but it did come up with reasons for opposing drug testing that went beyond its right-to-privacy and bodily-integrity arguments. However, its new approach proved to be similarly unpersuasive.

In 1988, Allan Adler, ACLU legislative counsel for the Washington Office, said that the Union would oppose mandatory drug testing in the commercial air, rail, and motor vehicle transportation industries. He complained that the bills before Congress failed to define such terms as "post-accident," would preempt state and local laws, were costly to implement, and would result in "a massive regulatory scheme" certain to "produce nightmares for the agencies that must administer it."[45]

Adler's first objection was perfunctory. But his other concerns have much merit to them. There is a problem, however, in expecting people to believe that the same ACLU that supports federal legislation for comparable worth cannot back other public-policy programs on the grounds that they might preempt state and local laws, cost too much money, and result in an administrative nightmare. Surely principled civil libertarians must see these inconsistencies as readily as anyone.

Like drug testing, sobriety road checks are aimed at stopping accidents before they happen. The ACLU opposes them as well.[46] And that's not all. "The administration of a breathalyzer test to detect intoxication in drivers," says official ACLU policy, "is a search and seizure within the meaning of the Fourth Amendment." Such tests can be used "only when the police have probable cause to believe a *particular* driver is under the influence of an intoxicant." What might pass as "probable cause" the Union does not say. But what is clear is that even when passengers are killed by a reckless driver, the Union remains steadfast in its opposition to blood tests. The ACLU reasons that "the compelled taking of blood from a criminal suspect is per se unreasonable under the Fourth Amendment, and unduly invades the privacy interest in bodily integrity."[47]

In the 1980s, a California law was passed permitting sobriety checkpoints. According to Paul Glastris, the aim of the test was to "nab drivers with gin-soaked breath, not those with copies of *Das Kapital* or *The Watchtower* stashed in the glove compartment." There were no body cavity searches, no right of the police to give citations for broken headlights or an expired inspection sticker. In addition, the police were denied the right to ask for the driver's license, save for instances when there were noticeable signs of intoxication or drugs. Even the date, and in some cases the precise location, of the checkpoint had to be publicized in newspapers and on TV and radio. And as a final precautionary measure, a lit sign was posted well in advance of the checkpoint notifying motorists of the impending test, allowing ample opportunity to turn around. But this wasn't reasonable enough for the ACLU, so it sued.[48]

The ACLU lost in California Supreme Court but did not give up the fight to have sobriety road checks declared unconstitutional. In Michigan, it found a case that it argued all the way to the U.S. Supreme Court. What happened in Michigan was that at the checkpoint, police conducted a brief discussion with the drivers and then waved them on if they detected no violation. If the driver appeared intoxicated, a breathalyzer test was administered. The average delay, including waiting in line, was about 90 seconds. This experiment was tried only once, for about one hour, before the ACLU went into court to challenge it.[49]

Sensing defeat, Loren Siegel expressed the ACLU's position by saying that if the Michigan statute were upheld, "then by the same reasoning the police may conduct suspicionless searches and seizures to deal with the equally serious problems of unlicensed firearms and stolen goods."[50] But the danger that a drunk driver poses is imminent, thus warranting a minimal intrusion into the privacy of the individual; he or she is also readily detectable. The same cannot be said of persons who harbor unlicensed firearms and stolen goods. As it turned out, the ACLU lost in a 6-3 decision in *Michigan v. Sitz*.[51] Since that time, the ACLU has not reported any instances of cops breaking and entering people's homes looking for contraband.

Ever consistent on these matters, the ACLU thinks that public drunkenness should be declared a civil liberty.[52] More revealing is its attitude toward alcoholic veterans who fail to take advantage of the GI Bill. The ACLU maintains that such persons should be given an extension of their ten-year time limit to use education benefits. For the ACLU, being an alcoholic constitutes a "handicapped status," not "willful misconduct"; the Supreme Court did not see it that way.[53] Now put the ACLU's position on this issue with its opposition to granting anything less than an honorable discharge to all military personnel (it does not matter if treason or murder was committed on duty),[54] and it tells volumes about the Union's concept of moral responsibility.

Crime Control

The family has more to do with crime control than the law, and much the same could be said of the schools and churches. But when mediating institutions fail—as they too often do these days—then there is nothing left but the naked power of the law. A social conception of liberty favors strong mediating institutions and an effective criminal justice system. Due process is not unimportant, but it is not the whole of the issue, either. The atomistic school to which the ACLU subscribes is singularly concerned about due process; it essentially sees the issue of order as someone else's problem.

No modern society can have meaningful crime control without a well-trained police force. The ACLU would not dispute this, though its idea as to what constitutes well-trained is not widely shared. It surely wants to limit the discretionary authority of the police. Moreover, its official policy statements indicate a greater interest in cop control than crime control, raising legitimate questions about whether the Union bears an animus against the police. Make no mistake about it, there are some in the ACLU who are plainly biased against the police. How many it is difficult to say, but the following section leaves no doubt that at least some are.

In the 1960s, the Supreme Court issued several landmark decisions on crime and civil liberties, including the exclusionary rule and the right of the accused to be read his or her rights upon arrest. These decisions had the effect of putting constraints on the police and have remained controversial even after a generation of usage. Prior to the 1960s, the police surely had more authority, and it is fair to ask whether they had too much. But few would claim that in the 1950s the police were largely out of control. Among the few is Samuel Walker, ACLU house historian. "With few Supreme Court rulings on police conduct," writes Walker, "American police were therefore essentially lawless."[55] Walker's perception of the police, it is fair to say, may not be widely shared among the public at large, but it is a fair representation of the views of many civil libertarians.

Any amount of police misconduct is a problem, and that is why no one objects to efforts that provide more professionalism and accountability. It is still an open question, however, as to how this should be achieved. The ACLU favors empowering civilian review boards,[56] panels that investigate charges of police wrongdoing. More debatable is why the ACLU, concerned as it purportedly is about police misconduct, finds it necessary to defend the right of police officers to belong to the Ku Klux Klan.

In 1990, when the town of Newfields, New Hampshire, learned that one of its police officers, Thomas Herman, belonged to the Ku Klux Klan, it had him fired. In stepped the ACLU to rescue Herman, citing freedom of association. For Clare Ebel, the New Hampshire executive director of the Civil Liberties Union, it was a clear case of discrimination on the basis of political affiliation. Boston columnist Don Feder saw things differently: "Once again the First Amendment fetishists are letting their fixation blind them to reality, in this case the reality of police work. If Klan members are allowed to infest police departments, how can a black, a Jew, an Hispanic, or an Oriental have any confidence in the operations of the same?"[57]

Feder's column was met by criticism by Colleen O'Connor of the New York office. "If town officials in New Hampshire have the right to bar Klansmen from their police force," wrote O'Connor, "what's to stop officials in another town from barring members of the NAACP from their ranks?"[58] For O'Connor, then, there is no distinct difference between avowed racists and terrorists joining the police force and those who belong to a sometimes controversial civil rights organization. But to get to the point, O'Connor still needs to address Feder's central issue: If a quality police force is desirable, then how much sense does it make to allow Klan members to join it? NAACP members do not have a history of racism and violence, and that is why their inclusion on the police force does not present a problem.

The Union's reaction to the beating of Rodney G. King, the black man who was beaten by white Los Angeles police officers after a high-speed chase on March 3, 1991, provides another look at how civil libertarians see the world of the police. The King beating, which was videotaped by a citizen, triggered a meeting of the Executive Directors Council (EDC) of the ACLU. The EDC, founded in 1974 as a forum for information exchange among affiliate directors, met in the aftermath of the King beating "to devise an action plan regarding the persistent problem of police brutality."[59]

For Ira Glasser, the King episode proved "what we have been saying for decades: that police brutality is an all-too-common occurrence, that it is often tinged with racism." Indeed, Glasser says that during his long association with the ACLU, "no other civil liberties complaint has been more common and steady" than police brutality. He charges that police brutality "is systemic and not an aberration" and elsewhere refers to the problem as "generic."[60]

Ramona Ripston of the Southern California affiliate agrees with Glasser, charging that the King affair was business as usual. Ripston, who quickly called for the resignation of Los Angeles police chief Daryl Gates, said her office averages 50 complaints a week from people objecting to LAPD tactics. She says the LAPD is a "highly mechanized police department with a great deal of state-of-the-art technology and a history of reliance on paramilitary style of law enforcement." Ripston blames the "cowboy mentality" of Gates and others in the police force for what happened.[61]

Now if Glasser and Ripston are right—racism and brutality are pervasive among urban police—why do they continue to defend the right of the police to belong to the Ku Klux Klan? By making this defense, the ACLU nullifies whatever remedies it recommends to combat racism and brutality on the police force. All the seminars and workshops on prejudice are not likely to matter in the end if the police know they can sign up with the Klan whenever they want. Moreover, it would not comfort most blacks to know that their police officer neighbor has the right to be elected as the Imperial Wizard. Nor would it make much sense to blacks to learn that liberty might be endangered if we *didn't* allow their neighbors to become the Imperial Wizard. Most reasonable persons might rightly wonder what kind of definition of liberty is at work.

When the officers who beat Rodney King were acquitted by a jury on April 29, 1992, a riot erupted in Los Angeles. It lasted for five days and left 60 people dead, causing an estimated $850 million in damages. On August 5, 1992, federal prosecutors announced that the four defendants in the case had been indicted on charges of violating Mr. King's civil rights.

The ACLU was caught in a dilemma. It had recently voted to oppose a 1992 Supreme Court decision permitting someone to be prosecuted by the federal government in cases where an acquittal had been reached in a state court for the same offense. Policy dictated that the ACLU oppose the federal prosecution of King, while politics dictated the opposite. Initially, politics triumphed over principle. On June 21, 1992, the national board of the ACLU voted to "suspend" its opposition to the Supreme Court decision, thus clearing the way for the federal prosecutors.[62] But on April 4, 1993, the board reversed itself and voted 37-29 against approving an exception to the double-jeopardy rule. Significantly, all 10 black members who were present voted to allow for the second trial of the implicated police officers.[63]

The Southern California affiliate has a history of letting politics dictate its behavior toward the LAPD. In 1984, the affiliate won a $1.8 million settlement against the LAPD. The Union had represented 144 left-wing organizations and individuals who complained that they had been the targets of illegal surveillance. In a second suit, the affiliate went after Western Goals, a private, conservative foundation that was used as a depository for some of the police files. The Southern California CLU charged Western Goals with "illegal storage and dissemination," meaning that it objected to the dissemination of information on political activists through the foundation's newsletter. This put the ACLU, defender of the publication of the Pentagon Papers, on the side of wanting to censor Western Goals. But would the ACLU have sued the police and Western Goals if the information had contained reports on South African intelligence operatives? Henry Holzer of Brooklyn Law School thinks not,[64] and there is ample reason to conclude that he is correct.

The case of policeman Richard Long demonstrates that the Southern California affiliate has long had it in for the police. In 1980, Long attended a public meeting held by the ACLU at Newport Harbor High

School. Long was not in uniform but was spotted by some ACLU officials nonetheless and was summarily ejected from the meeting. It was Linda Valentino, an operative with the American Friends Police Surveillance Program, who called attention to Long's presence, and it was ACLU attorney Rees Lloyd who confronted the Newport Beach policeman. Long charged that he was publicly humiliated and illegally ejected by Rees and Valentino.[65] Long's attorney, Jeffrey M. Epstein, cited the Unruh-Ralph law which bars business organizations from discriminating on the basis of arbitrary classification. The ACLU's response to this was to cite its right to free speech and freedom of association.

In 1987, the jury ordered the ACLU to pay Long $92,000; the figure was later pared back to $35,000. It is ironic to note that although it was ACLU attorney Rees Lloyd who was found guilty of Gestapo-like tactics, it was none other than Lloyd himself who charged that the jury's verdict reminded him of Nazi Germany in 1936. "It's probably appropriate in Germany in 1936," said Lloyd, "but certainly not in the United States in 1987."[66] After the trial, the ACLU settled its case, but Lloyd refused to quit and filed an appeal challenging the damages set against him. In 1990, the California Supreme Court declined to review the jury's assessment of the $46,000 in damages against Lloyd for harassing and ejecting Long.[67]

The Southern California CLU's war on Richard Long ended in embarrassment. Looking back at it now, it puts the affiliate's strong response to what happened to Rodney King in perspective. At issue is more than police misconduct. To be certain, police misconduct should be roundly condemned wherever and whenever it occurs. But reasonable people have a right to expect that those throwing the first salvos should not be tainted with a historical vendetta against the police.

Serious crime-control measures must come to grips with the issue of gun control. Whether gun control is effective is highly debatable. New York and Washington have among the toughest gun control laws in the country and also set annual records for the number of people killed by guns; the nation's capital has properly been dubbed the "murder capital of the world." "We get half our guns through trade-ins with dope fiends," confesses a gang member in Chicago's South Side. "If you wanted a gun right now, we could put in an order and you'd have it. It's like going through the drive-through window. 'Give me some fries, a Coke and a 9-millimeter.'" Rev. Paul J. Hall, founder of a community center in his name, agrees: "Getting a gun in Chicago is as easy as jumping into Lake Michigan."[68]

Just as controversial are the constitutional issues surrounding gun control. The Second Amendment simply says "A well regulated Militia, being necessary to the security of a free State, the right of the people to keep and bear Arms, shall not be infringed." Whether this means that only those in the army are allowed to own guns or whether every citizen has a right to bear arms has been the subject of a running debate. The ACLU, which favors an absolutist interpretation of the First Amendment, noticeably retreats on the Second Amendment, stating that "except for lawful police and military purposes, the possession of weapons by individuals is not constitutionally protected."[69]

From a social perspective on liberty, there is much merit to the argument that the states should have the right to regulate the sale and distribution of arms. In this regard, the ACLU's willingness to consider something other than individual rights is a refreshing departure from established procedure. However, how the ACLU came to its position is not without its own problems.

Official ACLU policy holds that "the setting in which the Second Amendment was proposed and adopted demonstrates that the right to bear arms is a collective one, existing only in the collective population of each state for the purpose of maintaining an effective state militia."[70] This is not an indefensible position to take, but it is a rather odd one for the ACLU to be sponsoring. As many examples in this book have already shown (for example, freedom of speech and religion), the historical context in which the Bill of Rights was written has never been of much interest to the ACLU. In short, the Union's reasoning seems forced and altogether expedient.

The Due Process Committee of the ACLU has been largely responsible for framing Union policy on gun control. In 1982, after much consideration, the members of that committee concluded that "no acceptable civil liberties rationale could be developed for affirmative support of gun control legislation."[71] Perhaps this is why the ACLU regards gun control as a question of social policy and not as a matter of civil liberties,[72] notwithstanding the fact that the Second Amendment addresses the issue. According to Jacob Sullum of *Reason* magazine, it is officials like Ira Glasser who are most responsible for this position. "If civil libertarians such as Glasser have difficulty understanding why law-abiding people would want to arm themselves against the government," comments Sullum, "it's because they have strayed so far from the philosophy of natural rights that underlies the Constitution."[73]

Sullum has a good point. ACLU interest in the Second Amendment has little to do with natural rights principles or with questions regarding "the setting" in which the Second Amendment was framed. In fact, such a concern might logically lead the ACLU to take the opposing position, namely that the right to bear arms is constitutionally protected. British common law, for example, long supported the right of citizens to bear arms. The Founders also had no qualms about this matter. In *The Federalist*, Madison wrote that "the advantage of being armed, which the Americans possess over the people of almost every other nation," provides them with an almost "insurmountable" barrier to tyranny. George Mason held that "to disarm the people . . . [is] the best and most effectual way to enslave them." Richard Henry Lee went further, arguing that "to preserve liberty, it is essential that the whole body of the people always possess arms and be taught alike, especially when young, how to use them."[74]

Edward J. Erler and Daniel C. Palm offer an interpretation of the Second Amendment that the ACLU resists hearing. "A commonsensical reading of the Second Amendment," they instruct, "is readily available: 'Since militias are necessary to the security of a free state, the people must therefore have the right to keep and bear arms.'" Individual citizens, they remind us, are what constitutes a militia, "and part of being a citizen of a free state is service in the militia."[75] So why doesn't the ACLU accept this line of reasoning? According to constitutional scholar and ACLU member Sanford Levinson, it is because the ACLU is ideologically predisposed against such arguments. Levinson charges that for the ACLU, the Second Amendment is "profoundly embarrassing."[76]

Even more embarrassing to the ACLU is Norm Siegel's objection to a New York legislative proposal to evict public-housing tenants who *illegally* possess firearms. "What they would have to show, in our opinion," said Siegel of the New York affiliate, "would be activity that interferes with other tenants and their rights."[77] But Siegel is not unaware of the hundreds who are wounded and killed each year in New York's housing projects. So on the one hand it is perfectly fine to ban guns, but on the other hand it is wrong to ban illegally owned guns in the housing projects. This may make sense to civil libertarians, but certainly not to those who live in the projects.

Worse than embarrassing is the ACLU's opposition to metal detectors in the airports. In 1973, the airlines began using metal detectors to screen for metal objects at the airports. The strategy has paid off as the number of hijackings has declined significantly over the past few decades. But the ACLU stands fast, holding to the conviction that metal detectors are a gross violation of the Fourth Amendment ban on unreasonable searches and seizures. Though the Union rarely discusses this issue today, and though it has long since given up on trying to have metal detectors banned (it says blacks and people with long hair are no longer singled out),[78] its opposition to the devices is still official ACLU policy. To those who maintain that without metal detectors we might all be endangered, the Union simply replies, "Regrettably, we live in dangerous times."[79]

If it is true that we live in dangerous times, it is doubly true for children. While the ACLU is not responsible for the conditions that give rise to crime, the course of action it follows makes it more difficult to create conditions of safety. Consider curfew ordinances. On occasion, when cities are plagued with a killing spree—especially involving youngsters—laws are passed forbidding minors from being in public late at night. The ACLU summarily sues. Official policy says that "the Union opposes juvenile curfew restrictions as unjustifiable government intrusions on the rights of children and young people and on parental rights to control and direct the movements of their children."[80]

The ACLU's approach to the issue of curfew ordinances is nothing if not atomistic. Its concern is solely with those children, and their parents, who don't want the curfew. That the public weal might be ill-served by not having the ordinance seems not to count. But in cities across the country, and especially in cities with black mayors and city councilmen, the sentiment has been different. In Philadelphia,[81] Washington,[82] and Atlanta,[83] black officials have passed curfew ordinances, reflecting the position of the overwhelming majority of their constituents.

The Atlanta curfew was passed in 1990, after two years of late-night crime left 25 young people dead. Mayor Maynard Jackson signed the law, which set a curfew of 11 p.m. on weekdays and midnight on weekends for youths under 17 years old. Parents who were cited could face up to 60 days in jail and $1,000 in fines. But according to ACLU spokeswoman Ellen Spears, the law was draconian: "It deprives teenagers of their rights unconstitutionally, and it goes further in penalizing parents without a showing that they contributed to what the child did." But Councilwoman Daveeta Johnson, the sponsor of the law, said the ACLU's concerns were misplaced.[84] As was the case for other black officials, Ms. Johnson's biggest fear was for the life of black youngsters, something she saw as even more important than even civil liberties.

Cruising is another problem involving youth, and it is one which the ACLU works hard to defend. The Union contends that bans on cruising are illegitimate, offering little solace to neighborhood residents who feel their rights are being abused. But when gays seeking sex, or drug users seeking a fix, cruise in their cars back and forth in front of homes—at all hours of the night—it is only logical that residents will push for an end to this kind of public nuisance. And it is predictable that when they do, in will step the ACLU, as it has done in Milwaukee and elsewhere. When the residents of the Pittsburgh community of Oakland complained in 1991 of noisy radios and engines and of people having sex in cars, they were accused of being anti-gay by Marion Damick, the local affiliate director.[85]

Far more serious than cruising is gang warfare. Here again, the ACLU's idea of what constitutes liberty is in stark contrast to what ordinary citizens mean. For example, the public supports police sweeps designed to clear public space, such as parks, from gang ownership. But for the ACLU, "Police sweeps strike at the heart of a citizen's First Amendment right to freely associate."[86] Ironically, it is precisely because law-abiding citizens are denied their First Amendment right to freely associate in public parks that police sweeps are instituted in the first place. The citizens of San Fernando know this better than anyone.

On July 3, 1991, a young mother and her three children were caught in the crossfire of two gangs in Las Palmas Park in San Fernando. Wounded, they became the center of public outcry over the terrorism that regularly marked the park. On September 16, the San Fernando City Council passed an ordinance prohibiting active members of street gangs from entering the park. A $250 fine was authorized for any active gang member that had been tied to convictions for two or more serious criminal offenses in a three-year period. The law was specific beyond reproach: no gang member could be prosecuted for entering the park unless he had received prior police notice and warning of the prohibition's application to him. If the gang member renounced his membership before walking into the park, he could enter unimpeded. But all these civil liberties guarantees carried little weight with the ACLU. So it sued.

The Hispanics who populate San Fernando enthusiastically favored the ban on gang members from its park. It worked. Within a few months, the gang members had disappeared and the park was restored to law-abiding citizens. Ramona Ripston was one of the few who were unhappy. "In order to achieve security," the ACLU official said, "people have been frequently willing to sacrifice their constitutional protections." But to a young mother who was free to return to the park, this was hard to understand. "All I know is it's better now," she said.[87]

To legal scholar Bruce Fein, the ACLU's suit was emblematic of its "litigating lunacy." "The ACLU should be cheering, not condemning, the San Fernando ordinance," Fein said. He called attention to the fact that the law "expands individual liberty—namely, the right to enjoy a public park without risking life and limb."[88] Fein's point is well taken: the ACLU's notion of liberty is so concentrated on due process that it has forgotten that the most elementary liberty is the right to live in peace and security.

Effective crime control often benefits from state-of-the-art technology. But it is critical that civil liberties are not endangered in the process. "Caller ID" is a case in point. This new technology enables the subscriber to view the numbers of incoming calls on a special display unit; it also allows callers to suppress their phone numbers in order to prevent them from being shown. The ACLU is not wrong to suggest that there are privacy interests on both sides of the issue. The devices could discourage people from calling hotlines when in need. But they could also serve to deter obscene phone calls. The Union's official policy holds that Caller ID "should not be made available unless callers are given the ability to control when, if ever, their number is displayed on the receiving end."[89] Though a case for the alternative conclusion could be made, the reasoning that the policy offers, as well as Janlori Goldman's testimony before a House subcommittee, was measured and sensitive to the multiple issues involved.[90]

Unfortunately, the ACLU's willingness to look at all sides of the Caller ID issue does not generally extend to other matters. Take, for example, its hostility to antistalking legislation. To the ACLU, such laws are an invitation to overly zealous prosecutors. But there are ways of ensuring against misuse without throwing out antistalking measures altogether.

Women, in particular, are glad that more states are passing them. They want to be spared the experiences of people like Erin Tavegia of Meriden, Connecticut.

When Erin was 15 years old, a man started following her back and forth from her high school. He parked his car outside her home and would appear at all hours of the day and night. When she left her house, he would drive slowly behind her, occasionally asking her to join him in the car. Everywhere she went, he followed. The cops could do nothing: without an antistalking law, there was no crime to charge him with. When such a law was passed in 1992, Phil Gutis of the local ACLU registered his complaints, stating that the legislation was poorly defined.[91] But to women who have been terrorized like Erin, any assistance the law could give to their situation was long overdue. Their idea of liberty was much broader than Mr. Gutis's.

The police also wonder about the ACLU's idea of freedom. In 1989, the mayor and the police commissioner of New York were aghast to learn that policeman Edward Byrne was killed after a contract was placed on him by an arrested drug dealer calling from a jail phone. Almost no one, other than Norm Siegel of the New York affiliate, thought it appropriate that the phone was made accessible. Siegel contended that the accused need access to a phone in the event that they want to talk their lawyer. Fine; but did it ever occur to civil libertarians that this legitimate request could easily be accomplished by having someone at the station house call the lawyer for the accused or have a message left for the attorney to call his or her client? Are we left with no other choice but to allow arrested drug dealers to phone in their hit?[92]

It is clear that the ACLU has given much attention to the rights of the accused. That is what a civil-liberties organization should do. It is legitimate to question, however, whether the Union's interpretation of due process serves the best interests of justice *of all those involved in the criminal justice system*. After all, the public, as well as the alleged crime victim, has a stake in seeing to it that the scales of justice do not tip too far toward the rights of the accused. Too much tipping, either way, may ensure one party's justice at the other party's expense. When that happens, it's a net loss for justice.

The ACLU's reaction to crime control legislation brings this issue into sharp focus. When it comes to crime-control bills, the ACLU almost always registers its opposition.[93] Any bill that broadens coverage of capital punishment, limits the number of appeals available to those convicted of a capital offense, allows for preventive detention, expands the meaning of "good faith" exception, narrows the exclusionary rule, or in any way authorizes more discretionary police power will automatically trigger intense opposition from the ACLU.

One of the best examples of how unyielding the ACLU can be on crime-control bills is its reaction to the Crime Control Act of 1990. Over a period of months, the Union had sought and won many important deletions from the bill, clearing the way for civil libertarian approval. Dropped from inclusion in the final bill were (a) an expansion of the application of the death penalty, (b) language making postconviction denial of federal benefits a matter of judicial discretion, (c) habeas corpus reform, (d) a narrowing of the exclusionary rule, (e) a provision allowing the attorney general to use tents as temporary prisons, (f) a provision allowing housing agencies to evict drug dealers from housing projects, and (g) a provision allowing drug testing of prisoners on probation, supervised release, or parole. But all this wasn't enough to satisfy the ACLU.

Why did the Union still oppose S.3266, a bill that won easily in the Senate? The ACLU's objections centered on three provisions: (a) a victim's-right provision allowing children to offer testimony via closed-circuit video or televised deposition, (b) increased penalties for those involved in the child pornography industry, and (c) a provision making it difficult to obtain release pending sentencing or appeal in drug or violent crime cases.[94] It is doubtful that many outside the ranks of the ACLU would have found these provisions sufficient grounds to reject the crime control bill, especially after having succeeded in obtaining the excision of seven other provisions.

Contrary to appearance, the Union's aversion to punishment is not ubiquitous. For example, in 1984 the Pennsylvania affiliate backed a bill making spousal rape a violation of law, admitting that the ACLU "does not generally advocate expanding the list of criminal offenses."[95] In this case, its overriding commitment to legislation favored by feminists proved to be determinative; not even the vagueness of the statute was sufficient to deter Union support.

More recently, the Union was "in the forefront" of lobbying efforts that resulted in the passage of the Congressional Hate Crimes bill,[96] a law much demanded by gay activists. And in a document critical of the

FBI, the ACLU said that "government officials and agents should face criminal liability for the willful violation of the statute and guidelines." It added that criminal penalties are needed because "they add an extra deterrent on anyone contemplating an illegal investigation."[97] Once again, the element of Union politics was evident; it almost never pushes for additional penalties for any crime, including serial crime, but in this instance it was the FBI that was being taken to task, and that apparently made all the difference in the world.

Punishing Criminals

Notwithstanding the three cases just cited, it is fair to say that in general the ACLU is essentially opposed to punitive measures. Indeed, it does not exaggerate to say that the ACLU has a phobia about punishment. This phobia stems from two sources: (a) its belief that many victimizers have been victimized by society and (b) its disinterest in matters of individual responsibility.

Loren Siegel provides as good an insight into the ACLU's phobia as anyone in the organization. Siegel complains that "people of color are in the majority behind bars." What never seems to be asked is whether a majority of those who commit crimes against persons and property are also "people of color," or whether a disproportionate number of crime victims are "people of color." Also found objectionable by the ACLU is the fact that in New York, 85 percent of the women behind bars "are mothers, many are pregnant when arrested, most are heads of families, and most are African-American."[98] Again, we are left with the impression that someone must have contrived this distribution, unjustly selecting black women who are single parents for imprisonment. The point about pregnant women being imprisoned might carry some weight were it coming from an organization that recognized the life of the unborn. But this complaint is coming from an organization that rejects gender-specific laws and sees no state interest in protecting the life of the unborn.

The ACLU's policy on "Sentencing" is the clearest statement of the Union's antipathy to punishing criminals. As is true of other policies, this one is no mere platitude: it informs the actions of affiliates throughout the country.

Ira Glasser gets upset when people charge that the ACLU believes that few crimes should be punished by a prison sentence. Glasser denies it wholesale: "That is not the ACLU position. We merely think that probation should be an option available to trial judges in appropriate cases."[99] Glasser has also denied that the ACLU believed, up until recently, that no one should go to prison except for such serious crimes as murder or treason.[100] He is twice wrong.

"Deprivation of an individual's physical freedom is one of the most severe interferences with liberty that the state can impose. Moreover, imprisonment is harsh, frequently counterproductive, and costly." This explains why the ACLU holds that "a suspended sentence with probation should be the preferred sentence, to be chosen generally unless the circumstances plainly call for greater severity." The Union favors alternative sentencing and lists the reintegration of the offender into the community as "the most appropriate correctional approach." Here's the clincher: "Probation should be authorized by the legislature in every case and exceptions to the principle are not favored."[101] Prior to 1991, when this policy was revised, the Union said that only such serious crimes as "murder or treason" should qualify as exceptions.[102] The explicit referencing of those two crimes was deleted because of the public embarrassment it caused the organization.[103]

Official ACLU policy, then, does not support Glasser's contention that all the Union wants is merely for judges to be given the option of probation in appropriate cases. No, official policy is not so nuanced. The record shows that the ACLU is presumptively opposed to prison sentences. Probation is preferred, and most of those in prison should be given alternative sentences. That is what the ACLU says.

Notice, too, that the ACLU says that one of the most severe interferences with liberty that the state can impose is the deprivation of an individual's physical freedom. It also complains that prison life is "harsh." It is correct on both counts. But of course, the reason why the state interferes with the physical liberty of criminals is because the offenders have interfered with the physical liberty of their victims. And it is not clear how justice could prevail if the state, in determining the conditions of prison life, simply ignored the harsh treatment accorded the victims of crime.

The ACLU lists several reasons why probation is preferable to imprisonment. Reason number one says it all: "Probation maximizes the liberty of the individual while at the same time vindicating the authority of the law and protecting the public from further violations of law."[104] Unfortunately, the Union does not explain why sentencing should make a priority out of maximizing the liberty of the guilty when it is the liberty of innocents that has been minimized. Moreover, it is not evident how the law is vindicated and the public protected if offenders aren't incarcerated.

Here's another reason why the ACLU favors probation: "Probation may minimize the impact of the conviction upon innocent family members of the offender."[105] This statement highlights the ACLU's selective distribution of compassion. A few pages later, in the same policy, the Union says that "a sentence should not be enhanced by, and the sentencing judge should not be informed of or consider victim impact statements."[106] Somehow the ACLU's supply of compassion for innocents seems to apply only to the family of the offender and not to the family of the victim. It is positions like this that seal the charge being made here: the ACLU's conception of liberty is narrowly and abstractly drawn, earning the label "atomistic."

ACLU talk about alternative sentencing is also suspect; it depends on what is meant by the term. It certainly wants nothing to do with the alternative of "boot camps." The Union opposes state boot-camp shock-incarceration programs on the grounds that they may be abusive.[107] An acceptable alternative sentencing program that even the Union approves of is electronic monitoring of convicted criminals. But even here the ACLU specifies its demands. Any such program must "(a) comport with equal protection guarantees, (b) provide Fourth Amendment protections, and (c) include objective legal standards so that individuals are not subject to electronic monitoring for the purpose of restricting movement/house arrest who would normally qualify for bail, release on personal recognizance, probation or parole."[108] Knowing how the ACLU interprets "equal protection," and what constitutes an "unreasonable" search and seizure, it is fair to say that its idea of electronic monitoring is not the conventional one.

The kinds of alternative sentencing favored by the Union are fines and restitution. Just what the appropriate fine should be for an ordinary mugging, the ACLU does not say. Nor does it say where the mugger is likely to get the money needed to make restitution. And what if the mugger can't afford to repay his victim? Anticipating this issue—the Union calls it economic discrimination—the "amount and terms of payment should be set according to a defendant's ability to pay."[109] So if the mugger can pay back only a fraction of what he stole, that will have to do. Should he be put in prison if he doesn't pay at all? It depends on whether the nonpayment was willful. If it was nonwillful, then incarceration should be prohibited and community service should be "encouraged." The Union does not say what should be done in the event the encouragement fails.

The ACLU opposes mandatory sentencing on the grounds that it "unduly restricts the judge's ability to engage in individualized sentencing."[110] But what about some particularly heinous crimes; shouldn't there be a minimum sentence imposed? Such was the sentiment in 1990 when Senator Rudy Boschwitz recommended mandatory minimum sentences for kidnapping, sexual abuse of children, and the use of children in pornography. The ACLU opposed Senator Boschwitz's proposal because it allegedly lacked evidence showing the deterrent effect of a minimum sentence of 30 years.[111]

The Union's advocacy of an indeterminate sentence includes the right of the judge to set a presumptive parole release date, one that can be postponed by parole authorities "only when justified by a finding that the prisoner committed serious disciplinary infractions during the period of confinement."[112] In other words, the assessments of psychiatrists and other professionals should not count in determinations of a release date. Only if a "serious disciplinary infraction" has taken place should there be any schedule change.

"Whenever appropriate," ACLU policy instructs, "a prison sentence should require only partial confinement, thereby allowing an offender to maintain community ties."[113] The problem here is that criminals typically seek reintegration in the same neighborhoods as their victims. This policy idea may sound attractive to those who do not live in high-crime areas, but to those who do it is as unconvincing as it is unrealistic. It is just as unrealistic for the ACLU to say that "whenever appropriate, sentences of incarceration should either provide for work release during the period of confinement or for the confinement to take place only on those days of the week when the offender is not employed."[114] Now put yourself in the shoes of the offender's victim, who may be an unemployed single parent. She learns that the man who robbed her is going to return to her neighborhood *with a job* and be allowed to stay out of prison on weekdays. Who could blame her if she just gave up on the criminal justice system altogether?

Procedural safeguards in the sentencing process should, of course, be a staple concern for civil libertarians. But here again there is evidence of inconsistency. For instance, official policy holds that at the time of sentencing, "the defendant must be permitted to present any and all aspects of his or her record and offense which she or he believes are mitigating." The policy lists lack of prior criminal record as its first example. However, if the defendant has a criminal record, the ACLU says such information should be withheld. The policy reads that "the sentencing judge should not be informed of or consider, prior arrests, prior bad acts, or any charges that have not resulted in conviction."[115] That crime victims and their families might find fault with this construction of procedural fairness would hardly come as a surprise.

There are other mitigating circumstances that the ACLU has found to be compelling. The Union says that at the time of sentencing, if it is appropriate, it should be mentioned that the defendant suffered from the "effects of mental or emotional disturbance, mental disease or defect, or intoxication through alcohol or drug ingestion at the time of the offense." Also appropriate for comment are extenuating circumstances, "effects of duress or domination by another person at the time of the crime," and the defendant's role as an accomplice to the principal perpetrator.[116]

Cumulatively, these "mitigating" circumstances tell volumes about the ACLU's idea of personal responsibility. They also say something else. The same ACLU that says that people who suffer from mental problems or have a history of drug or alcohol abuse should be understood as persons who do not have full command of their will, stands in the way of municipal authorities trying to rescue such persons from freezing to death on city streets and sidewalks.

The federal government has tried to bring some needed uniformity to sentencing. To that end, it has offered guidelines that recommend that the nature of the offense and prior criminal history ought to be made a priority. The ACLU objects, saying it gives "insufficient attention to individual offender characteristics" and "unduly restricts judicial discretion." But what really incenses the Union are the federal guidelines that recommend that attention be given to the "criminal livelihood" of the defendant. The ACLU holds that "factors relating to the nature of the crime victim, public concern over the crime and defendant's acceptance of responsibility" are of "questionable legitimacy."[117] Federal guidelines also say that those who derive a "substantial portion of income" from a "pattern of criminal conduct" should have their sentences enhanced. This would clearly target mobsters and drugkingpins, among others. Again, the ACLU objects. It finds the idea vague and says it has the potential to discriminate against the poor.[118] That the poor have been discriminated against by mobsters and drugkingpins seems not to register with civil libertarians.

Prisoners' Rights

Given the ACLU's disposition toward crime and punishment, it is only fitting that it would take an aggressive stand on prisoners' rights. Since 1972, the ACLU has run the National Prison Project, dedicated to strengthening the constitutional rights of prisoners. Mainly focused on litigation, the National Prison Project also drafts model legislation, coordinates activities with other like-minded organizations, publishes a journal, and engages in educational outreach programs. It has won a number of important court cases affirming prisoners' rights and has succeeded in holding public officials accountable for prison conditions.

There is nothing incongruous about a civil-liberties organization protecting the rights of prisoners. But as we have seen, the ACLU is fundamentally opposed to putting most criminals in prison, and it is this bias against incarceration that drives the National Prison Project. From the very beginning, the National Prison Project has traveled a highly politicized course, using creative legal techniques to dismantle the prison system. The key players in this operation have been Philip Hirschkop and Alvin J. Bronstein. Bronstein took over from Hirschkop and is mostly responsible for the work of the National Prison Project. He is also a recipient of a MacArthur Foundation Fellowship (the foundation is a major contributor to the ACLU) and an exponent of the idea that "a polluter's actions [are] a more serious offense than a violent murderer's."[119]

It was at the University of Virginia in the mid-1960s that Hirschkop and fellow colleague Alan Ritter teamed up to create the Virginia Prison Project, the forerunner of the National Prison Project. With funding from the Ritter Family Foundation, Hirschkop and Ritter took aim at prison conditions in Virginia, receiving advice from their friend William Kunstler.[120] It didn't take long before Hirschkop managed to appear before a Senate judiciary subcommittee making sensational comments about the alleged brutality of the Virginia prison system. At the time,

Hirschkop was a cooperating counsel to the newly organized Virginia affiliate of the ACLU. His attack was roundly criticized by nine members of the affiliate's Richmond chapter, a group that included six college and seminary professors, the editor of the "Presbyterian Outlook," a doctor, and a businessman. They publicly labeled Hirschkop's remarks "an intemperate outburst."[121]

The nine who questioned Hirschkop's gambit paid a dear price. "To those who think the ACLU as a haven of free expression and dissent," writes Dr. Lawrence Cranberg, "it may come as a shock to learn that after a bitter factional struggle, the Richmond Nine were censured and they resigned en masse from the organization."[122] Cranberg was cofounder, along with Hirschkop, of the Virginia CLU. To this day, Cranberg has drawn the invective of ACLU officials whenever he exposes Union misdeeds.

The tone of the ACLU's approach to prisoners' rights was set by Hirschkop in a 1969 article he wrote with Michael A. Millemann in the *Virginia Law Review.* The title of the piece, "The Unconstitutionality of Prison Life," was aptly named, as it provided an accurate reflection of ACLU thinking on the subject. Claiming that the conditions in Virginia prisons were "similar to those described by Franz Kafka,"[123] Hirschkop recommended new legal strategies to reform the prison system. Unsupervised conduct by guards could be seen as "arbitrary and unreasonable treatment of criminals" and thus could "easily [be] categorized as a denial of liberty or life without due process of law." It was therefore recommended that the proper focus of judicial challenges shift from Eighth Amendment violations to abuses of the Fourteenth Amendment.[124] The Fourteenth Amendment was also best suited to challenge "some vague offense such as 'agitation.'"[125]

Now it is one thing to claim that abuses of civil liberties occur in prison, quite another to maintain that prison life is itself unconstitutional. "It is the secret exercise of vast power over lives and human rights and the unsupervised delegation of control that makes prison life as it exists today unconstitutional." Hirschkop and Millemann add that "prison life at present is unconstitutional because the system fosters violation of the public trust and because there is no means of redressing legitimate grievances."[126] Nowhere do the authors indicate what the effect might be on public safety if the prisons were declared unconstitutional.

Hirschkop's dream of declaring all prisons unconstitutional did not come true, but nearly two decades after his article was published, the National Prison Project, under the direction of Al Bronstein, did succeed in getting Federal District Judge Frank M. Johnson to declare the entire Alabama prison system unconstitutional.[127]

Another partial victory was the Union's effort to transform the power structure in the prisons. No longer do the guards run the prisons: it is generally conceded that those who hold the greatest power in the prisons today are the most brutal inmates. But unfortunately, living conditions have actually worsened, with more violence now than ever before.[128] The ACLU's response to this condition has been to sue the authorities for not separating the vulnerable prisoners from the strong ones.[129]

It is not always clear what the source of prison problems is. From Maryland, we hear complaints about "the overwhelming stench of human waste," "incredible filth," and "deafening noise."[130] From Ohio, we hear about "excessive" noise levels, "filthy" restrooms, and the like.[131] Just who created these conditions never seems to be mentioned. Was it the guards? If so, they should be punished. But if it was the prisoners, then what does the ACLU want to do about that? After all, when guards cover the cells with plexiglass to prevent being hit with feces, it is not their feces they are protecting themselves against. To be exact, how much sense does it make to sue a prison for violating the rights of inmates when in many instances it is the inmates who have created the "illegal" conditions?

Overcrowding does create poor conditions, and in those instances, prison officials should be held accountable. But it is not clear how justice is served when the ACLU succeeds in obtaining a court order to reduce the prison population. Who should be let out seems never to be never addressed. Nor is much attention paid to those innocent citizens who have been victimized by a released criminal; what recourse they should have against the state is left undetermined. These are issues that deserve an answer. One thing is certain: overcrowding, poor sanitation, and violence in the prisons are not, per se, a violation of the Constitution. The high court said in 1991 that before such conditions are declared unconstitutional, proof must exist that the prison administration has acted with "deliberate indifference" to basic human needs. The ACLU participated in a losing effort in this case.[132]

What kinds of rights should prisoners have? The ACLU has fought in court for many kinds of rights, but in its official policy on the subject, it emphasizes such rights as (a) the right to a law library in prison, (b) no censorship of letters, (c) no listening devices in visiting booths, (d) the need for a search warrant to examine reading materials, and (e) the right to vote.[133] This is what we would expect: heavy on rights, absent on responsibilities. The ACLU is not unaware that restrictions on the free flow of communication are designed to guard against potential trouble. It is just that that is not a good enough reason to justify monitoring of any kind.

More needs to be said about the right of prisoners to vote. In 1988, in *Human Events*, I wrote the following: *Do you believe that all prisoners should have the right to vote, regardless of the nature of their offense, and that they should be allowed out of prison to vote at the last place of residence prior to confinement? The ACLU does.*[134] Glasser denied this was true, writing that "we do think prisoners ought to be allowed to vote—by absentee ballot—but you can't find a word in our Policy Guide to suggest that we think prisoners ought to be let out to do so."[135]

Here again, for the record, is official ACLU policy on the subject: "Persons convicted of any offense, whether or not incarcerated, should not be deprived of the right to vote. Prisoners should be authorized to vote at their last place of residence prior to confinement unless they can establish some other residence in accordance with rules applicable to free citizens."[136] The policy says nothing about absentee voting and verifies my charges exactly.

It is true that the public is not gravely concerned about the plight of prisoners, but it is also true that ACLU trivialization of the subject doesn't make matters any better. When people read that the ACLU has sued over such infractions as slow elevators in a New York City prison[137] and meal schedules in Wyoming[138] (the Union once sued over the scheduling of meat loaf for 21 consecutive days),[139] it does little to elevate the seriousness of the issue. Even the first case ever brought by the National Prison Project in 1972 was hardly on the order of provoking serious public awareness: it sued the Federal Bureau of Prisons challenging restrictions on sexually explicit homosexual publications. Since that time, the Union has moved to secure pornographic reading rooms in the prisons, complete with copies of *Hustler* and the *Advocate*, a gay porn publication.[140]

Some rights seem benign until scrutinized in the context of prison life. Take religion. The only publicly funded place in which the ACLU fights hard to secure freedom of religion is in prison. Bible reading and prayer groups are especially defended as a First Amendment right.[141] This from an organization that fights against the right of students to stage a religious play. It should be obvious that something else must be at stake besides religious freedom.

It is well known to penologists that prayer groups in prison are often a front for convening a strategy session outside the purview of guards. By declaring a constitutional right to religious expression, inmates can secure quarters to make the kinds of plans that the authorities can do little about. Though there is no hard evidence explaining the ACLU's motive for defending prayer groups in prison, its traditional hostility to religious expression, coupled with its extremist interpretation of prisoners' rights, is sufficient to raise the eyebrow of any serious observer.

In another interesting departure from policy, the ACLU sees family bonding as a necessity for inmates and their families. It seeks to have family visitation centers available in prison so that parents can maintain strong ties with their children.[142] As with the issue of prayer groups in prison, the Union's position on this issue is at once commendable and suspicious. After all, we hear so little from the ACLU about the need for family bonding outside the context of prisoners' rights. Is it because the Union has as its objective the reduction of disparities between life in prison and life outside? If so, that is a goal that deserves an airing, and it is one that ought to include the input of families of crime victims as well.

Gay and lesbian inmates have not been overlooked by the ACLU. The Union has fought for visitation rights and other amenities, always seeking to equalize conditions between heterosexuals and homosexuals. It has also fought against penalties for AIDS-infected inmates who bite prison guards. When New Jersey inmate Gregory Dean Smith was sentenced to 25 years in prison for trying to murder a prison guard by biting him (Smith had AIDS), Judy Greenspan of the ACLU protested by saying that "the defendant was not sentenced to more than 20 years in prison for biting or because of his prior prison record, but for having the AIDS virus."[143] Greenspan did not explain why, if this were true, Smith was not arrested before he intentionally bit one of the guards.

Not all of the ACLU's actions taken in behalf of prisoners have been liberating. Ask inmates what they think of the ACLU's lawsuits demanding the nonsegregation of AIDS-infected inmates from the rest of the prison population. Despite all the talk about civil liberties that people like Greenspan like to vent,[144] most prisoners think segregation is a good thing. In the late 1980s, 300 inmates in a Colorado prison blamed the ACLU for what they considered the worst thing that ever happened to them: The authorities in Colorado stopped testing and segregating inmates with AIDS.[145]

In 1992, the ACLU won an important victory when the Supreme Court held that a beating or other use of excessive force by a prison guard may violate the Constitution even if it does not result in a serious injury to the prisoner.[146] But ironically, the ACLU has not been free of the charge of fomenting prison violence itself. In 1990, Utah inmate David Jolivet fingered Michele Parish-Pixler, the state director of the ACLU, as the person who told him that prison officials were planning to murder him. Jolivet and other inmates rioted after learning of Ms. Parish-Pixler's alleged remarks. The ACLU official denied the accusation.[147]

One might think that given the ACLU's unrelenting criticism of the current prison system, almost any alternative would be supported. But the Union's criticisms are apparently not weighty enough to overcome its objections to the privatization of prisons. Calling private prisons "time bombs just waiting to go off,"[148] Union official Barry Steinhardt has been as critical of privatization as any ACLU operative. In 1986 and 1987, Steinhardt got what he wanted when the board of directors issued a formal policy opposing private prisons. What was most striking about the policy was its complete lack of supporting evidence. Six reasons are advanced stating why privatization is not a good idea, and every one of them reads that private prisons "are likely" to result in all kinds of abuses.[149] This is one of those rare instances where the likelihood of abuse is sufficient to trigger ACLU policy.

The ACLU maintains that upon release from prison, there should be no denial of federal benefits. Its reasons include the prospects for rehabilitation and reintegration in the community. The ACLU evidently thinks that federal benefits are a sinecure, not contingent on the character of the recipient. This was the approach taken by Janlori Goldman in her 1989 statement before the House Republican Study Committee; she invoked both sociological and constitutional reasons why ex-cons should not be denied any of the amenities afforded the law-abiding. Even when a bill was introduced making the denial of federal benefits mandatory after the third offense, Goldman objected.[150]

Capital Punishment

It would be an understatement to say that the ACLU is against capital punishment, for to do so would mask the vast amount of resources the organization expends annually to halt executions. The strategies it chooses to stop capital punishment are themselves controversial. For example, it has tried to discredit psychiatrists like Dr. James P. Grigson of Dallas (he is a "menace") simply because he does not render judgments regarding the mental state of defendants that accord with the ACLU's view.[151] The Union much prefers to work with people like Federal Appellate Judge Stephen Reinhardt, one of the most liberal members of the Ninth Circuit Court; Judge Reinhardt, a strong opponent of capital punishment, is married to Ramona Ripston, the executive director of the Southern California CLU.[152]

There was a time when even the ACLU did not find fault with capital punishment. In the 1950s, the board of directors said there was no civil-liberties problem with the scheduled execution of Ethel and Julius Rosenberg, convicted of conspiracy to commit espionage.[153] But in 1963, the board asked Norman Dorsen to prepare a memorandum on the subject outlining the pros and cons of capital punishment. Two years later, the Union came out officially against the death penalty;[154] it has never wavered since.

There are legal, moral, and social reasons for opposing or defending capital punishment. The ACLU invokes all three, though a moral objection alone renders the other arguments moot. The legal objection that the Union makes is that capital punishment is a violation of the Eighth Amendment prohibition of "cruel and unusual punishment."[155] This was not, interestingly, the ACLU's initial grounds for opposition. In his 1963 memo, Dorsen said the ACLU should oppose capital punishment "even if it does not transgress any provision of the Bill of Rights." It was enough, he reasoned, that capital punishment was "inconsistent with the spirit of civil liberties."[156] The board accepted his logic and said in 1965 that "capital punishment is so inconsistent with the underlying values of a democratic system that the imposition of the death penalty for any crime is a denial of civil liberties."[157]

Whatever one thinks of the ACLU's initial opposition to capital punishment, it was not jurisprudentially suspect. It did not try to say then what it says now, namely that the Constitution's ban on "cruel and unusual punishment" precludes the use of the death penalty. But those were the days when fanciful ideas about "updating" the meaning of the Constitution to fit "modern needs" were seen for what they were: contrived reasons used to justify a particular ideological agenda. Moreover, even if one takes the view that the Constitution ought to be afforded a "contemporary reading," it is not certain why this would negate support for the death penalty. Why is it not more likely that, given the unprecedented rates of crime we are experiencing in the 1990s, a "contemporary reading" would support the death penalty now more than ever before?

The ACLU favors a "contemporary reading" of the Constitution because it knows that the Founders had no problem with capital punishment. The same persons who wrote the Eighth Amendment also expressly allowed for the death penalty; it was routinely used during their time. What was meant by "cruel and unusual punishment" was torturous and barbarous acts, such as disembowelment or breaking at the wheel (smashing someone's bones with a crowbar on a wheel). By denying these acts while permitting death by hanging, the Framers sought to distinguish between those forms of punishment in which pain was not incidental to the act (wanton punishment) and those in which it was. And recall that the Fifth Amendment bars the taking of life *without due process of law*, suggesting that if due process were provided, executions were acceptable.

It should be noted as well that the Supreme Court has never declared capital punishment to be a violation of the Eighth Amendment, though some justices have demurred. In 1972, in *Furman v. Georgia*, the Supreme Court did strike down every existing statute allowing capital punishment, but not because it was violative of the Constitution; the Court ruled that since the states had applied the death penalty in such an inconsistent manner, it could not countenance its use, as then administered. Four years later, in *Gregg v. Georgia*, the high court reinstated capital punishment (its previous objections had been relieved). More important, the Supreme Court explicitly rejected the argument that the death penalty was violative of the Constitution.

The moral case against capital punishment was first broached by Norman Dorsen. In his 1963 memo on the subject, Dorsen contended that "the sanctity of human life" was not only "the indispensable condition for all other rights," it was "the *raison d'être* of the ACLU."[158] Similarly, official ACLU policy today says that "contemporary ideas of the significance of human life make imposition of the death penalty cruel and unusual punishment, which is prohibited by the Constitution."[159] All this from the nation's number one litigant on behalf of abortion on demand.

The moral argument against the death penalty needs to address the question of justice: If the punishment should be proportionate to the gravity of the offense, then why should serial murderers be exempted from the fate of their victims? Some say that life imprisonment, without the possibility of parole, accomplishes the same ends as capital punishment, without the bloodletting. But what if the condemned kill in prison? In any event, this is not a question the ACLU needs to answer. It is already on record opposing life imprisonment without parole as an alternative to capital punishment.[160] It is fair to say that by opposing even life imprisonment, the ACLU seriously undermines its case against capital punishment and calls into question its conception of justice.

When opposing various crime bills, the ACLU has remarked that "capital punishment is fundamentally inconsistent with the principle of human dignity, the basic concept underlying the Eighth Amendment."[161] This was the position of former Supreme Court Justice William Brennan, and it is one that all of his colleagues, save Thurgood Marshall, found wanting. Surely it is credible to argue that capital punishment is a violation of human dignity, but to ground such a position in the Eighth Amendment is another matter altogether.

Human dignity is a philosophical construct, not a constitutional one; offenses to human dignity take place every day without ever triggering a constitutional debate. Moreover, it is a slippery argument to maintain that the death penalty is an affront to human dignity. Kant and Hegel both argued, quite persuasively, that execution affirms the humanity of the executed by giving full recognition to conscious human action. And as former New York Mayor Ed Koch has said, "In the original Hebrew . . . the Sixth Commandment reads 'Thou Shalt Not Commit Murder,'" not "Thou Shalt Not Kill"; in addition, the Torah specifies capital punishment for a variety of offenses.[162]

"Under no circumstances should a juvenile ever be subject to the death penalty."[163] In one sense this official ACLU policy is superfluous: if it opposes the death penalty in all circumstances, then no exceptions can be made for minors. But there is more to this than meets the eye. If the ACLU, citing the special status of juveniles, makes a separate case against capital punishment, then how does it answer its critics who charge that when it comes to young girls seeking an abortion, the ACLU has no problem treating minors as adults? This dilemma came to a head in 1988 in a brief the ACLU drafted in behalf of William Wayne Thompson, a Death Row candidate who committed murder at age 15.

The ACLU brief, written by Henry Schwarzchild of the Union's Capital Punishment Project, maintained that juveniles do not have the same mental and moral development as adults. Due to the "diminished capacity" of juveniles, Schwarzchild said, they should be exempted from the death penalty. But the brief was never filed because of opposition from Janet Benshoof, head of the ACLU's Reproductive Freedom Project.

Benshoof knew what the stakes were: "Schwarzchild argues that teens have the incapacity to make moral, even rational decisions. In order to oppose restrictions on abortion, he forces me to favor the hanging of teenagers."[164] Schwarzchild saw it just the other way around, complaining that Benshoof's logic "forces me to say that in order to oppose restrictions on abortion, I have to favor hanging 15-year-old girls."[165]

Internal splits are not uncommon in any organization, but what makes this case especially interesting is that it was the natural outcome of having so many special "Projects" within the ACLU. Perhaps most telling was the fact that Benshoof prevailed. What this suggests, as Nat Hentoff has said, is that the death penalty was made "subservient to abortion."[166]

Another moral argument the ACLU makes against capital punishment is that the "irreversibility of the death penalty means that error discovered after the penalty has been imposed cannot be corrected."[167] This is technically true, but the number of innocent people who have been executed is so few as to lend little support to the abolitionist position (just the opposite may well be the case). While no one can be exact, it is estimated by *anti-capital punishment* experts that of the more than 7,000 executions that have taken place in this century, 25 people were wrongfully executed.[168] This number, it should be noted, is undoubtedly inflated, as it includes people like the anarchists Sacco and Vanzetti;

Bruno Hauptmann, convicted of kidnapping and killing the baby of Charles Lindbergh; and Ethel and Julius Rosenberg. Now aside from Vanzetti and Ethel Rosenberg (they *may* have been innocent), there is little doubt as to the guilt of the others.

The central question is whether capital punishment can be justified given the likelihood that some innocent people, however few in number, will unintentionally lose their lives as a result. As social scientist Ernest van den Haag has said, the same question might appropriately be asked of many social policies. For example, since both automobile traffic and surgery also result in the loss of innocent human life, should we opt to ban them as well? "These activities are justified, nevertheless," van den Haag answers, "because benefits (including justice) are felt to outweigh the statistical certainty of unintentionally killing innocents." More to the point, van den Haag stresses that "if innocent victims of future murderers are saved by virtue of the death penalty imposed on convicted murderers, it must be retained, just as surgery is, even though some innocents will be lost through miscarriages of justice—as long as more innocent lives are saved than lost."[169]

The social arguments that the ACLU advances against capital punishment center on issues of equality and deterrence. The Union finds it objectionable that a disproportionate number of those who have been executed in the twentieth century have been poor and members of minority communities.[170] Again, van den Haag is helpful: "Punishments are imposed on persons, not on racial or economic groups. Guilt is personal. The only relevant question is: does the person to be executed deserve the punishment? Whether or not others who deserved the same punishment, whatever their economic or racial group, have avoided execution is irrelevant."[171] Moreover, there is no kind of demographic distribution that would ever satisfy the ACLU.

The Union also claims that capital punishment does not deter crime.[172] But it is not easy to settle this issue since so few are executed. While today we execute about 25 people a year (there are more than 20,000 homicides committed each year), in 1935 an American convict was executed every 44 hours. What we do know about the deterrent effect of the death penalty, when employed on a fairly steady basis, is that it does deter crime. The work of Isaac Ehrlich, who studied the relationship between the execution rate and the homicide rate between the years 1933 and 1969, showed that for every execution, eight additional homicides were prevented.[173] Even more impressive is the fact that when Ehrlich's data were extended to the 1980s (after executions resumed), the evidence that capital punishment deters was even stronger.[174] Also noteworthy are the findings of David Phillips, a British social scientist,[175] and Auburn University sociologist Steven Stack.[176] Both independently support the claim that when executions are well publicized, there is a strong deterrent effect.

But none of this matters to the ACLU. It prefers to cast itself in noble raiments while viewing its critics as Philistines. "It's very important for American officials to see that enlightened people all over the universe abhor capital punishment." Mr. Schwarzchild can believe this if he wants to,[177] but the fact remains that support for capital punishment in the United States hovers around 75 percent, and the absence of capital punishment in Europe is no indication of public sentiment on the issue.

If the ACLU has been unsuccessful in getting capital punishment declared unconstitutional, it has succeeded greatly in tying up the system with endless appeals. Chief Justice William Rehnquist was correct to say that the seven-to-eight-year lag between sentence and execution in the average death penalty case represents a "serious malfunction in our legal system."[178] More than half of all state court death sentences are overturned by federal courts during habeas corpus proceedings, thanks in large part to the ACLU.

Cooper Union professor Fred Siegel has said that there was a time when the ACLU could be counted on to make a positive contribution to the issue of crime and civil liberties. "But today its libertarian vision of license for all, regardless of the consequences," writes Siegel, "has both reduced the liberties of the law-abiding and undercut faith in our civic institutions, including the police and the courts."[179] The ACLU has come to this stage in its history primarily because of its flawed vision of liberty. It cannot see beyond the rights of the accused and the convicted and wants nothing to do with studying the consequences of its actions on innocent people. It does not seem to understand that freedom cannot move forward if people's lives move backward as a result of crime. Only a more comprehensive appreciation of liberty can turn the organization around, and that is not something that will happen overnight.

Notes

1. Jeffrey T. Leeds, "Impeccable Judgments or Tainted Policies?" *New York Times Magazine*, September 10, 1989, p. 74.
2. Dorothy Ehrlich, "The 'Criminals' Lobby' Dissents," *ACLU News*, October 1981, p. 4.
3. Daniel J. Popeo, *Not OUR America . . . The ACLU Exposed* (Washington: Washington Legal Foundation, 1989), 36.
4. The exchange with Neier took place at ACLU headquarters on June 19, 1978. Dr. Cranberg relayed the information to me on several occasions.
5. Quoted in "Affiliate Notes," *Civil Liberties*, Fall/Winter 1989, p. 10.
6. ACLU Memo on Senate Amendments to the Crime Bill, Washington Office, July 10, 1990, p. 3.
7. *Payne v. Tennessee*, 111 S.Ct. 1407 (1991).
8. Quoted in "Thinking the Unthinkable," *Time*, May 30, 1988, p. 15.
9. Nadelmann made his remarks at the 1989 ACLU Biennial Conference session on Drugs (available on cassette).
10. James Q. Wilson and Richard Herrnstein, *Crime and Human Nature* (New York: Simon and Schuster, 1985), 366.
11. Quoted in "Thinking the Unthinkable," *Time*, May 30, 1988, p. 16.
12. See James Q. Wilson, "Against the Legalization of Drugs," *Commentary*, February 1990, p. 25; and William E. McCauliff, "Psychoactive Drug Use Among Practicing Physicians and Medical Students," *New England Journal of Medicine*, September 25, 1986, p. 805.
13. Policy #210, "Victimless Crimes."
14. Ibid.
15. See the exchange Glasser and I had on this issue, as well as others, in "ACLU and Donohue Square Off," *Human Events*, October 15, 1988, pp. 12–13.
16. Martin Tolchin, "Kemp Vows to Oust Tenants Over Drugs," *New York Times*, March 8, 1989, p. 10.
17. Ibid.
18. Statement of Wade J. Henderson, Associate Director, Washington National Office of the ACLU, and Jacqueline Berrien, Staff Attorney of the ACLU, on behalf of the ACLU on "Drugs in Federally Assisted Housing" before the Subcommittee on Housing and Urban Affairs, Committee on Banking, Housing and Urban Affairs, United States Senate, July 20, 1989.
19. Dirk Johnson, "Housing Gangs Are Given a Licking," *New York Times*, May 20, 1989, p. 9.
20. "HUD's Kemp Cracks Down on Crime," *Human Events*, April 20, 1989, p. 5.
21. Quoted in "Closing the Vagrancy Circle," *Wall Street Journal*, April 6, 1989, p. A18.
22. Loren Siegel, "A War on Drugs or on People?" *Civil Liberties*, Fall/Winter 1989, p. 4.
23. "AARR to Defend Drug Loitering Law," *Rights and Responsibilities*, (the newsletter of the American Alliance for Rights and Responsibilities), July 1990, p. 1.
24. Quoted by L. Gordon Crovitz, "The New Civil Rights: ACLU vs. Maxine Clark," *Wall Street Journal*, September 5, 1990, p. A15.
25. Glasser's fund-raising letter, sent to all ACLU members, was sent in October 1989.
26. "The Other Drug War," *Rights and Responsibilities*, July 1990, p. 3.
27. Mark S. Campisano, "Card Games," *New Republic*, October 31, 1988, p. 11.
28. "No Comment," *Rights and Responsibilities*, April 1991, p. 6.

29. Ira Glasser, fund-raising letter entitled "ACLU 1990 Workplan," sent to members in May 1990.
30. ACLU Memorandum, Washington Office, "Senate Amendments to the Crime Bill," July 10, 1990, p. 3.
31. "Drugs," *Rights and Responsibilities*, October 1991, p. 4.
32. Ibid.
33. *Harmelin v. Michigan*, 111 S.Ct. 2680 (1991).
34. William A. Donohue, "The ACLU's Policy on Drugs," *Legal Backgrounder* of the Washington Legal Foundation, March 9, 1990.
35. "Drug Testing for Discounts," *Rights and Responsibilities*, November–December 1990, p. 4.
36. Lynn Paltrow, Kary Moss, and Judy Crockett on behalf of the ACLU on "The President's National Drug Abuse Strategy," before The Subcommittee on Health and the Environment of the United States House of Representatives Committee on Energy and Commerce, April 30, 1990, pp. 20, 23.
37. See Washington Office Memoranda, "McCollum Amendment Requiring Mandatory Drug Testing as a Condition of Federal Parole, Probation or Supervised Release," July 9, 1990 and "Senate Amendments to the Crime Bill," July 10, 1990.
38. Policy #214, "State Control of Drugs and Alcohol."
39. Policy #320, "Discrimination in Employment Against Alcohol and Substance Users."
40. Paul Glastris, ". . . One That Should Be The Best, *But Isn't*," *Washington Monthly*, March 1988, p. 27.
41. For an overview of the ACLU's cases on drug testing, see Loren Siegel, "State and Federal Courts Struggle With the Constitutionality of Drug Testing," *Civil Liberties*, Winter 1988, pp. 6–7.
42. Jeanne M. Woods, "Time to End the Cold War At Home," *First Principles*, August 1990, p. 7.
43. Glastris has an account of this in his article ". . . One That Should Be The Best," pp. 31–32.
44. See Glasser's letter to the editor, in reply to an article by Amitai Etzioni, in the *Wall Street Journal*, November 1, 1991, p. A15.
45. Memorandum from Allan Adler, "Transportation Industry Employee Drug Testing," June 28, 1988.
46. Policy #217, "Drunk Driving Roadblocks."
47. Policy #260, "Chemical Tests of Drivers."
48. Paul Glastris, ". . . One That Should Be the Best, *But Isn't*," pp. 30–31.
49. "Two Views on Rights and Responsibilities in Connection with Traffic Sobriety Checkpoints," a Special Report of *Rights and Responsibilities*, March 1990.
50. Loren Siegel, "Michigan ACLU's Roadblock Case Goes to Supreme Court," *Civil Liberties*, Spring 1990, p. 6.
51. *Michigan v. Sitz*, 496 U.S. 444 (1990).
52. Policy #216, "Alcoholism and Public Drunkenness."
53. *Mc Kelvey v. Traynor*, 485 U.S. 535 (1988).
54. Policy #253, "Military Justice."
55. Samuel Walker, *In Defense of American Liberties: A History of the ACLU* (New York: Oxford University Press), 247. It is worthy of note that the only citation Walker presents to buttress his case is a previous book he wrote on the police.
56. Policy #205, "Civilian Review Boards."

57. Don Feder, "ACLU Defends N.H. Cop for Klan Ties," *Boston Herald*, August 16, 1990, p. 53.

58. Colleen O'Connor, "Defending the Unpopular." O'Connor's piece was distributed by Heritage Features Syndicate (the outlet that distributes Don Feder's work) on September 18, 1990. A copy of O'Connor's article was sent to me by Andy Seamans, managing editor of the Syndicate.

59. "Directors Council Now A Major Player In ACLU Internal Affairs," *Civil Liberties*, Spring/Summer 1991, p. 7.

60. Ira Glasser, "In the Wake of Savagery, Change?" *Civil Liberties*, Spring/Summer 1991, p. 16.

61. Ripston's remarks were made in an interview with Bob Blanchard, "We Can't Rely on the Courts Anymore," *Progressive*, August 1991, p. 32.

62. This was first reported in "The ACLU's New Cut," *Wall Street Journal*, July 20, 1992, p. A14.

63. Neil A. Lewis, "A.C.L.U. Opposes Second Trial for Same Offense," *New York Times*, April 5, 1993, p. A8.

64. John C. Boland, "An ACLU Unit Loosens Up to Prior Restraint," *Wall Street Journal*, June 26, 1984, p. 24.

65. John Spano, "Police Officer Wins Lawsuit Against ACLU," *Los Angeles Times*, July 24, 1987, Part II, p. 1.

66. "ACLU Pays for Violating Rights of Cop," *San Jose Mercury News*, November 15, 1988, pp. 1C, 3C.

67. "Officer's Award Stands Against ACLU Attorney," *Insight*, May 21, 1990, p. 53.

68. Quoted by Don Terry, "How Criminals Get Guns: In Short, All Too Easy," *New York Times*, March 11, 1992, pp. A1, A12.

69. Policy #47, "Gun Control."

70. Ibid.

71. Ibid. See the footnote to the policy.

72. See the ACLU reply to a letter by Victor Viviano in *Civil Liberties*, Summer/Fall 1986, p. 2.

73. Jacob Sullum, "Gun-Shy Judges," *Reason*, May 1991, pp. 47–49.

74. See Edward J. Erler and Daniel C. Palm, "The Serious Case Against Criminalizing Semi-Autos," *Proposition*, March 1989.

75. Ibid.

76. Sanford Levinson, "The Embarrassing Second Amendment," *Yale Law Journal* 99 (December 1989): 637–59.

77. See William A. Donohue and James Taranto, "The Assault on Public Order," *City Journal*, Winter 1992, p. 45.

78. See the letter to the editor by Norman Dorsen and Ira Glasser, "An Exchange On The ACLU," *New Republic*, December 12, 1988, p. 22.

79. Policy #270, "Airport Searches." See also the discussion by Paul Glastris, ". . . One That Should Be The Best, *But Isn't*," pp. 27–29.

80. Policy #206, "Curfew Ordinances."

81. "Whither Curfews?" *Civil Liberties Record* (of PA), December 1985, p. 6.

82. "ACLU Opposes Curfews," *Capital Liberties*, Fall/Winter 1987, p. 8.

83. Ronald Smothers, "Atlanta Sets a Curfew for Youths, Prompting Concern on Race Bias," *New York Times*, November 21, 1990, p. A1.

84. Ibid.

85. Andrew Sheehan, "ACLU Opposes Cruising Ban," *Pittsburgh Post-Gazette*, July 4, 1991, p. 4. For the ACLU's reaction to the Milwaukee case, see "For Young

Drivers in Milwaukee, Ban on Cruising Is Un-American," *New York Times*, August 7, 1990, p. A12.

86. Washington Office Memorandum, "Police 'Sweeps' for Gangs and Drugs," June 20, 1988.

87. Richard Perez-Pena, "Barring Gangs From Park Raises Some Legal Issues," *New York Times*, January 10, 1992, p. B9.

88. Bruce Fein, "ACLU Gangs Up on the Public and Safety in a California Park," *Insight*, March 9, 1992, p. 21.

89. Policy #254a, "Caller ID."

90. Testimony of Janlori Goldman, legislative counsel, on Behalf of the ACLU, before the House Subcommittee on Courts, Intellectual Property, and the Administration of Justice, In Support of H.R. 4340, September 19, 1990.

91. Constance Hayes, "If That Man Is Following Her, Connecticut Plans to Follow Him," *New York Times*, June 5, 1992, p. A8.

92. William A. Donohue, "Civil Liberties, Civility and Community," *Legal Backgrounder* of the Washington Legal Foundation, March 9, 1990.

93. For a good account of ACLU opposition to various crime bills, see the publication *Civil Liberties Alert*, published by the Washington Office. It details ACLU opposition to virtually every crime bill introduced by Congress.

94. "Passage of Anti-Crime Legislation Sees Controversial Provisions Ousted," *Civil Liberties Alert*, November/December 1990, p. 1.

95. "Override Urged On Spousal Rape Bill," *Civil Liberties Record* of Pennsylvania, November 1984, p. 3.

96. Jan Phillips, "Hate Crimes: Getting Communities Off the Dime," *Civil Liberties*, Winter 1990–91, p. 9.

97. Gary M. Stern, *The FBI's Misguided Probe of CISPES*, June 1988, p. 34.

98. Loren Siegel, "A War on Drugs or on People?" *Civil Liberties*, Fall/Winter 1989, p. 4.

99. See Glasser's letter to the editor, *Wall Street Journal*, October 13, 1988, p. A17.

100. See Glasser's reply to my July 16, 1988, criticisms of the ACLU published in *Human Events*. His remarks appear in the October 15, 1988 edition of *Human Events*, p. 12.

101. Policy #242, "Sentencing."

102. See Policy #242, "Sentencing," before the 1991 revision. The 1986 policy guide contains the previous policy.

103. During the 1988 presidential campaign, when the ACLU became a major issue, I was deluged with phone calls from reporters asking for proof of my charge that the ACLU believes that no one should go to prison save for such crimes as treason and murder. I provided the proof and this put additional pressure on the ACLU to revise its policy. See my piece, "Where Does the ACLU Stand on the Issues?" *Human Events*, July 16, 1988.

104. Policy #242, "Sentencing."

105. Ibid.

106. Ibid.

107. Memorandum from the Washington Office, "Senate Amendments to the Crime Bill," July 10, 1990, p. 4.

108. Policy #242a, "Electronic Monitoring of Prisoners."

109. Policy #242, "Sentencing."

110. Ibid.

111. Memorandum from the Washington Office, "Senate Amendments to the Crime Bill," July 10, 1990, pp. 1-2.
112. Policy #242, "Sentencing."
113. Ibid.
114. Ibid.
115. Ibid.
116. Ibid.
117. Ibid.
118. Ibid.
119. Daniel J. Popeo, *Not OUR America . . . The ACLU Exposed*, p. 35.
120. Lawrence Cranberg, "We Can Thank ACLU For Costly, Dangerous Prison Reform Ideals," *New York City Tribune*, June 12, 1989, p. 11.
121. Lawrence Cranberg, "It Began With the ACLU Prison Project," *West Austin News*, February 26, 1987, p.6.
122. Ibid.
123. Philip J. Hirschkop and Michael A. Millemann, "The Unconstitutionality of Prison Life," *Virginia Law Review* 55, (1969): 839.
124. Ibid., pp. 820-21.
125. Ibid., p. 833.
126. Ibid., p. 835.
127. "National Prison Project Works to Eliminate Barbaric Conditions," *Civil Liberties*, Fall 1987, p. 4.
128. See chapter 14 in my book, *The New Freedom: Individualism and Collectivism in the Social Lives of Americans* (New Brunswick, New Jersey: Transaction Press, 1990).
129. "ACLU Sues Three Shore Jails," *Free State Liberties* (of Maryland), Spring 1988, p. 4.
130. Ibid., p. 1.
131. Eileen Hershenov, ""Diverse Issues Confront Court; Souter Stance Remains Elusive," *Civil Liberties*, Winter 1990-91, p. 12.
132. *Wilson v. Seiter*, 111 S.Ct. 2321 (1991).
133. Policy #241, "Prisoners, Parolees, Probationers, and Ex-Offenders."
134. William A. Donohue, "Where Does the ACLU Stand on the Issues?" p. 17.
135. Ira Glasser's response to my article appeared in the October 15, 1988 edition of *Human Events*, p. 12.
136. Policy #241, "Prisoners, Parolees, Probationers, and Ex-Offenders." This particular policy was passed on January 28-29, 1984.
137. Mark S. Campisano, "Card Games," p. 11.
138. "Affiliate Notes," *Civil Liberties*, Spring 1990, p. 14.
139. Daniel J. Popeo, *Not OUR America . . . The ACLU Exposed*, 39.
140. See tape 7 of the 1985 Biennial Conference section on "Gay Rights."
141. See the 1989 Biennial Conference tape on "Prisoners' Rights."
142. The ACLU was one of several groups to issue a memorandum on the subject. See the Washington Office Memorandum entitled "Family Unity Demonstration Projects for Children and Their Incarcerated Parents," July 26, 1990.
143. Joseph F. Sullivan, "25-Year Sentence for Biting Guard," *New York Times*, May 19, 1990, p. 10.
144. Judy Greenspan, "HIV Infection among Prisoners," *Focus: A Guide to AIDS Research and Counseling*, May 1989, pp. 1-2.
145. See the tape of the 1989 Biennial Conference section on "Prisoners' Rights."

146. *Hudson v. McMillian*, 112 S.Ct. 995 (1992).
147. "Prison: Did ACLU Director Cause Disturbance?" *Salt Lake City Tribune*, January 3, 1990, p. B1.
148. Barry Steinhardt, "Prisons for Profit?" *Civil Liberties Record* (of Pennsylvania), May 1985, p. 2.
149. Policy #243, "Delegation of Prison Operations to Private Bodies."
150. Statement of Janlori Goldman, on behalf of the ACLU, on "Post-Conviction Denial of Benefits," before the House Republican Study Committee, May 17, 1989.
151. Lisa Belkin, "Expert Witness Is Unfazed by 'Dr. Death' Label," *New York Times*, June 10, 1988, p. B9.
152. Richard C. Paddock, "Federal Judge Criticizes High Court Over Execution," *Los Angeles Times*, April 26, 1992, p. A3.
153. William A. Donohue, *The Politics of the American Civil Liberties Union*, 266–67.
154. Norman Dorsen, *Frontiers of Civil Liberties* (New York: Pantheon Books, 1968), 269.
155. Policy #239, "Capital Punishment."
156. Dorsen, *Frontiers of Civil Liberties*, 275.
157. Ibid., 278.
158. Ibid., 277.
159. Policy #239, "Capital Punishment."
160. Memorandum from the Washington Office, "Senate Amendments to the Crime Bill," July 10, 1990, p. 2.
161. "The Death Penalty: An Intolerable Violation of Civil Liberties," *Civil Liberties Alert*, May 1986, p. 3.
162. Edward Koch, "The Death Penalty," in Thomas Draper, ed., *Capital Punishment* (New York: H.W. Wilson Co., 1985), p. 139.
163. Policy #272, "Children's Rights."
164. Quoted by Sharon Edelson, "The ACLU's Teen Problem," *Savvy Woman*, September 1989, p. 20.
165. Quoted by Ron Rosenbaum, *New York Times Magazine*, March 12, 1989, p. 60. See the box insert for the quote.
166. Nat Hentoff, "Two Cheers for the ACLU," *Washington Post*, March 3, 1990, p. A25.
167. Policy #239, "Capital Punishment."
168. The survey was done by Professor Hugo Adam Bedau (an ACLU member) and Michael Radelet and covered all executions between 1900 and 1985. See my pamphlet, "The Death Penalty and the Release of Convicted Criminals," published by the Washington Legal Foundation in 1990.
169. Ernest van den Haag, *Punishing Criminals* (New York: Basic Books, 1975), 219–20.
170. Policy #239, "Capital Punishment."
171. Ernest van den Haag, "The Ultimate Punishment: A Defense," *Harvard Law Review* 99 (May 1986).
172. See ACLU Briefing Paper, "Crime and Civil Liberties," No. 2.
173. Isaac Ehrlich, "The Deterrent Effect of Capital Punishment: A Question of Life and Death," *American Economic Review* (1975): 397–417.
174. James A. Yunker, "The Relevance of the Identification Problem to Statistical Research on Capital Punishment," 28 *Crime and Delinquency*: 96–124.
175. David P. Phillips, "The Deterrent Effect of Capital Punishment: New Evidence on an Old Controversy," 86 *American Journal of Sociology* (1980): 139–48.
176. Steven Stack, "Publicized Executions and Homicide, 1950–1980," 52 *American Sociological Review* (1987): 532–40.

177. Quoted in "Amnesty International Assails U.S. on Executions," *New York Times*, February 19, 1987, p. A17.
178. Quoted in "Rehnquist Urges Curb on Appeals of Death Penalty," *New York Times*, May 16, 1990, p. A1.
179. Fred Siegel, "Civil Liberties on the Block," *Newsday*, October 14, 1988, p. 88.

Conclusion
The Radical Cast of Liberty

Throughout this book the case has been made that the cause of liberty is ill served by defending an extremist interpretation of individual rights. Some defenders of the ACLU might well argue that it is the courts, not the ACLU, that determine the final outcome. Others might maintain that we need the ACLU to defend individual rights against the government, even if on occasion extremism prevails. Without the ACLU, the argument goes, who is there to defend our constitutional rights? These positions deserve a response.

To begin with, the cause of liberty would be better served if we had a more moderate and temperate ACLU, one that took due consideration of the social context in which freedom thrives. In its formative years, the 1920s and 1930s, the ACLU was hopelessly partisan, thus minimizing whatever contribution it stood to make to the fund of liberty. As this book has shown, most recently (since the late 1960s to be exact) the Union's highly atomistic vision of liberty has led it to discount the value of other important properties that make for freedom. It was in the 1940s, 1950s, and early 1960s that the ACLU was at its level best, trying hard to be evenhanded in its operations. It wasn't perfect, and honest scholars can disagree whether the ACLU compromised its position too much during this period. But compared to what preceded it, and to what followed, those were years of prudence and judiciousness.

The courts may decide what the final outcome of any civil-liberties battle is, but when the ACLU files its briefs, its work is hardly academic. When the ACLU wins, it does not win a debating contest; it scores a judicial victory that has consequences for the entire society. Furthermore, the ACLU does not go into court to play devil's advocate; it truly believes that freedom is best served when its views are adopted by the courts and imposed on society.

Think of it another way. If an organization dedicated to an extremist interpretation of the rights of businessmen were to surface, wouldn't it make sense to question whether such an enterprise really contributed to liberty, properly understood? Would it do to say that businessmen have rights too? Wouldn't we say that it is irresponsible to push the rights of businessmen to extremes? Would it be satisfactory to say that it's the courts, not the organization, that settle matters in the end? Wouldn't we want to scrutinize the agenda of such an organization and question its worth? Why, then, when the ACLU makes an extremist defense of the rights of, say, students, do we balk at criticism? And does not an extremist defense of individual rights—it matters not a whit which individuals are being defended—run counter to what is termed "ordered liberty"? Finally, with well over 800,000 lawyers in the United States, can it really be maintained that were it not for the ACLU, constitutional rights would go by the wayside?

Let it be said that any fair-minded assessment of the ACLU's history, including the ACLU of the 1990s, will find much to admire. Any organization that takes an expansive interpretation of a principled value, and acts on it, is bound to include in its portfolio much that is good. The problem with the ACLU is not its goal of defending civil liberties—that is its strength—it is its unwillingness to see that individual rights do not alone make for liberty. The refusal to understand that limits must be set, even when addressing noble causes, is the heart of the problem.

For reasons that are self-evident, the ACLU does not see itself as defending many extremist causes. Even less so does it see itself as unwittingly working against the process of liberty. On the contrary, it thinks its vision of liberty can be historically validated. More than that, it sees its vision as offering the greatest hope for the future. It is not unfair to say that the Union prefers to see itself as the last bastion of liberty left in the nation, struggling against the forces of darkness. By way of example, consider the way it continues to portray the Reagan-Bush years.

Skewing the Truth

President Reagan wasn't in office two months when the ACLU charged that "unless massive support for constitutional rights is mounted," the administration would make "radical changes" threatening our liberties. After Reagan completed his first year in office, it was said: "1981 was a bad year for civil liberties. 1982 could be worse." Just as predicted, one year later the Union was convinced that the Reagan administration had turned out to be an "implacable" foe of freedom.[1]

When Reagan was reelected, Ira Glasser sounded the alarms, claiming that "we have some dark days ahead—*a period of moral McCarthyism.*"[2]

Glasser repeated this theme in the annual report for 1984–85, this time contending that "these are not normal times for the country or the ACLU."[3] At about the same time, Glasser further charged that "I don't think there has ever been such a concerted assault on so many fundamental liberties at once." The Reagan administration, he said, was trying to accomplish "nothing less than the overturning of several basic values that this country was founded on."[4] In 1985, Glasser upped the ante by holding that the Reagan administration was at war with the Bill of Rights and that "the infamous W. Bradford Reynolds" (Associate Attorney General) had turned the Justice Department into the "enemy of civil rights."[5]

The fact that Reagan won 49 of 50 states in 1984 evidently left Glasser unimpressed. It was clear to him, if to no one else, that at the close of 1985 the White House had been taken over by "extremists," people who in previous times, he said, were regarded as "kooks" and "zealots."[6] Midway through 1986, Glasser opined that "President Reagan's personal charm had somehow managed to camouflage the sinister agenda of the extremists."[7] In the closing months of Reagan's second term, Glasser took aim at Attorney General Edwin Meese's record and concluded that *"the Reagan Administration will leave a frightening legacy of harm, if not irreparable damage, to the First Amendment!"* It was Meese's enforcement of the obscenity statutes that most upset Glasser.[8]

When Bush won, Norman Dorsen exclaimed that we had entered a "new and dangerous era."[9] Glasser chimed right in, saying we live "under extraordinary and frightening circumstances."[10] After the *Webster* decision was rendered (it allowed some state restrictions on abortion), Glasser went into high gear. He immediately issued an EMERGENCY BULLETIN, wherein he said that the Supreme Court had "handed America a shocking and frightening decision on the eve of July 4—leaving the Bill of Rights in shreds."[11] A few months later, at the end of Bush's first year in office, Glasser issued another EMERGENCY BULLETIN, this time saying that "Our enemies are now moving their anti-liberties agenda into the legal system."[12]

Notice that the Republicans (that is who Glasser meant by the "enemies" of the ACLU) were accused of having an "anti-liberties agenda." This is a far cry from saying that there are honest differences of opinion between the way the ACLU interprets civil liberties and the way the Republicans do. It is one thing to blast the Republicans for having an intellectually bankrupt approach to constitutional issues, quite another to charge them with harboring an agenda subversive to liberty.

The demagoguery only got worse in the 1990s. In May 1990, Glasser warned that "it is difficult to believe that the next decade will be even worse."[13] By year's end, Glasser let that *"these are not normal times for the ACLU,"* a comment that was as predictable as it was inexplicable. Wasn't this what he said in the 1980s? This being so, wasn't it normal for the ACLU to be living in abnormal times? This also helps to explain why in the 1990s Glasser is averaging three EMERGENCY BUL-LETINS a year. Given this stance, it is not surprising to learn that the ACLU regards itself as the *"only organization capable of defending liberties today."*[14]

Most of these statements were made for the purpose of fund raising. Now it is no secret that many prospective donors will not part with their money unless they feel moved to do so. So a certain amount of hype is to be expected in letters of this sort, and it would be unfair not to consider the context in which these remarks were made.Nonetheless, there are two questions that need to be raised. One is whether the ACLU is letting the prospect of big money influence its policies. The other is whether the ACLU really thinks that it holds a monopoly on the correct reading of the Bill of Rights.

It has not gone unnoticed that there is a striking similarity between the agenda of the ACLU and the agenda of People for the American Way, Norman Lear's organization. The two organizations not only address many of the same issues, and from the same perspective, they draw on like persons: somewhere between 40 to 45 percent of the ACLU's members also belong to People for the American Way. This makes fund raising difficult as many of the same foundations, individual donors, and members are asked to give to both organizations. To Morton Halperin, this raises a serious question for both organizations: "To what extent do people give money because of fear?"[15] This, of course, raises the issue of demagogic appeals.

To Mark Lambert, legislative director of the Iowa Civil Liberties Union, the biggest problem with the ACLU's fund-raising strategy is its effect on principle. So attractive is the lure of money, says Lambert, that it has led to a new ACLU philosophy: "Let's do whatever will raise the maximum amount of money to support the organization and ignore any loss in philosophical integrity." Alan Dershowitz agrees, charging that "the ACLU has become too crassly commercial. It's too concerned about its pocketbook."[16] Bad as this is, it is even more disturbing to learn that the ACLU's self-image is so inflated, so riddled with hubris, that the fund-raising hype is not hype at all: the leadership of the ACLU really believes that those who disagree with its positions are the enemies of liberty.

It has become something of a cliché among ACLU officials to refer to the Union as "the most conservative organization in America."[17] It is, of course, anything but conservative in its politics. What these officials really mean is that there is nothing more conservative than conserving the Constitution. Nothing too controversial about that, except that the Union's reading of the Constitution shows little regard for conserving the intentions of the Founders. But far more significant is the fact that the ACLU literally equates itself with the Bill of Rights.

"*We are the ignition for the constitutional engine*, the key that makes it run." This is how Ira Glasser, in the late 1980s, summarized the ACLU's legacy since its founding in 1920.[18] In 1988, Glasser accused then-Vice President Bush of bashing the Bill of Rights when he criticized the Union. Glasser said "now comes George Bush, for what I guess he sees as a short-term political advantage, and he attacks the ACLU, and he attacks his opponent. But Bush is attacking something else. He's attacking the fabric of that great principle of liberty. He's attacking the Bill of Rights itself." McCarthyite smears were not out-of-bounds for Glasser either: "If he [Bush] is against all of the rights we protect, if he is in fact against most of what the ACLU does, then he is against most of the Bill of Rights, and he has aligned himself with the darkest forces in America, which from time to time arise to repress those rights."[19]

Norman Dorsen made the same comment in 1988 when he said, "Vice President Bush says he's opposed to most of our positions and if that's true, he's opposed to the Bill of Rights."[20] For Nadine Strossen, there is nothing quite like the ACLU anywhere in the world: "I think this is the most important organization in the country, if not the world. To say what we're doing is controversial is to say the Bill of Rights is controversial."[21] Samuel Walker's effrontery has also been recorded: "Critics who accuse the ACLU of taking the Bill of Rights to extremes are, in effect, voicing a more fundamental complaint about the Constitution, the courts, and some of the deepest impulses in American society."[22]

None of these statements had anything to do with fund raising; they are the true convictions of the ACLU's top brass. They would have us believe that the only correct reading of the Constitution is the one they ascribe to. Moreover, the only legitimate way for friends of liberty to view the ACLU is favorably. Those who disagree are either showing their ignorance or actively engaged in subverting the cause of liberty. It's just that simple.

There are occasions when the ACLU's leaders find it difficult to reconcile its past behavior with its inflated image of itself. On such occasions, it helps to shade the record a bit. One example will suffice.

The internment of the Japanese during World War II was an egregious violation of civil liberties. Unfortunately, there were few voices—either from the left or the right—that openly complained about this travesty at the time. But contemporary ACLU revisionists offer a different story.

Ira Glasser likes to boast today that "the ACLU was the only national organization to condemn the internment and help fight it in court."[23] In point of fact, the national organization did not enter a brief in *Korematsu*. It was the Northern California affiliate that did so, and it did so over the objections of its membership[24] and over the objections of the national office. The national organization protested the manner in which the evacuations took place but not the right to evacuate. "The government in our judgment has the constitutional right in the present war to establish military zones and to remove persons, either citizens or aliens, from such zones when their presence may endanger national security, even in the absence of a declaration of martial law."[25]

Even less will Glasser confess that the national organization actually threatened the Northern California chapter with disaffiliation for its role in *Korematsu*. In response to this outrage, the executive director of the Northern California affiliate, Ernest J. Besig, refused to participate in revenue sharing with the national ACLU. Not until Besig's retirement in 1971 did this change.[26] But don't look for Samuel Walker or other ACLU officials to say much about this.

A Flawed Conception of Liberty

In the end, however, it is not the missed opportunities that most scar the ACLU's record. It is its flawed conception of freedom. An alternative vision, a social conception of liberty, offers a more contextual and sociologically realistic way of thinking about freedom. There are three basic elements to this perspective: (a) individual rights are not exhaustive of liberty, (b) individual responsibilities are the necessary corollary of individual rights, and (c) mediating institutions are functional to the cause of liberty.

Those who reject the social conception of liberty think that individual rights are a necessary and sufficient condition of liberty. Perhaps no one in the ACLU holds this position more dearly than Ira Glasser. Glasser deplores current talk about "too many rights," contending that such a perception is quite removed from the world view of the Founders.[27] Indeed, Glasser believes that, for the Founders, "government's primary objective was to promote individual rights."[28]

It is interesting to note that Glasser provides not a single citation to buttress his case, nor does he explain why the Constitution had to be amended before this "primary objective" was encoded into law. It would be more correct to say that the Founders were interested in securing "the blessings of liberty" (among other things) and that a means toward this end was the rights of the individual.

Glasser would have us believe that the Founders were all engaged libertarians, but as noted civil-libertarian scholar Leonard Levy has written, such a view does not square with the historical record: "The evidence drawn particularly from the period 1776 to 1791 indicates that the generation that framed the first state declarations of rights and the First Amendment was hardly as libertarian as we have traditionally assumed." In fact, as Levy demonstrates, "If the Revolution produced any radical libertarians on the meaning of freedom of speech and press, they were not present at the Constitutional Convention or the First Congress which drafted the Bill of Rights."[29]

Glasser's belief to the contrary, the Founders did not see the promotion of individual rights as the primary objective of government. "Why has government been instituted at all?" asked Hamilton. "Because the passions of men will not conform to the dictates of reason and justice without constraint."[30] Not only is this sentiment not reflective of the Bill of Rights, it is not the kind of idea that the ACLU would ever choose to be associated with. In fact, the ACLU works directly against this government objective by warring on the mediating institutions, the only social reservoir capable of constraining the individual.

Madison and Jefferson were no different. Madison, the author of the First Amendment, made it clear that "Justice"—not individual rights—

"is the end of government."[31] And though Jefferson is sometimes seen as the advocate of individual rights, par excellence, Sidney Hook's analysis of the author of the Declaration of Independence is more nuanced. Hook saw Jefferson as committed to plural values, ranging from individual rights to public safety.[32] Indeed, it was Jefferson who maintained that if the security of the nation were at stake, a strict adherence to individual rights might very well have to be suspended. Again, this is not the kind of position that the ACLU is likely to take.

If there is a single source that best expresses what the Founders believed to be the prime objective of government, it is the Preamble to the Constitution. The Preamble lists a series of collective goals: the need to (a) form a more perfect union, (b) establish justice, (c) ensure domestic tranquility, (d) provide for the common defense, (e) promote the general welfare, and (f) to secure the blessings of liberty. Implicit in these goals is not so much an emphasis on civil liberties but a need to provide for more collective ends, all of which are predicated on a modicum of order.

There is a reason why the ACLU doesn't make a practice of citing the collective goals of the Constitution: It sees individual rights as exhaustive of both liberty and the Constitution. This vision of liberty is decidedly atomistic, lacking a real-life social context. It envisions aggregates of individuals, each armed with state-awarded rights, going about their business in a solitary fashion. It is not for nothing that Mary Ann Glendon sees the "rights-bearer as a lone autonomous individual" as representative of a peculiarly American conception of freedom. This trait, she says, is closely bound up with the tendency to see rights as absolute.[33] Once again, there is no better organizational example of this frame of mind than the ACLU.

Nadine Strossen claims the ACLU isn't absolutist. The president of the Union says that "the A.C.L.U. has never taken a position that any constitutional right is absolute, nor does the Constitution."[34] But that doesn't square with the ACLU's house historian, Samuel Walker. "The commands of the Bill of Rights were absolutes." According to Walker, that was the way civil libertarians came to view rights in the 1960s. "It had taken the ACLU over forty years to come to grips with the ramifications of that idea, but in the decade of the 1960s it moved from a hesitant to an ashamed embrace of the absolutist position."[35] And here is Morton Halperin, testifying before the Senate Select Committee on Intelligence: "The ACLU is deeply troubled by the notion that there is a national security exception to the Fourth Amendment or any part of the Bill of Rights. We regard those rights as fundamental and absolute."[36]

In actual fact, the ACLU occasionally recognizes limits to individual rights (intimidating phone calls are not seen as free speech, nor is perjury or incitement to riot), but they are few and far between. It would be more accurate to say that the ACLU comes closer to the absolutist position than any organization in the nation. As such, it departs widely not only from mainstream legal thought but from the position of the Founders. As Sidney Hook has written, Jefferson was "much too intelligent" to believe that any rights were absolute.[37] Hook shows how absurd it is to think that the Bill of Rights contains absolutes: Since all rights can arguably conflict, it makes no sense to cast them as absolute.

That the ACLU has a natural penchant for seeing rights as absolute is not an issue. From libel law to obscenity, the Union takes the most extreme interpretation of free speech, seeing virtually every form of expression as entitled to First Amendment protection. What explains the ACLU's reasoning is its utter lack of interest in interpreting the First Amendment according to the historical context in which it was written. However, when it comes to the Second Amendment, "the setting in which the Second Amendment was proposed and adopted" becomes determinative.[38] Why this philosophy of jurisprudential reasoning is not applied to the First Amendment, the ACLU does not say.

As Francis Canavan has argued, to understand the original meaning of freedom of speech is to understand that it—like all other rights—has limits. It is limited by the purposes it was designed to serve. And in the case of free speech, its central purpose was to allow for the free reign of political discourse so that the best interests of society could be served. To say that speech, or expression, is the end, and that all expression is equally valuable, is preposterous. "If expression need serve no goal beyond itself," writes Canavan, "if all expressions are on the same level because they are all identical in the only essential respect, that of being expressions, then to say that they are all equally valuable is tantamount to saying that they are all equally valueless."[39]

That the ACLU refuses to set limits can be seen most clearly in its eagerness to defend terrorists. Roger Baldwin once admitted that the ACLU occasionally defended Nazis and Klansmen because it kept the courts free to defend its real political interests.[40] Similarly, former ACLU official Larry Freedman charges that such cases are undertaken not out of commitment to the issue but for headline grabbing purposes.[41] There is truth to both assertions. But it is also true that some civil libertarians defend Nazis and Klansmen out of fidelity to an absolutist interpretation of the First Amendment. It is this position that requires a response.

To the absolutist, there is no distinction between Nazis and those who engage in other kinds of unpopular speech. But it is not the unpopularity of Nazi speech that is at issue, it is the right of a paramilitary terrorist organization to exploit the laws of a democracy so that it might prove triumphant. Nazis and Klansmen are not just another dissident voice seeking to be heard. They are bent on the dissolution of freedom and democracy through whatever means available. That is why it will not do to say that if Klansman are barred from marching, so might be a Martin Luther King: King sought to expand rights, while Klansmen seek to annihilate them (and the sponsors of liberty, as well). If these elementary distinctions cannot be made, then the fight for freedom is indeed in jeopardy. Furthermore, if the Europeans have managed to preserve their liberties by outlawing various neo-Nazi organizations, there is no reason to believe that the United States would ineluctably descend the slippery slope to repression if we decided to do likewise.

Some say that the best response to a Klan march is for the people to organize and not show up, thereby depriving the hooded thugs of an audience. But what if, after a no-show bust, the Klansmen apply for a second permit? In 1990, they did just that in Pulaski, Tennessee, seeking to march on Martin Luther King Jr.'s birthday. Was the ACLU right to sue the town after an ordinance was passed limiting the number of parades per month?[42] Was the cause of liberty really advanced by allowing those who would destroy liberty the right to pervert the meaning of the First Amendment? Is the purpose of the Constitution fulfilled by allowing the exponents of liberticide an equal opportunity to win?

It is said that the Supreme Court has allowed Klansmen and Nazis full First Amendment rights and that therefore the ACLU is only following the high court's lead. That is true, and it remains to be seen whether conditions might ever force the Supreme Court to rethink its wisdom. But there are those in the ACLU who would go further still, beyond anything the Supreme Court has countenanced or would countenance.

Does free speech give one the right to scream fire falsely in a crowded theater? This famous example of Oliver Wendell Holmes is apparently not enough to dissuade some ACLU officials. In 1988, in a radio debate

I had with Louis Rhodes, the president of the Arizona CLU, Rhodes was pressed to see how far he was willing to go in defense of free speech. The talk show host, Barry Young, wondered if Rhodes was willing to defend the right of a radio announcer to falsely tell listeners that a missile was heading toward Phoenix and that everyone should immediately evacuate the city. Young was stunned when Rhodes glibly asserted that he would certainly defend the announcer.[43] It was simple: Free speech was at stake, and the First Amendment makes no exceptions.

Here's another example. In a segment of the PBS television series "The Constitution: That Delicate Balance," hosted by Fred Friendly, a telling scenario was put to Jeanne Baker, former general counselor of the Massachusetts Civil Liberties Union. Harvard Law professor Arthur Miller asked Baker to consider a situation where a radical left-wing group, the National People's Alliance, is prepared to square off against a recently reorganized chapter of the Ku Klux Klan. There has already been a series of deaths and both groups want to confront each other in a demonstration. Baker said she had no problem defending the groups and would challenge any law that would bar them from marching. Professor Miller then loaded the deck, adding that there have already been twelve fistfights at a press conference, a cross burning at the head of the NAACP, a gun cache, and the like. Here's what followed:

Ms. BAKER: You need more than that.
PROF. MILLER: The presence in town of somebody on the Ten Most Wanted list.
Ms. BAKER: You need more than that. You need—and it might happen in a particular case—
PROF. MILLER: Do I have to bring in an A-bomb?
Ms. BAKER: I don't think bringing in an A-bomb would change it—if all you did was bring in the A-bomb. What you have to do is show facts that if these permits—
PROF. MILLER: Have we allowed doctrine to run riot here?
Ms. BAKER: No, no, you haven't tied any of the facts that you've presented into an imminence of danger at the location of the marches at the time of the marches.

The discussion ends when Judge William J. Bauer of the U.S. Court of Appeals for the Seventh Circuit says he would have no problem issuing an injunction, based on the evidence.[44] The difference between Ms. Baker and Judge Bauer is plain: she's an absolutist and he's not.

The absolutist position runs into additional problems when it is applied to groups' rights as well as individual rights. As Dr. Lawrence Cranberg has perceptively noted, "when the ACLU speaks of 'rights' today, after its transformation in the late '60s to its present 'activist' role, it breaks down society into its component parts. Students, prisoners, enlisted men, secularists, etc., are addressed separately, and almost invariably in terms of belligerent antagonism to other segments of society, such as teachers, prison guards, military officers, religionists, etc." The result, Cranberg points out, is a variation of the Marxist "class war" strategy, with one group pitted against the other. "Law," writes Cranberg, "instead of being an instrument of order and peace, becomes an instrument of permanent turmoil and conflict."[45] Unnecessarily.

Responsibility (Should) Matter

Mary Ann Glendon perceptively notes that those who ascribe to an absolutist interpretation of rights typically show very little interest in seeing that individual responsibilities are tied to them.[46] That is certainly true of the ACLU, and it is just the opposite of what a social conception of liberty extols. There are some civil libertarians, like Burt Neuborne, who openly say that individual responsibility is not the charge of the ACLU.[47] Offering a social perspective on liberty, Harry Jaffa maintains that "civil liberties are, as their name implies, liberties of men in civil society. As such, they are to be correlated with the duties of men in civil society, and they are therefore subject to that interpretation which is consistent with the duty of men to preserve the polity which incorporates their rights."[48] But this is not acceptable to Gara LaMarche, former head of the Texas CLU. In 1987, he proudly announced that at the national celebration of the Constitution's bicentennial he was going to "sit out the pledge." To LaMarche, those who say the pledge have got it all wrong: "The Pledge of Allegiance is not the essence of the Constitution. *Not* pledging is."[49] To take the pledge would have meant a commitment, an expression of duty to country, and to those preoccupied with rights this is simply too much to bear.

Though the ACLU will not acknowledge it, rights that become un-hinged from responsibilities threaten the prospects for liberty. Rights, when exercised by morally responsible persons, can be liberating; they are debilitating when used by morally depraved persons. As Edmund Burke once counseled, "The effect of liberty to individuals is that they may do as they please; we ought to see what it will please them to do before we risk congratulations, which may be soon turned into com-plaints."[50] Surely the officers in the ACLU must understand the veracity of Burke's remark: the ACLU's headquarters is right around the corner from Times Square.

It would be a relief to hear the ACLU mention that pregnant women have a duty not to deliberately abuse their bodies in a way that is likely to cause harm to their unborn children. It would be a relief to hear the ACLU say that those who use illegal drugs and work in safety-sensitive jobs should never use drugs while at work or come to work stoned. It would be a relief to hear the ACLU tell veterans who are alcoholics that if they continue their practice for ten years after they've been discharged, they will lose their right to use the GI Bill to pay for their college education. It would be a relief to hear the ACLU say that if a military person acts dishonorably, then a dishonorable discharge is warranted.

It would be a relief to hear the ACLU tell students that they should be as informed of their responsibilities as they are their rights. It would be a relief to hear the ACLU say that the public has a right to require able-bodied persons to work, as a condition of receiving public assistance. It would be a relief to hear the ACLU tell convicted felons that when they violated the rights of others, they gave up certain rights for themselves, including the right to vote. It would be a relief to hear the ACLU counsel homosexuals and drug users to practice restraint. And it would be a relief to hear the ACLU counsel the media and the judiciary to practice the same degree of restraint it expects from the police.

To put it differently, consider the consequences to liberty if responsibility is not practiced. For example, it makes little sense to proclaim fidelity to free speech while at the same time defending the most extreme interpretation of students' rights. If it is true that the educated are in a much better position to exercise their free-speech rights than are the uneducated (through both oral and written communication), and if it is true that education is conditioned on the right of principals and teachers to insist on a measure of discipline in the schools then it is counterproductive to allow students' rights to take priority over the legitimate exercise of authority. When ACLU lawyers object to metal detectors in violence-laden schools, or protest locker searches in search of drugs or guns, while at the same time defending obscene T-shirts in the classroom, they are not contributing to the kind of milieu wherein serious learning is likely to take place. Therefore, it is as unfortunate as it is true that when the ACLU wins, too often the net result is a diminution of the First Amendment's potential value.

Mediating Institutions and Liberty

It is not enough that an absolutist interpretation of rights be rejected in favor of a more contextual reading of civil liberties. Nor is it sufficient to include a strong and lasting interest in individual responsibility. A social conception of liberty embraces one other quality: respect for mediating institutions and an enlightened skepticism of the role of government.

This book has shown numerous examples of the ACLU's desire to displace social authority with the authority of the state. ACLU officials know that their goal of reordering society cannot take place without the right and ability of government to substantially penetrate both mediating institutions and the private sector. One of the ways they seek to accomplish their goal is by justifying an ever-increasing role for the federal government. It is for this reason that Ira Glasser finds the original Constitution wanting, contending that the Bill of Rights contained "a major flaw" because it was not made applicable to the states.[51] His complaint is not a new one among ACLU activists: in 1939, Raymond L. Wise argued that the Constitution should be amended to make the Bill of Rights binding on the states.[52]

The complaints of Wise and Glasser are directed at the system of federalism that the Founders crafted. What they find troublesome—the so-called "flaw" in the Bill of Rights—is state autonomy, the right of the people in the states to determine their own destinies. But as Leonard Levy has written, the First Amendment (and the Bill of Rights more generally) was seen by the Founders as "more an expression of federalism than of libertarianism."[53] In fact, as University of Maryland historian Herman Belz notes, "scholars generally agree that the purpose of the first ten amendments to the Constitution was to allay the apprehensions of states' rights supporters concerning the extent of the power of the national government."[54]

The "flaw" that Glasser sees was the product of reasoned design. The Bill of Rights, though made applicable to the states in the twentieth century, was for good reason not supposed to be superimposed on the states. Federal judge and legal scholar Richard A. Posner explains why: "The Bill of Rights was intended to weaken the federal government; apply the Bill of Rights to the states through the due process clause and you weaken the states tremendously by handing over control of large areas of public policy to the federal judges, whose interpretations of the Bill of Rights are (short of constitutional amendment) conclusive of its meaning."[55] A plural structure, one that allows for liberty to reign, is what the founders wanted. The ACLU, whose interest is power, sees a plural structure as an obstacle, a hindrance to its goal.

ACLU opposition to state autonomy stems from the same reason that it finds problematic the autonomy of mediating institutions: anything that competes with the authority of the federal government makes it difficult to redistribute power. The same logic explains ACLU hostility to property rights. Since the 1930s, the ACLU has maintained that property rights— considered by many to be the nucleus of liberty—have "nothing to do with the maintenance of democratic processes."[56] Though property rights are clearly delineated in the Bill of Rights (Fifth Amendment), and though the ACLU claims that "its only client is the Bill of Rights," the Union continues to downgrade their significance. It is worth noting, too, that while the ACLU vigorously defends substantive due process with regard to First Amendment rights, it is nakedly hostile to such considerations as they affect Fifth Amendment rights.

If the roots of ACLU activism in pursuit of power extend back to its early years, it wasn't until the late 1960s that the pursuit went into high gear. Beginning with the New York affiliate, and led by what were to be the next two executive directors of the ACLU, Aryeh Neier and Ira Glasser, the Union moved toward what was described as an "enclave theory" of law. The goal was to bring every nook and cranny of American life under the aegis of the state. Neier made it clear that there wasn't a social issue that couldn't be redefined as a civil-liberties matter, declaring that "nothing seemed beyond the reach of litigation."[57]

It is the voice of statism, not civil liberties, that proclaims that nothing is outside the reach of litigation. In the minds of ACLU officials, it is acceptable for the judiciary to thrust itself onto the body social and invade every institution in its path, providing only that the end result is an expansion of some individual's rights. Yet as Sidney Hook has observed, the Founders never endorsed judicial supremacy. Hook adds that "those who defend the theory of judicial supremacy cannot easily square their position with any reasonable interpretation of the theory of democracy."[58] That is why accusations of majoritarianism fail to satisfy: We need to know how democracy is supposed to proceed if every time the expressed sentiments of the people are challenged by a dissident voice—asserting a constitutional objection—the ACLU answers the alarm.

As a result of ACLU tactics, many in society have sought to find their liberty by running from the reach of the Constitution. When truly private colleges are taken to court because they do not accept federal hegemony over their own internal matters, when private voluntary movie ratings systems are challenged for advising parents on the appropriateness of certain films for children, and when private employers are sued for setting their own standards of conduct and appearance, unreflecting persons might be forgiven if they conclude that constitutional rights have become the enemy of liberty. Though civil libertarians will not be persuaded, the attempt to "constitutionalize" society in service to libertarian ideals is no less threatening to freedom than the more familiar examples of state bullying done throughout the ages.

It is this same mindset that entices Nadine Strossen to look to international law as a means of establishing more rights. But bringing unelected world judicial bodies to bear on the affairs of Peoria will not advance civil liberties so much as it will advance imperialism. Strossen's fixation on individual rights as the determinant of liberty is itself problematic, but when contempt for the democratic process is added to it, the result is a view of liberty that surely the Founders would never recognize.

The ACLU's excessively legalistic approach to the subject of freedom is sorely neglectful of the social and cultural bases of liberty. Burke, like Hamilton, understood that there could be no freedom if society had not first found a way to put a restraint on the passions of the individual. What this required, above all else, was a robust and lively center of social authority, a place where the individual could take anchor; it was to the mediating institutions of society that Burke looked to accomplish this goal. If Burke is correct, then the enervation of social authority needs to be factored into the account of civil liberties.

It is true that neither the Constitution nor the Bill of Rights speaks to questions of character, virtue, duty, and individual responsibility. But that hardly means that the Founders were indifferent to such considerations. Madison understood something ACLU officials seem never to grasp: "No theoretical checks—no form of government can render us secure. To suppose that any form of government will secure liberty or happiness without any virtue in the people, is a chimerical idea."[59] If virtue counts, then it is only logical that we inquire into the sources of virtue and do what we can to strengthen them. That is why shielding the family, schools, churches, and voluntary associations from state penetration is fundamental to the cause of liberty: they are the most fundamental sources of virtue in society.

The vision of liberty favored by the ACLU shares much in common with the perspective of Rousseau. For Rousseau, the claims of the individual and the state were exhaustive of liberty. As for mediating institutions, it was from their clutch that the state sought the liberation of the individual. Yet as Robert Nisbet has argued, "The existence of authority in the *social* order staves off encroachments of power from the political sphere."[60] Nisbet is not unmindful of the abridgments to individual liberty that his position entails; it is just that his concern for keeping the state at bay matters most. To be sure, oppression can and does take place within the mediating institutions of family, schools, churches, and community associations. That, however, does not give the state carte blanche permission to intervene, for if it did, the inflation of state authority that would result would be an even greater menace to the process of liberty. It is possible to restrain—and even to escape—social authority, but how does one restrain or escape the reach of the state?

The imposition of state control into the recesses of a democratically designed social order is what deTocqueville called democratic despotism; it was no oxymoron. Indeed, what deTocqueville labeled as the "strangest paradox" has unveiled itself in the West, and most especially in America: freedom in the sphere of politics and despotism in the administrative sphere.[61] The democratic despotism that he lamented referred to the fruits of inordinate administrative centralization, the kind of government that was "meddlesome in detail."[62] When government busied itself with "trivial matters,"[63] when it explored the minutiae of social life, when it sought to penetrate the crevices of private associations, it annihilated pluralism and thus destroyed freedom.

deTocqueville believed that if freedom were to be safeguarded in a democracy, we not only had to guard against encroachments of the state on society, we had to guard against the kinds of social and cultural forces that propelled the individual to seek incorporation in the state. A free society depends as much on the capacity of the individual to find contentment in the interstices of society as it does in assuring that the government satisfies itself with the interests of the nation. This requires social stability and a recognition that there is something called the common good. Without a sense of community, and a certain willingness on the part of the individual to bow to the needs of society, collective goals cannot be pursued.

The Common Good

The idea that individual rights might conflict with the common good is wholly resisted by the ACLU. Glasser, in particular, maintains that there is no such tension, holding that for the Founders, "individual liberty was the fundamental social value most to be cherished and protected. Far from being antagonistic to the common good, individual liberty was seen as part of the common good, indeed as the highest common good."[64] It is one thing, of course, to make such an extravagant claim, quite another to impute it to the Founders. Clinton Rossiter, in his introduction to The Federalist Papers, more accurately captured the central message of the Founders: "no happiness without liberty, no liberty without self-govern-ment, no self-government without constitutionalism, no con-stitutionalism without morality—and none of these great goods without stability and order."[65]

While it would be an exaggeration to say that there is a zero-sum relationship between individual liberty and the common good, it remains true that the two properties often collide. The rights of the accused need to be respected, but the social interest in maintaining order is also legitimate. There are instances when the needs of national security might require significant control over civil liberties. We have metal detectors in airports—over the objections of the ACLU—solely to accommodate the common interest in public safety. There may be a right to sell sexually explicit literature, but there is also a rightful purpose in limiting its distribution. Begging on the street is legitimate, but so too are laws that proscribe begging in subway stations. People have a right to live in neighborhoods of their own choosing, but neighbors also have a right to pass zoning ordinances that define their collective interests.

It is one thing to say that in a free society there is a common interest in protecting individual rights, quite another to insist that individual rights are the highest expression of the common good. The common good, or the public weal, is not reducible to the rights of the individual or to any individual pursuit. Its meaning derives from its transcendent qualities, that is, from its ability to override the importance of any single individual in society. Not even the cause of civil liberties—noble as it is—can always be permitted to override the common good—not, at least, if freedom is to be maintained. That there are instances when the common good should be checked is certain, and the Bill of Rights addresses those instances. But that only underscores the delicate balance that exists between the common good and individual liberty.

So as not to be misunderstood, it needs to be said that the most common threats to liberty have historically come from those who would sacrifice individual rights in exchange for a measure of security and order. Put differently, appeals to the common good have often been so extreme that expressions of individualism have been summarily negated. That is why a vigorous defense of civil liberties is a must in any society that aspires to be free. But having said that, it is also important to understand that the maximization of individual rights does not equate with the maximization of liberty. That would only be true if there were a one-to-one relationship between the two properties. Liberty, however, is just as dependent on making adequate provisions for the common good as it is on ensuring an adequate enforcement of civil liberties.

Morris Ernst, one of the ACLU's most famous attorneys, once confided that he "would hate to live in a world with utter freedom."[66] What he had in mind was a world where every debased appetite could find expression, all in the name of liberty. The same sentiment has often been voiced by contemporary ACLU officials, and some, like Burt Neuborne, have flatly stated that "I would not want to live in a world where the ACLU won all its cases."[67]

It is certainly strange that those who most champion liberty would not want to live in a world with "utter freedom" or where "the ACLU won all its cases." Is it because, deep down, even they can't stomach unbounded liberty? No matter; it clearly seems that the ACLU's self-doubt is testimony to the failure of an atomistic conception of liberty to satisfy. Unfortunately, the lesson to be learned—that absolute rights are corrosive of freedom—seems never to be understood. The problem is not with liberty but with those who give it a radical cast.

Notes

1. William A. Donohue, *The Politics of the American Civil Liberties Union* (New Brunswick, New Jersey: Transaction Press, 1985), 330.
2. Fund-raising letter, received November 1984.
3. Ira Glasser, "Executive Director's Message," Annual Report, 1984–85, p. 6.

4. Ira Glasser, "The Reagan Administration Is Moving America Away From Civil Liberties," *Civil Liberties*, Winter 1985, p. 3.

5. Memorandum from Ira Glasser sent to "Special Friends of the ACLU," July 12, 1985.

6. Fund-raising letter, December 1985.

7. "THE STATE OF CIVIL LIBERTIES IN THE UNITED STATES," A Special Midyear Report, June 1986, p. 3.

8. Memorandum by Ira Glasser, "Double-Barreled First Amendment Assault," May 1988.

9. Memorandum by Norman Dorsen to ACLU members, December 1988.

10. Fund-raising letter, February 1989.

11. EMERGENCY BULLETIN by Ira Glasser, July 1989.

12. EMERGENCY BULLETIN by Ira Glasser, November 1989.

13. Fund-raising letter by Ira Glasser to ACLU members, May 1990, that accompanied the Union's 1990 WORKPLAN.

14. ACLU Membership Acceptance Form, March 1992.

15. Quoted by Anne Kornhauser, "Do 'Fraternal Twins' Have Sibling Rivalry?" *Legal Times*, April 4, 1988, p. 4.

16. Quoted by Charles Oliver, "The First Shall Be Last?" *Reason*, October 1990, pp. 24–25.

17. See for example the comments of Gara LaMarche and Robyn Blumner. LaMarche was formally with the New York and Texas affiliates and Blumner heads the affiliate in Florida. For LaMarche's remark see the story by Enedelia J. Obregon, "Texas Attitudes Challenge Civil Liberties Director," *Austin American-Statesman*, March 14, 1988, p. D1. Blumner's comment is cited by Ted Gest, "The Aging Bulldog of Civil Liberties," *U.S. News and World Report*, February 18, 1991, p. 57.

18. Annual Report for 1986–87, p. 9.

19. Ira Glasser made these remarks before the National Press Club on October 6, 1988.

20. Quoted by Philip Shenon, "A.C.L.U. Reports Rise in Membership Calls in Wake of Bush's Attacks," *New York Times*, September 27, 1988, p. 10.

21. Quoted by David Gonzalez, "A Guardian For Liberty," *New York Times*, January 28, 1991, p. A11.

22. Samuel Walker, *In Defense of American Liberties: A History of the ACLU* (New York: Oxford University Press, 1990), 5.

23. Glasser's remark was before the National Press Club on October 6, 1988.

24. William Petersen, *Japanese Americans* (New York: Random House, 1971), 77–79.

25. ACLU Annual Report #21, p. 28.

26. Bill Blum and Gina Lobaco, "Fighting Words At The ACLU," *California Lawyer*, February 1990, pp. 45–46.

27. Ira Glasser, *Visions of Liberty: The Bill of Rights for All Americans* (New York: Arcade Publishing, 1991), 10.

28. Ibid., 33.

29. Leonard Levy, *Freedom of Speech and Press in Early American History: Legacy of Suppression* (New York: Harper and Row, 1963), xxi, 3.

30. The quote is found in Federalist #15. Alexander Hamilton, James Madison, and John Jay, *The Federalist Papers* (New York: Mentor Book, New American Library), 110.

31. Ibid., 324. Federalist #51.

32. Sidney Hook, *Paradoxes of Freedom* (Buffalo, New York: Prometheus Books, 1987), 18.

33. Mary Ann Glendon, *Rights Talk* (New York: Free Press, 1991), 45.

34. Quoted by Robin Pogrebin, "Does Civil Libertarian Hinder City Order?" *New York Observer*, March 9, 1992, p. 11.
35. Walker, *In Defense of American Liberties*, 320.
36. Prepared Testimony and Statement For The Record of Morton H. Halperin on S. 2726 The Counterintelligence Improvements Act Of 1990 and the Jacobs Panel Recommendations For The Enhancement of U.S. Counterintelligence Capabilities Before the Senate Select Committee On Intelligence, July 12, 1990, p. 35.
37. Hook, *Paradoxes of Freedom*, 17.
38. Policy #47, "Gun Control."
39. Francis Canavan, *Freedom of Expression: Purpose As Limit* (Durham, North Carolina: Carolina Academic Press, 1987), 145.
40. William A. Donohue, *The Politics of the American Civil Liberties Union*, 51.
41. Interview with Larry Freedman, Coral Ridge Ministries, for the television program "Taking Liberties: The Case Against the ACLU." Freedman offered his views during this interview, portions of which were shown on the Dr. D. James Kennedy program, CBN, April 21, 1991.
42. John Rosenthal, "The Day the Nazis Had a Party and Nobody Came," *Civil Liberties*, Spring 1990, p. 5.
43. Rhodes made his confession on the Barry Young Show, KFYI Phoenix, on September 28, 1988.
44. See the transcript (#109) for the series "The Constitution: That Delicate Balance." The show in question, "School Prayer, Gun Control, and the Right to Assemble," was first aired on PBS on November 13, 1984. It was a production of Media and Society Seminars, a program of Columbia University Graduate School of Journalism. See pp. 13–14 of the transcript.
45. Lawrence Cranberg, "ACLU: Party of Secret Privilege, Class Struggle," *New York City Tribune*, April 24, 1990, p. 9.
46. Glendon, *Rights Talk*, p. 45.
47. Neuborne said that those who criticize the ACLU for not concerning itself with issues of individual responsibility misunderstand what the organization is all about. He made his comment on *MacNeil-Lehrer Newshour*, PBS television, October 10, 1988.
48. Harry Jaffa, "On the Nature of Civil and Religious Liberty," in William F. Buckley, Jr., and Charles R. Kesler, eds., *Keeping the Tablets* (New York: Harper and Row, 1988), 147.
49. Gara LaMarche, "Why I Won't Be Pledging Today," *Austin American-Statesman*, September 16, 1987.
50. Edmund Burke, in Ross J.S. Hoffman and Paul Levack, eds., *Burke's Politics* (New York: Knopf, 1967), 285.
51. Glasser, *Visions of Liberty*, 54–55.
52. Raymond L. Wise, "We Still Need a Bill of Rights," *Nation*, March 11, 1939, pp. 291–93.
53. Levy, *Freedom of Speech and Press in Early American History*, ix.
54. Herman Belz, "Liberty and Equality for Whom? How to Think Inclusively About the Constitution and the Bill of Rights," *History Teacher*, May 1992, p. 264.
55. Richard A. Posner, *The Federal Courts* (Cambridge: Harvard University Press, 1985), 195.
56. Annual Report #16, p. 15.
57. Walker, *In Defense of American Liberties*, 299. See chapter 14 for a good account of this view.

58. Hook, *Paradoxes of Freedom*, 95.
59. Madison made his remark at the Virginia Convention, June 20, 1788. See Saul K. Padover, ed., *The Complete Madison: His Basic Writings* (New York: Harper and Row, 1971), 48–49.
60. Robert Nisbet, "Uneasy Cousins," in George W. Carey, ed., *Freedom and Virtue: the Conservative/Libertarian Debate* (Lanham, Maryland: University Press of America, 1984), 19.
61. Alexis de Tocqueville, *Democracy in America*, J.P. Mayer, ed. (New York: Anchor Books, 1969), 694.
62. Ibid., 539.
63. Ibid., 680.
64. Glasser, *Visions of Liberty*, 11.
65. Rossiter's introduction can be found in the 1961 Mentor/New American Library edition of *The Federalist Papers*, xvi.
66. Quoted by Walter Berns, "Pornography vs. Democracy: The Case for Censorship." *Public Interest* (Winter 1971), p. 6.
67. After debating Gara LaMarche on radio, he told me that Norman Dorsen held the same idea. For Neuborne's remark, see his article, "Confessions of an ACLU Lawyer," *Wall Street Journal*, October 20, 1988, p. A16.

Index